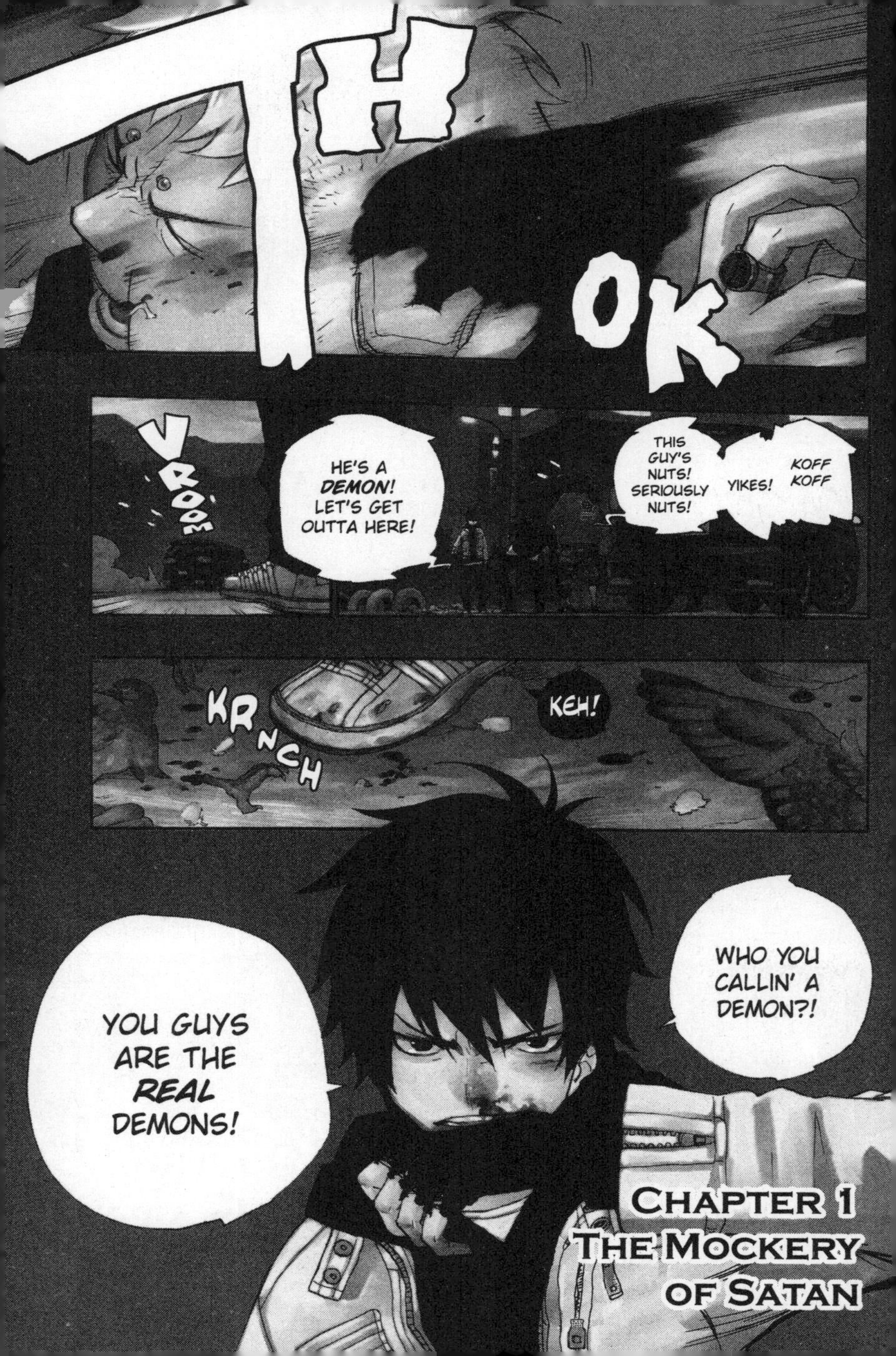
THOK
KOFF KOFF
YIKES!
THIS GUY'S NUTS! SERIOUSLY NUTS!
HE'S A DEMON! LET'S GET OUTTA HERE!
VROOM
KEH!
KRNCH
WHO YOU CALLIN' A DEMON?!
YOU GUYS ARE THE REAL DEMONS!
Chapter 1
The Mockery of Satan

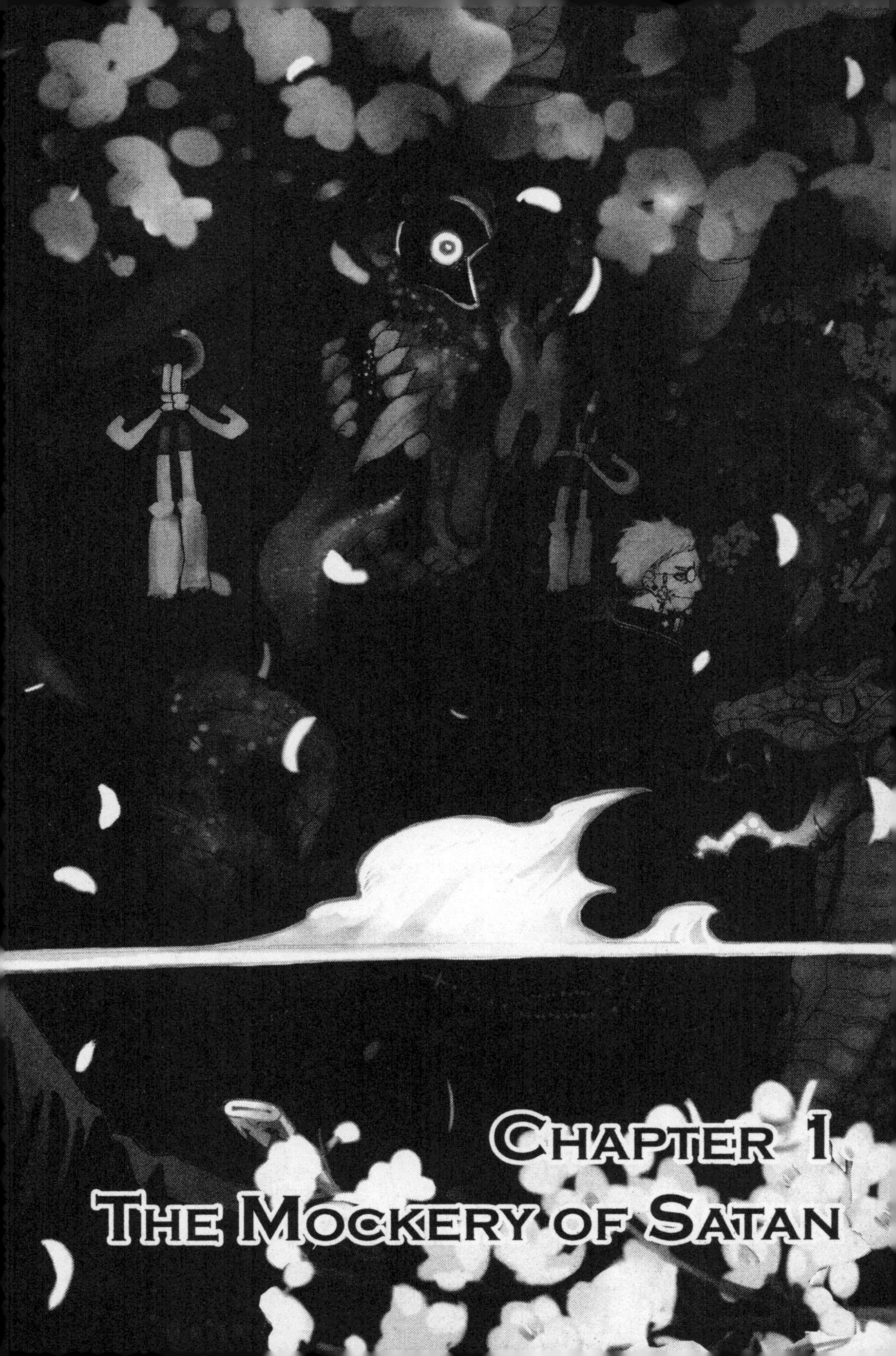
Chapter 1
The Mockery of Satan

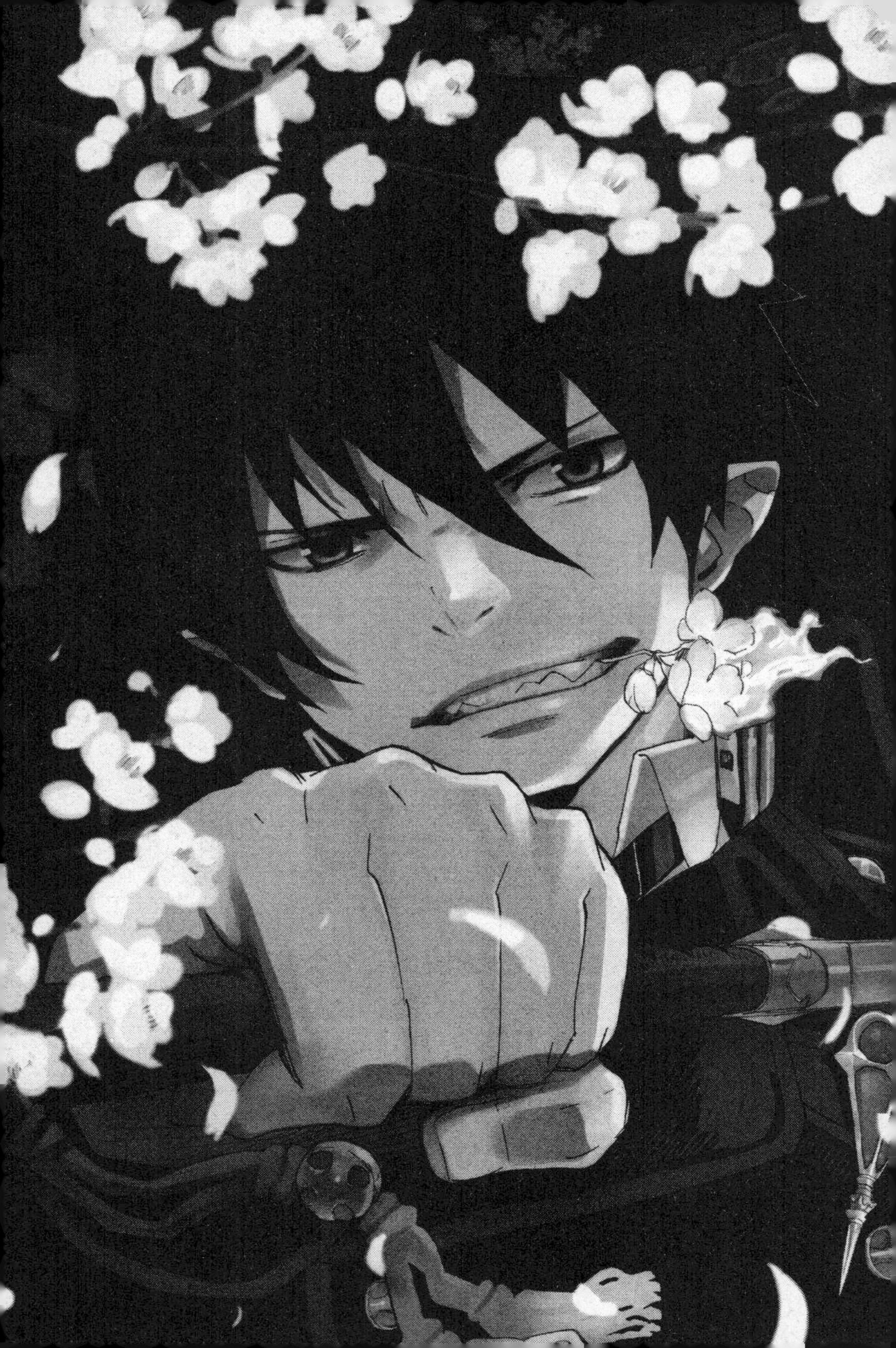

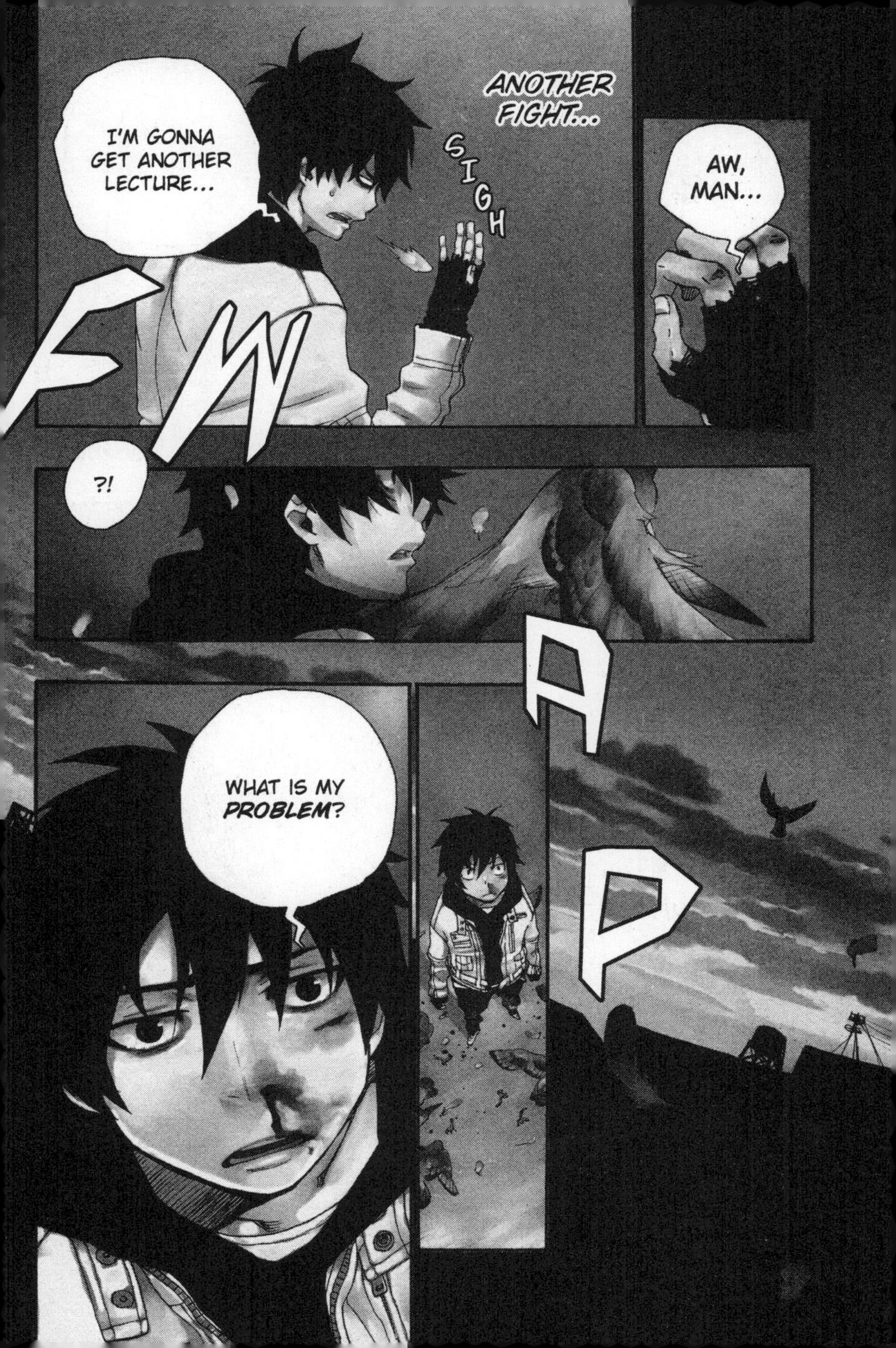
AW, MAN...
ANOTHER FIGHT...
SIGH
I'M GONNA GET ANOTHER LECTURE...
FW
?!
AP
WHAT IS MY *PROBLEM*?

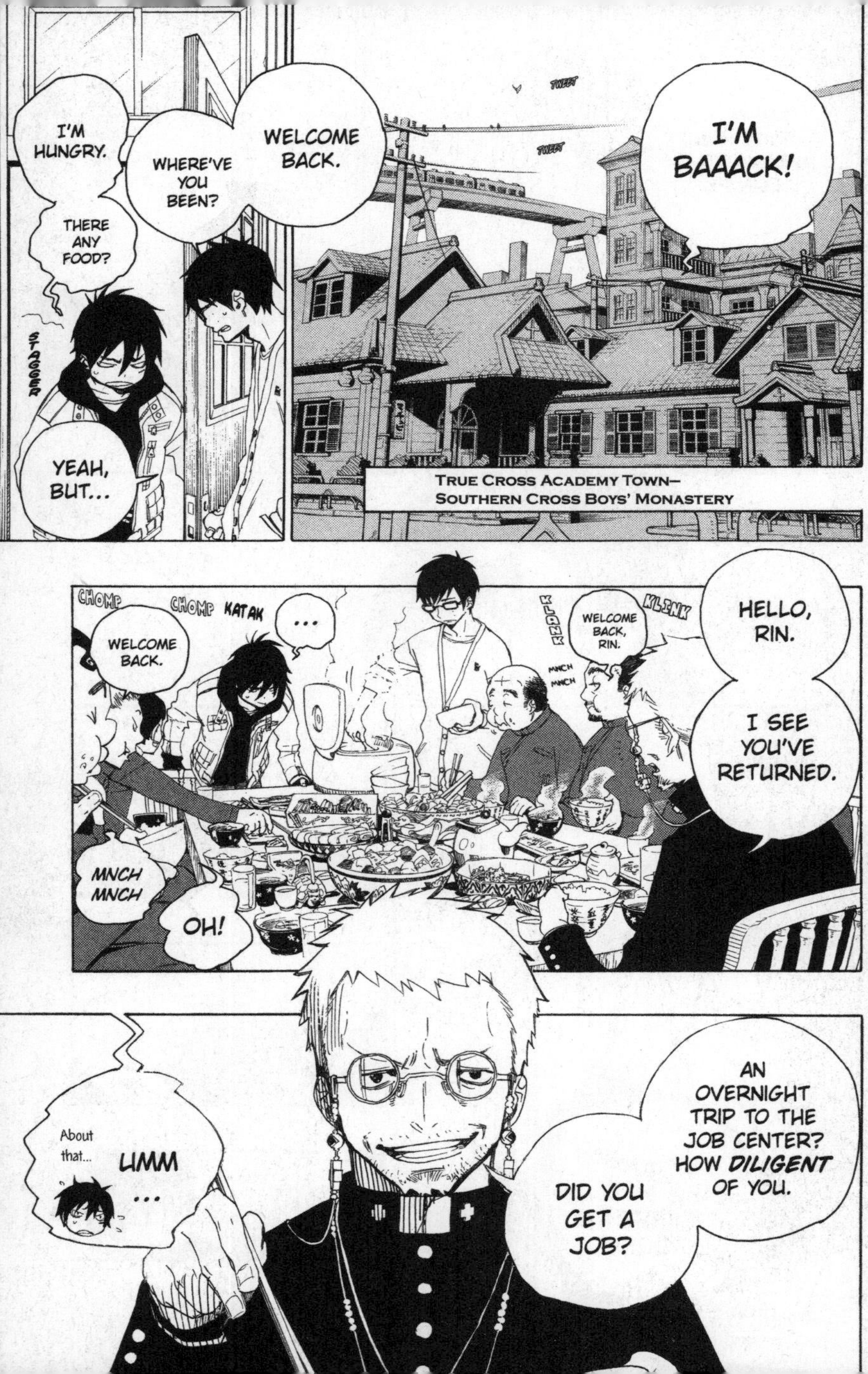
TWEET
TWEET
I'M BAAACK!
TRUE CROSS ACADEMY TOWN— SOUTHERN CROSS BOYS' MONASTERY
WELCOME BACK.
WHERE'VE YOU BEEN?
I'M HUNGRY.
THERE ANY FOOD?
STAGGER
YEAH, BUT...
HELLO, RIN.
I SEE YOU'VE RETURNED.
KLINK
WELCOME BACK, RIN.
KLANK
MNCH MNCH
...
KATAK
CHOMP
CHOMP
WELCOME BACK.
OH!
MNCH MNCH
AN OVERNIGHT TRIP TO THE JOB CENTER? HOW *DILIGENT* OF YOU.
DID YOU GET A JOB?
UMM ...
About that...

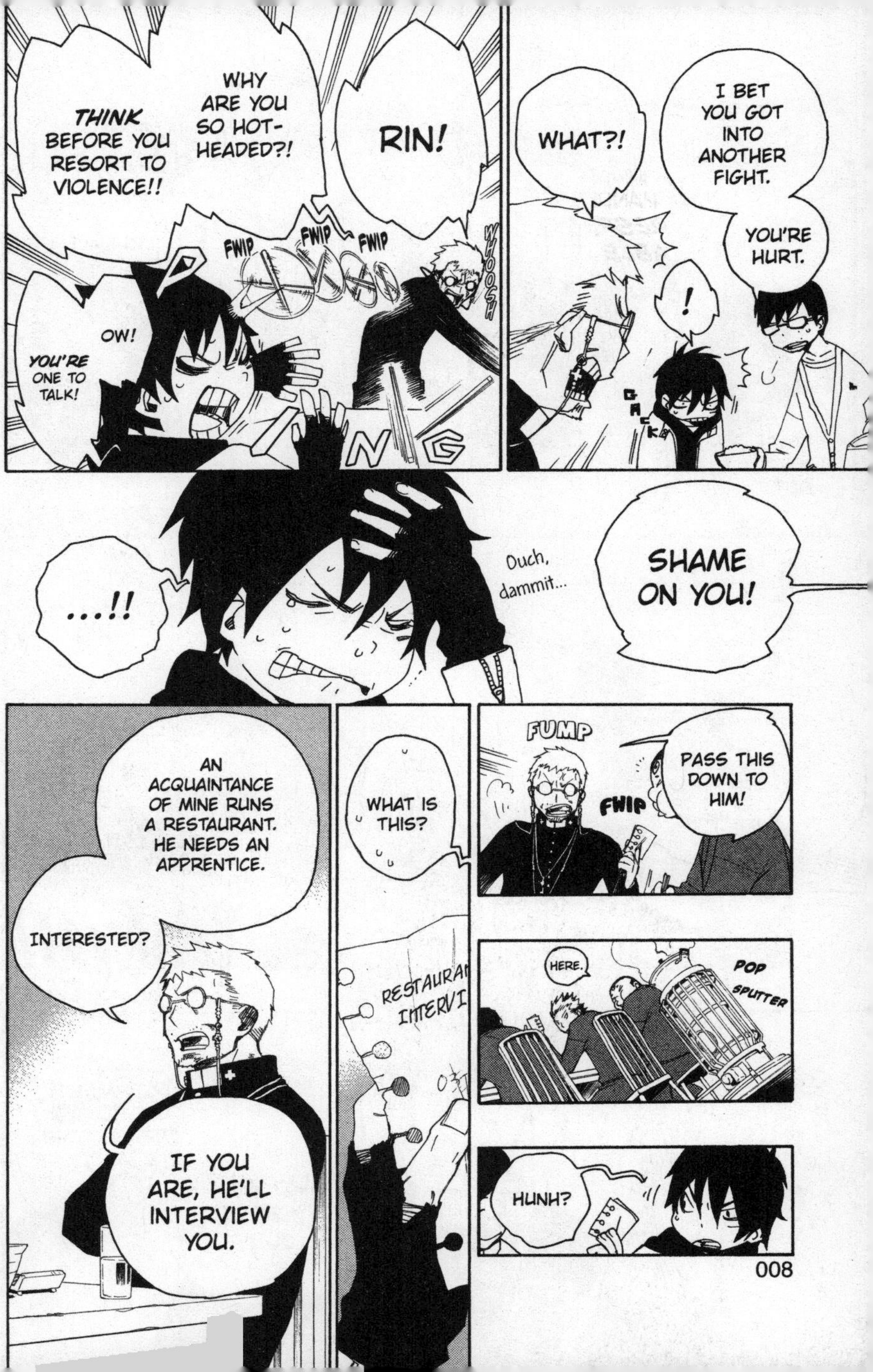
I BET YOU GOT INTO ANOTHER FIGHT.
YOU'RE HURT.
WHAT?!
!
GACK
RIN!
WHOOSH
WHY ARE YOU SO HOT-HEADED?!
THINK BEFORE YOU RESORT TO VIOLENCE!!
FWIP FWIP FWIP
OW!
YOU'RE ONE TO TALK!
NG
SHAME ON YOU!
Ouch, dammit...
...!!
FUMP
PASS THIS DOWN TO HIM!
FWIP
HERE.
POP
SPUTTER
HUNH?
WHAT IS THIS?
RESTAURAN
INTERVI
AN ACQUAINTANCE OF MINE RUNS A RESTAURANT. HE NEEDS AN APPRENTICE.
INTERESTED?
IF YOU ARE, HE'LL INTERVIEW YOU.

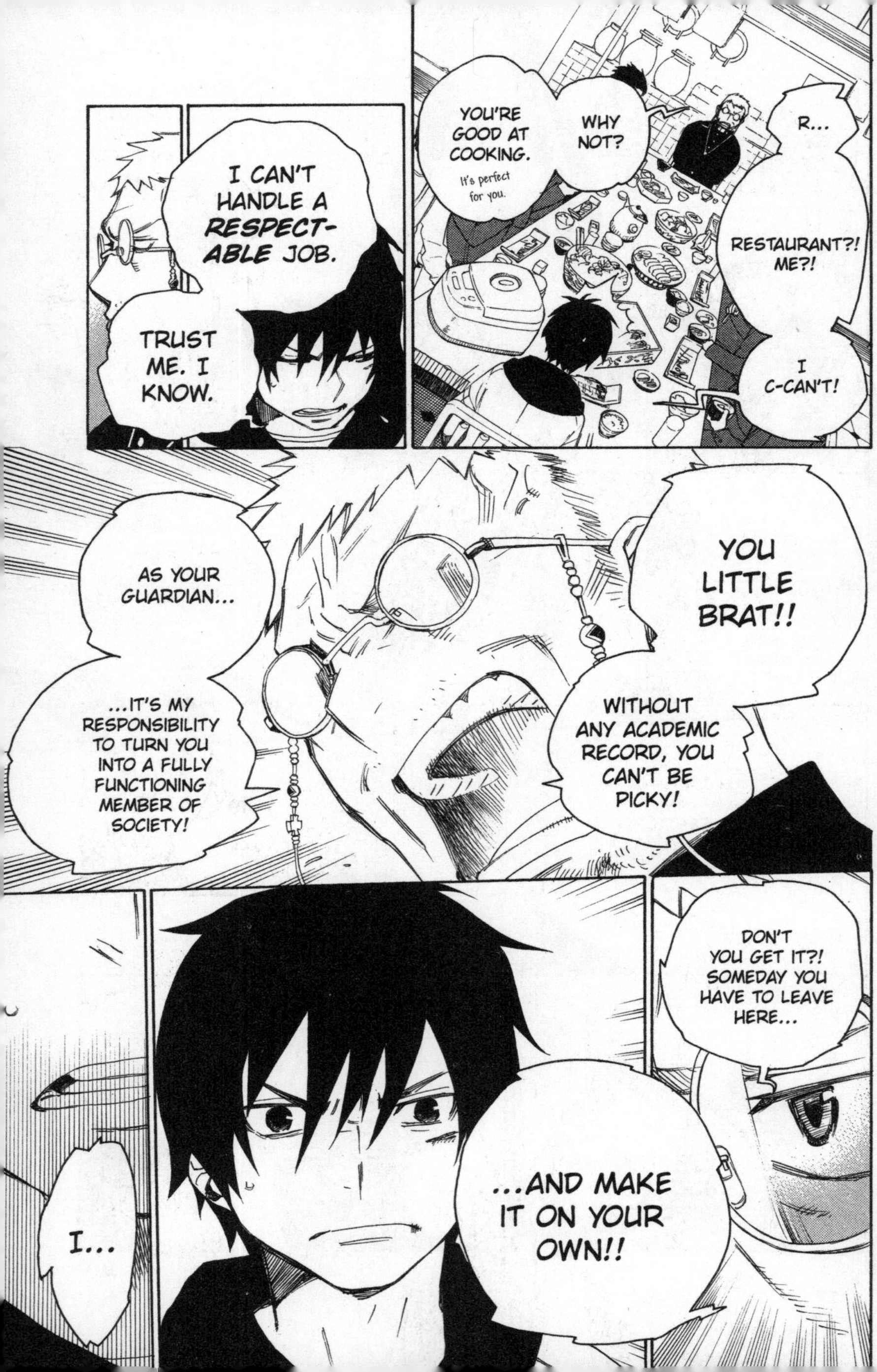
R...
RESTAURANT?! ME?!
I C-CAN'T!
WHY NOT?
YOU'RE GOOD AT COOKING.
It's perfect for you.
I CAN'T HANDLE A RESPECTABLE JOB.
TRUST ME. I KNOW.
YOU LITTLE BRAT!!
WITHOUT ANY ACADEMIC RECORD, YOU CAN'T BE PICKY!
AS YOUR GUARDIAN...
...IT'S MY RESPONSIBILITY TO TURN YOU INTO A FULLY FUNCTIONING MEMBER OF SOCIETY!
DON'T YOU GET IT?! SOMEDAY YOU HAVE TO LEAVE HERE...
...AND MAKE IT ON YOUR OWN!!
I...

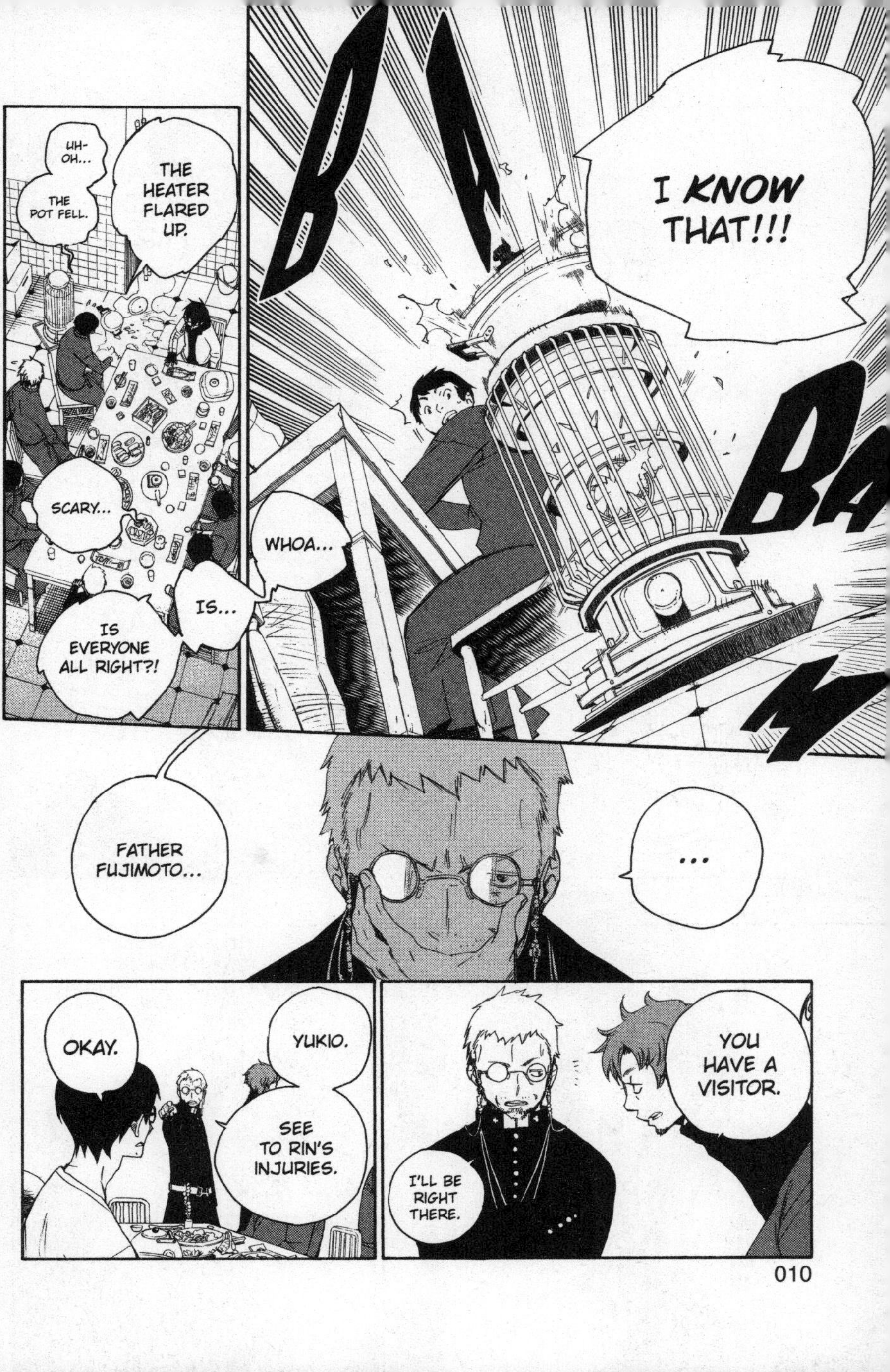
BA
I KNOW THAT!!!
BAM
WHOA...
THE HEATER FLARED UP.
UH-OH...
THE POT FELL.
SCARY...
IS...
IS EVERYONE ALL RIGHT?!
...
FATHER FUJIMOTO...
YOU HAVE A VISITOR.
I'LL BE RIGHT THERE.
YUKIO.
SEE TO RIN'S INJURIES.
OKAY.

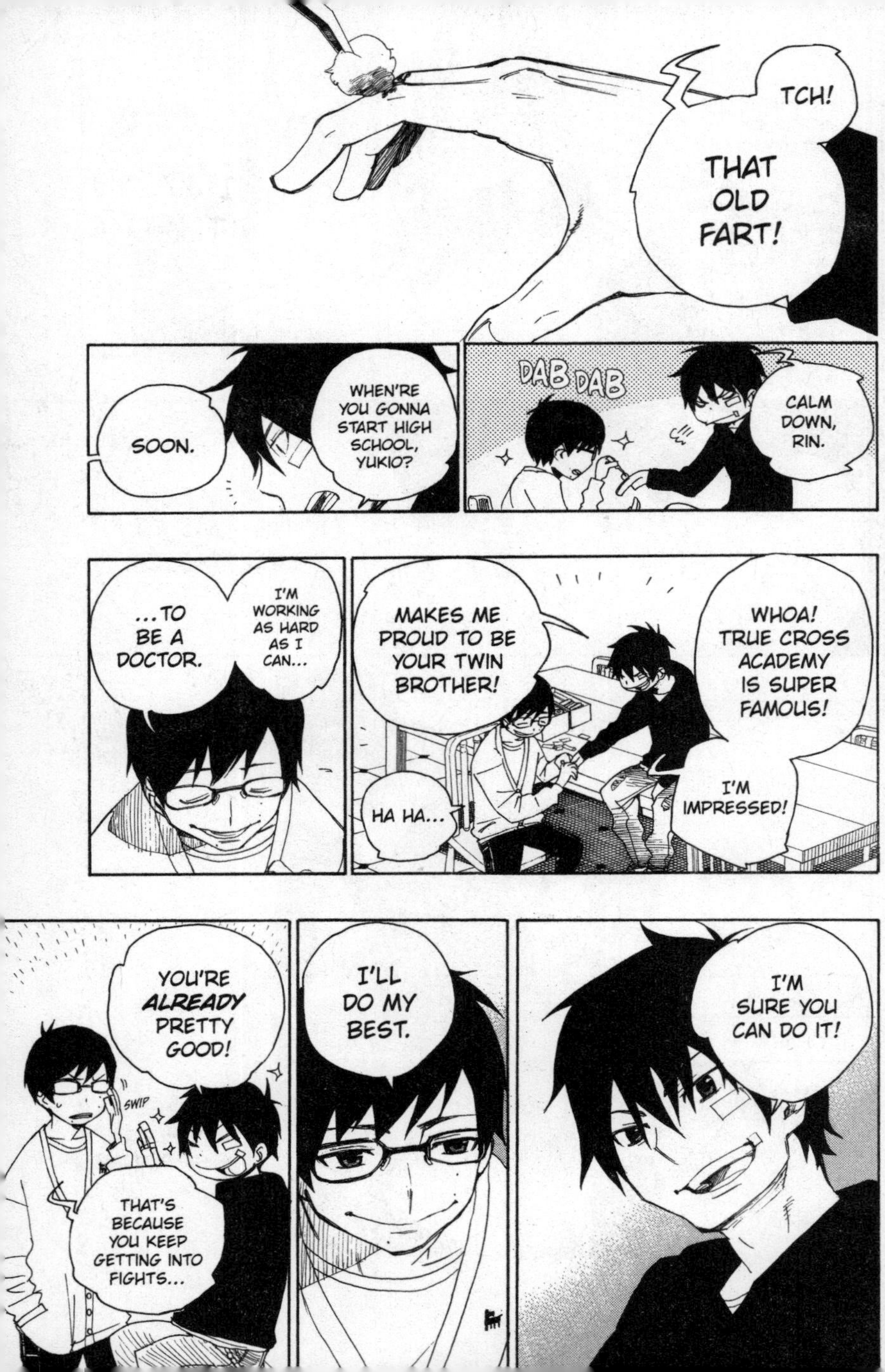
TCH!
THAT OLD FART!
DAB DAB
CALM DOWN, RIN.
WHEN'RE YOU GONNA START HIGH SCHOOL, YUKIO?
SOON.
WHOA! TRUE CROSS ACADEMY IS SUPER FAMOUS!
I'M IMPRESSED!
MAKES ME PROUD TO BE YOUR TWIN BROTHER!
HA HA...
I'M WORKING AS HARD AS I CAN...
...TO BE A DOCTOR.
I'M SURE YOU CAN DO IT!
I'LL DO MY BEST.
YOU'RE *ALREADY* PRETTY GOOD!
SWIP
THAT'S BECAUSE YOU KEEP GETTING INTO FIGHTS...

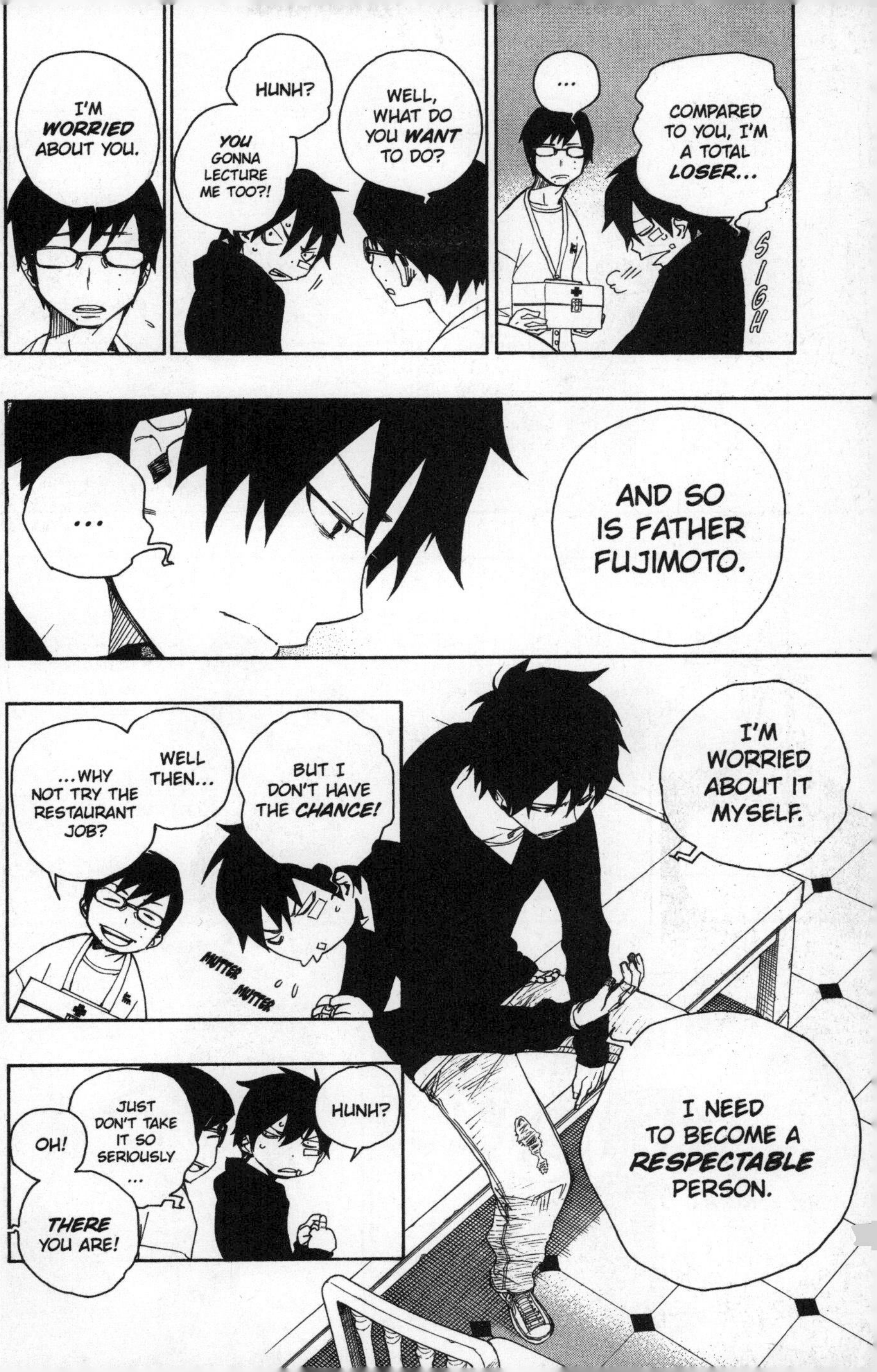
COMPARED TO YOU, I'M A TOTAL LOSER...
...
SIGH
WELL, WHAT DO YOU WANT TO DO?
HUNH? YOU GONNA LECTURE ME TOO?!
I'M WORRIED ABOUT YOU.
AND SO IS FATHER FUJIMOTO.
...
I'M WORRIED ABOUT IT MYSELF.
I NEED TO BECOME A RESPECTABLE PERSON.
BUT I DON'T HAVE THE CHANCE!
WELL THEN...
...WHY NOT TRY THE RESTAURANT JOB?
MUTTER MUTTER
HUNH?
JUST DON'T TAKE IT SO SERIOUSLY...
OH!
THERE YOU ARE!

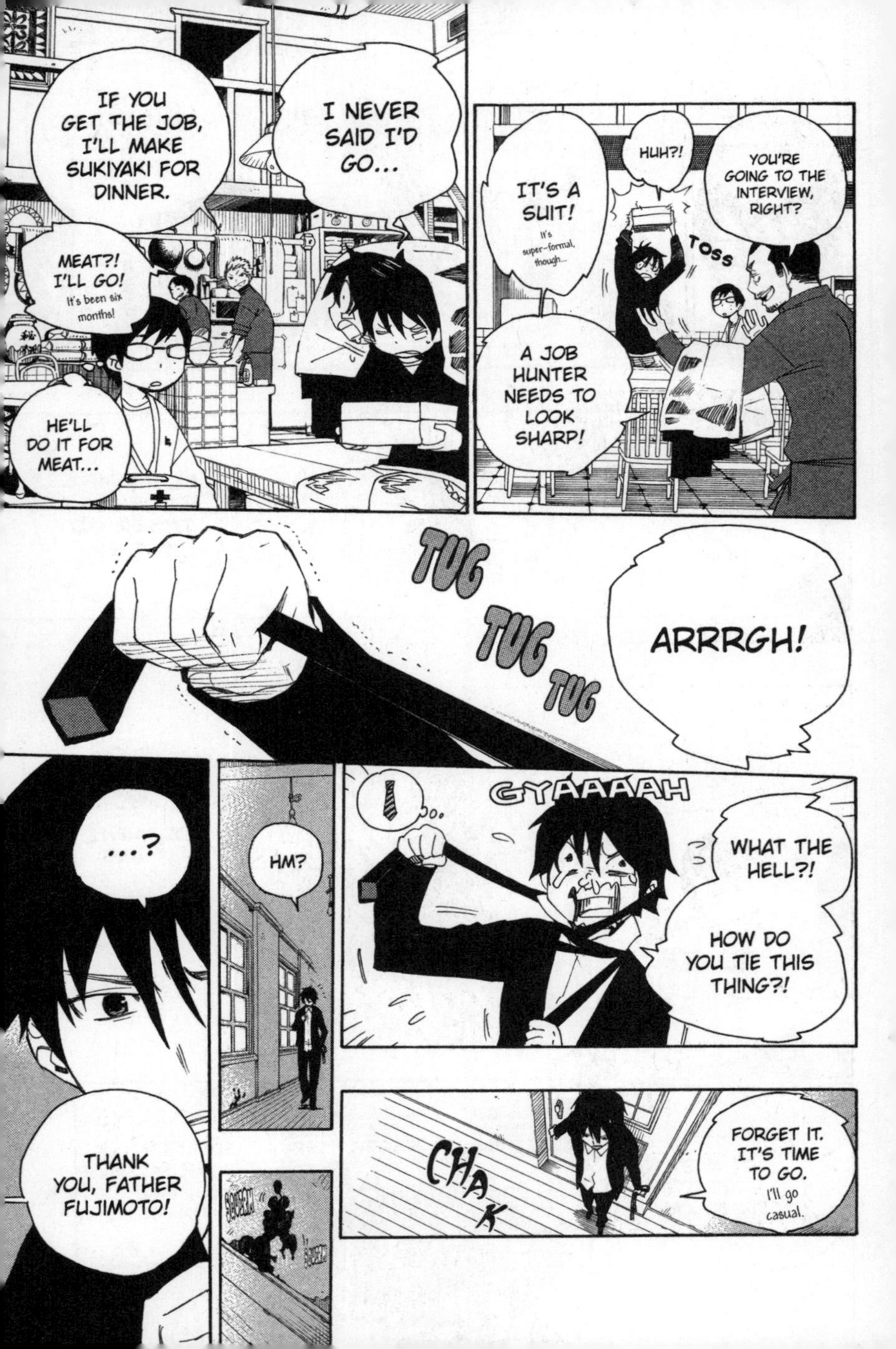
YOU'RE GOING TO THE INTERVIEW, RIGHT?
HUH?!
TOSS
IT'S A SUIT!
It's super-formal, though...
A JOB HUNTER NEEDS TO LOOK SHARP!
I NEVER SAID I'D GO...
IF YOU GET THE JOB, I'LL MAKE SUKIYAKI FOR DINNER.
MEAT?! I'LL GO!
It's been six months!
HE'LL DO IT FOR MEAT...
ARRRGH!
TUG
TUG
TUG
GYAAAAH
WHAT THE HELL?!
HOW DO YOU TIE THIS THING?!
FORGET IT. IT'S TIME TO GO.
I'll go casual.
CHAK
HM?
...?
THANK YOU, FATHER FUJIMOTO!

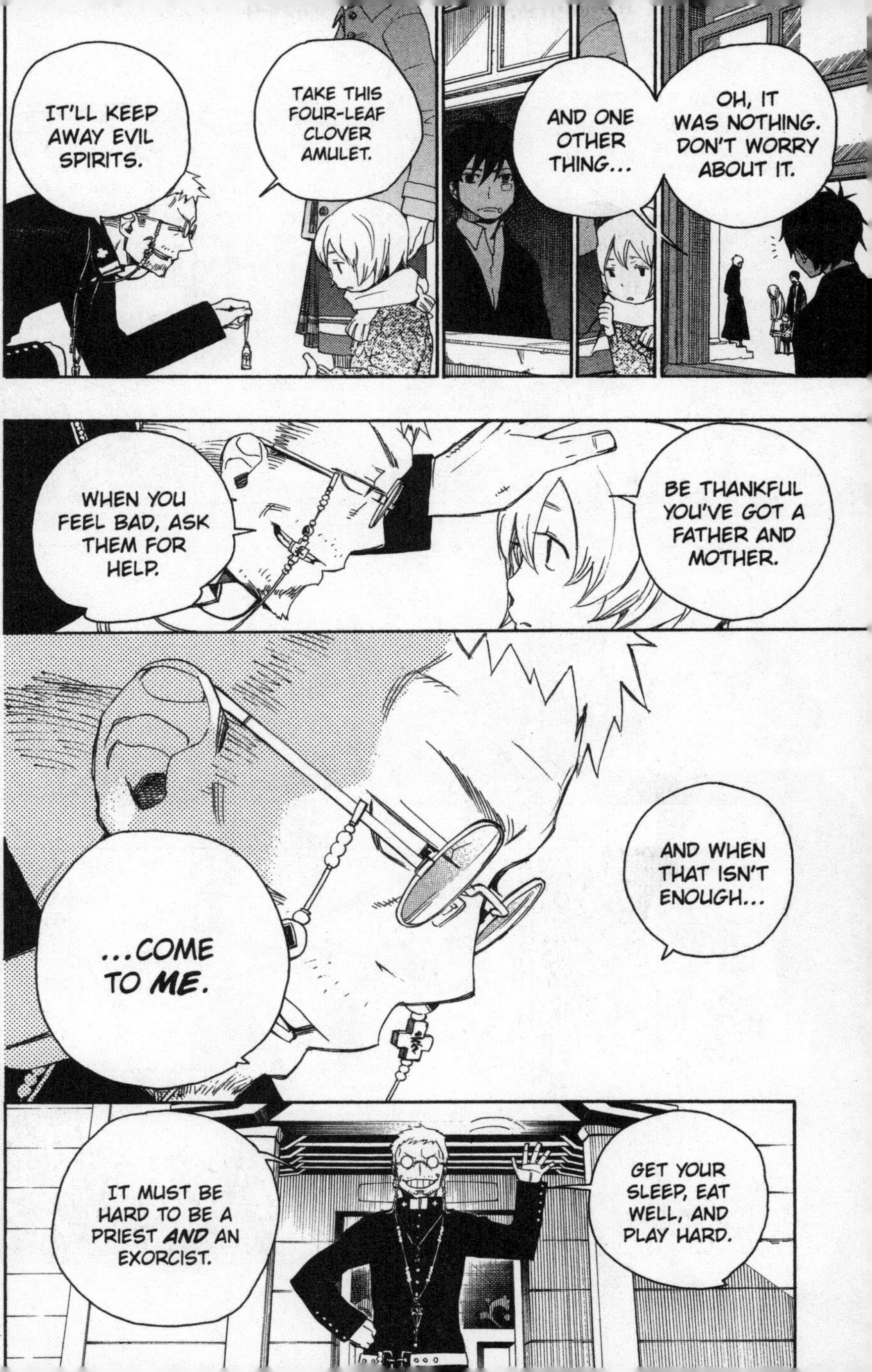
OH, IT WAS NOTHING. DON'T WORRY ABOUT IT.
AND ONE OTHER THING...
TAKE THIS FOUR-LEAF CLOVER AMULET.
IT'LL KEEP AWAY EVIL SPIRITS.
BE THANKFUL YOU'VE GOT A FATHER AND MOTHER.
WHEN YOU FEEL BAD, ASK THEM FOR HELP.
AND WHEN THAT ISN'T ENOUGH...
...COME TO *ME*.
GET YOUR SLEEP, EAT WELL, AND PLAY HARD.
IT MUST BE HARD TO BE A PRIEST *AND* AN EXORCIST.

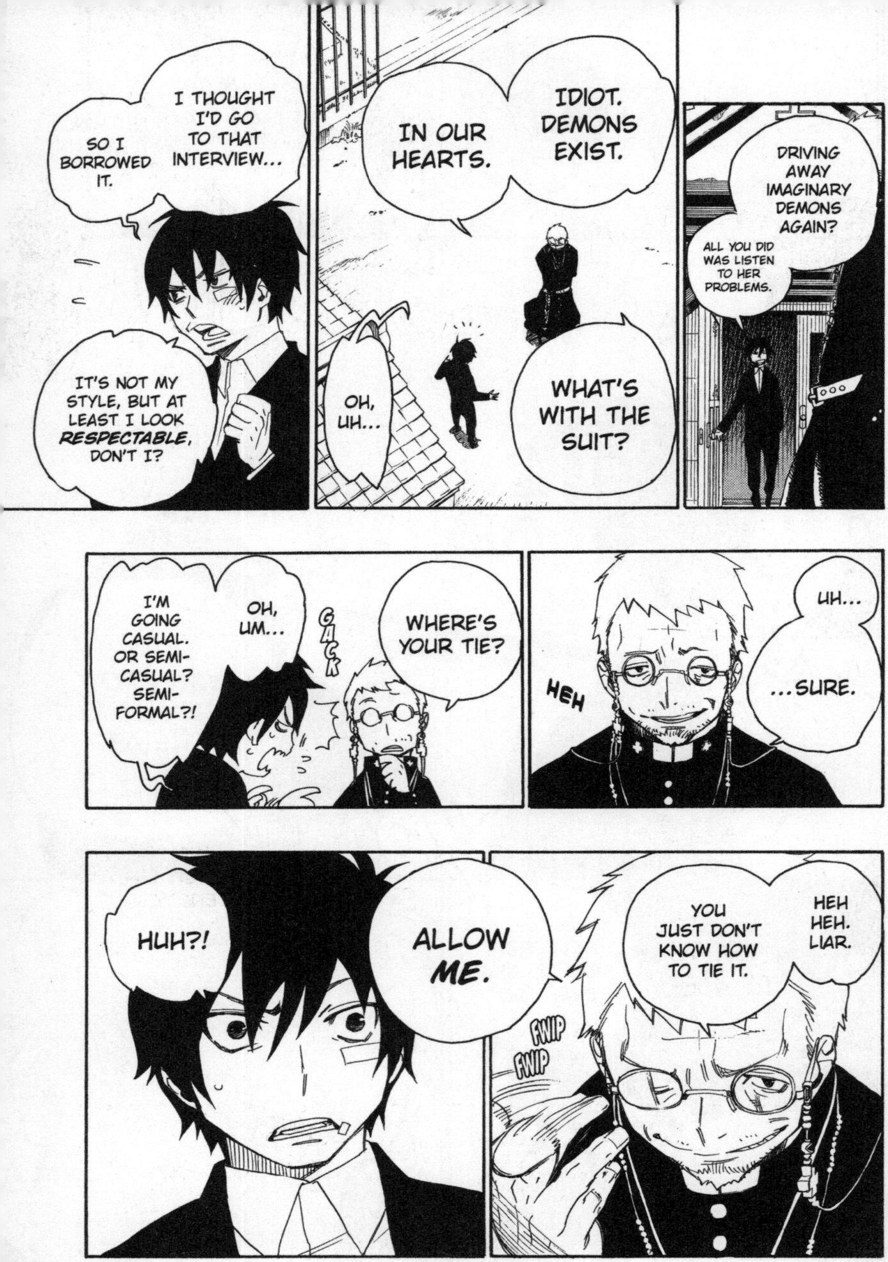
DRIVING AWAY IMAGINARY DEMONS AGAIN?
ALL YOU DID WAS LISTEN TO HER PROBLEMS.
IDIOT. DEMONS EXIST.
IN OUR HEARTS.
WHAT'S WITH THE SUIT?
OH, UH...
I THOUGHT I'D GO TO THAT INTERVIEW...
SO I BORROWED IT.
IT'S NOT MY STYLE, BUT AT LEAST I LOOK *RESPECTABLE*, DON'T I?
UH...
...SURE.
HEH
WHERE'S YOUR TIE?
GACK
OH, UM...
I'M GOING CASUAL. OR SEMI-CASUAL? SEMI-FORMAL?!
HEH HEH. LIAR.
YOU JUST DON'T KNOW HOW TO TIE IT.
FWIP
FWIP
ALLOW *ME*.
HUH?!

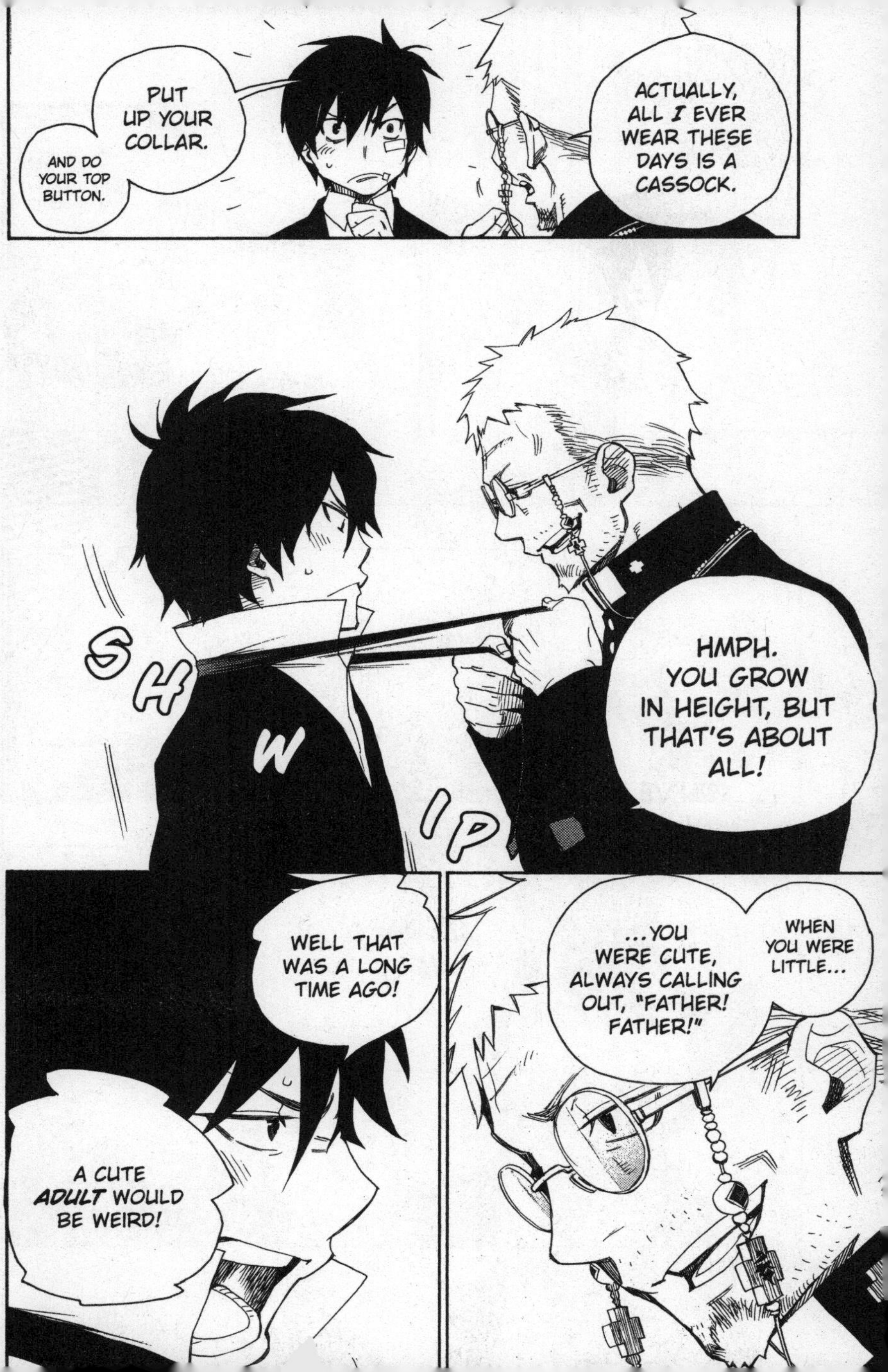
ACTUALLY, ALL I EVER WEAR THESE DAYS IS A CASSOCK.
PUT UP YOUR COLLAR.
AND DO YOUR TOP BUTTON.
HMPH. YOU GROW IN HEIGHT, BUT THAT'S ABOUT ALL!
SHWIP
WHEN YOU WERE LITTLE...
...YOU WERE CUTE, ALWAYS CALLING OUT, "FATHER! FATHER!"
WELL THAT WAS A LONG TIME AGO!
A CUTE ADULT WOULD BE WEIRD!

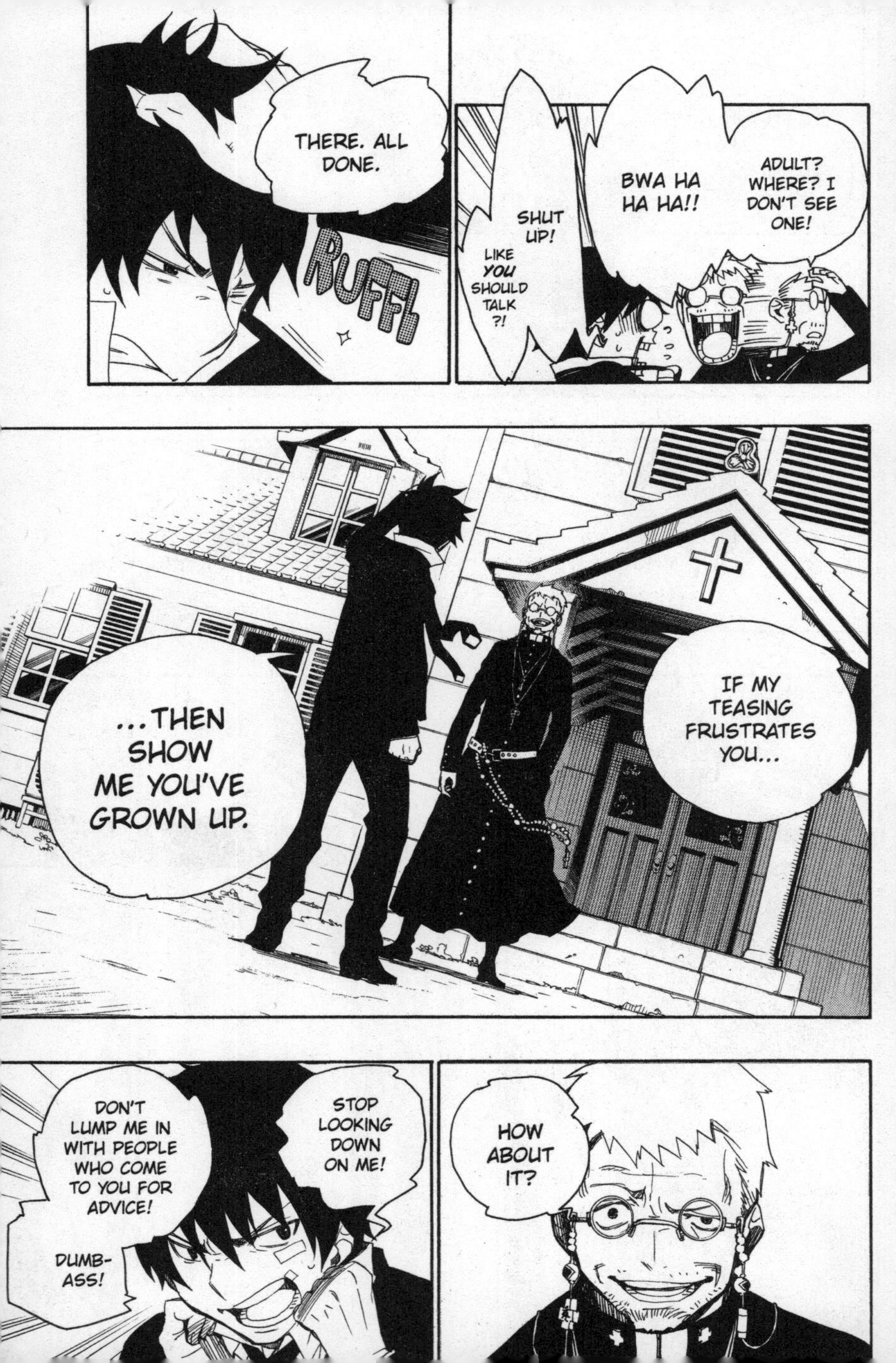
ADULT? WHERE? I DON'T SEE ONE!
BWA HA HA HA!!
SHUT UP! LIKE YOU SHOULD TALK?!
THERE. ALL DONE.
RUFFL
IF MY TEASING FRUSTRATES YOU...
...THEN SHOW ME YOU'VE GROWN UP.
HOW ABOUT IT?
STOP LOOKING DOWN ON ME!
DON'T LUMP ME IN WITH PEOPLE WHO COME TO YOU FOR ADVICE!
DUMB-ASS!

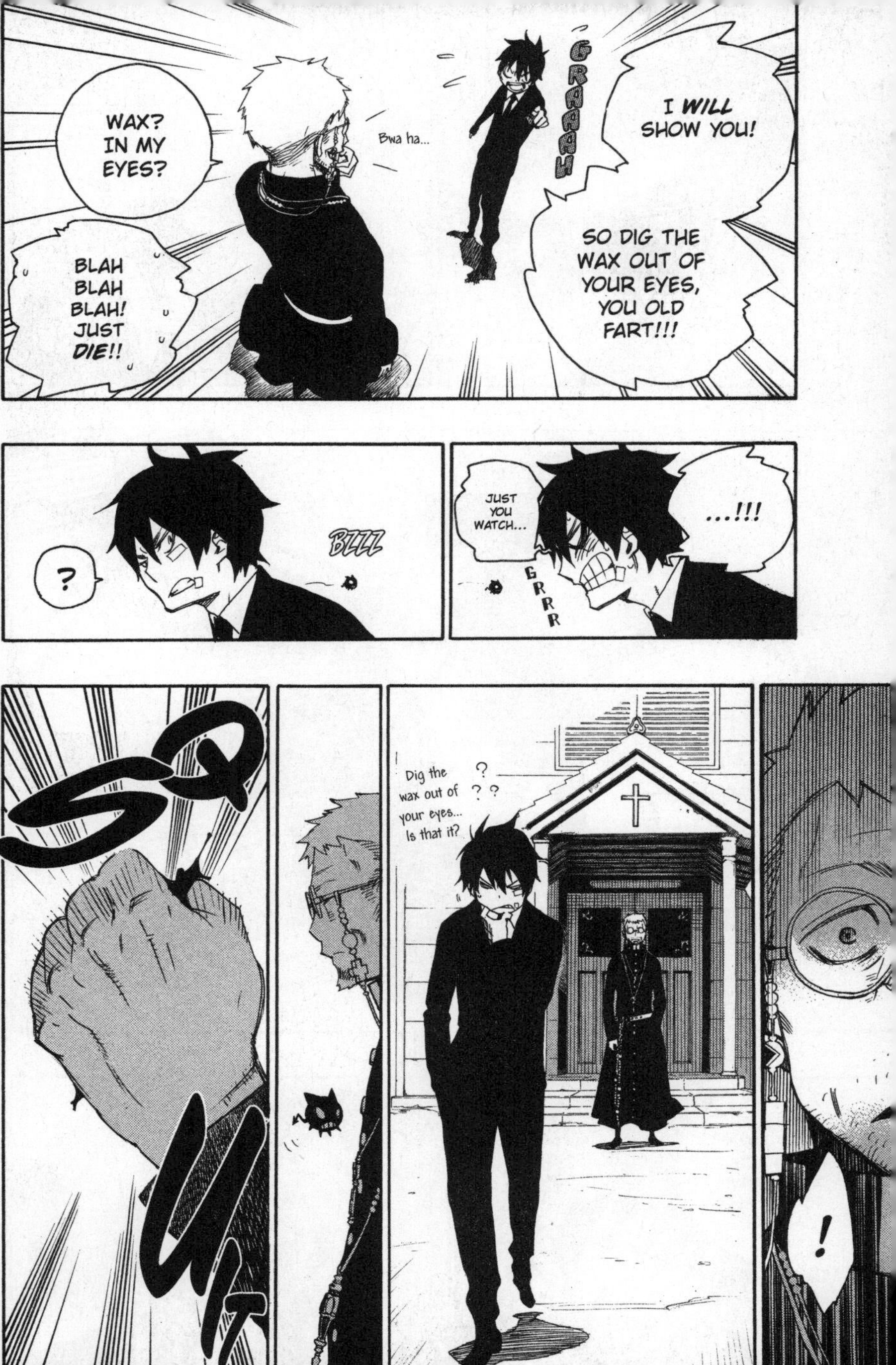
I WILL SHOW YOU!
GRAAAH
SO DIG THE WAX OUT OF YOUR EYES, YOU OLD FART!!!
Bwa ha...
WAX? IN MY EYES?
BLAH BLAH BLAH! JUST DIE!!
...!!!
JUST YOU WATCH...
GRRR
BZZZ
?
!
Dig the wax out of your eyes... Is that it?
? ? ?
SQUIT

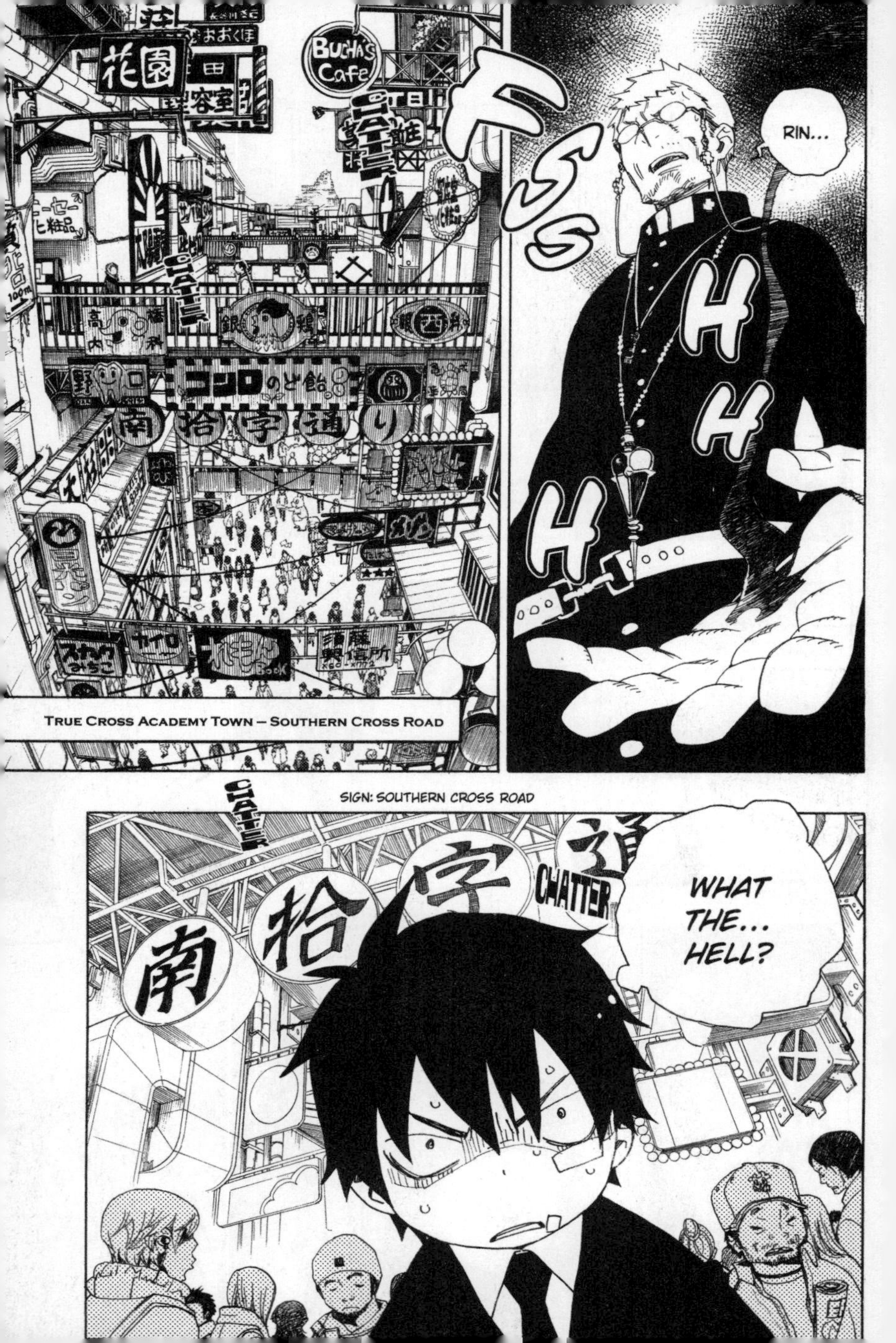
RIN...
FSSHHH
True Cross Academy Town – Southern Cross Road
BUCHA'S Cafe
花園
南拾字通り
CHATTER
Sign: Southern Cross Road
CHATTER
CHATTER
WHAT THE... HELL?

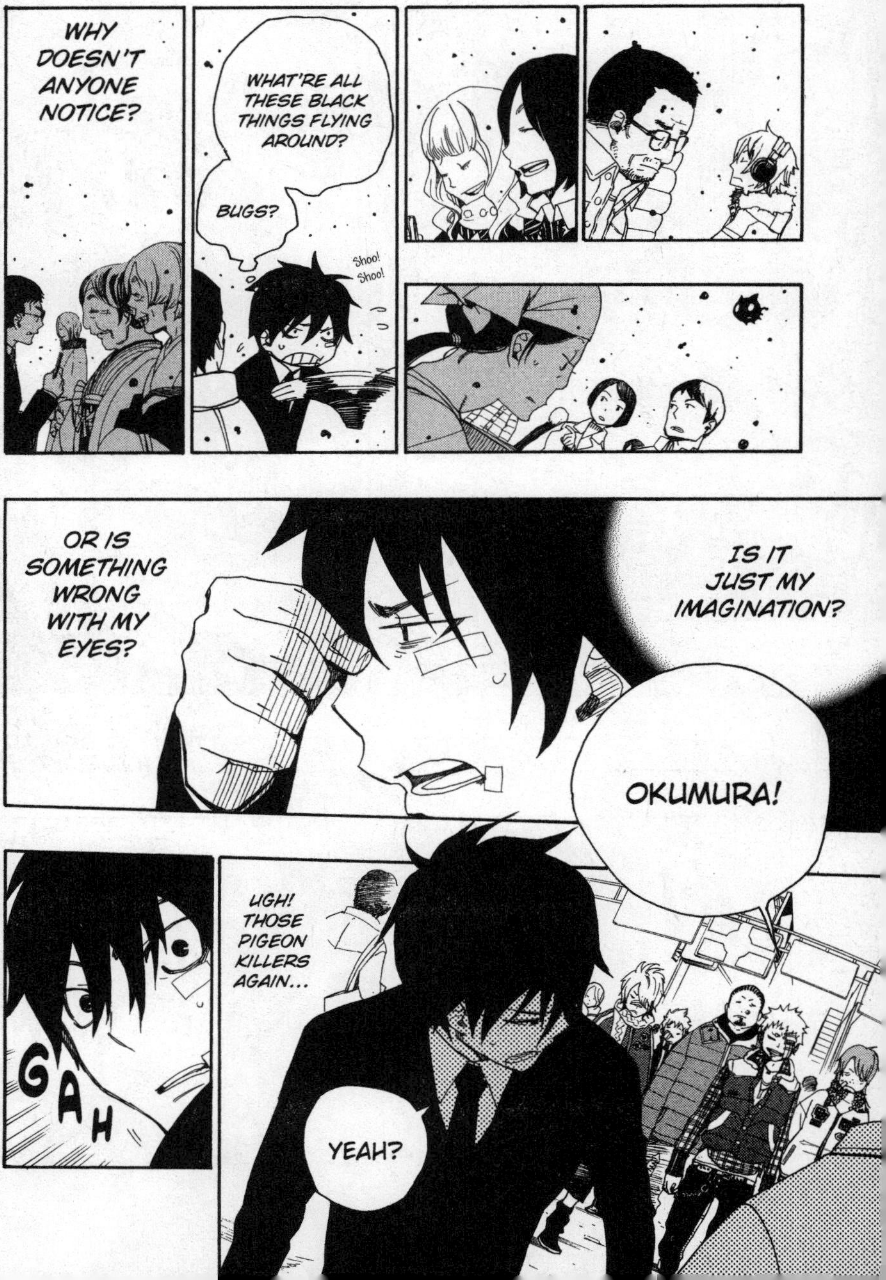
WHAT'RE ALL THESE BLACK THINGS FLYING AROUND?
BUGS?
Shoo! Shoo!
WHY DOESN'T ANYONE NOTICE?
IS IT JUST MY IMAGINATION?
OR IS SOMETHING WRONG WITH MY EYES?
OKUMURA!
UGH! THOSE PIGEON KILLERS AGAIN...
YEAH?
GAH

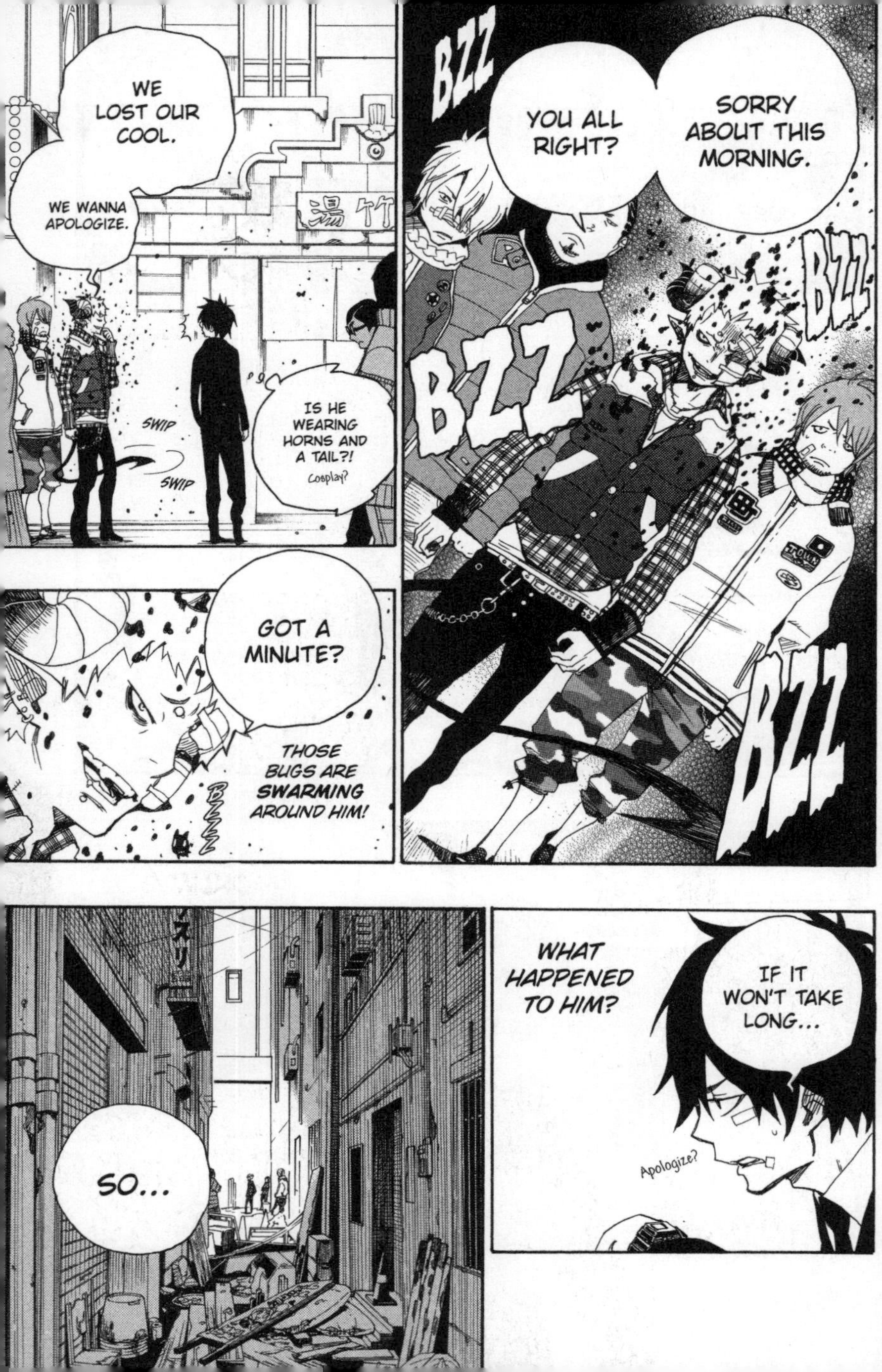
SORRY ABOUT THIS MORNING.
YOU ALL RIGHT?
BZZ
BZZ
BZZ
BZZ
WE LOST OUR COOL.
IS HE WEARING HORNS AND A TAIL?!
Cosplay?
WE WANNA APOLOGIZE.
SWIP
SWIP
GOT A MINUTE?
THOSE BUGS ARE SWARMING AROUND HIM!
BZZZ
IF IT WON'T TAKE LONG...
WHAT HAPPENED TO HIM?
Apologize?
SO...

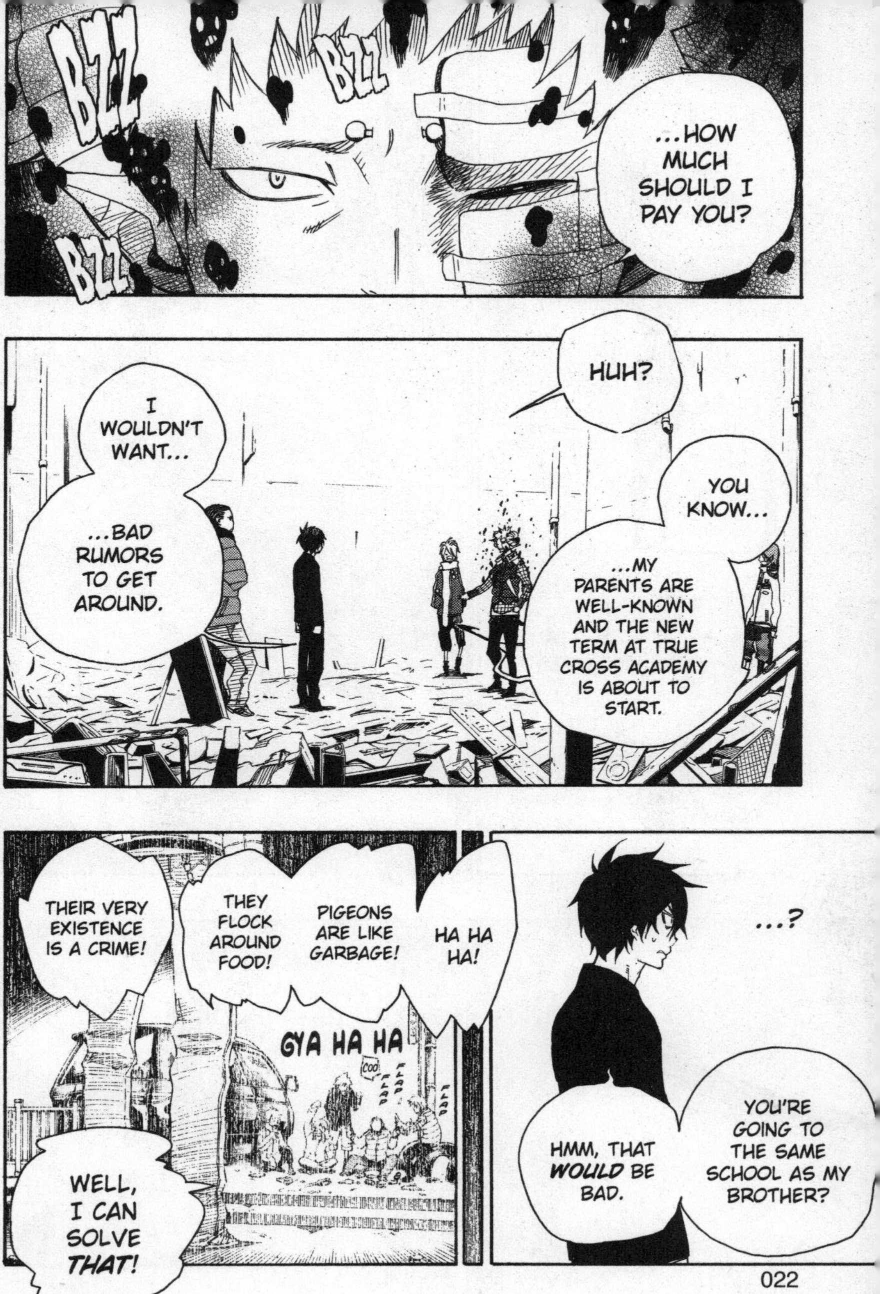
BZZ
BZZ
BZZ
...HOW MUCH SHOULD I PAY YOU?
HUH?
YOU KNOW...
...MY PARENTS ARE WELL-KNOWN AND THE NEW TERM AT TRUE CROSS ACADEMY IS ABOUT TO START.
I WOULDN'T WANT...
...BAD RUMORS TO GET AROUND.
...?
YOU'RE GOING TO THE SAME SCHOOL AS MY BROTHER?
HMM, THAT *WOULD* BE BAD.
HA HA HA!
PIGEONS ARE LIKE GARBAGE!
THEY FLOCK AROUND FOOD!
THEIR VERY EXISTENCE IS A CRIME!
GYA HA HA
COO
FLAP FLAP
FLAP
WELL, I CAN SOLVE *THAT*!

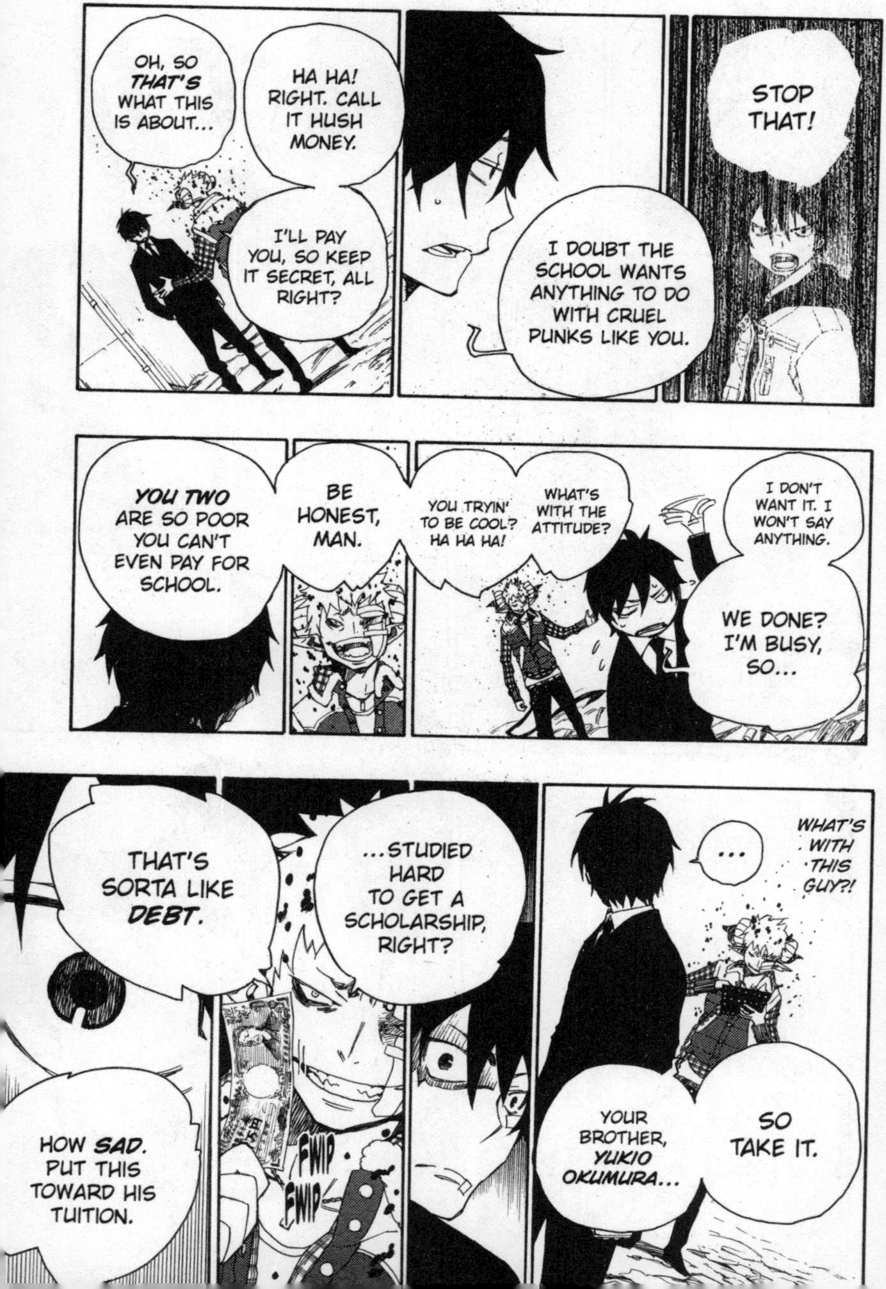
STOP THAT!
I DOUBT THE SCHOOL WANTS ANYTHING TO DO WITH CRUEL PUNKS LIKE YOU.
HA HA! RIGHT. CALL IT HUSH MONEY.
I'LL PAY YOU, SO KEEP IT SECRET, ALL RIGHT?
OH, SO *THAT'S* WHAT THIS IS ABOUT...
I DON'T WANT IT. I WON'T SAY ANYTHING.
WE DONE? I'M BUSY, SO...
WHAT'S WITH THE ATTITUDE?
YOU TRYIN' TO BE COOL? HA HA HA!
BE HONEST, MAN.
YOU TWO ARE SO POOR YOU CAN'T EVEN PAY FOR SCHOOL.
WHAT'S WITH THIS GUY?!
...
SO TAKE IT.
YOUR BROTHER, *YUKIO OKUMURA*...
...STUDIED HARD TO GET A SCHOLARSHIP, RIGHT?
FWIP
FWIP
THAT'S SORTA LIKE *DEBT*.
HOW *SAD*. PUT THIS TOWARD HIS TUITION.

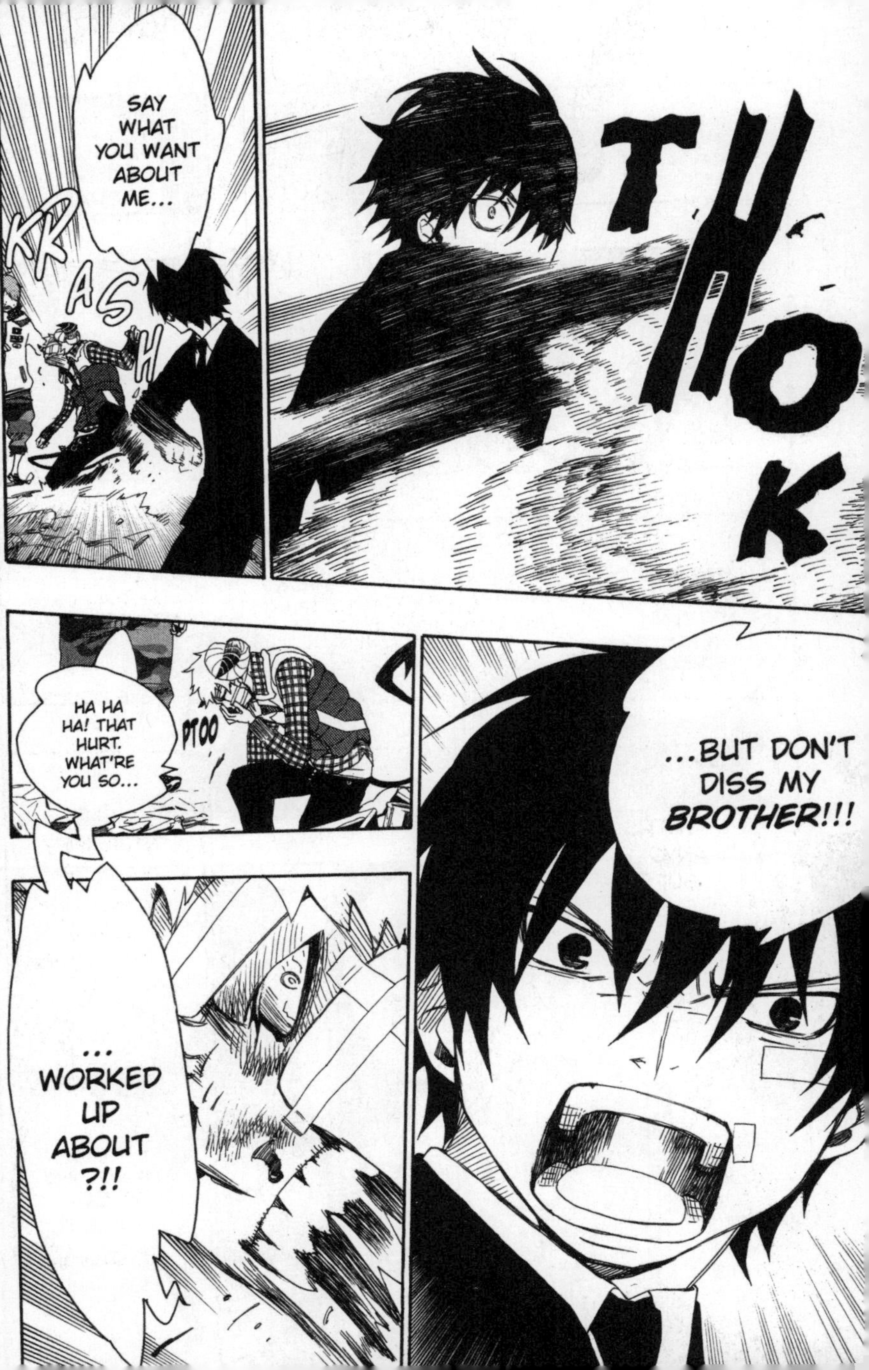
THOK
SAY WHAT YOU WANT ABOUT ME...
KRASH
...BUT DON'T DISS MY BROTHER!!!
HA HA HA! THAT HURT. WHAT'RE YOU SO...
PTOO
...WORKED UP ABOUT?!!

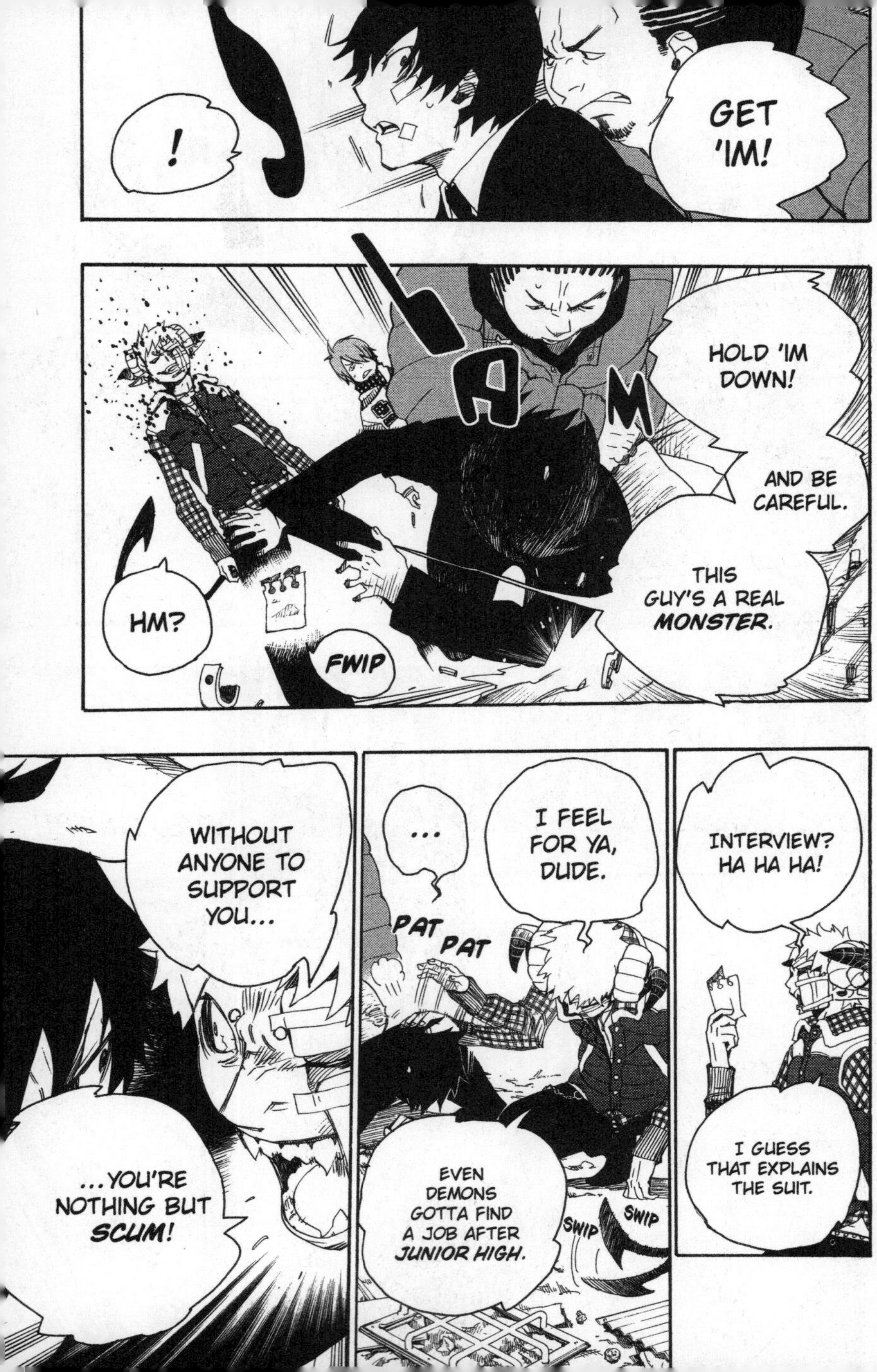
GET 'IM!
!
HOLD 'IM DOWN!
AND BE CAREFUL.
THIS GUY'S A REAL MONSTER.
HM?
FWIP
INTERVIEW? HA HA HA!
I GUESS THAT EXPLAINS THE SUIT.
I FEEL FOR YA, DUDE.
...
PAT PAT
EVEN DEMONS GOTTA FIND A JOB AFTER JUNIOR HIGH.
SWIP SWIP
WITHOUT ANYONE TO SUPPORT YOU...
...YOU'RE NOTHING BUT SCUM!

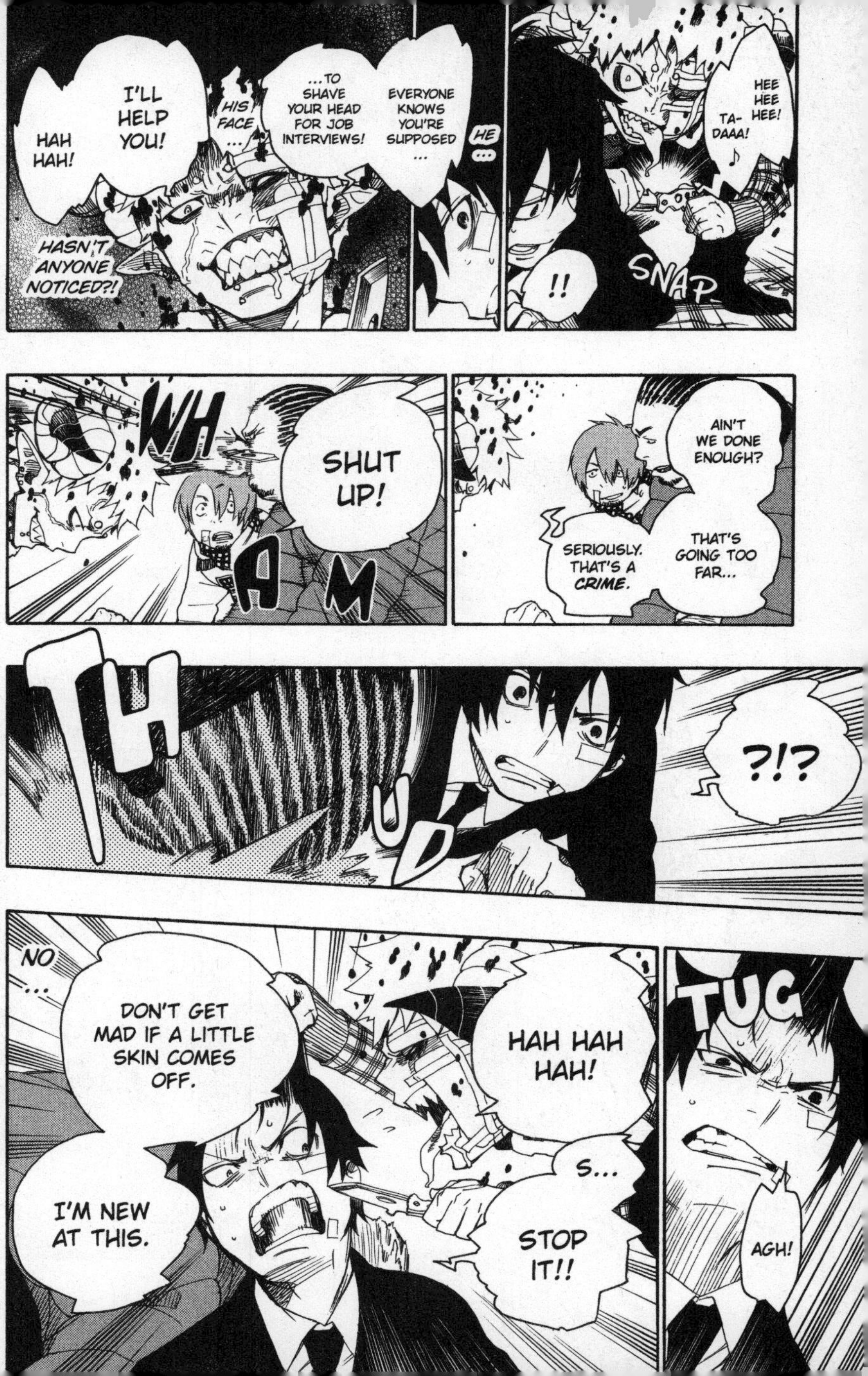
HEE HEE HEE!
TA-DAAA! ♪
SNAP
!!
HE...
EVERYONE KNOWS YOU'RE SUPPOSED ...
...TO SHAVE YOUR HEAD FOR JOB INTERVIEWS!
HIS FACE ...
I'LL HELP YOU!
HAH HAH!
HASN'T ANYONE NOTICED?!
AIN'T WE DONE ENOUGH?
THAT'S GOING TOO FAR...
SERIOUSLY. THAT'S A *CRIME*.
SHUT UP!
WHAM
?!?
THUD
TUG
AGH!
HAH HAH HAH!
S...
STOP IT!!
DON'T GET MAD IF A LITTLE SKIN COMES OFF.
NO...
I'M NEW AT THIS.

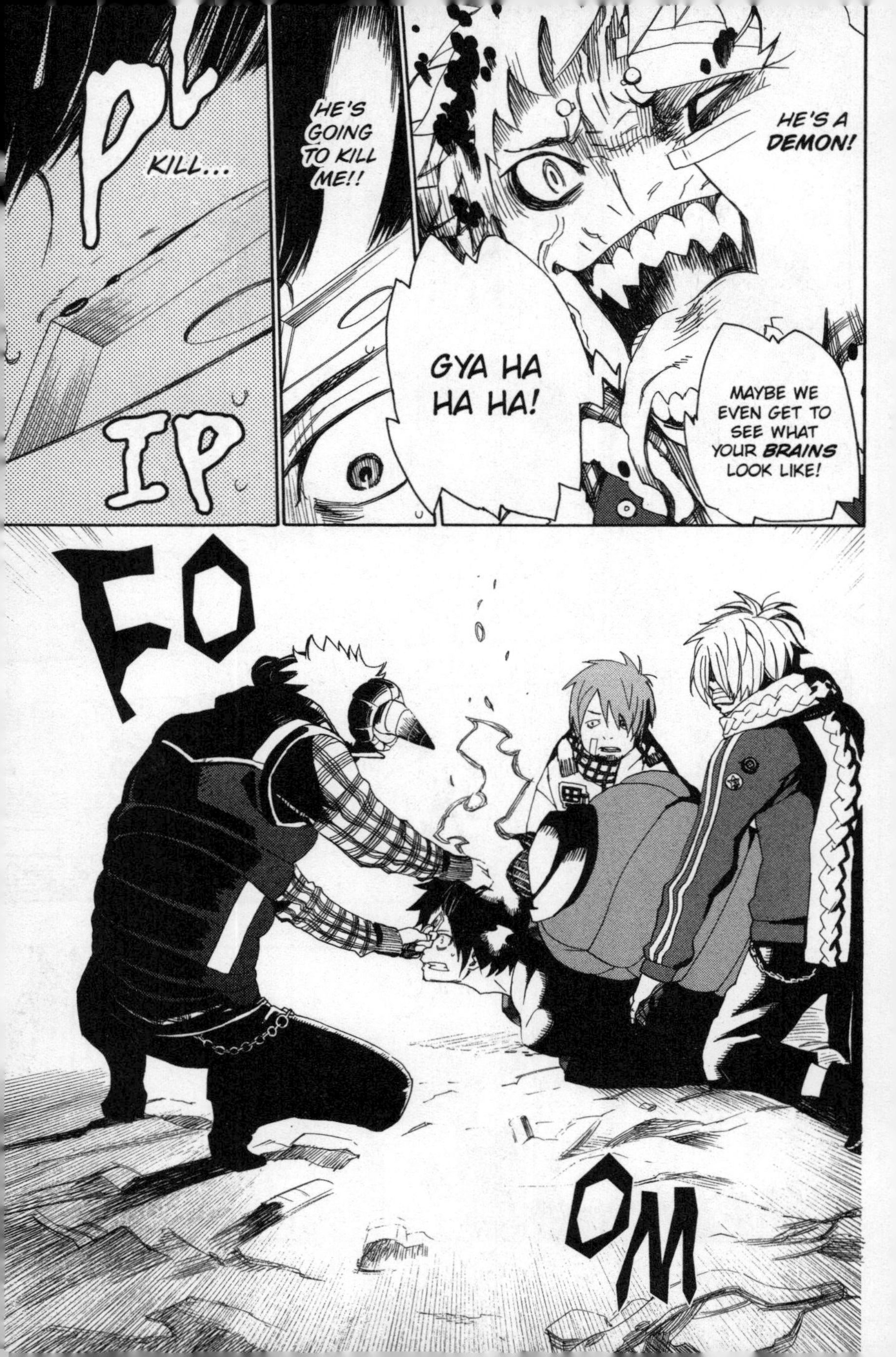
GYA HA HA HA!
MAYBE WE EVEN GET TO SEE WHAT YOUR BRAINS LOOK LIKE!
HE'S A DEMON!
HE'S GOING TO KILL ME!!
KILL...
DRIP
FOOM

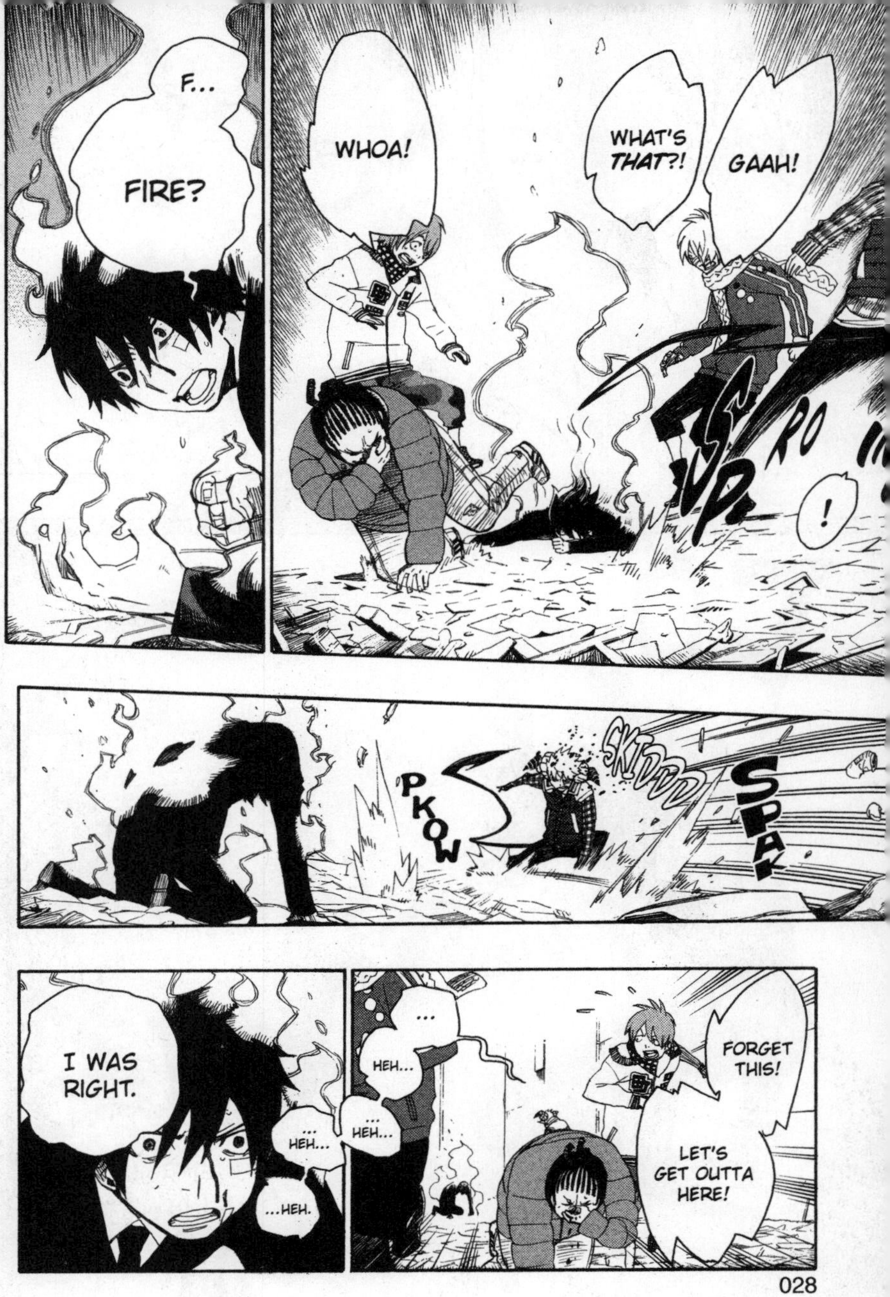
GAAH!
WHAT'S *THAT*?!
WHOA!
!
F...
FIRE?
SPAK
SKIDDDD
PKOW
FORGET THIS!
LET'S GET OUTTA HERE!
...
HEH...
... HEH...
... HEH...
...HEH.
I WAS RIGHT.

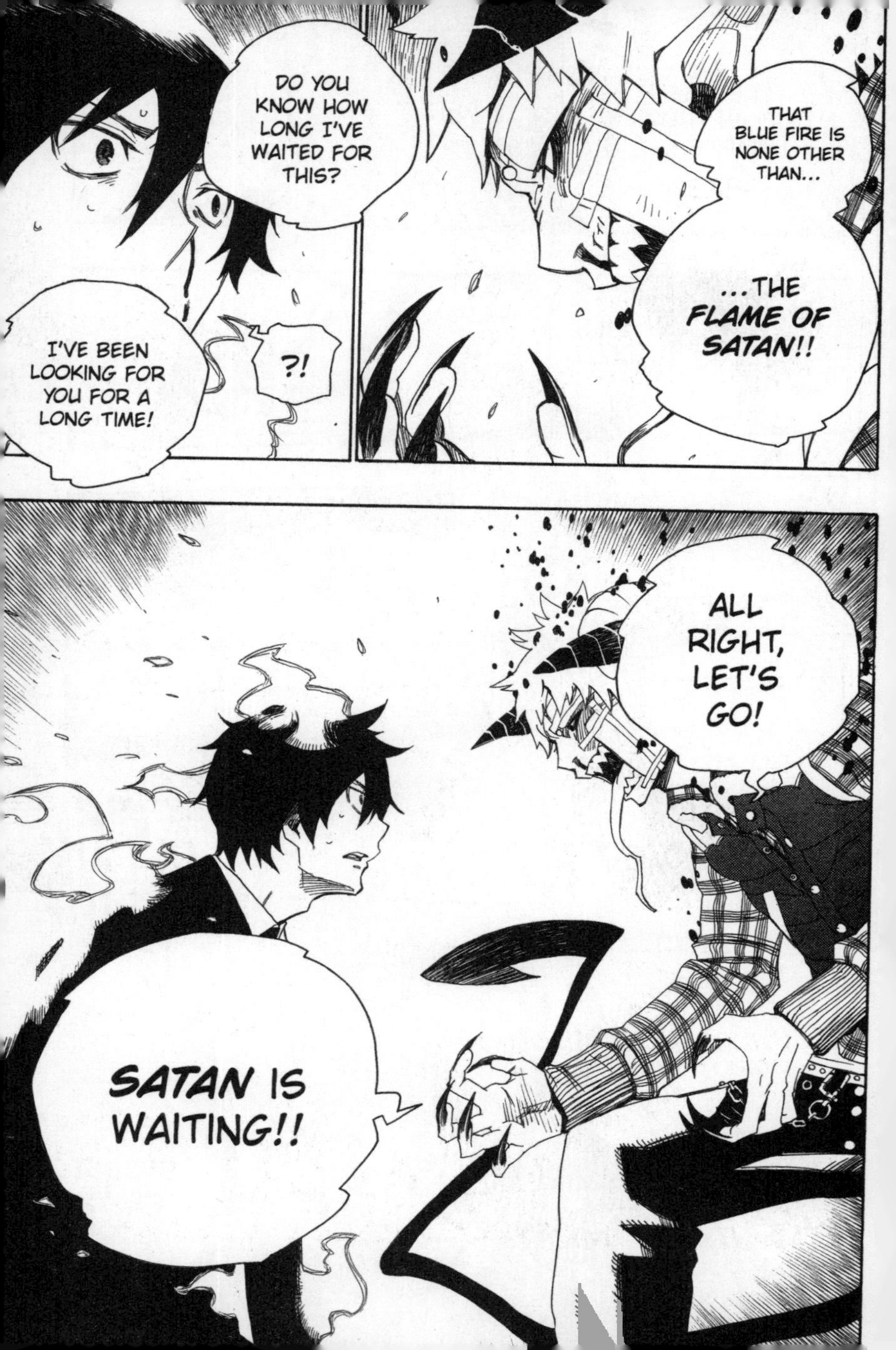
THAT BLUE FIRE IS NONE OTHER THAN...
...THE FLAME OF SATAN!!
DO YOU KNOW HOW LONG I'VE WAITED FOR THIS?
?!
I'VE BEEN LOOKING FOR YOU FOR A LONG TIME!
ALL RIGHT, LET'S GO!
SATAN IS WAITING!!

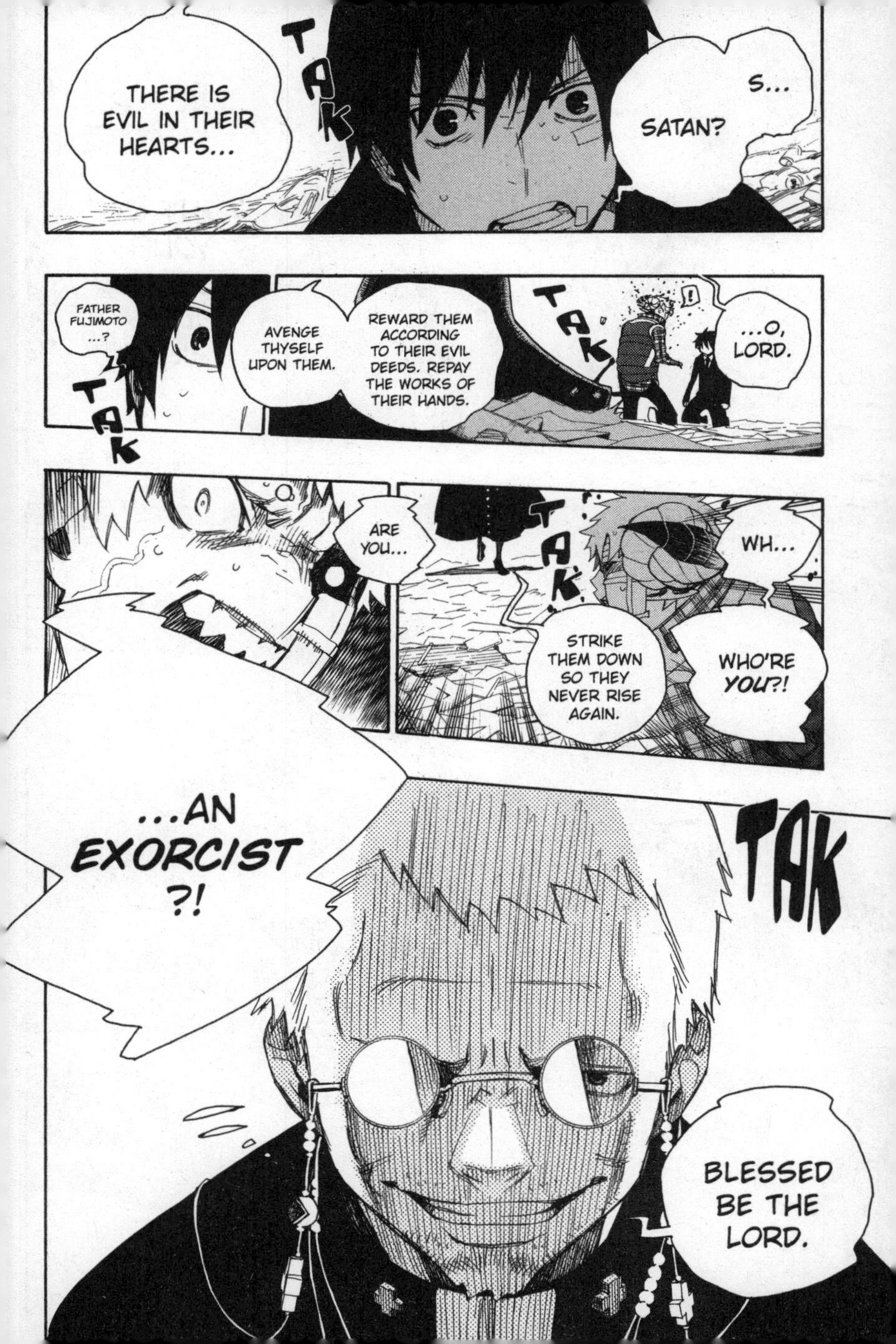
S...
SATAN?
TAK
THERE IS EVIL IN THEIR HEARTS...
...O, LORD.
!
TAK
REWARD THEM ACCORDING TO THEIR EVIL DEEDS. REPAY THE WORKS OF THEIR HANDS.
AVENGE THYSELF UPON THEM.
FATHER FUJIMOTO ...?
TAK
WH...
WHO'RE *YOU*?!
TAK
STRIKE THEM DOWN SO THEY NEVER RISE AGAIN.
ARE YOU...
TAK
BLESSED BE THE LORD.
...AN *EXORCIST* ?!

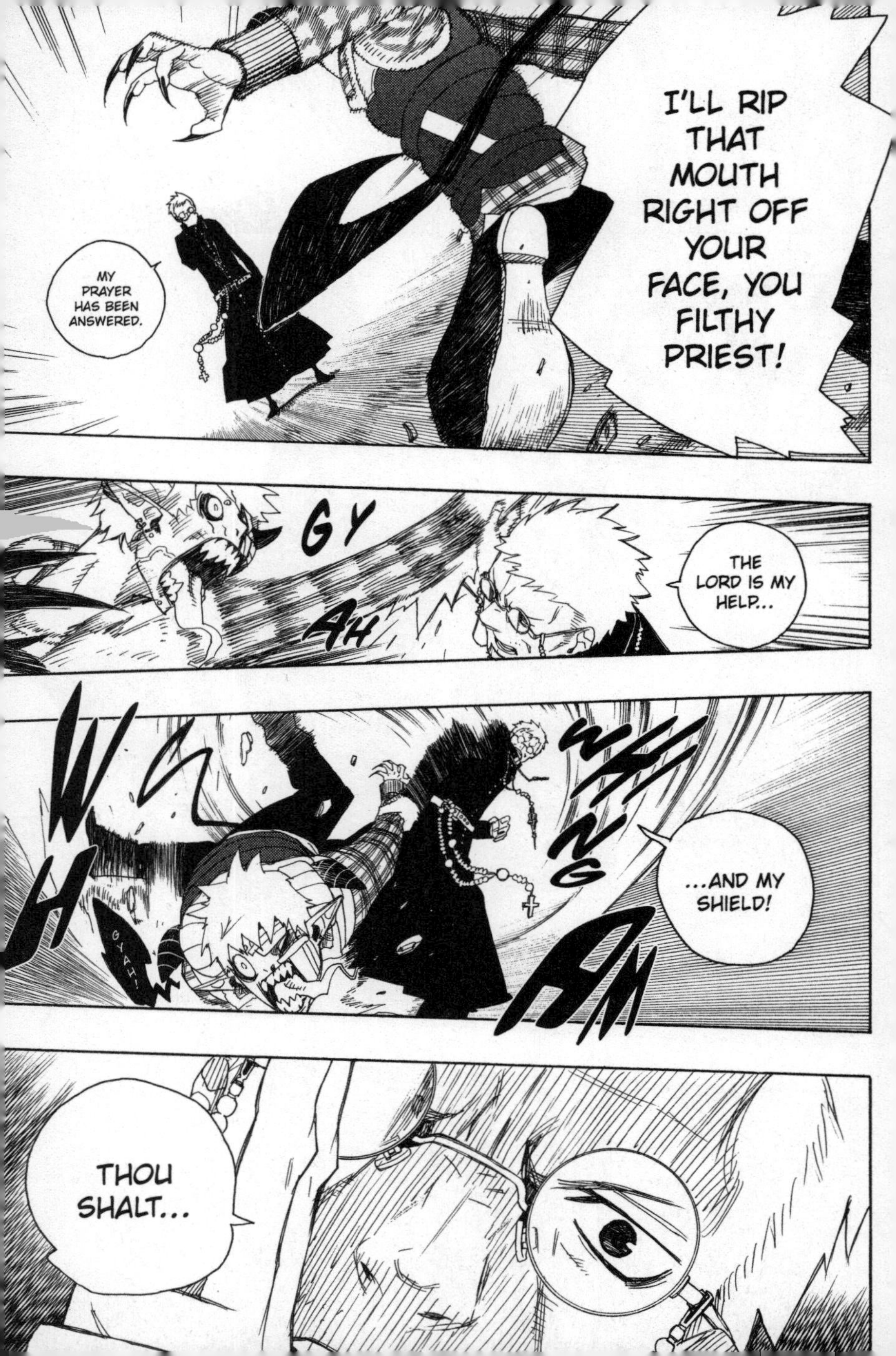
I'LL RIP THAT MOUTH RIGHT OFF YOUR FACE, YOU FILTHY PRIEST!
MY PRAYER HAS BEEN ANSWERED.
THE LORD IS MY HELP...
GY
AH
...AND MY SHIELD!
GYAH!
THOU SHALT...

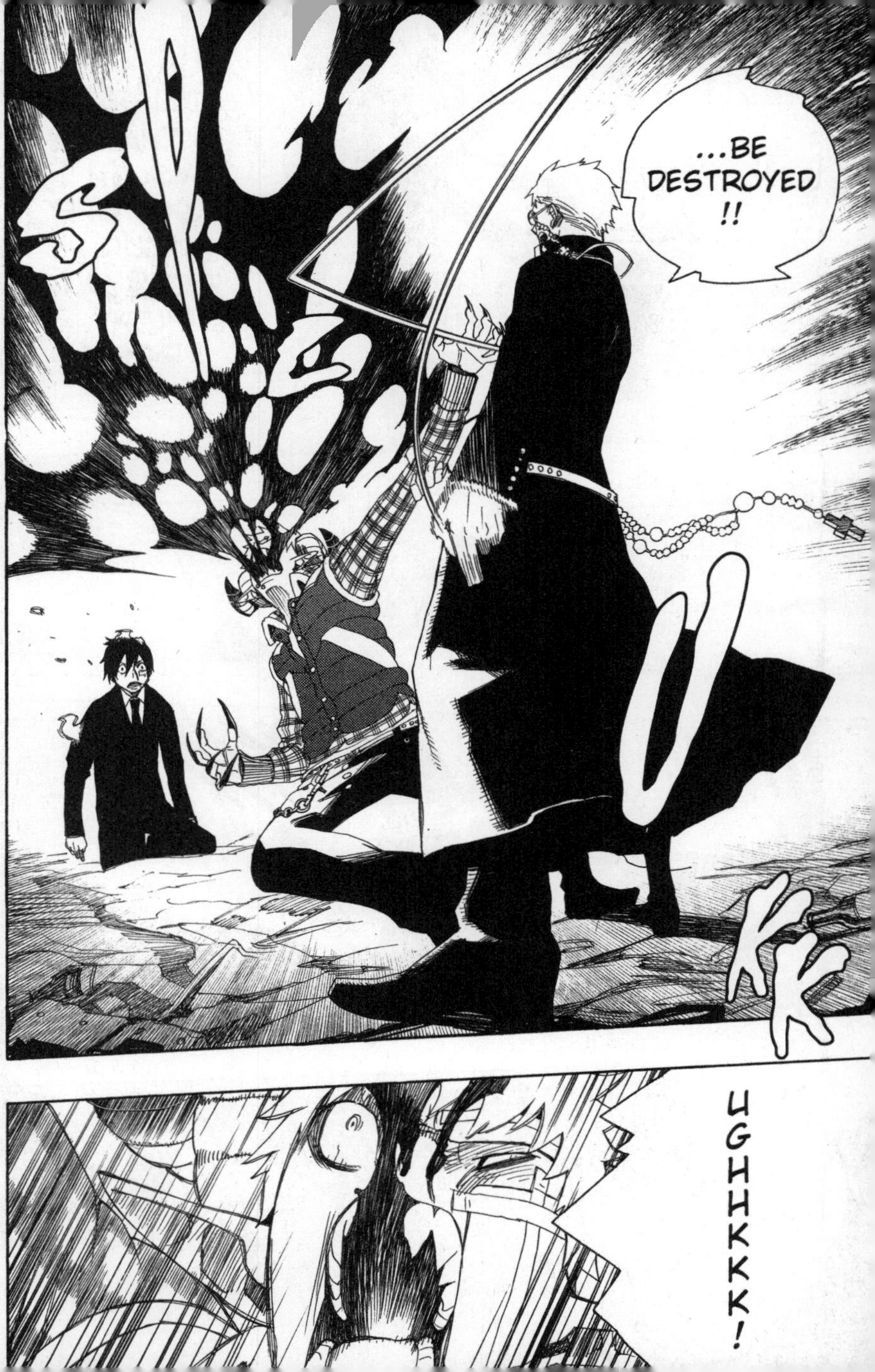
...BE DESTROYED !!
KK
UGHHKKK!

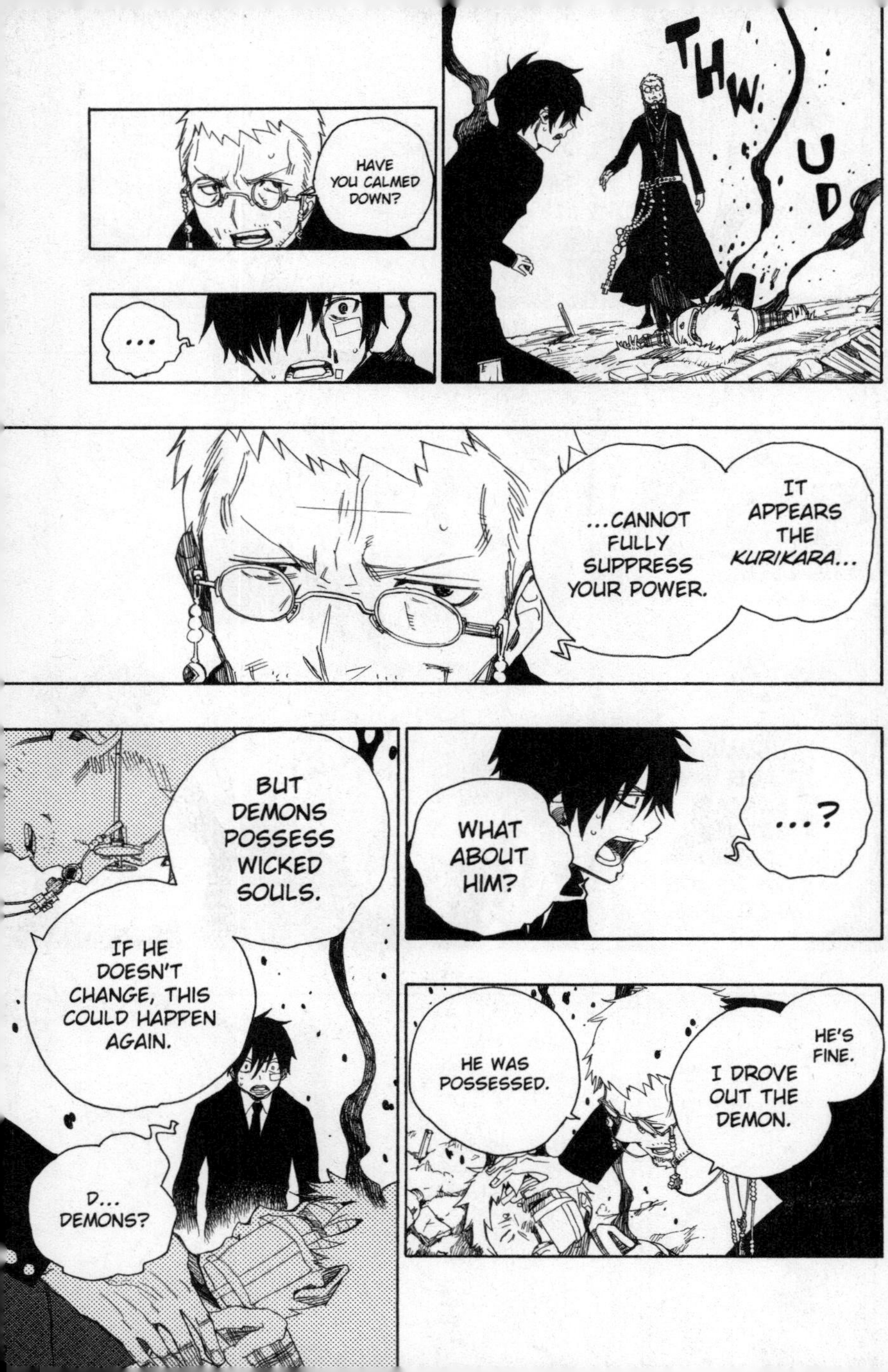
THW... UD
HAVE YOU CALMED DOWN?
...
IT APPEARS THE *KURIKARA*...
...CANNOT FULLY SUPPRESS YOUR POWER.
...?
WHAT ABOUT HIM?
HE'S FINE.
I DROVE OUT THE DEMON.
HE WAS POSSESSED.
BUT DEMONS POSSESS WICKED SOULS.
IF HE DOESN'T CHANGE, THIS COULD HAPPEN AGAIN.
D... DEMONS?

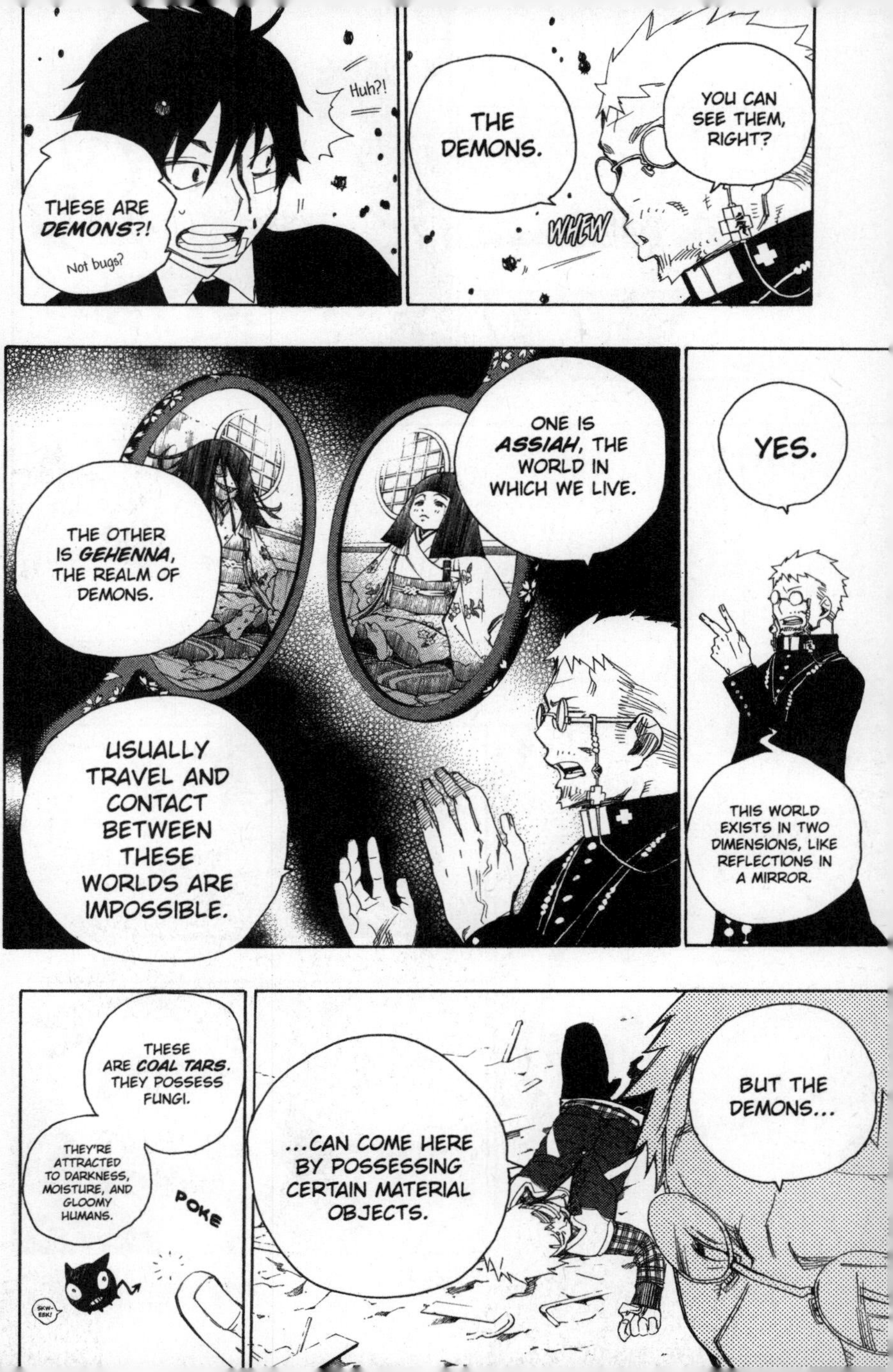
YOU CAN SEE THEM, RIGHT?
THE DEMONS.
WHEW
Huh?!
THESE ARE DEMONS?!
Not bugs?
YES.
THIS WORLD EXISTS IN TWO DIMENSIONS, LIKE REFLECTIONS IN A MIRROR.
ONE IS ASSIAH, THE WORLD IN WHICH WE LIVE.
THE OTHER IS GEHENNA, THE REALM OF DEMONS.
USUALLY TRAVEL AND CONTACT BETWEEN THESE WORLDS ARE IMPOSSIBLE.
BUT THE DEMONS...
...CAN COME HERE BY POSSESSING CERTAIN MATERIAL OBJECTS.
THESE ARE COAL TARS. THEY POSSESS FUNGI.
THEY'RE ATTRACTED TO DARKNESS, MOISTURE, AND GLOOMY HUMANS.
POKE
SKW-EEK!

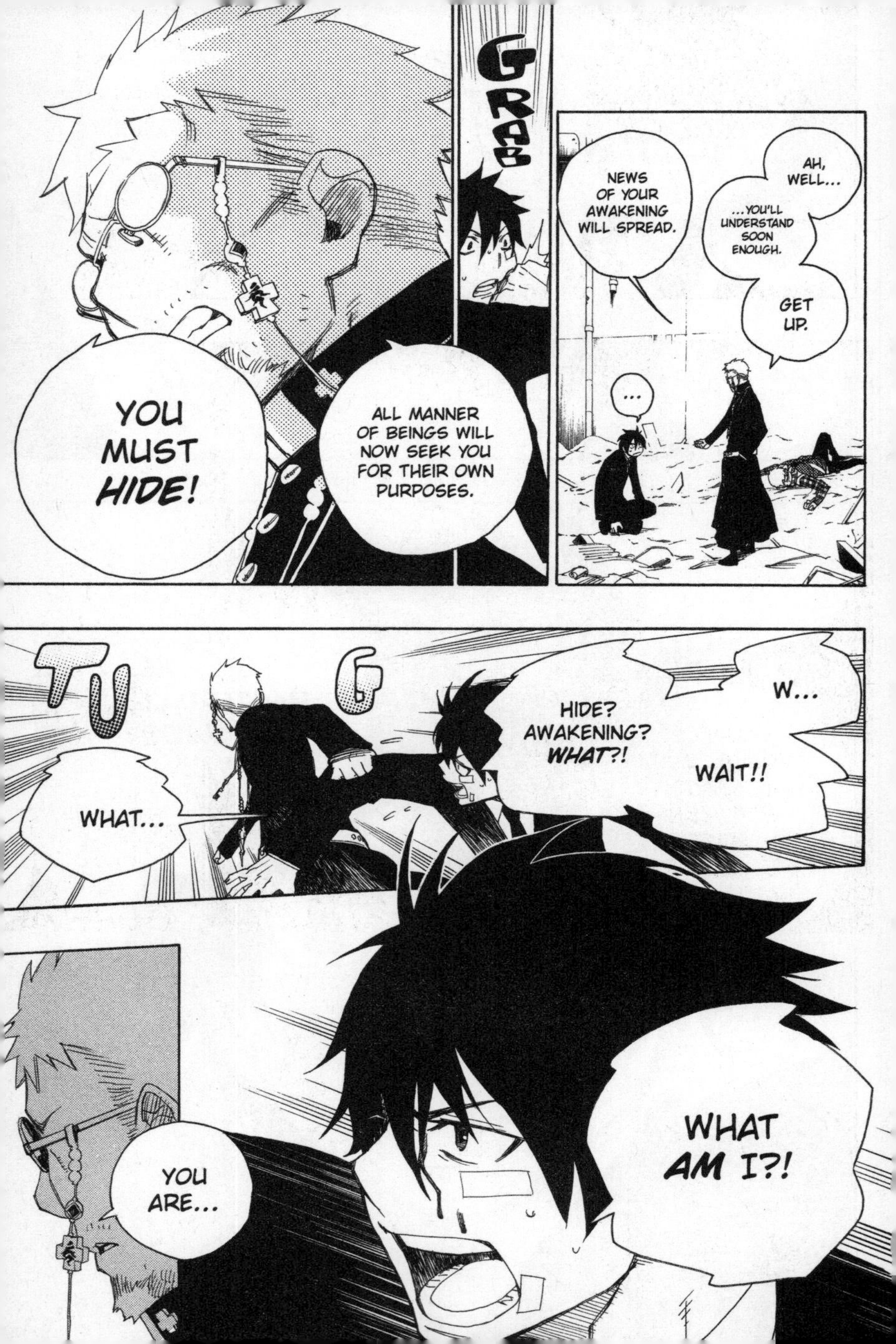
AH, WELL...
...YOU'LL UNDERSTAND SOON ENOUGH.
GET UP.
NEWS OF YOUR AWAKENING WILL SPREAD.
...
GRAB
ALL MANNER OF BEINGS WILL NOW SEEK YOU FOR THEIR OWN PURPOSES.
YOU MUST HIDE!
W...
WAIT!!
HIDE? AWAKENING? WHAT?!
TUG
WHAT...
WHAT AM I?!
YOU ARE...

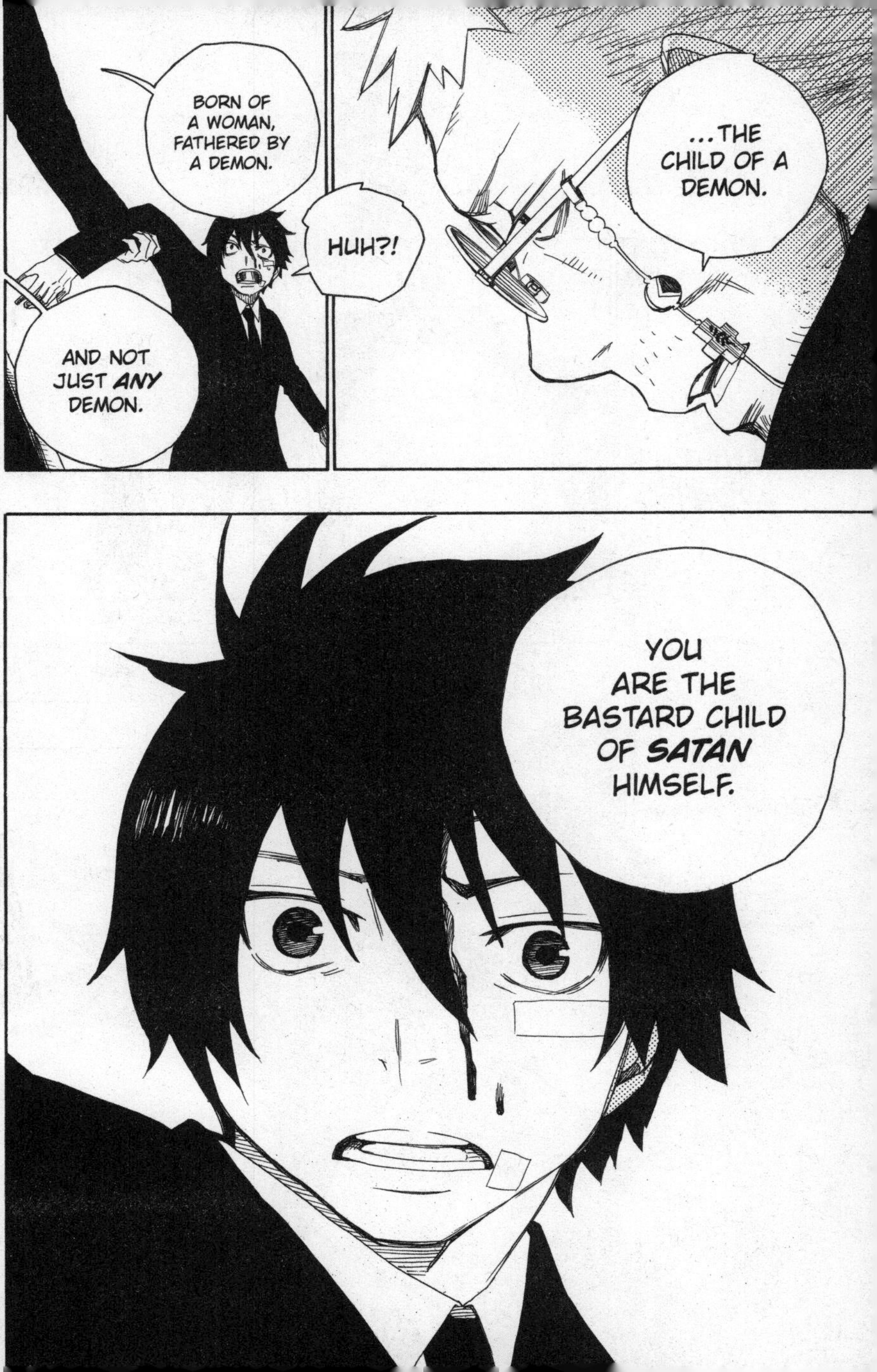
...THE CHILD OF A DEMON.
BORN OF A WOMAN, FATHERED BY A DEMON.
HUH?!
AND NOT JUST *ANY* DEMON.
YOU ARE THE BASTARD CHILD OF *SATAN* HIMSELF.

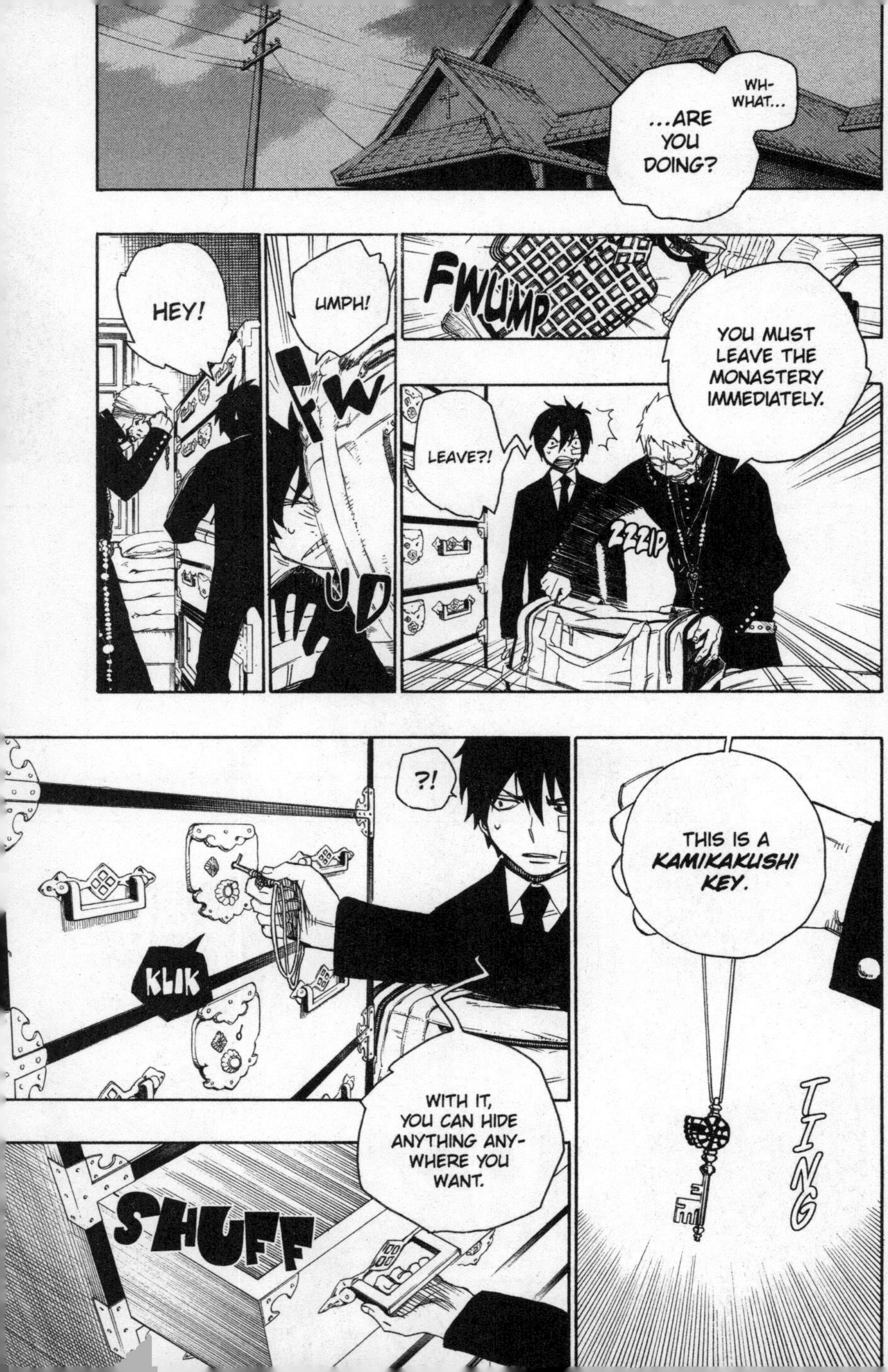
WH- WHAT...
...ARE YOU DOING?
FWUMP
YOU MUST LEAVE THE MONASTERY IMMEDIATELY.
LEAVE?!
ZZZIP
UMPH!
FWUD
HEY!
THIS IS A KAMIKAKUSHI KEY.
TING
?!
KLIK
WITH IT, YOU CAN HIDE ANYTHING ANY- WHERE YOU WANT.
SHUFF

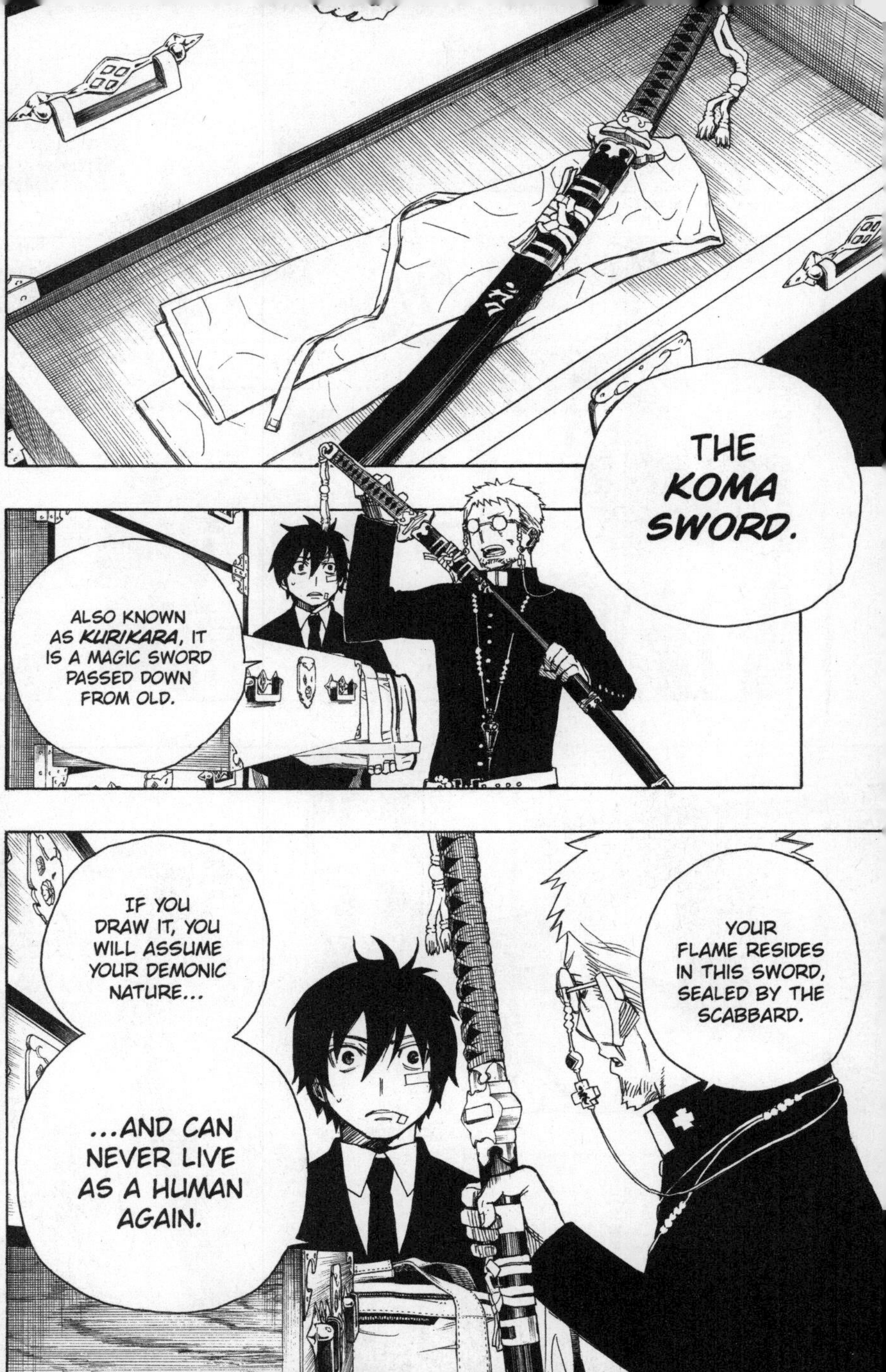

THE KOMA SWORD.
ALSO KNOWN AS KURIKARA, IT IS A MAGIC SWORD PASSED DOWN FROM OLD.
YOUR FLAME RESIDES IN THIS SWORD, SEALED BY THE SCABBARD.
IF YOU DRAW IT, YOU WILL ASSUME YOUR DEMONIC NATURE...
...AND CAN NEVER LIVE AS A HUMAN AGAIN.

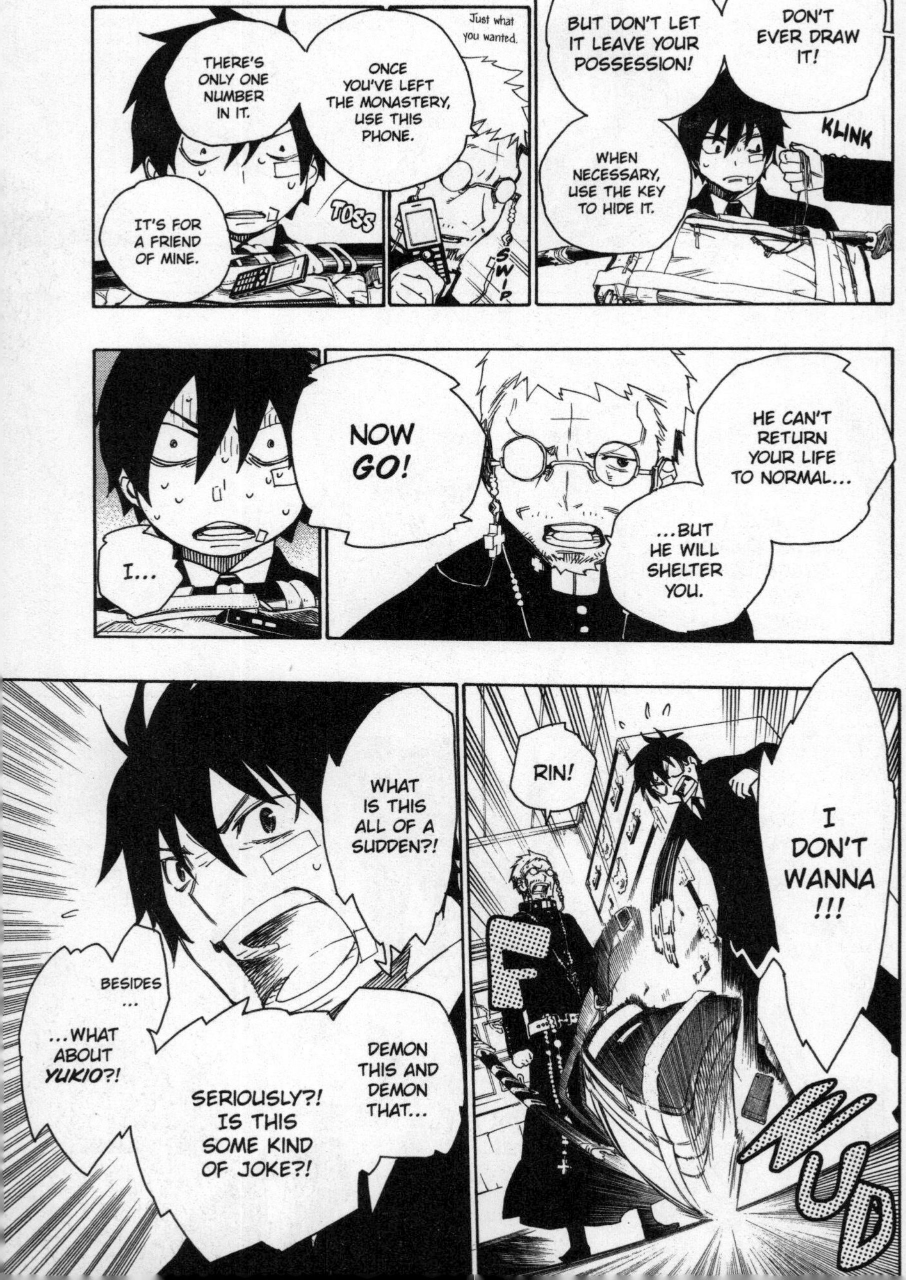
DON'T EVER DRAW IT!
KLINK
BUT DON'T LET IT LEAVE YOUR POSSESSION!
WHEN NECESSARY, USE THE KEY TO HIDE IT.
Just what you wanted.
ONCE YOU'VE LEFT THE MONASTERY, USE THIS PHONE.
SWIP
THERE'S ONLY ONE NUMBER IN IT.
TOSS
IT'S FOR A FRIEND OF MINE.
HE CAN'T RETURN YOUR LIFE TO NORMAL...
...BUT HE WILL SHELTER YOU.
NOW *GO!*
I...
I DON'T WANNA!!!
RIN!
F
WUD
WHAT IS THIS ALL OF A SUDDEN?!
DEMON THIS AND DEMON THAT...
SERIOUSLY?! IS THIS SOME KIND OF JOKE?!
BESIDES...
...WHAT ABOUT *YUKIO*?!

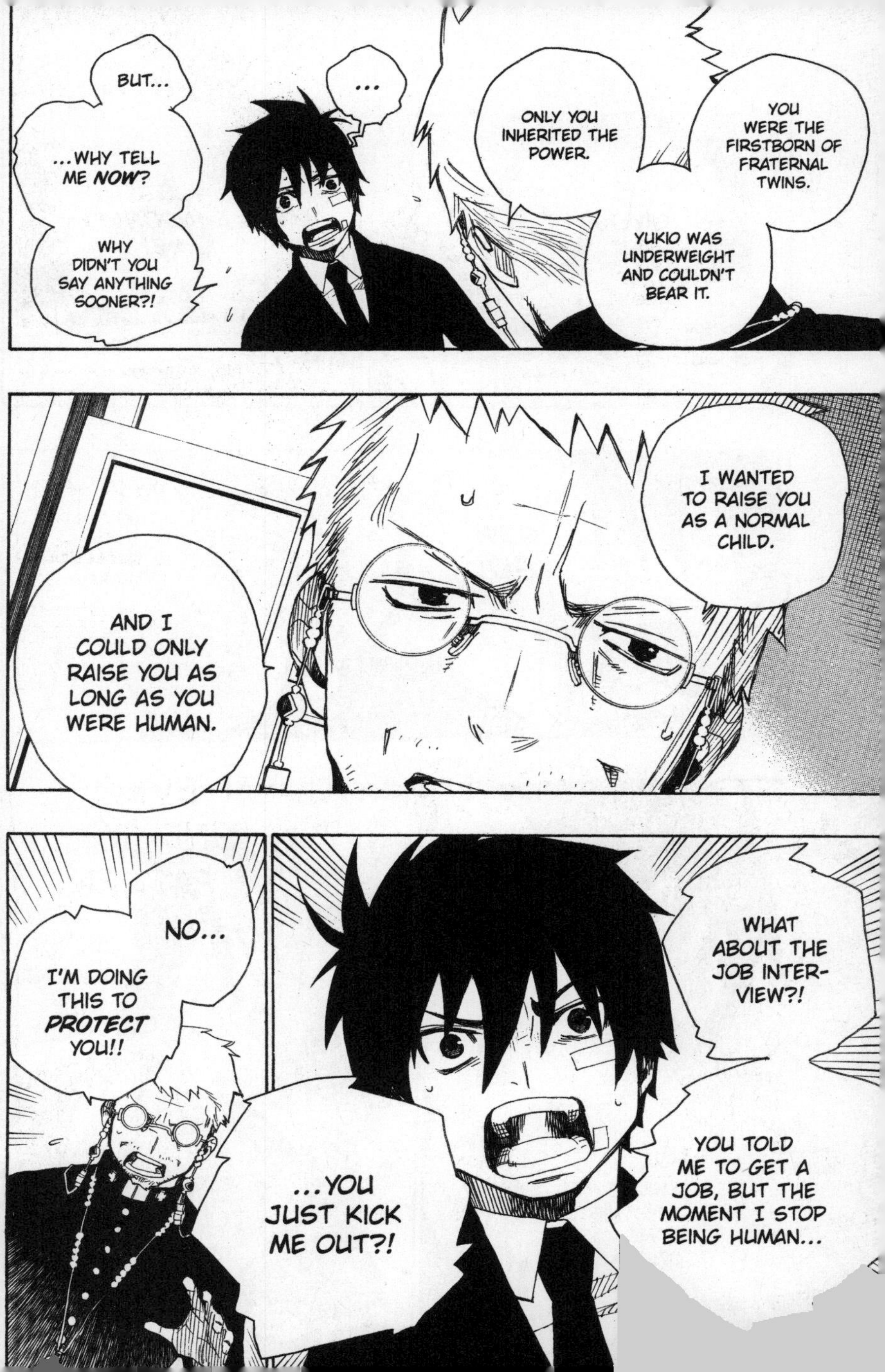
YOU WERE THE FIRSTBORN OF FRATERNAL TWINS.
ONLY YOU INHERITED THE POWER.
YUKIO WAS UNDERWEIGHT AND COULDN'T BEAR IT.
...
BUT...
...WHY TELL ME *NOW*?
WHY DIDN'T YOU SAY ANYTHING SOONER?!
I WANTED TO RAISE YOU AS A NORMAL CHILD.
AND I COULD ONLY RAISE YOU AS LONG AS YOU WERE HUMAN.
WHAT ABOUT THE JOB INTER-VIEW?!
YOU TOLD ME TO GET A JOB, BUT THE MOMENT I STOP BEING HUMAN...
...YOU JUST KICK ME OUT?!
NO...
I'M DOING THIS TO *PROTECT* YOU!!

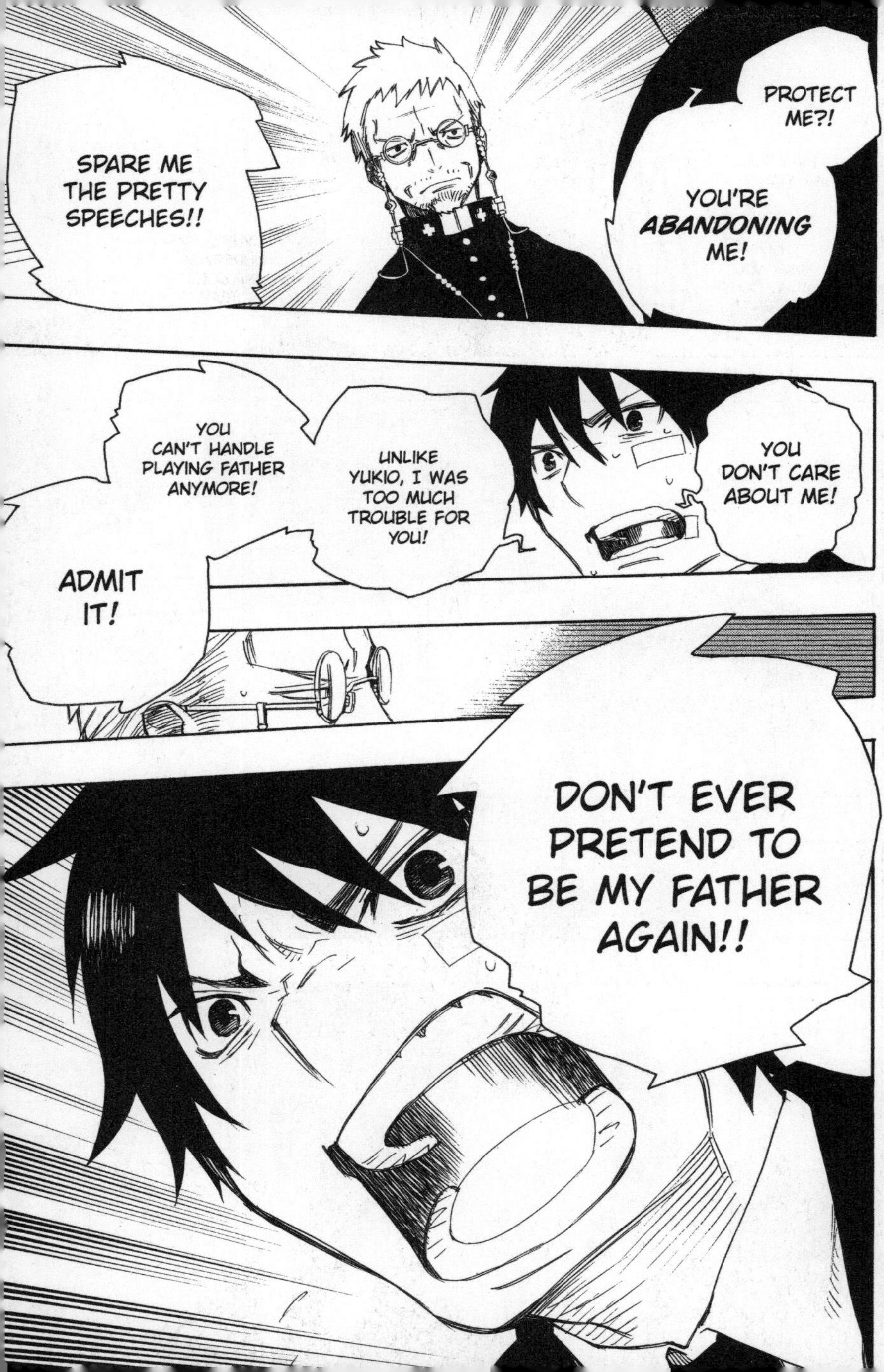
PROTECT ME?!
YOU'RE ABANDONING ME!
SPARE ME THE PRETTY SPEECHES!!
YOU DON'T CARE ABOUT ME!
UNLIKE YUKIO, I WAS TOO MUCH TROUBLE FOR YOU!
YOU CAN'T HANDLE PLAYING FATHER ANYMORE!
ADMIT IT!
DON'T EVER PRETEND TO BE MY FATHER AGAIN!!

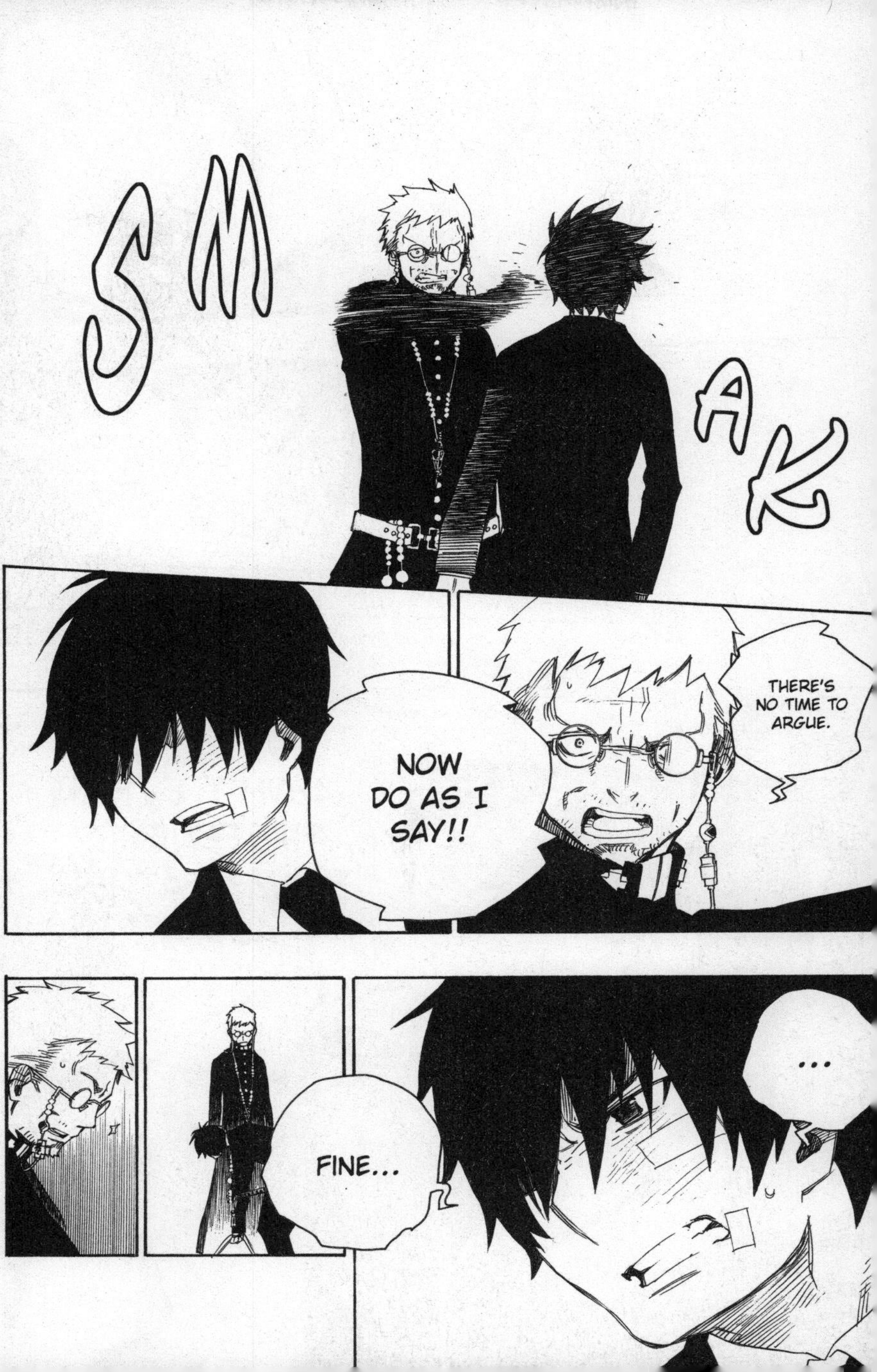
SMAK
THERE'S NO TIME TO ARGUE.
NOW DO AS I SAY!!
...
FINE...

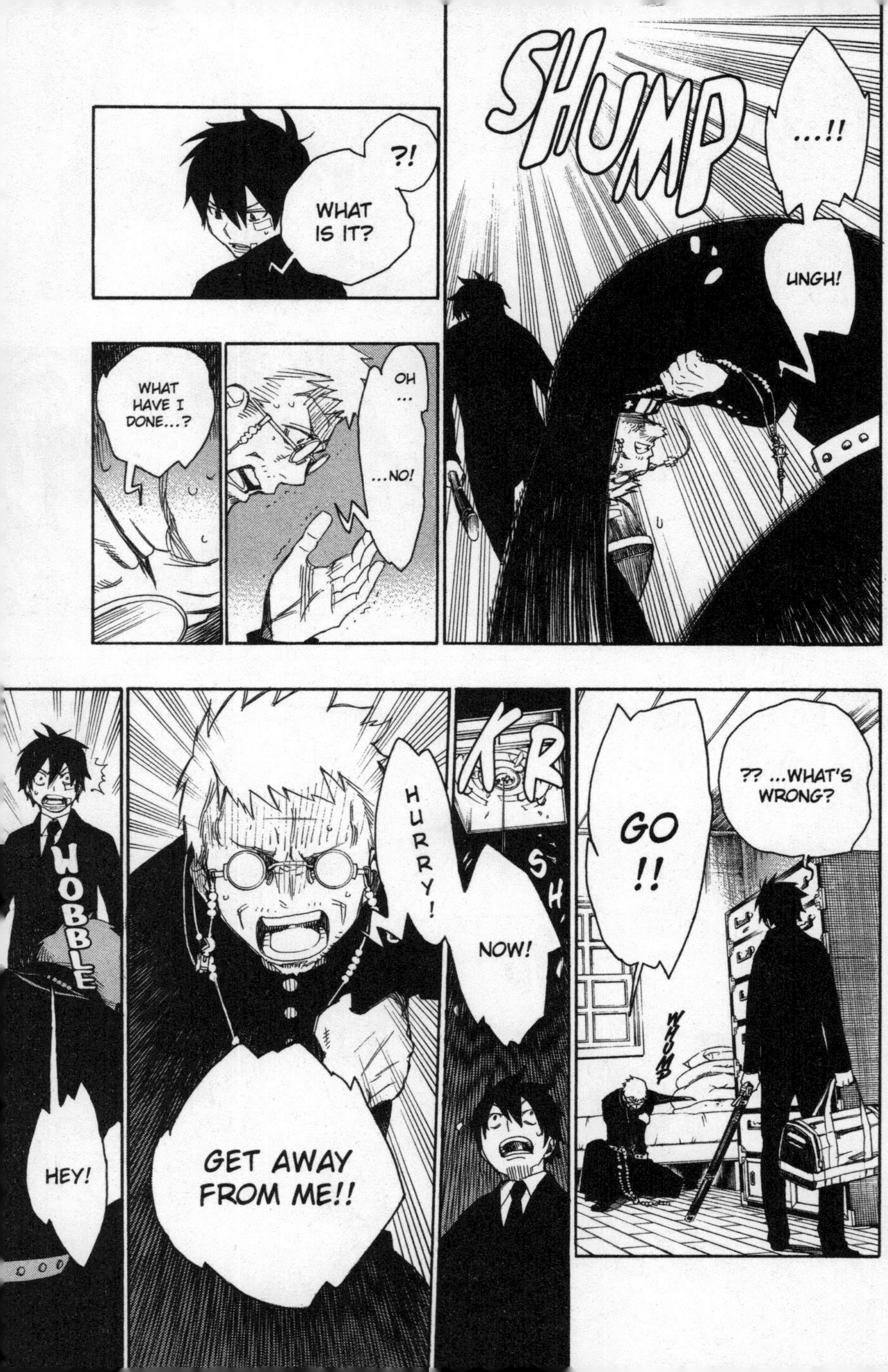
SHUMP
...!!
UNGH!
?!
WHAT IS IT?
OH ... ...NO!
WHAT HAVE I DONE...?
?? ...WHAT'S WRONG?
GO !!
WHUMP
KR
SH
HURRY!
NOW!
GET AWAY FROM ME!!
WOBBLE
HEY!

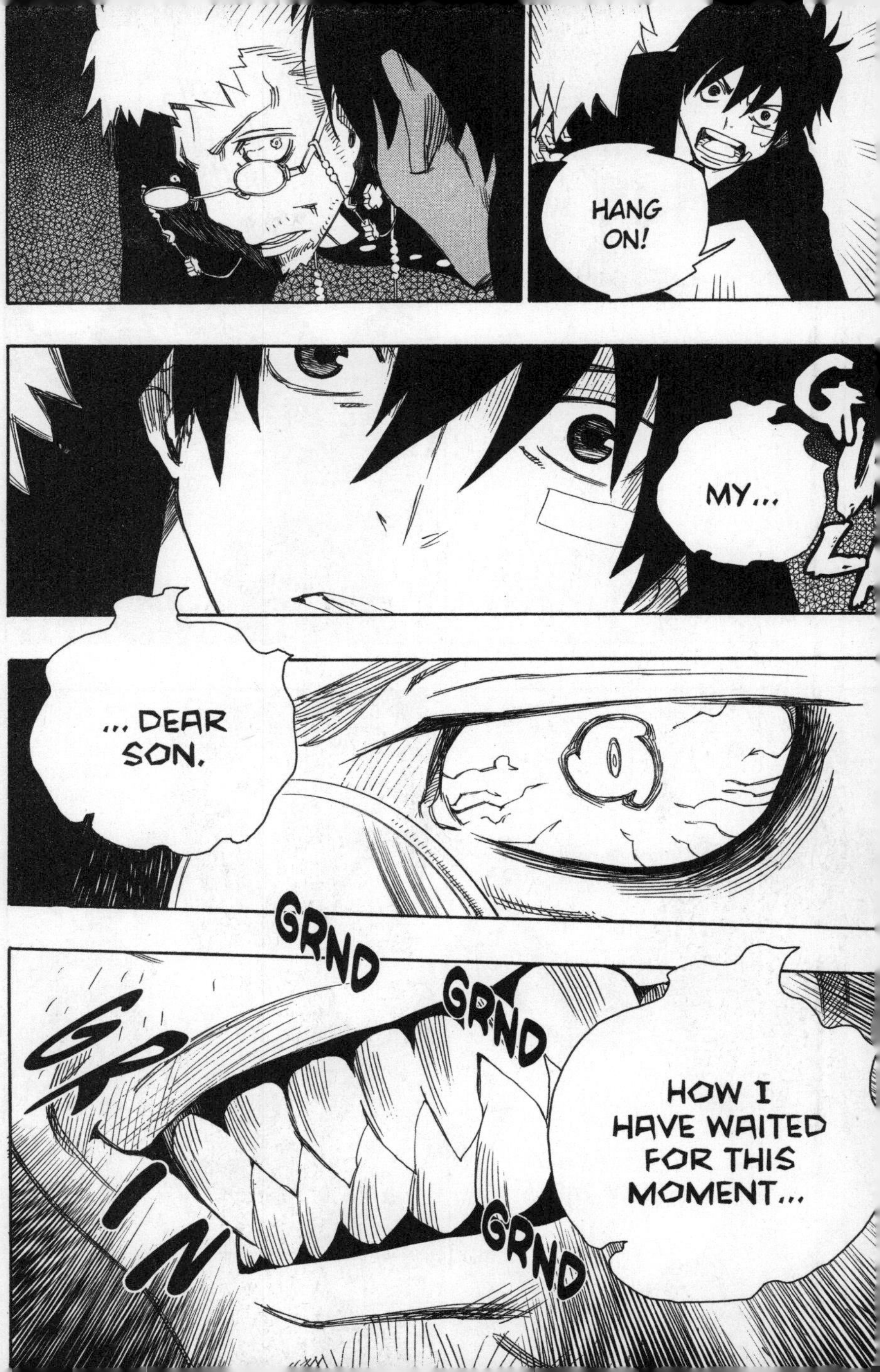
HANG ON!
MY...
...DEAR SON.
GRND
GRND
HOW I HAVE WAITED FOR THIS MOMENT...
GRND
GRIN

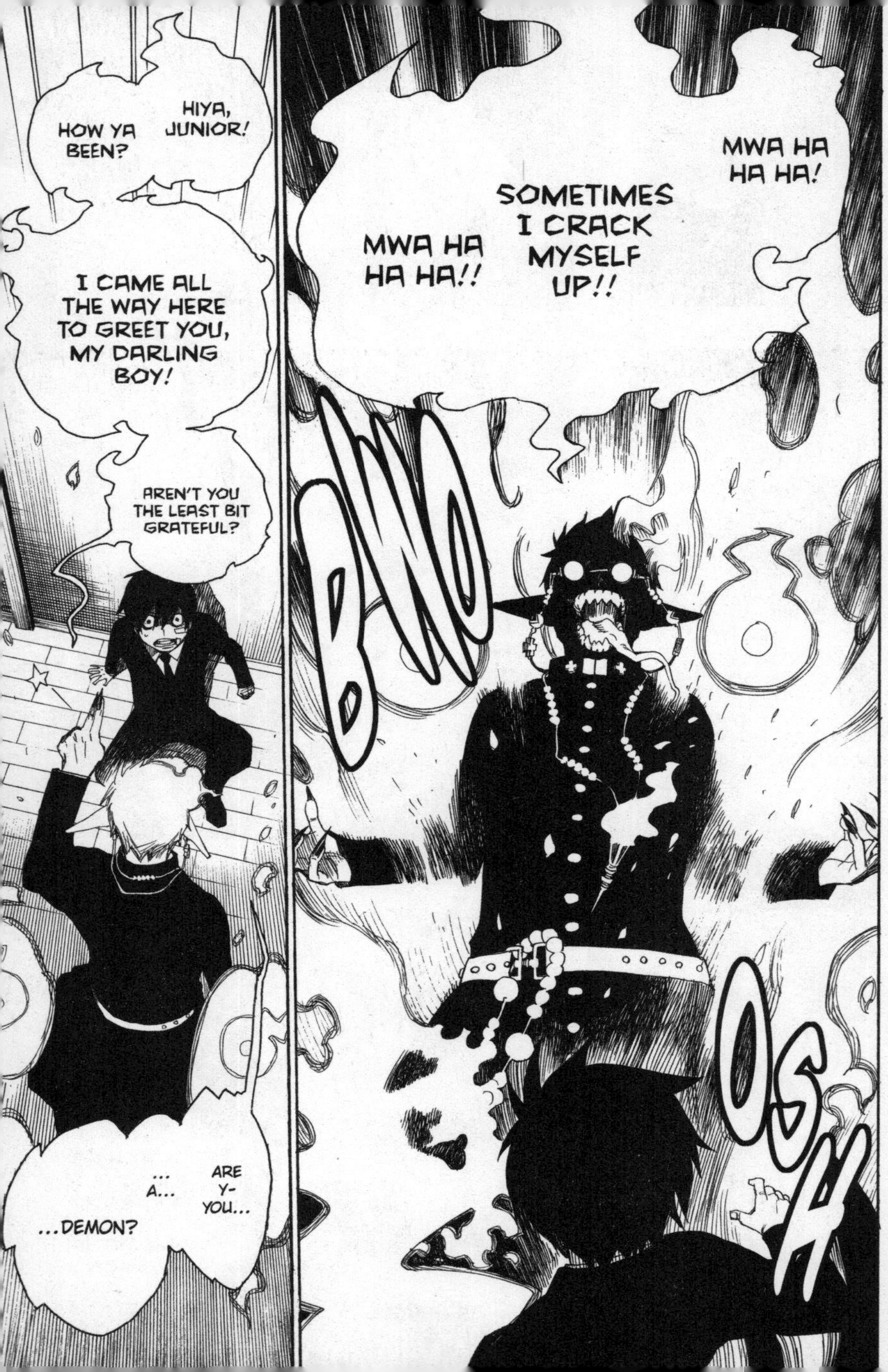
MWA HA HA HA!
SOMETIMES I CRACK MYSELF UP!!
MWA HA HA HA!!
HIYA, JUNIOR! HOW YA BEEN?
I CAME ALL THE WAY HERE TO GREET YOU, MY DARLING BOY!
AREN'T YOU THE LEAST BIT GRATEFUL?
ARE Y- YOU...
... A...
...DEMON?

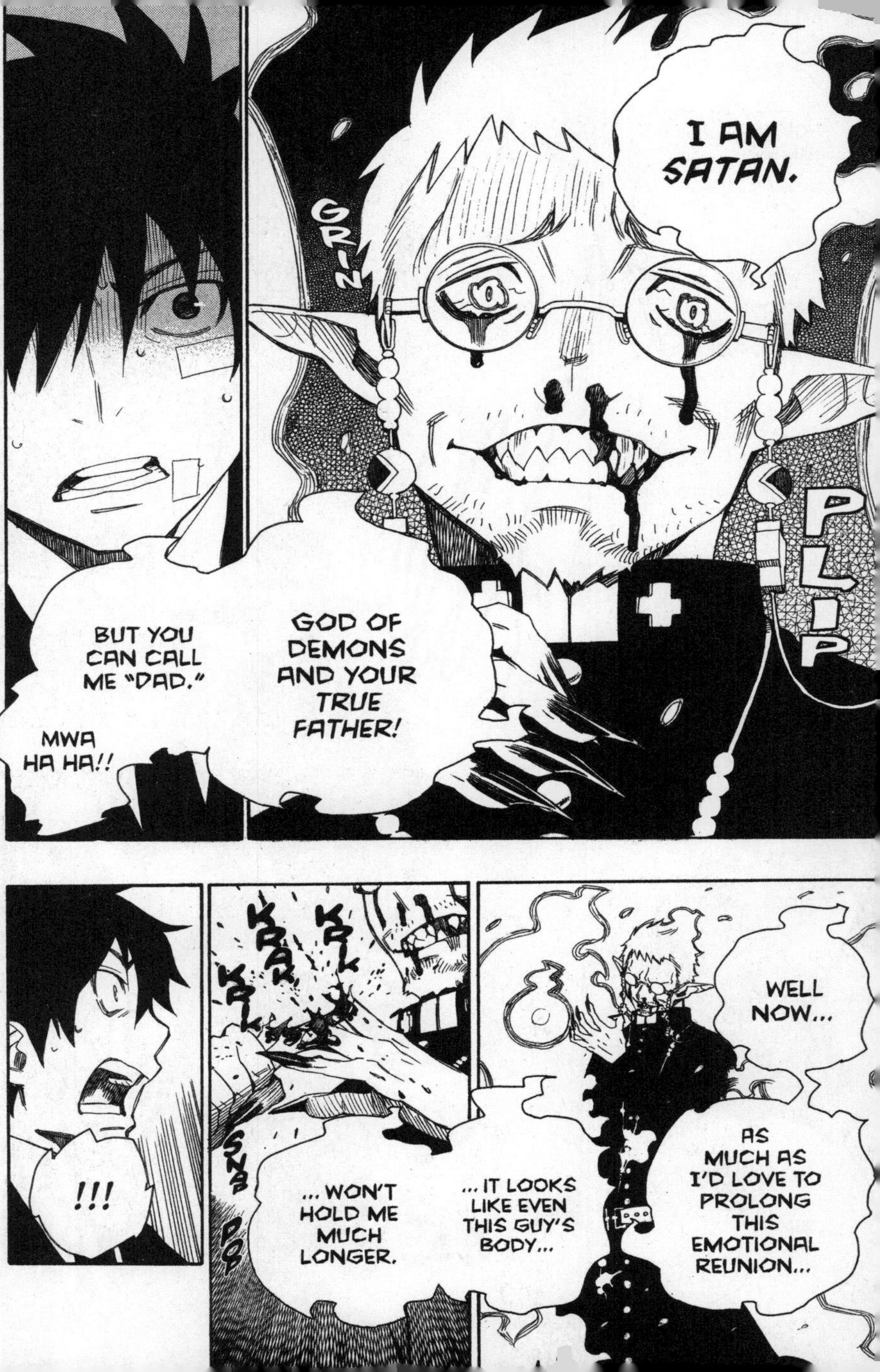
I AM SATAN.
PLIP
GRIN
GOD OF DEMONS AND YOUR TRUE FATHER!
BUT YOU CAN CALL ME "DAD."
MWA HA HA!!
WELL NOW...
AS MUCH AS I'D LOVE TO PROLONG THIS EMOTIONAL REUNION...
...IT LOOKS LIKE EVEN THIS GUY'S BODY...
...WON'T HOLD ME MUCH LONGER.
KRAK
KRAK
KRAK
!!!

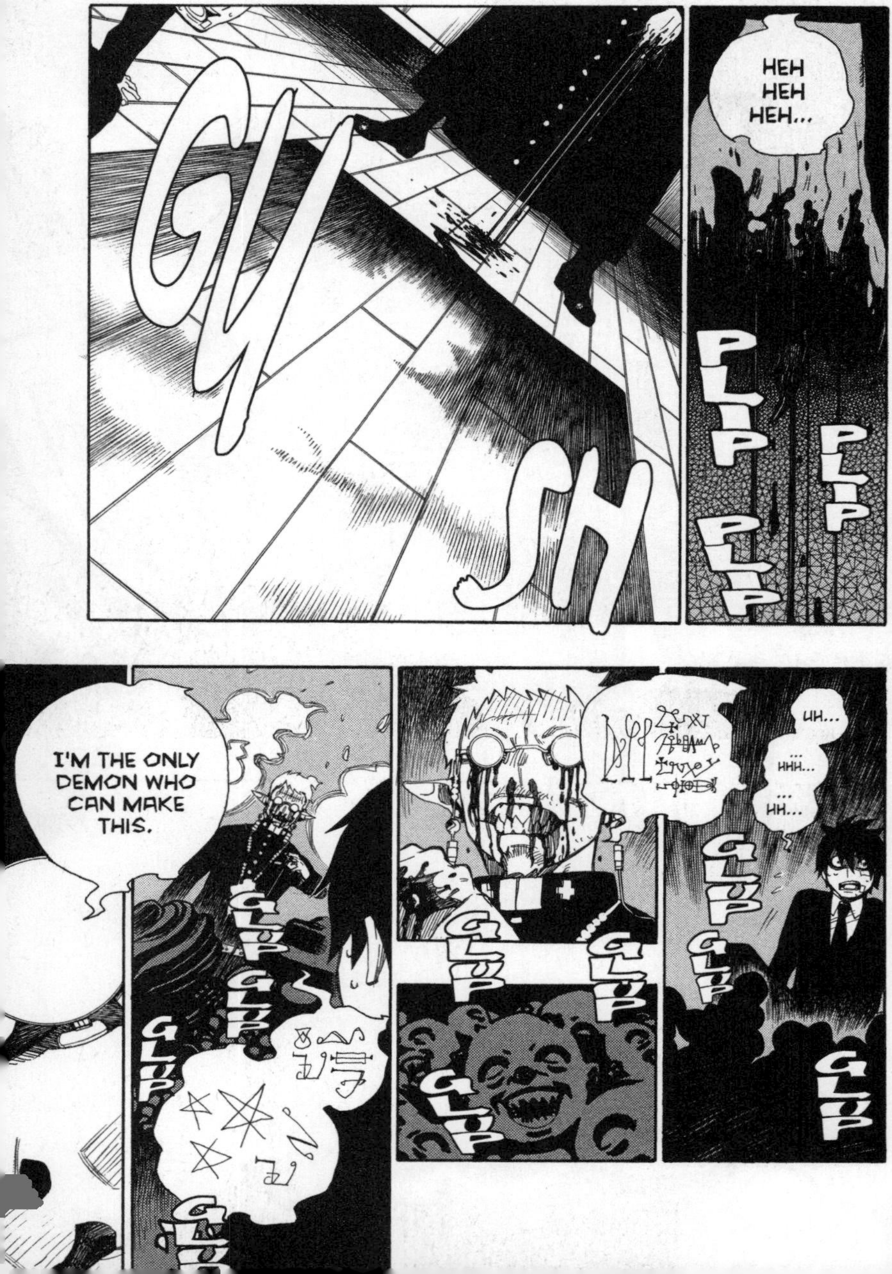
HEH HEH HEH...
PLIP PLIP
PLIP PLIP
GUSH
UH...
...HHH...
...UH...
GLUP GLUP GLUP
GLUP
GLUP
GLUP
I'M THE ONLY DEMON WHO CAN MAKE THIS.
GLUP GLUP GLUP

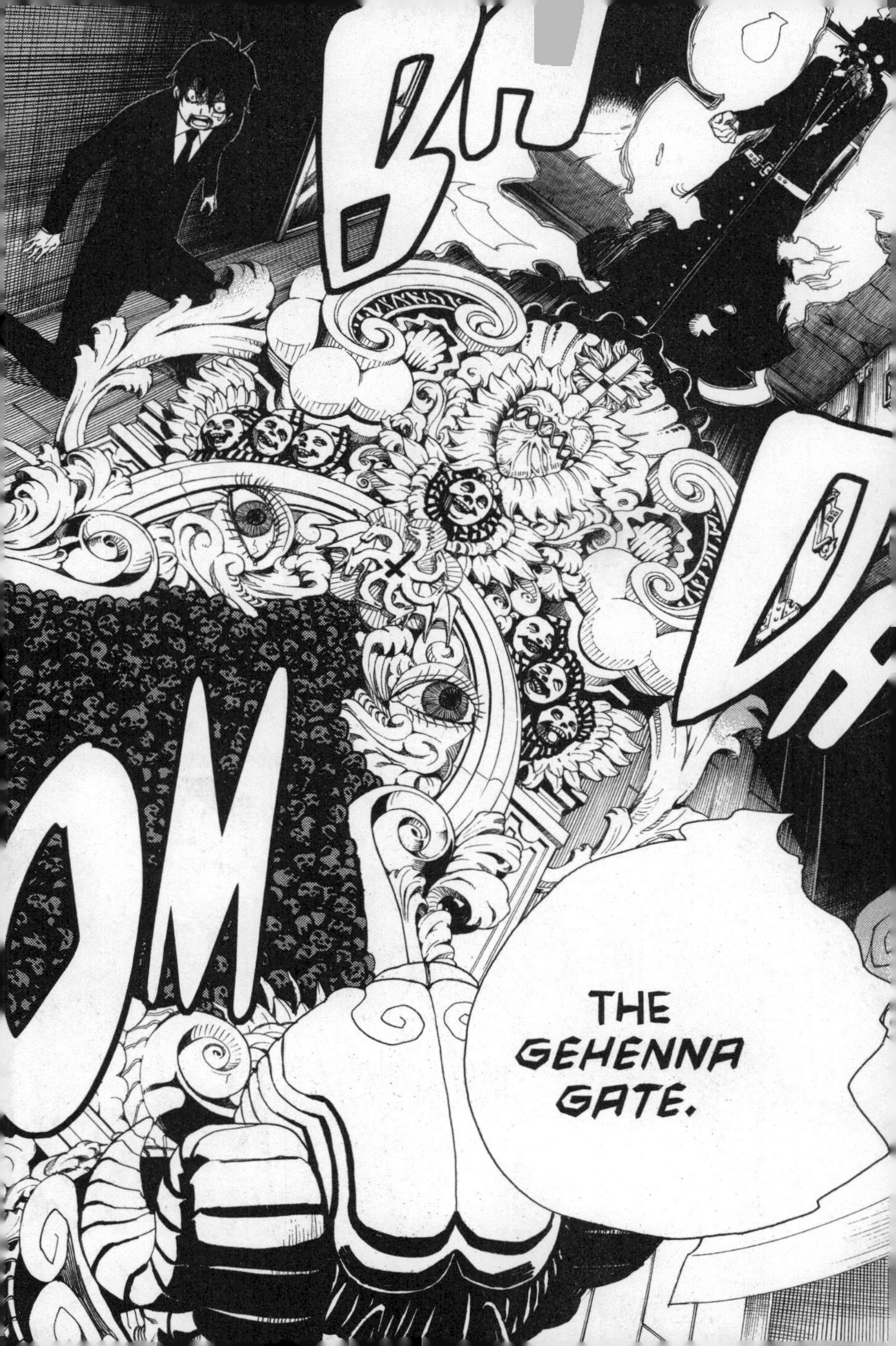
THE GEHENNA GATE.

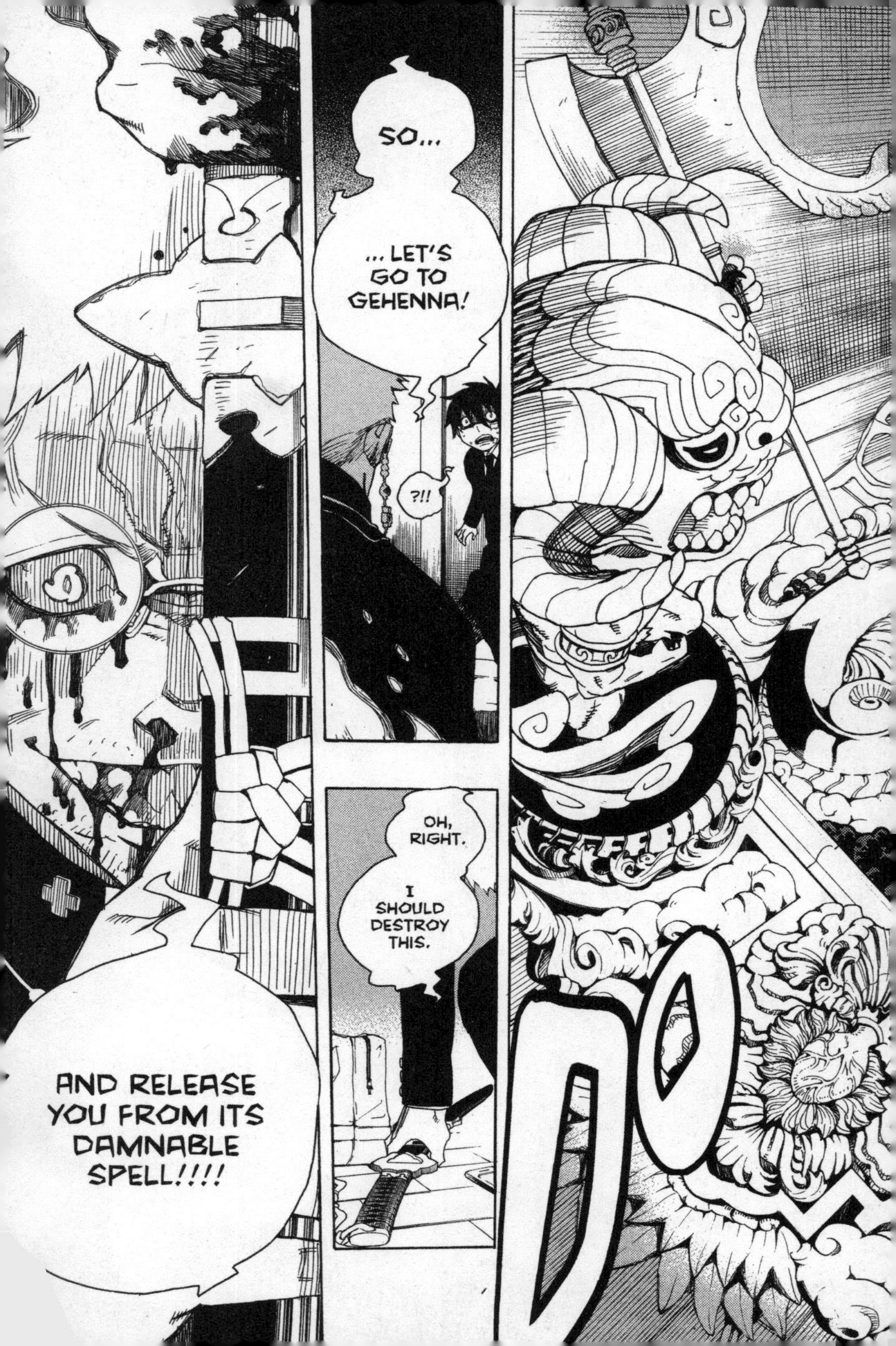
SO...
...LET'S GO TO GEHENNA!
?!!
OH, RIGHT.
I SHOULD DESTROY THIS.
AND RELEASE YOU FROM ITS DAMNABLE SPELL!!!!

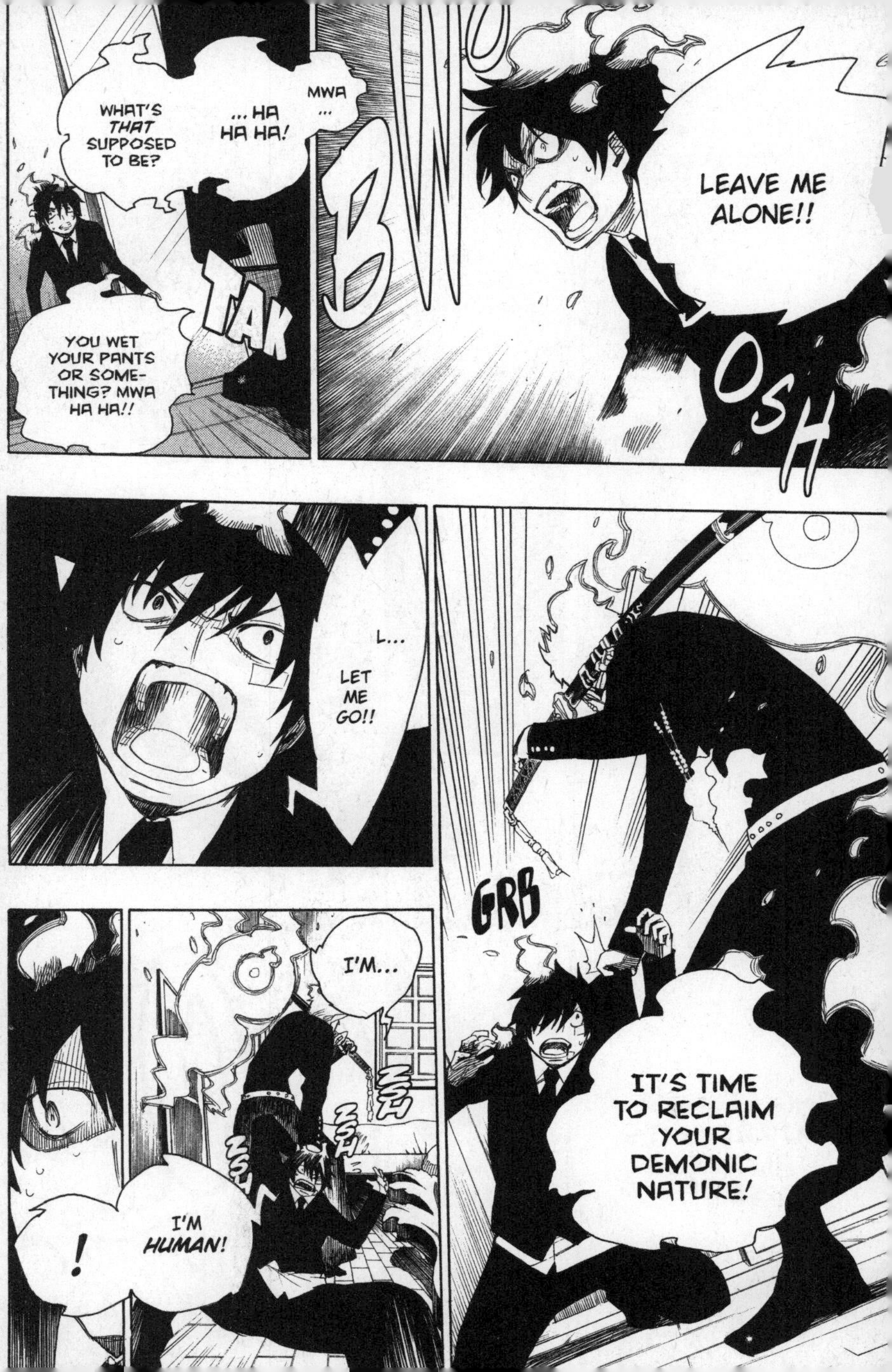
LEAVE ME ALONE!!
BWOOSH
MWA ...
... HA HA HA!
WHAT'S *THAT* SUPPOSED TO BE?
TAK
YOU WET YOUR PANTS OR SOME-THING? MWA HA HA!!
GRB
IT'S TIME TO RECLAIM YOUR DEMONIC NATURE!
L...
LET ME GO!!
I'M...
ZSH
ZSH
ZSH
I'M *HUMAN*!
!

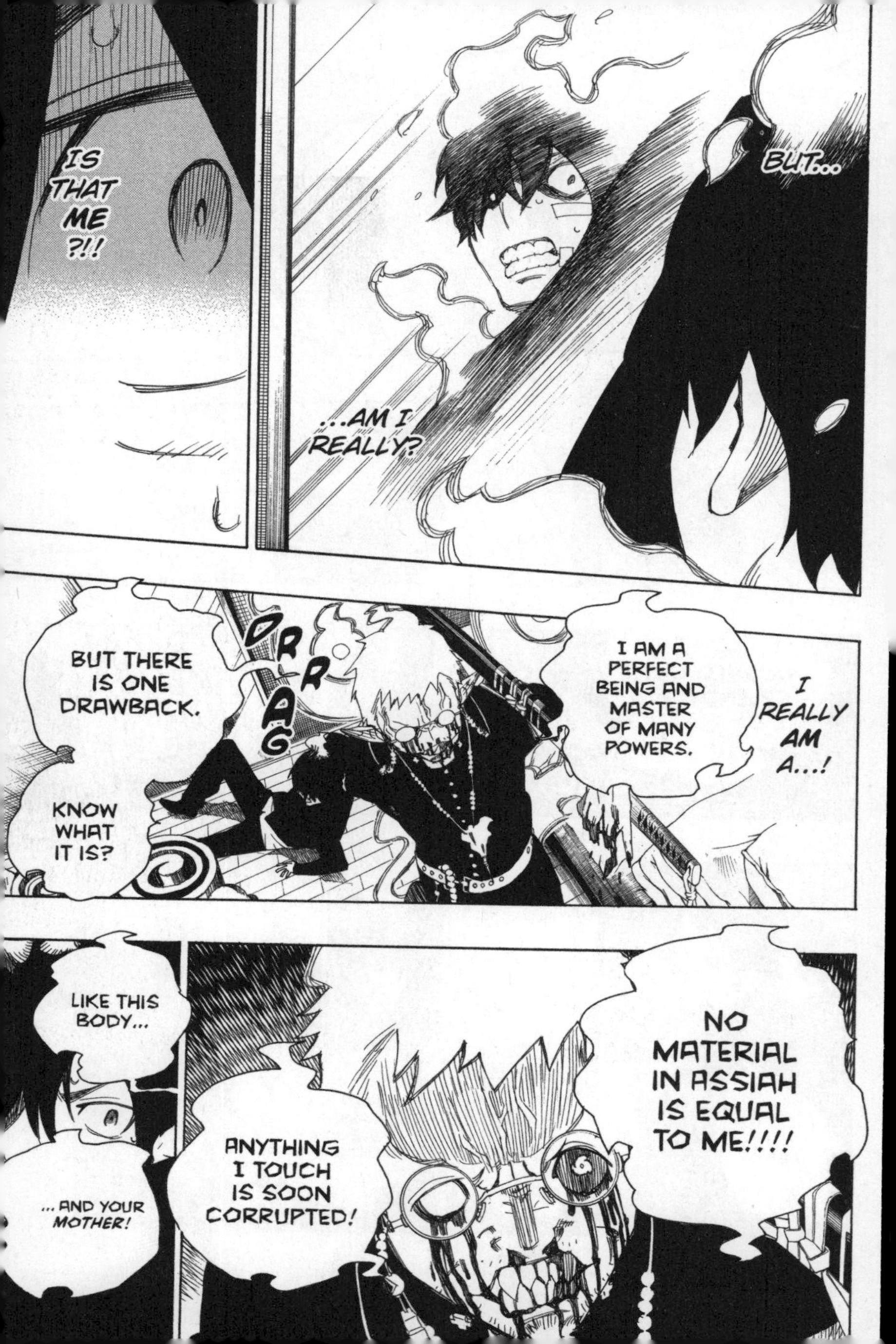
BUT...
...AM I REALLY?
IS THAT ME ?!!
I REALLY AM A...!
I AM A PERFECT BEING AND MASTER OF MANY POWERS.
DRRAG
BUT THERE IS ONE DRAWBACK.
KNOW WHAT IT IS?
NO MATERIAL IN ASSIAH IS EQUAL TO ME!!!!
ANYTHING I TOUCH IS SOON CORRUPTED!
LIKE THIS BODY...
...AND YOUR MOTHER!

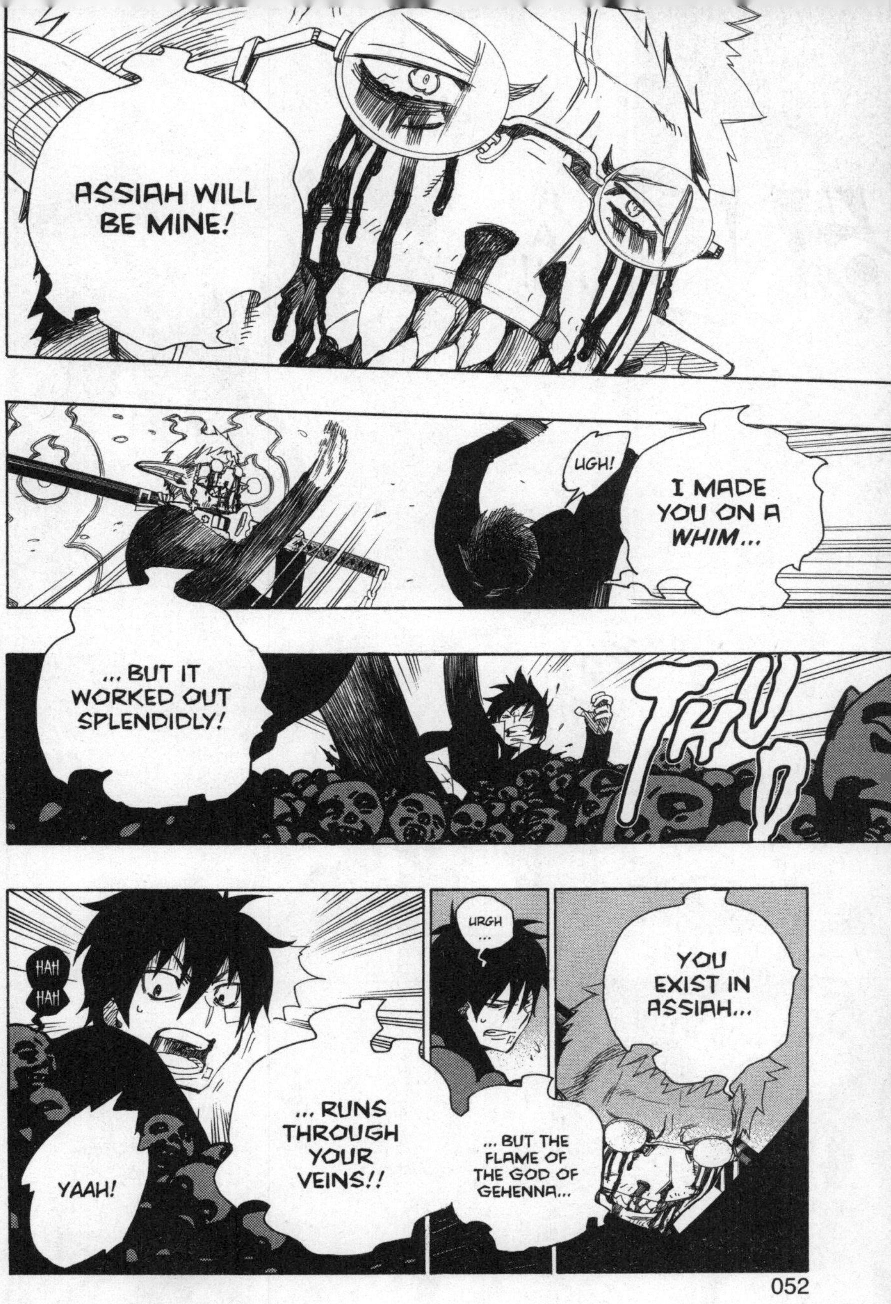
ASSIAH WILL BE MINE!
I MADE YOU ON A WHIM...
UGH!
THUD
... BUT IT WORKED OUT SPLENDIDLY!
YOU EXIST IN ASSIAH...
... BUT THE FLAME OF THE GOD OF GEHENNA...
URGH ...
... RUNS THROUGH YOUR VEINS!!
HAH HAH
YAAH!

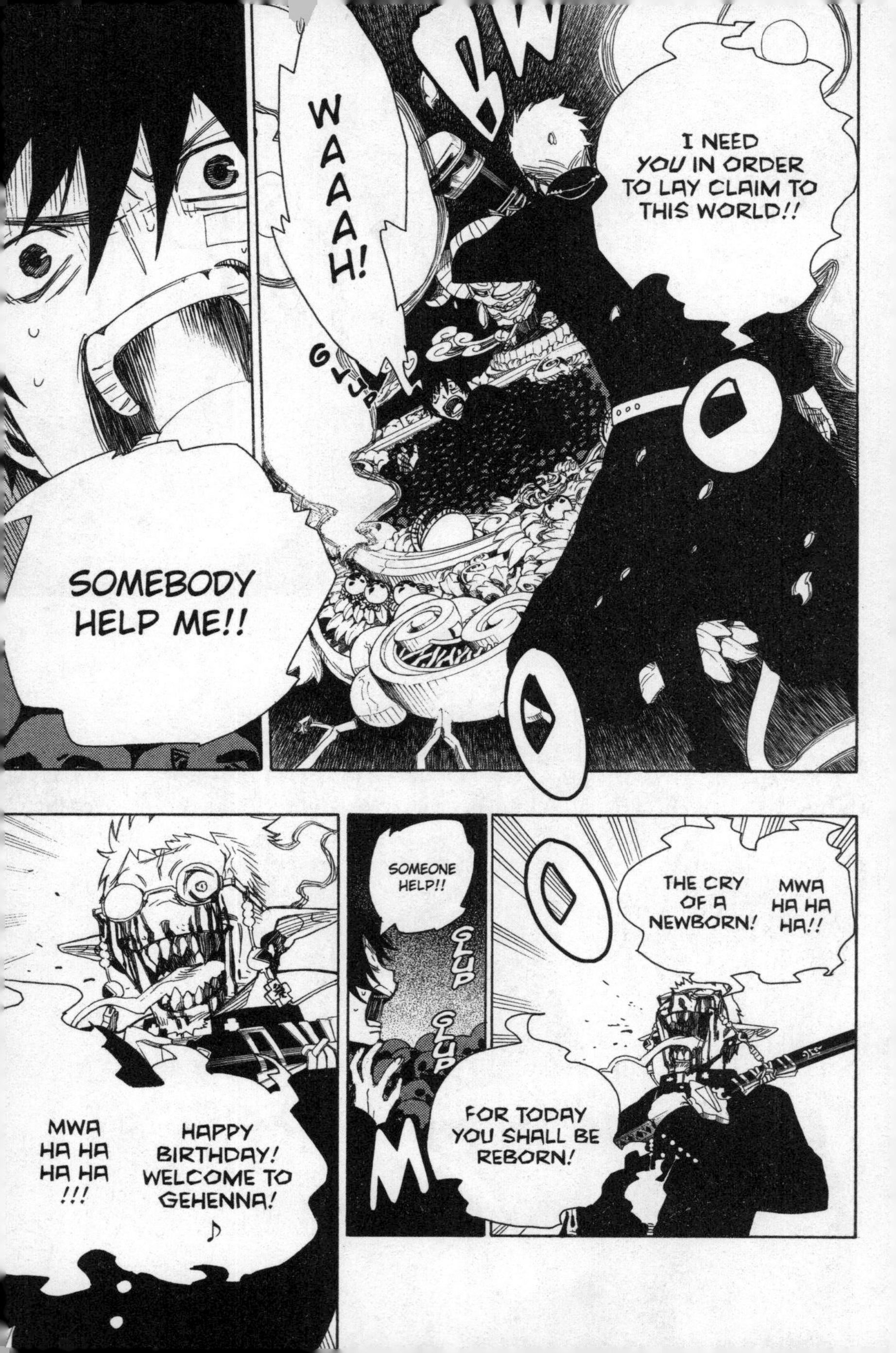
I NEED YOU IN ORDER TO LAY CLAIM TO THIS WORLD!!
WAAAAH!
GLUP
SOMEBODY HELP ME!!
MWA HA HA HA!!
THE CRY OF A NEWBORN!
FOR TODAY YOU SHALL BE REBORN!
SOMEONE HELP!!
GLUP GLUP
HAPPY BIRTHDAY! WELCOME TO GEHENNA! ♪
MWA HA HA HA HA !!!

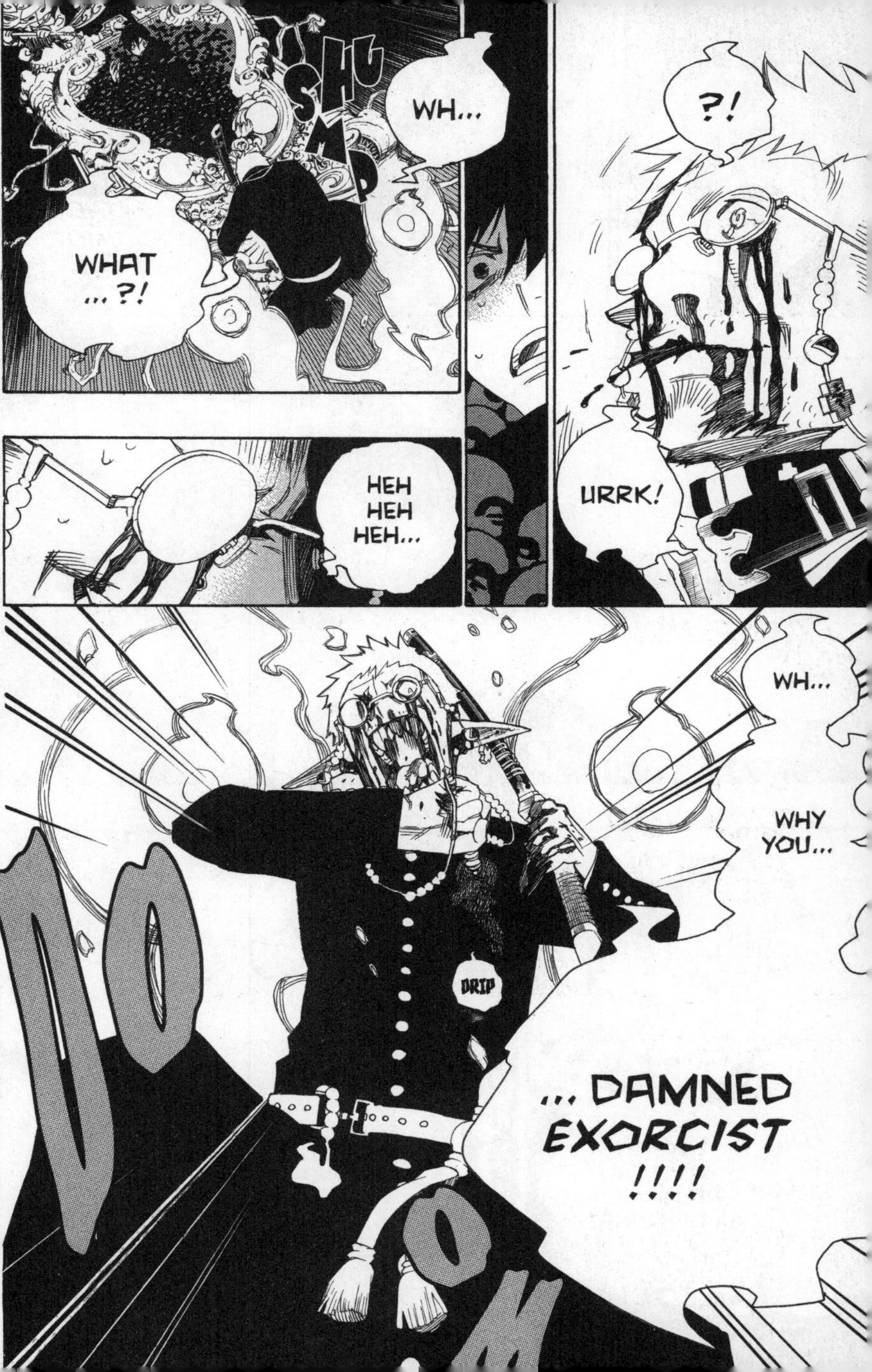
?!
URRK!
WH...
SHUMP
WHAT ...?!
HEH HEH HEH...
WH...
WHY YOU...
DRIP
... DAMNED EXORCIST !!!!
DOOM

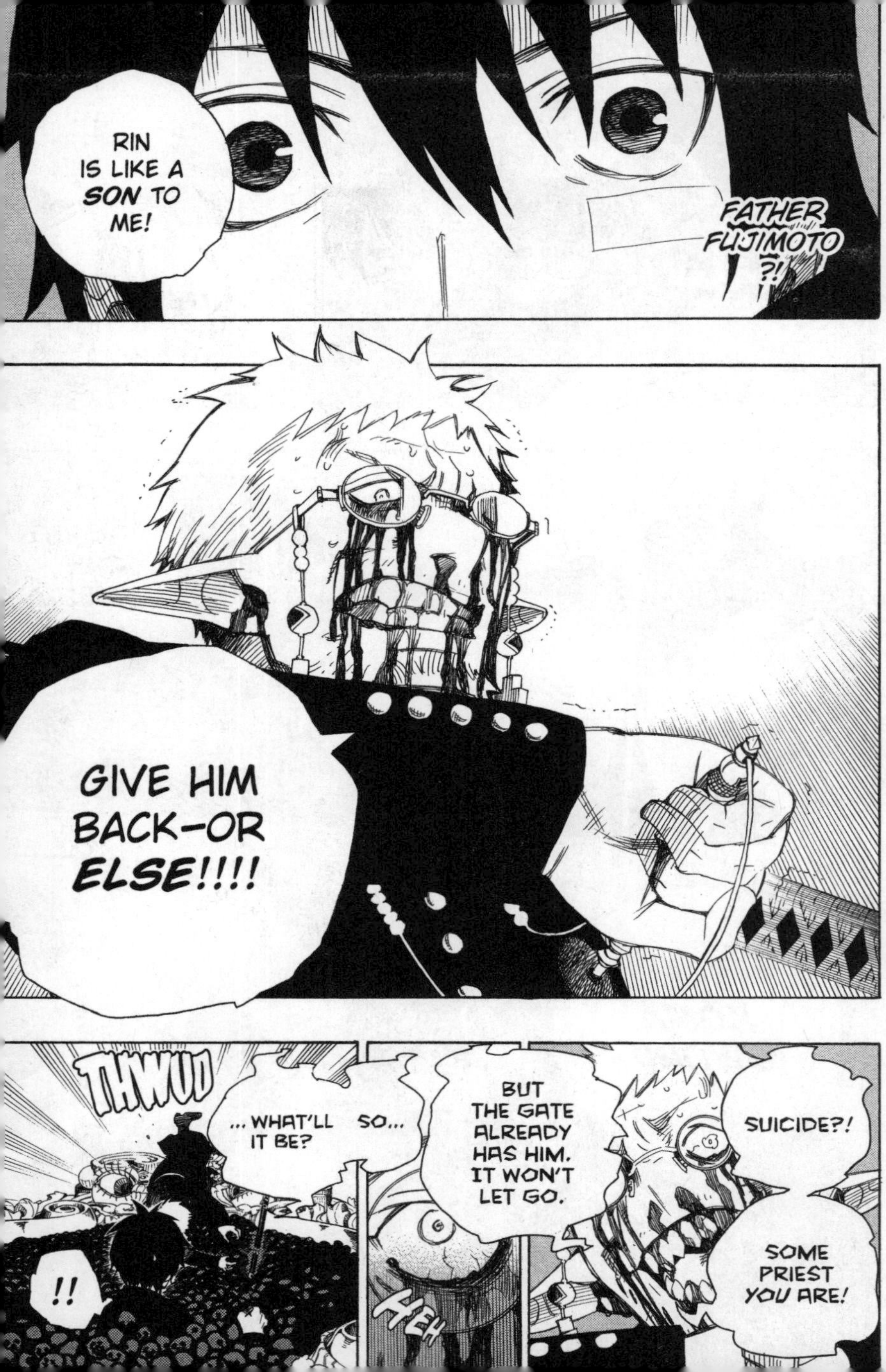
FATHER FUJIMOTO?!
RIN IS LIKE A SON TO ME!
GIVE HIM BACK—OR ELSE!!!!
SUICIDE?!
SOME PRIEST YOU ARE!
BUT THE GATE ALREADY HAS HIM. IT WON'T LET GO.
HEH
SO...
...WHAT'LL IT BE?
THWUD
!!

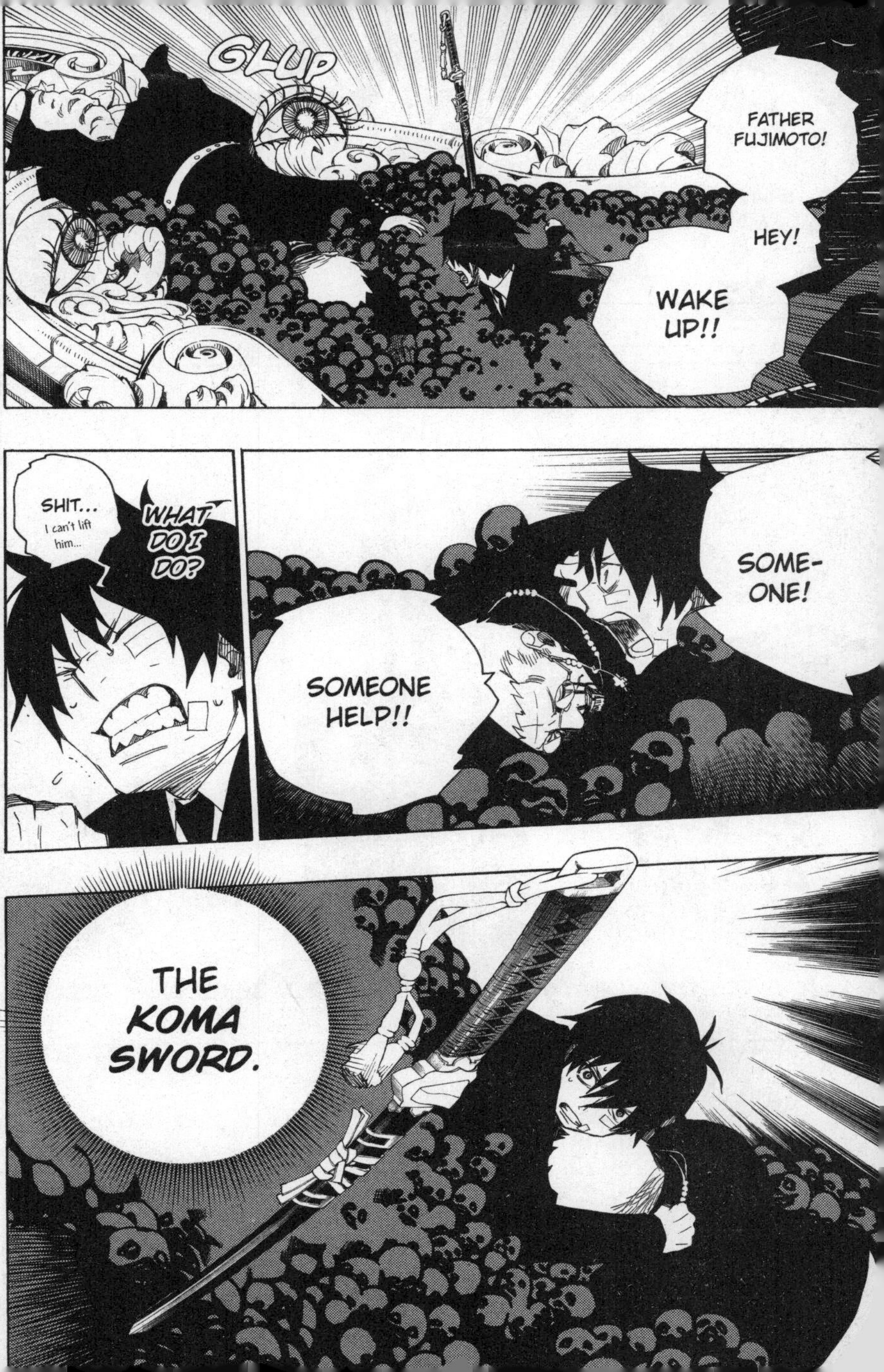
FATHER FUJIMOTO!
HEY!
WAKE UP!!
GLUP
SOME-ONE!
SOMEONE HELP!!
WHAT DO I DO?
SHIT...
I can't lift him...
THE KOMA SWORD.

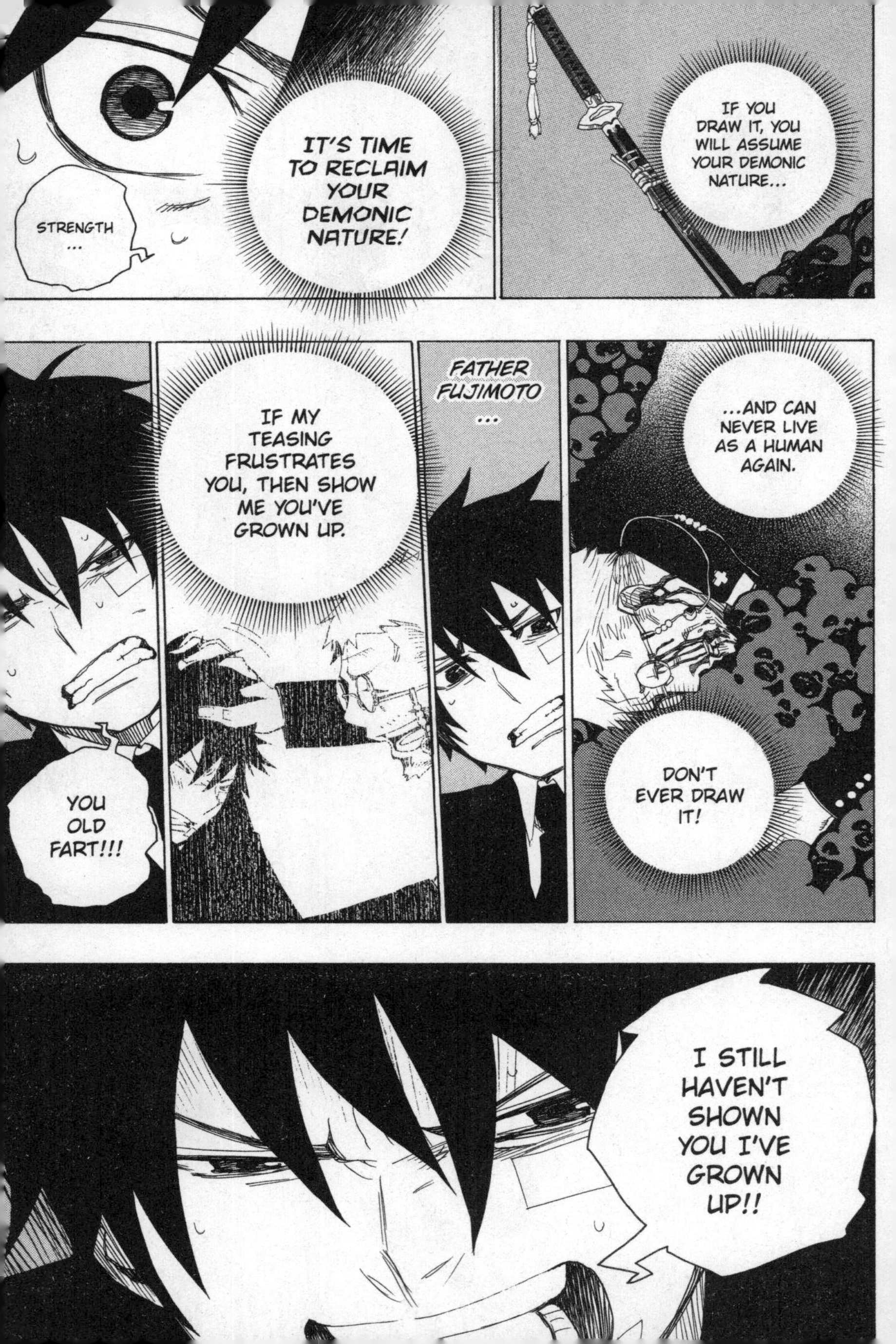
IF YOU DRAW IT, YOU WILL ASSUME YOUR DEMONIC NATURE...
IT'S TIME TO RECLAIM YOUR DEMONIC NATURE!
STRENGTH ...
...AND CAN NEVER LIVE AS A HUMAN AGAIN.
DON'T EVER DRAW IT!
FATHER FUJIMOTO ...
IF MY TEASING FRUSTRATES YOU, THEN SHOW ME YOU'VE GROWN UP.
YOU OLD FART!!!
I STILL HAVEN'T SHOWN YOU I'VE GROWN UP!!

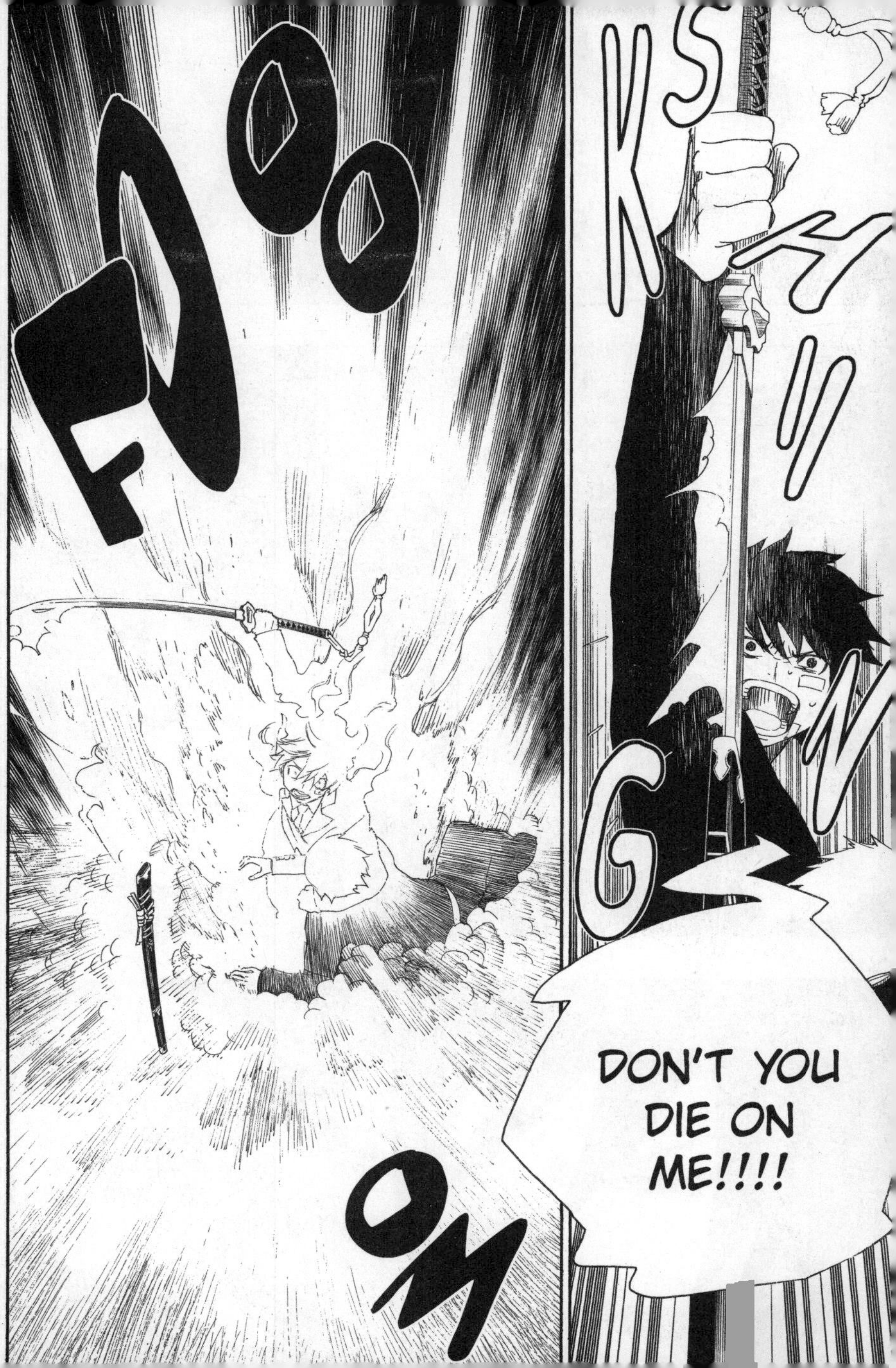
DON'T YOU DIE ON ME!!!!

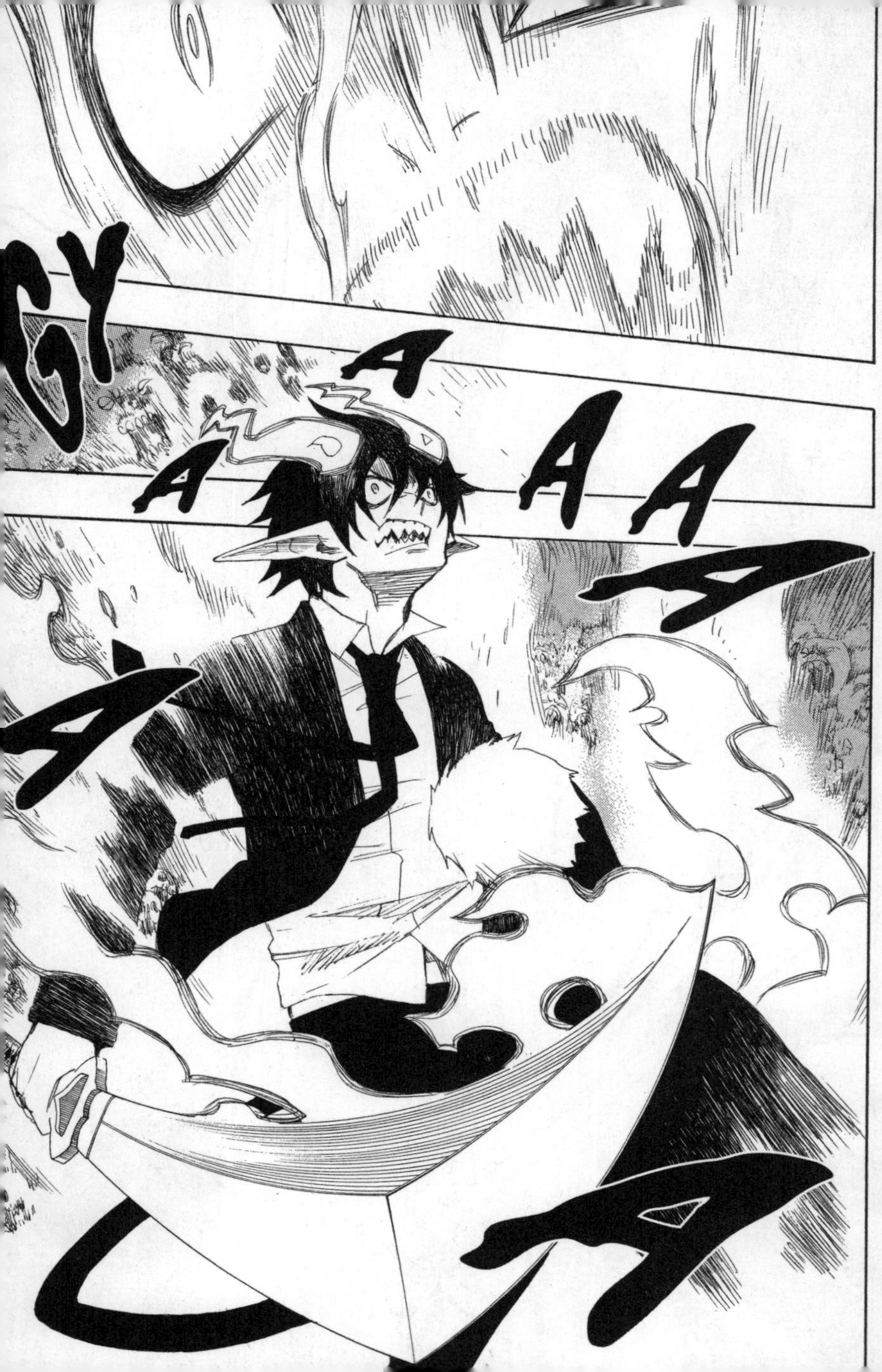
GYAAAAAAAA

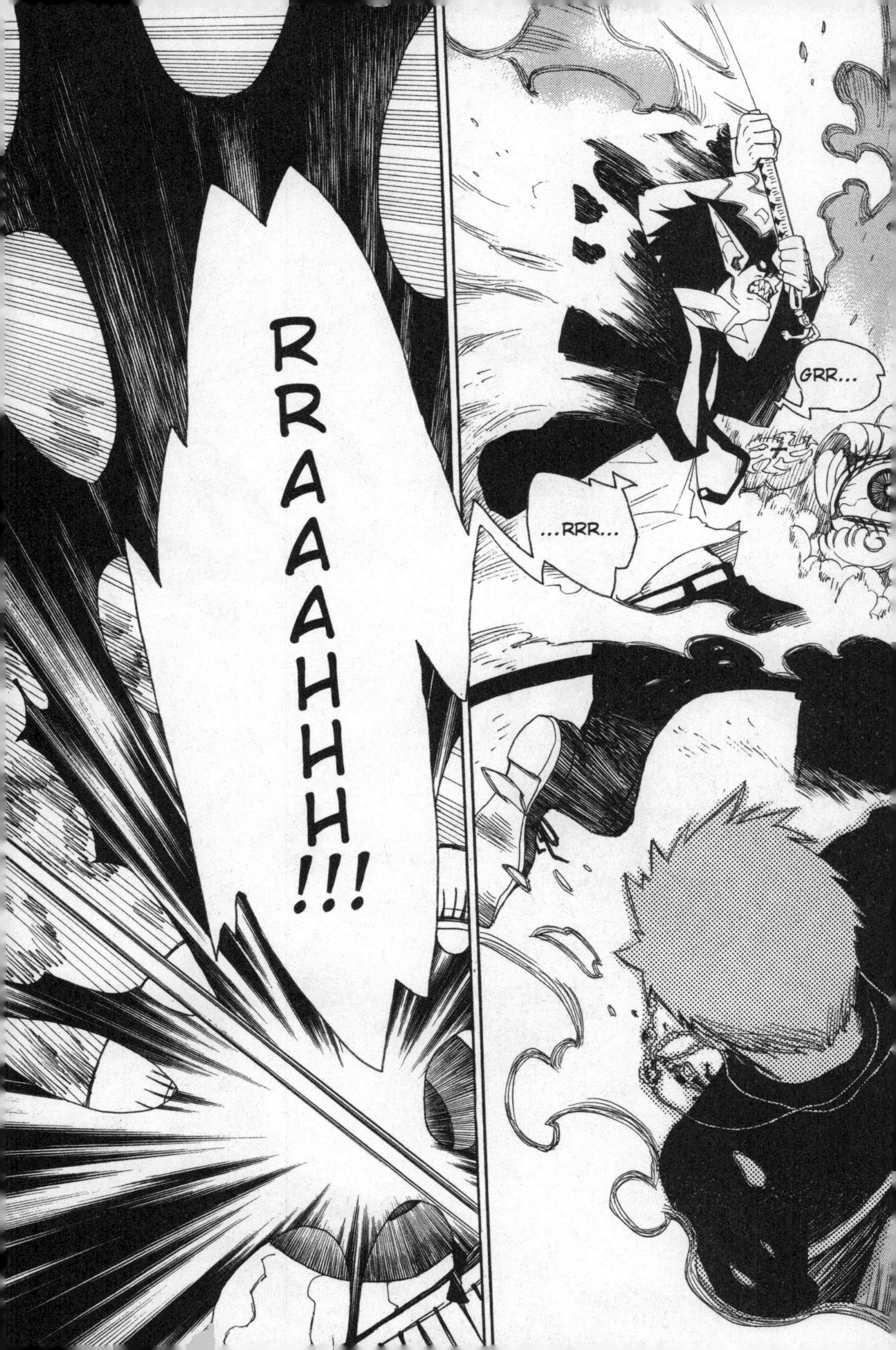
GRR...
...RRR...
RRAAAHHH!!!

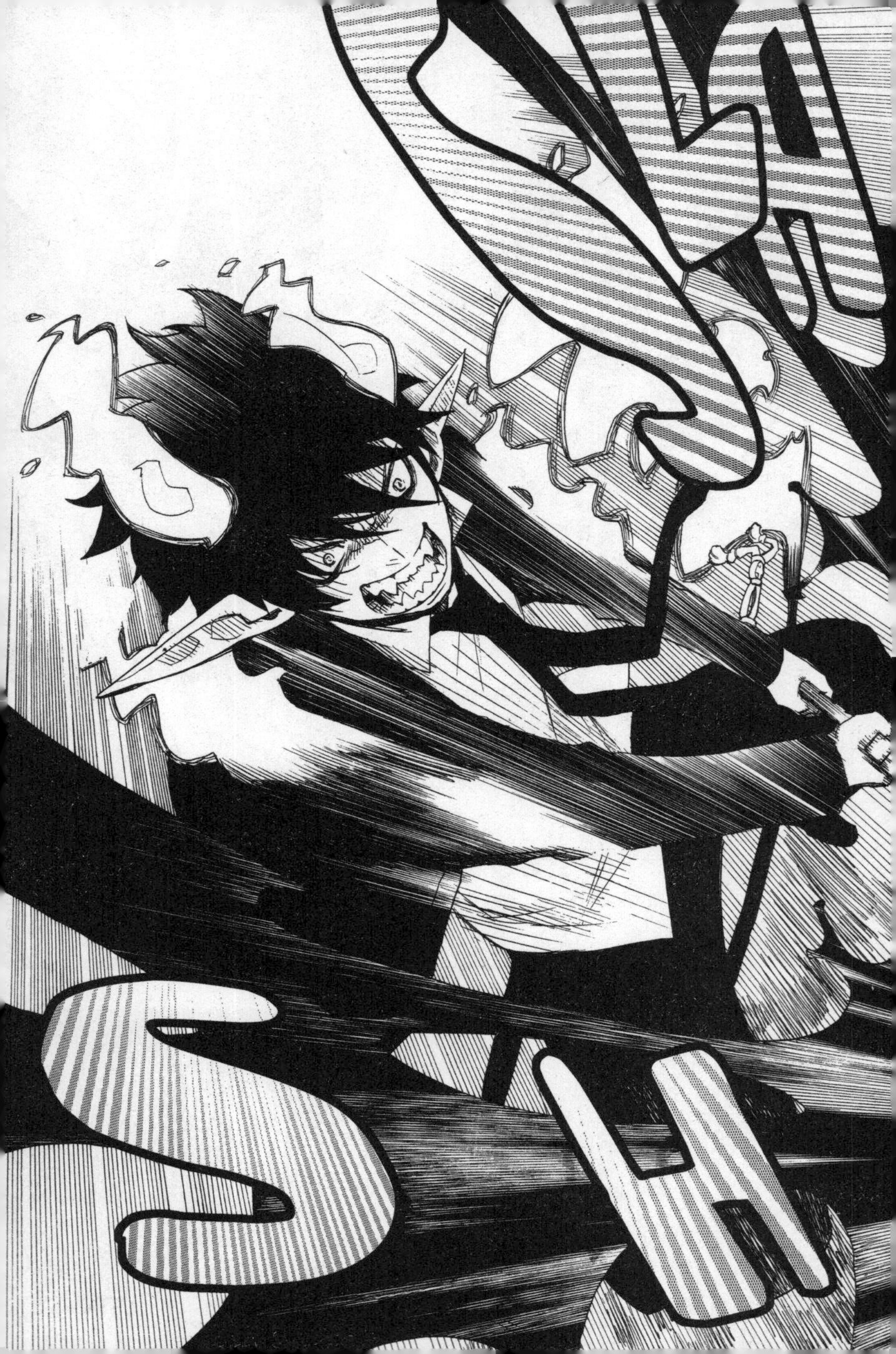

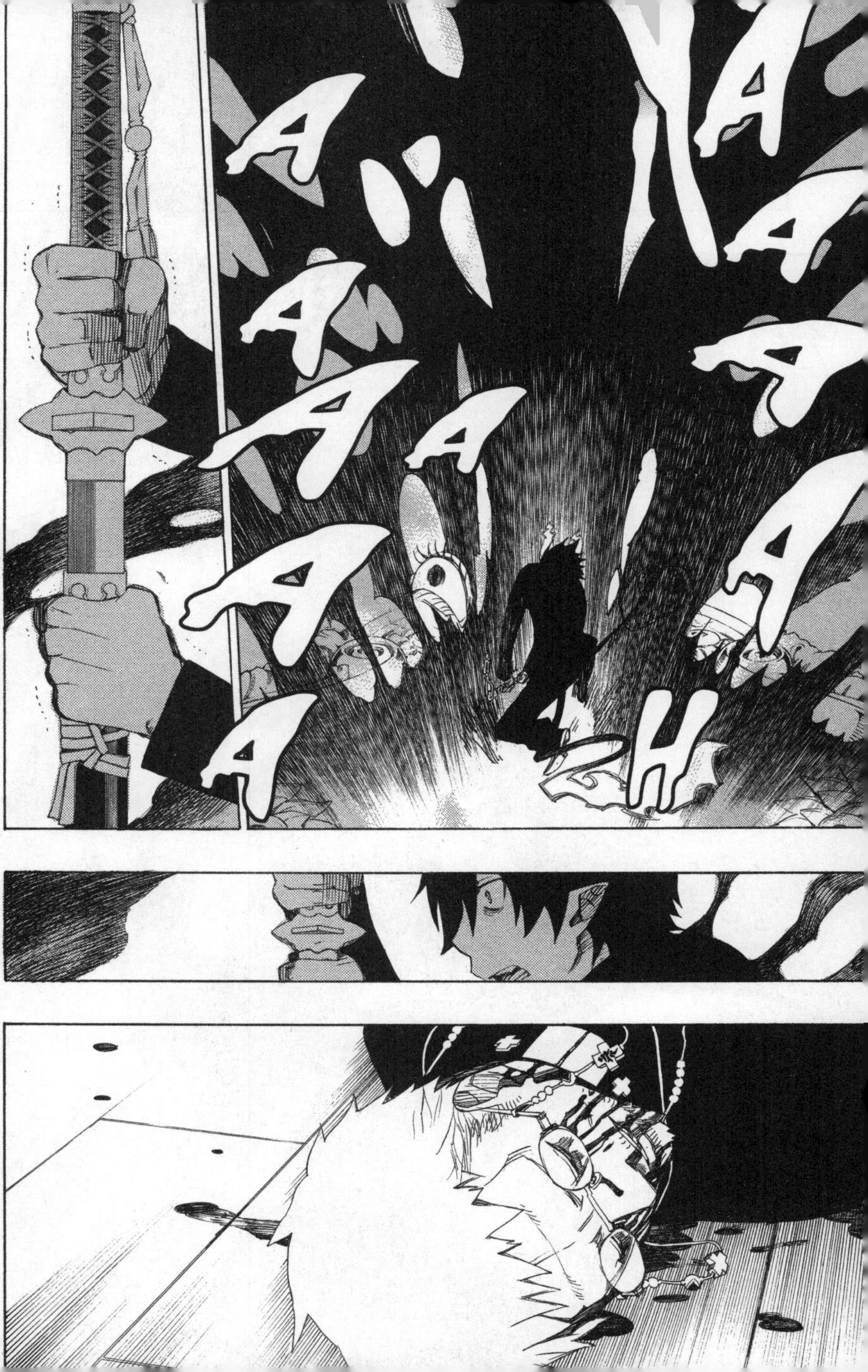
AAAAAAAAAAH

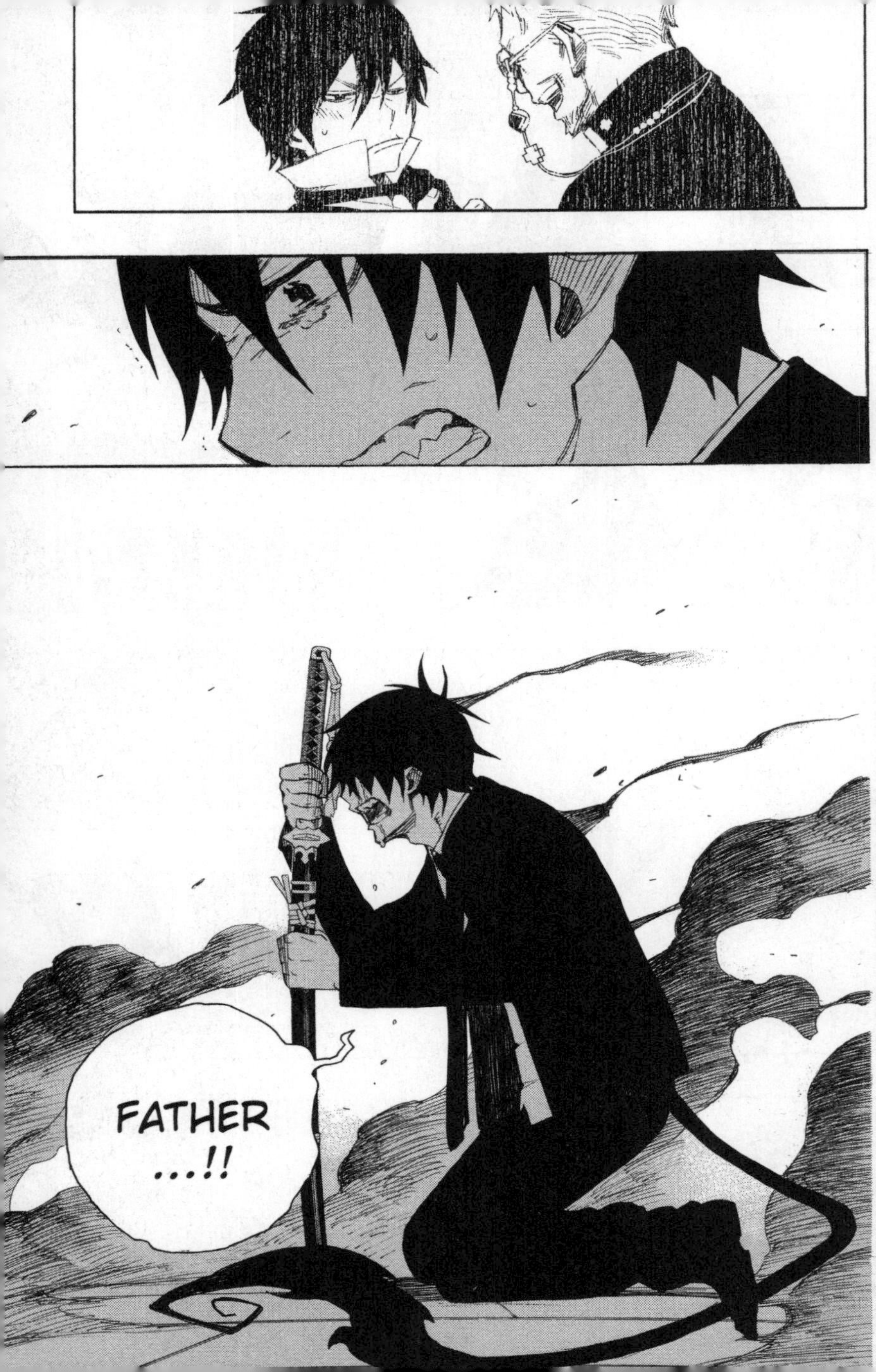
FATHER ...!!

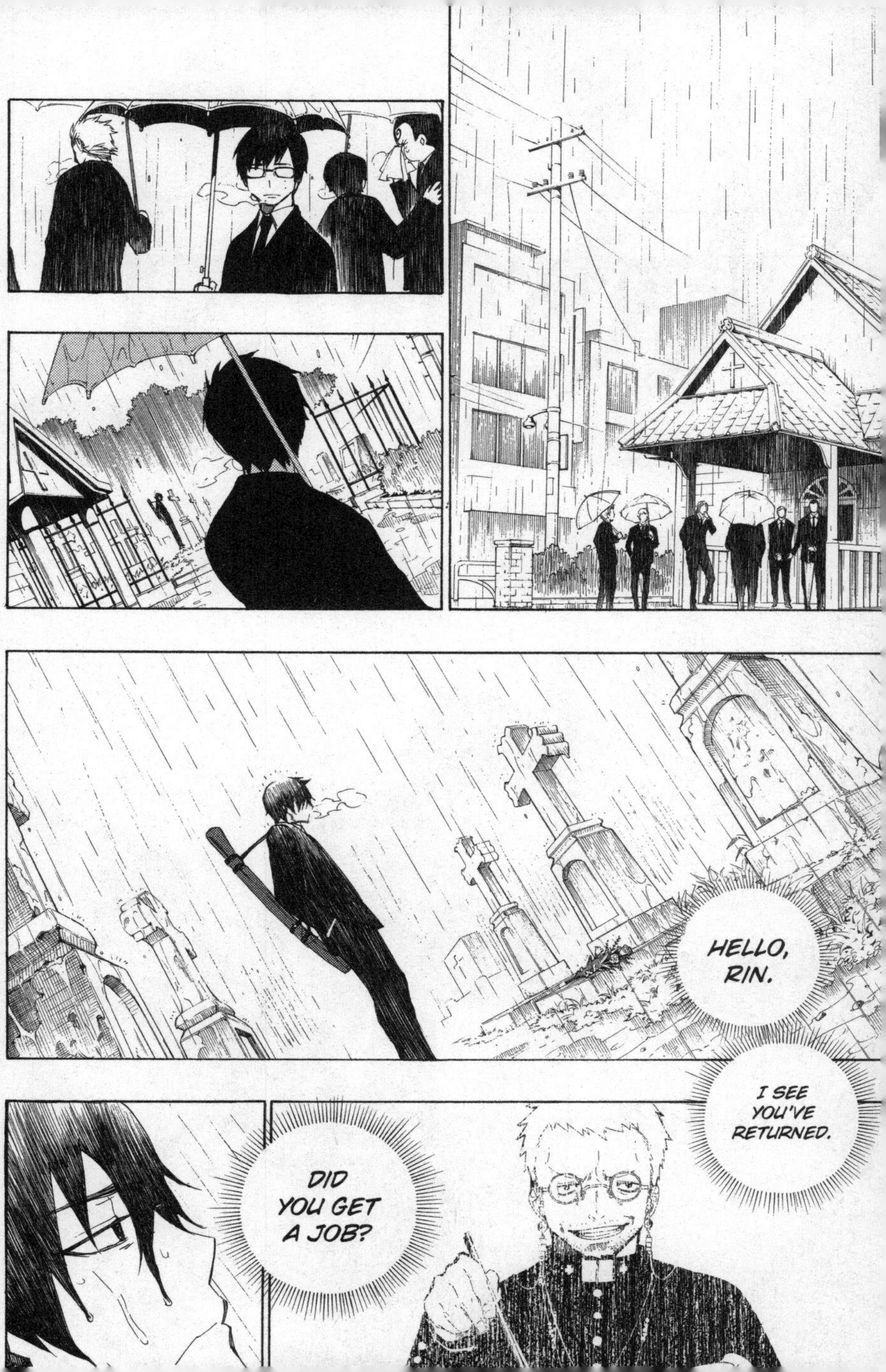
HELLO, RIN.
I SEE YOU'VE RETURNED.
DID YOU GET A JOB?

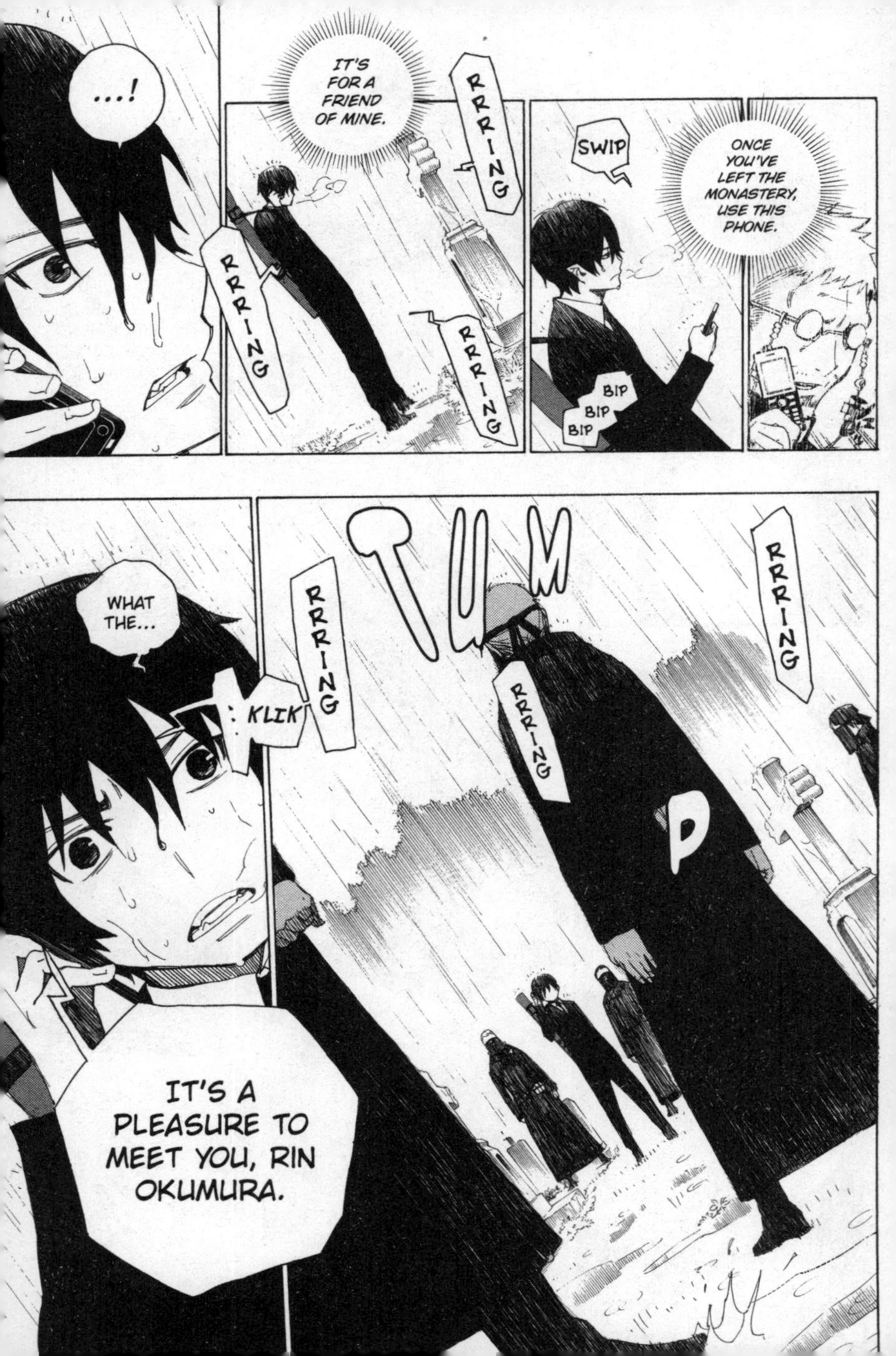
ONCE YOU'VE LEFT THE MONASTERY, USE THIS PHONE.
SWIP
BIP BIP BIP
RRRING
IT'S FOR A FRIEND OF MINE.
RRRING
RRRING
...!
TUM
P
RRRING
RRRING
RRRING
KLIK
WHAT THE...
IT'S A PLEASURE TO MEET YOU, RIN OKUMURA.

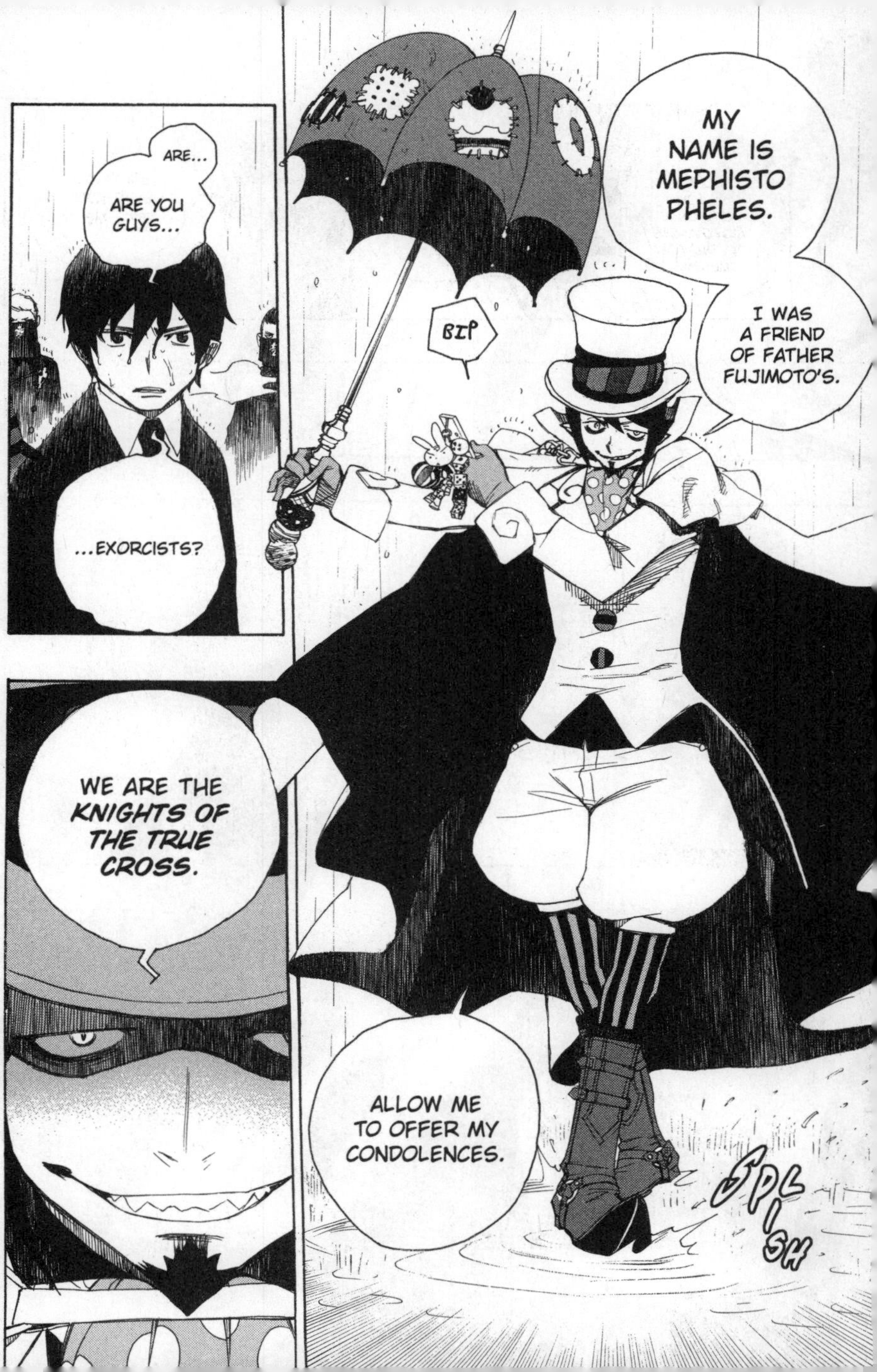
MY NAME IS MEPHISTO PHELES.
I WAS A FRIEND OF FATHER FUJIMOTO'S.
BIP
ALLOW ME TO OFFER MY CONDOLENCES.
SPLISH
ARE...
ARE YOU GUYS...
...EXORCISTS?
WE ARE THE *KNIGHTS OF THE TRUE CROSS*.

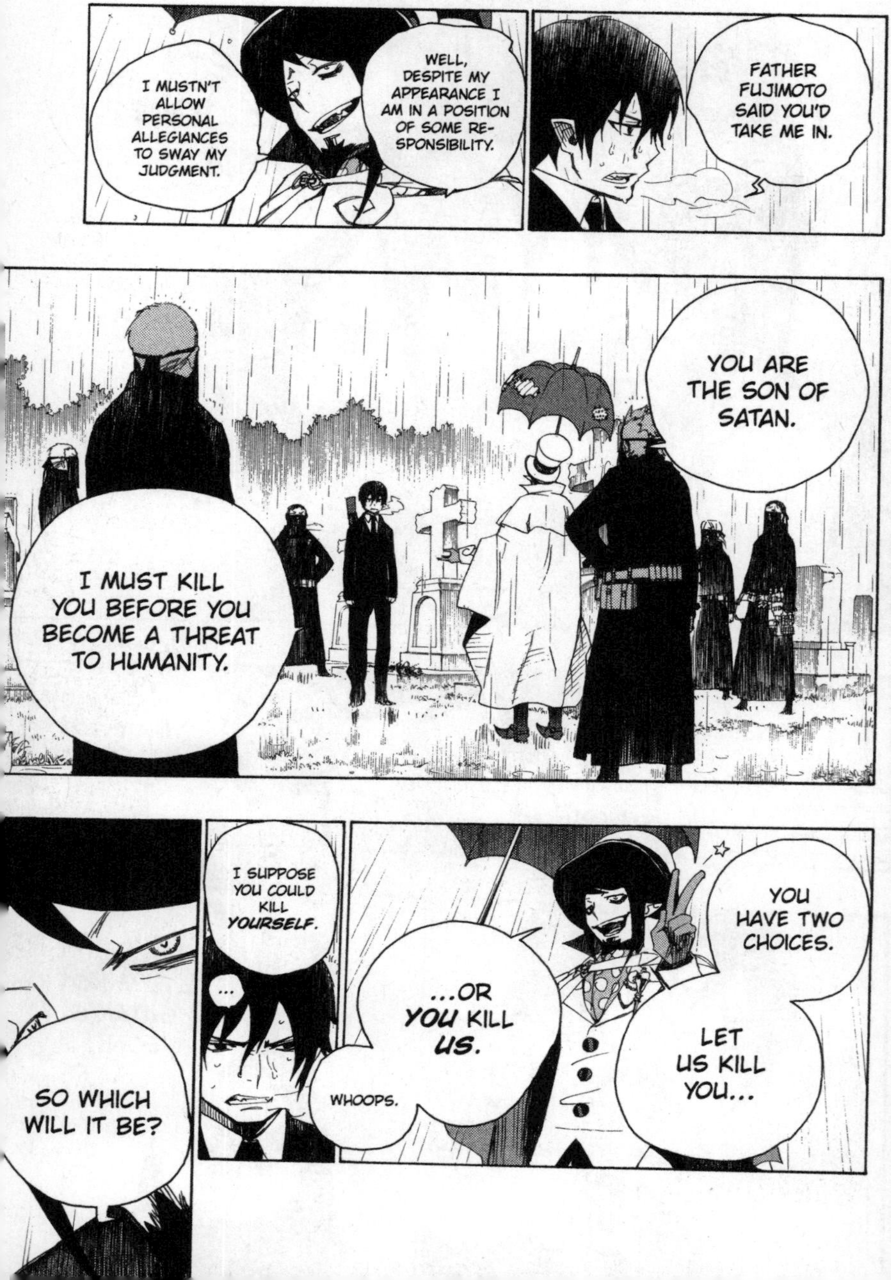
FATHER FUJIMOTO SAID YOU'D TAKE ME IN.
WELL, DESPITE MY APPEARANCE I AM IN A POSITION OF SOME RE-SPONSIBILITY.
I MUSTN'T ALLOW PERSONAL ALLEGIANCES TO SWAY MY JUDGMENT.
YOU ARE THE SON OF SATAN.
I MUST KILL YOU BEFORE YOU BECOME A THREAT TO HUMANITY.
YOU HAVE TWO CHOICES.
LET US KILL YOU...
...OR *YOU* KILL *US*.
WHOOPS.
I SUPPOSE YOU COULD KILL ***YOURSELF***.
...
SO WHICH WILL IT BE?

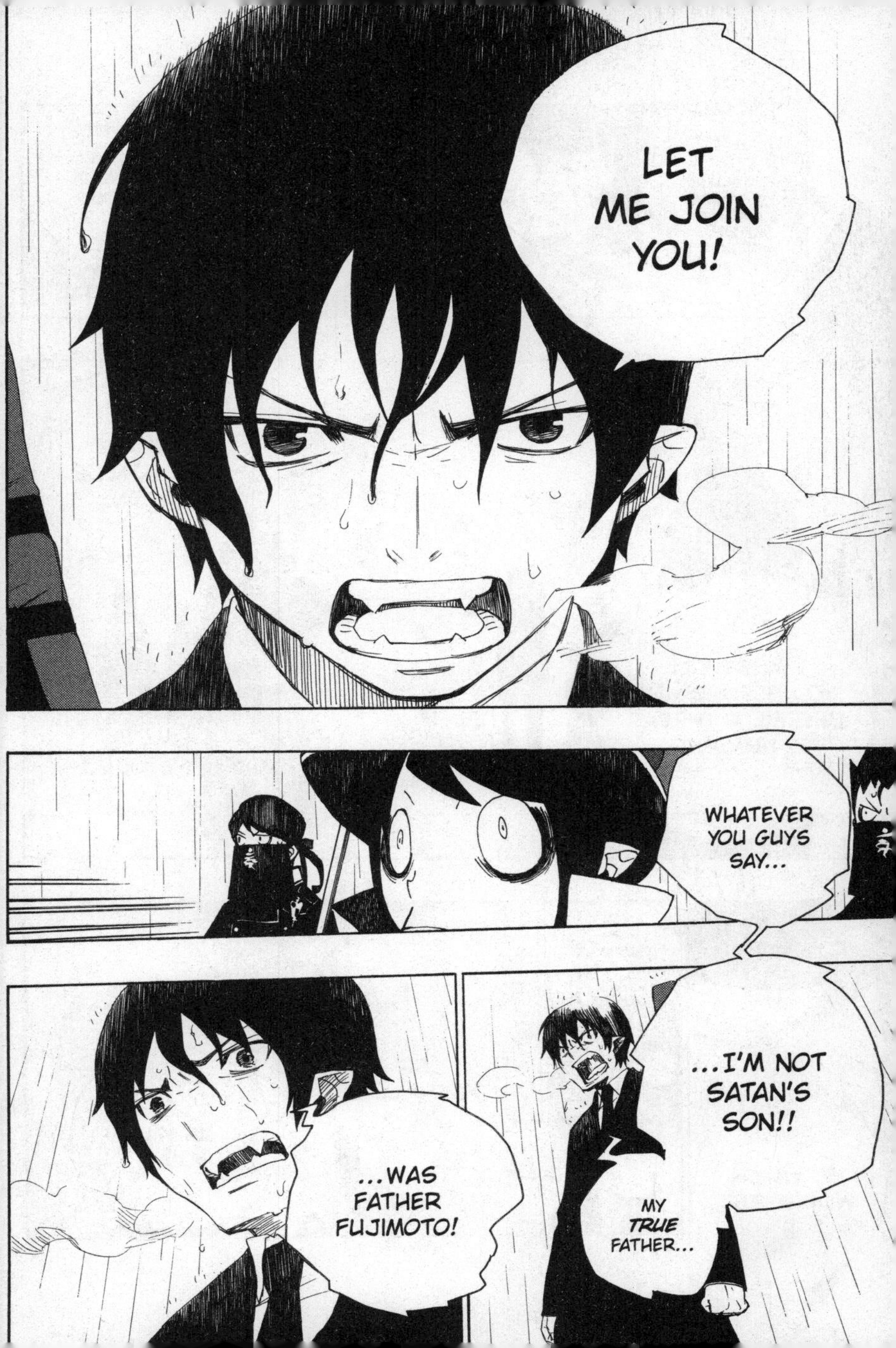
LET ME JOIN YOU!
WHATEVER YOU GUYS SAY...
...I'M NOT SATAN'S SON!!
MY *TRUE* FATHER...
...WAS FATHER FUJIMOTO!

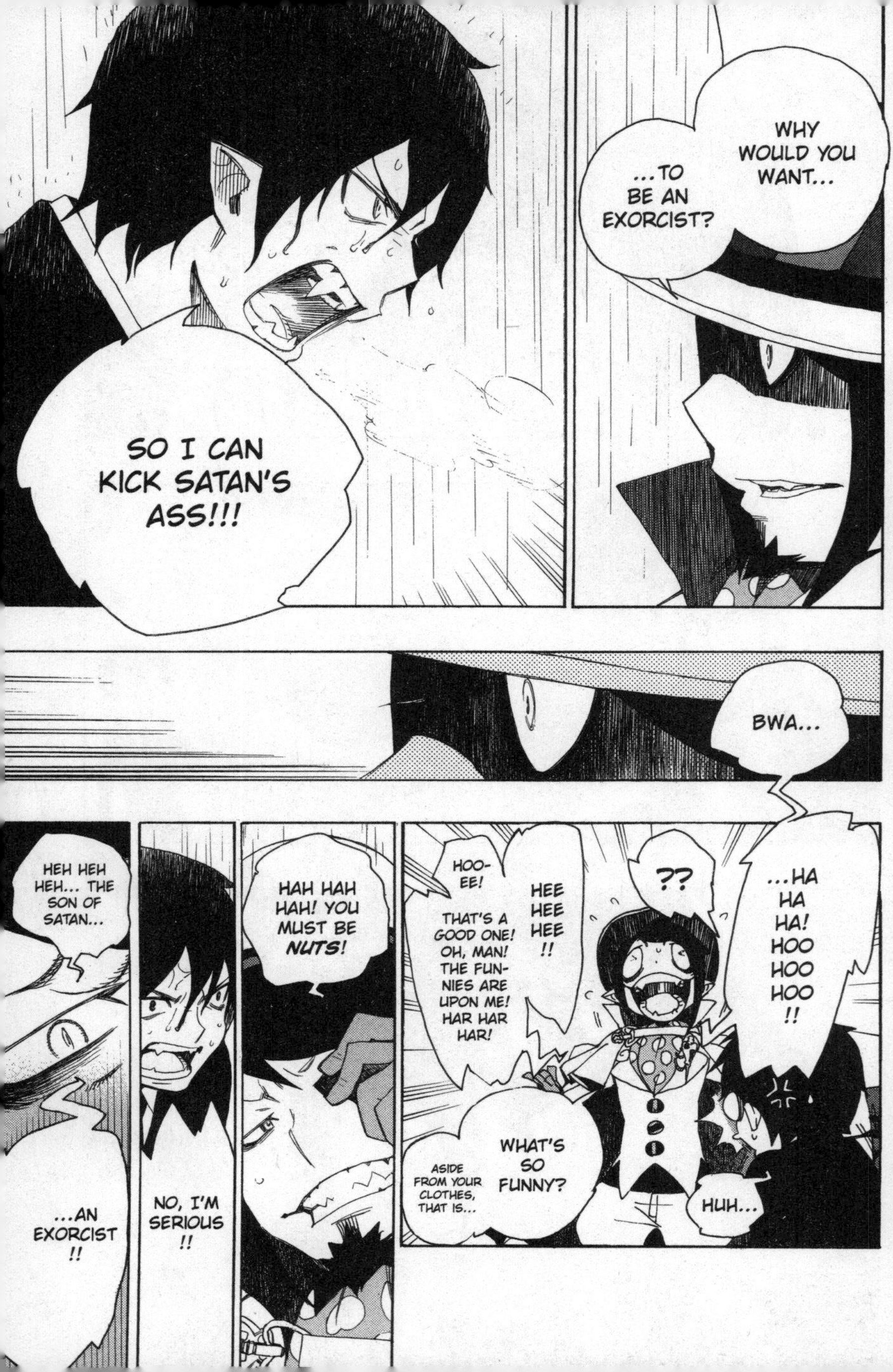
WHY WOULD YOU WANT...
...TO BE AN EXORCIST?
SO I CAN KICK SATAN'S ASS!!!
BWA...
...HA HA HA! HOO HOO HOO!!
??
HEE HEE HEE!!
HOO-EE! THAT'S A GOOD ONE! OH, MAN! THE FUNNIES ARE UPON ME! HAR HAR HAR!
HUH...
WHAT'S SO FUNNY?
ASIDE FROM YOUR CLOTHES, THAT IS...
HAH HAH HAH! YOU MUST BE NUTS!
NO, I'M SERIOUS!!
HEH HEH HEH... THE SON OF SATAN...
...AN EXORCIST!!

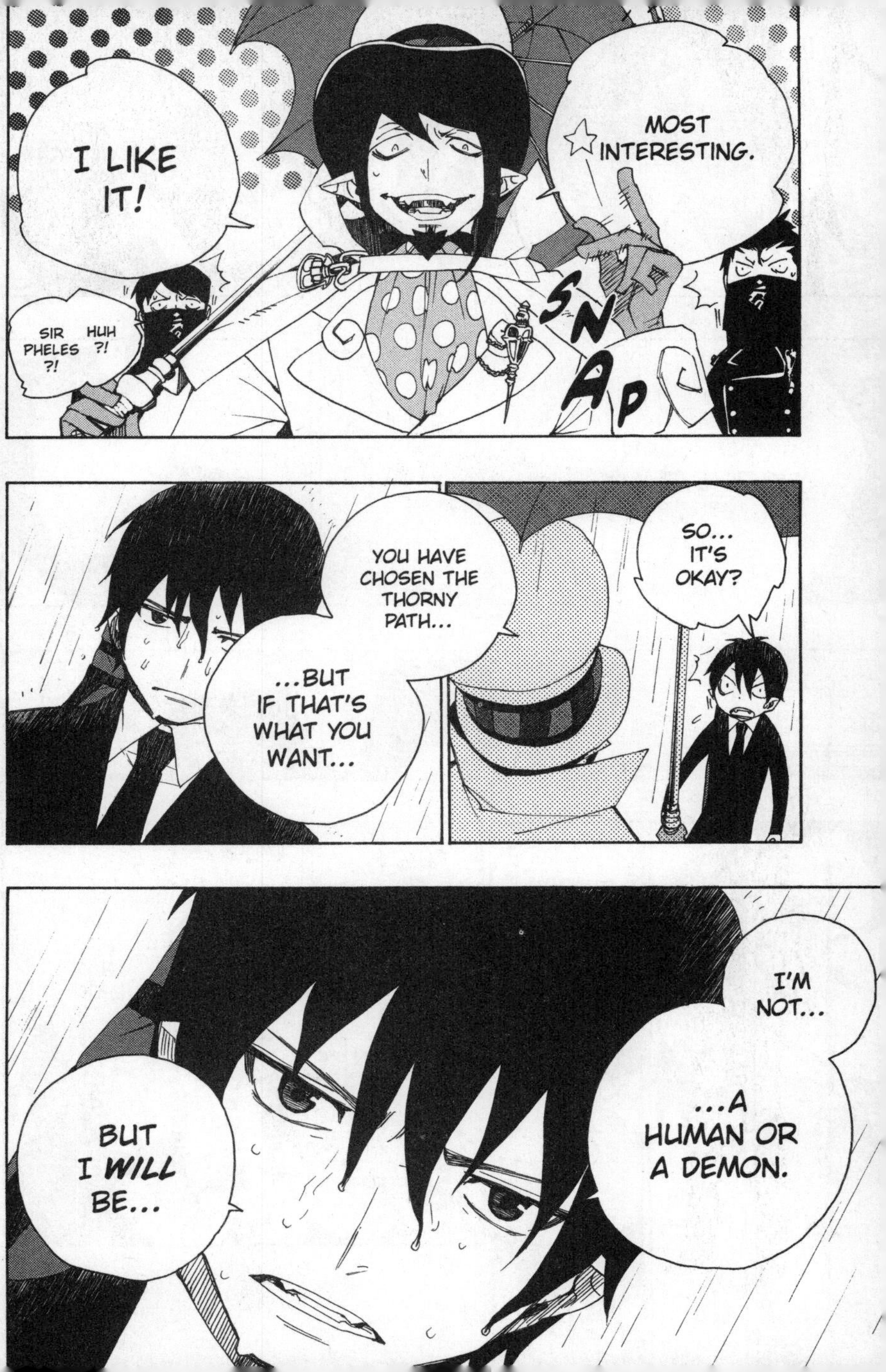

MOST INTERESTING.
I LIKE IT!
SNAP
HUH ?! SIR PHELES ?!
SO... IT'S OKAY?
YOU HAVE CHOSEN THE THORNY PATH...
...BUT IF THAT'S WHAT YOU WANT...
I'M NOT...
...A HUMAN OR A DEMON.
BUT I *WILL* BE...

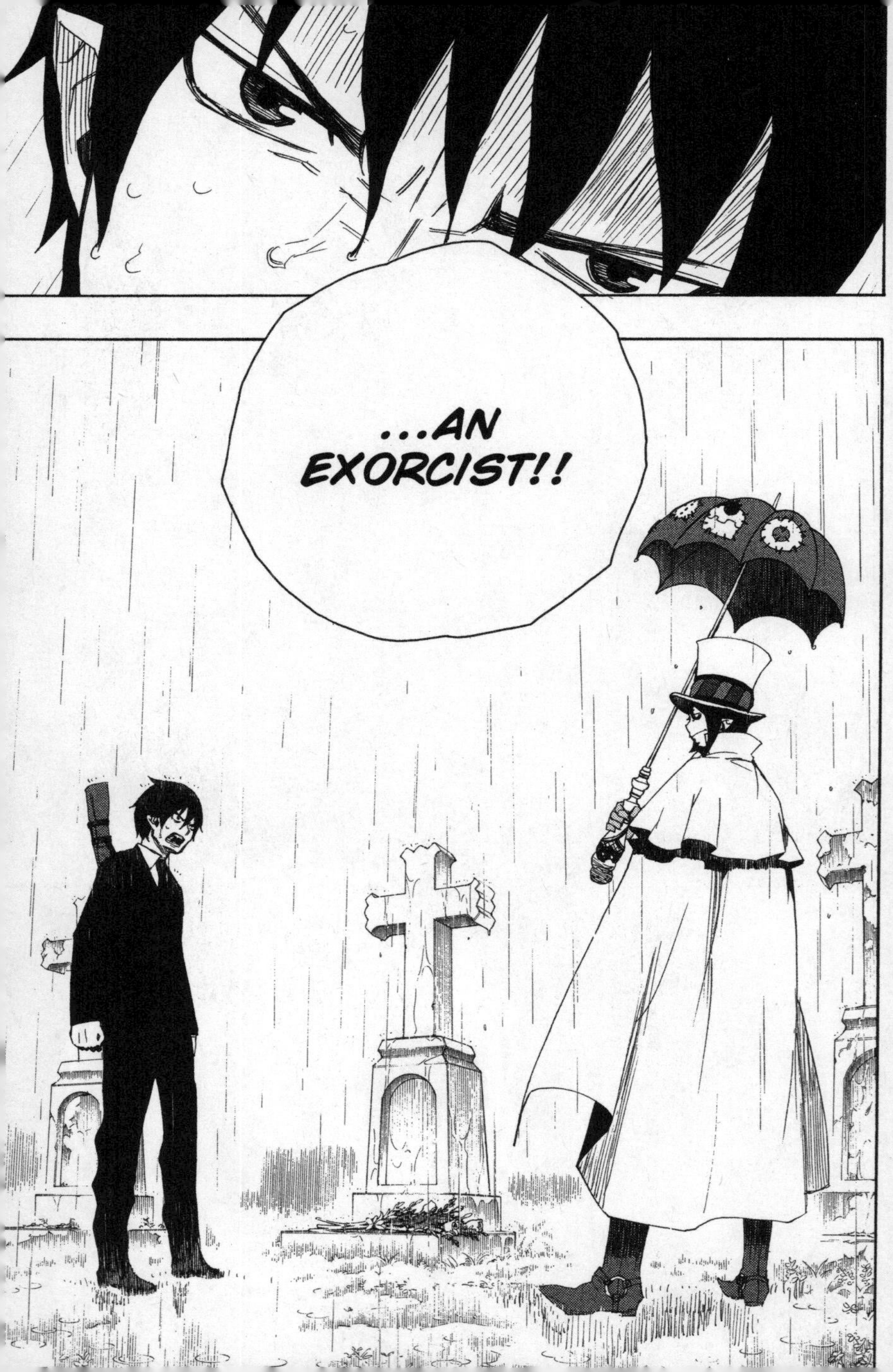
...AN EXORCIST!!

Chapter 1 The Mockery of Satan

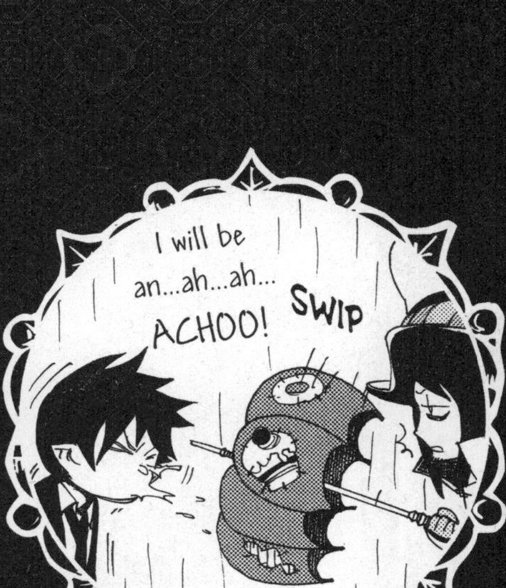
I will be an...ah...ah... ACHOO!
SWIP

Chapter 2
Big Brother, Little Brother

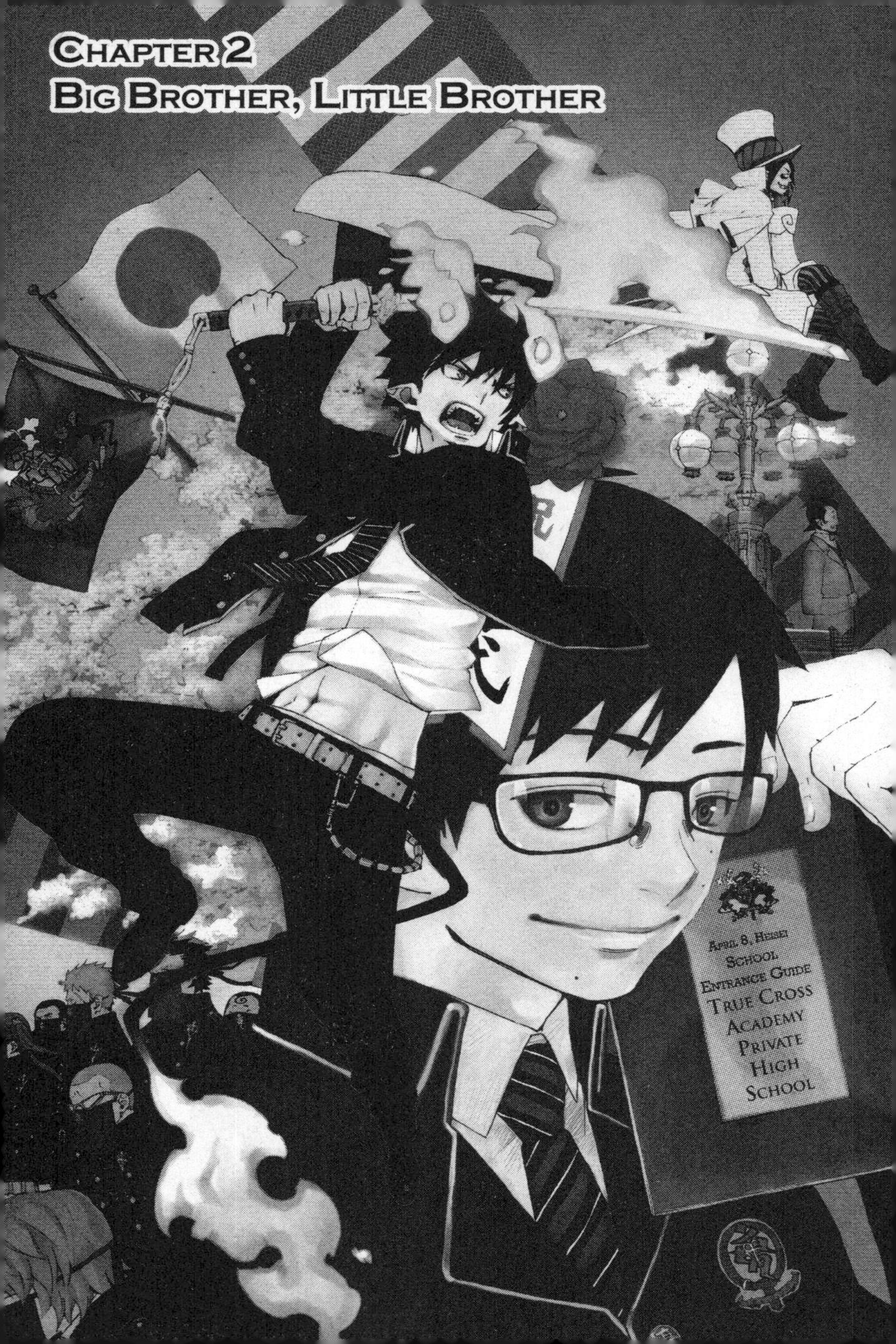
April 8, Heisei
School
Entrance Guide
True Cross
Academy
Private
High
School

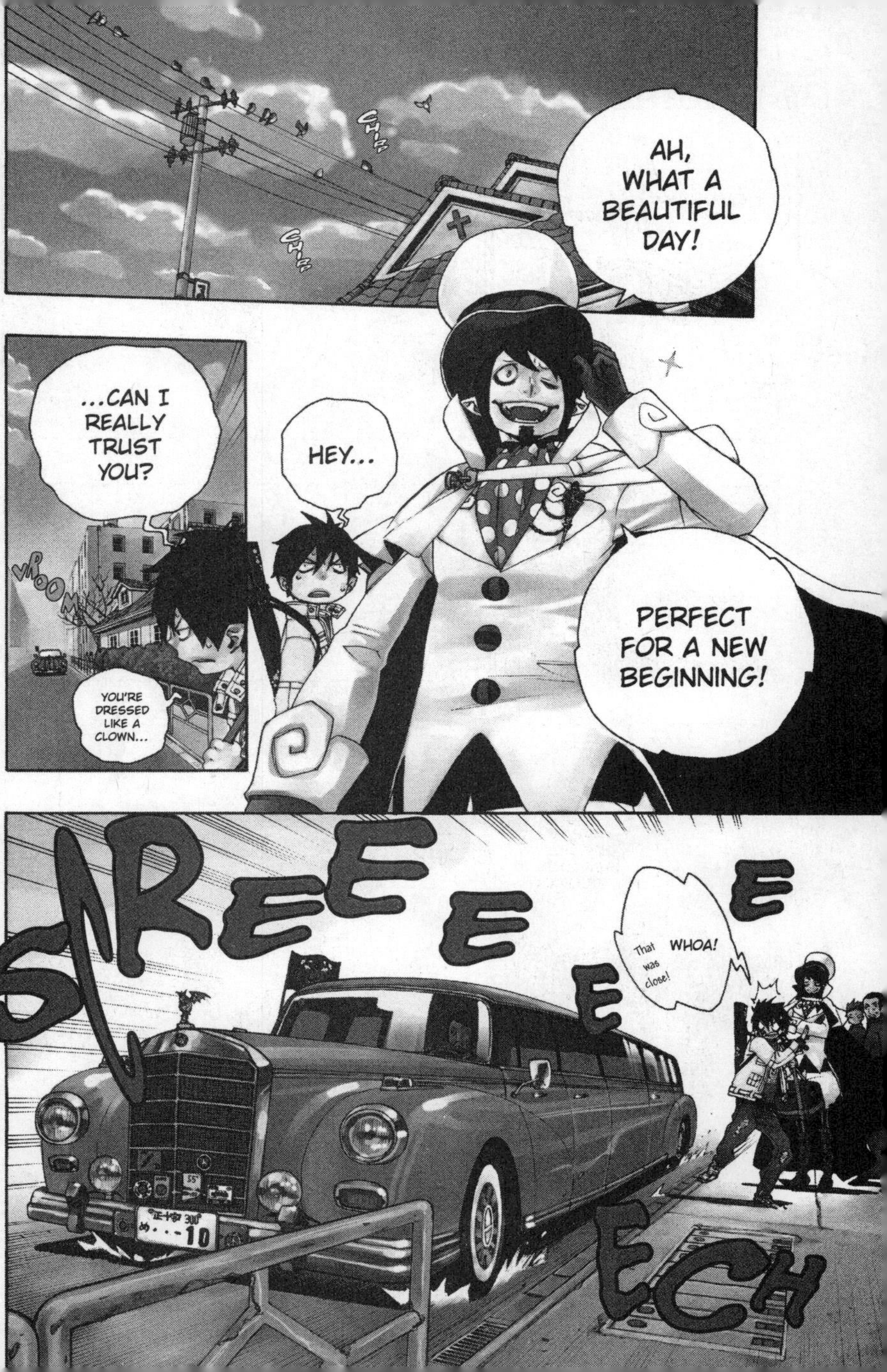
CHIP
CHIP
AH, WHAT A BEAUTIFUL DAY!
PERFECT FOR A NEW BEGINNING!
HEY...
...CAN I REALLY TRUST YOU?
VROOM
YOU'RE DRESSED LIKE A CLOWN...
SREEEEEEEECH
WHOA!
That was close!

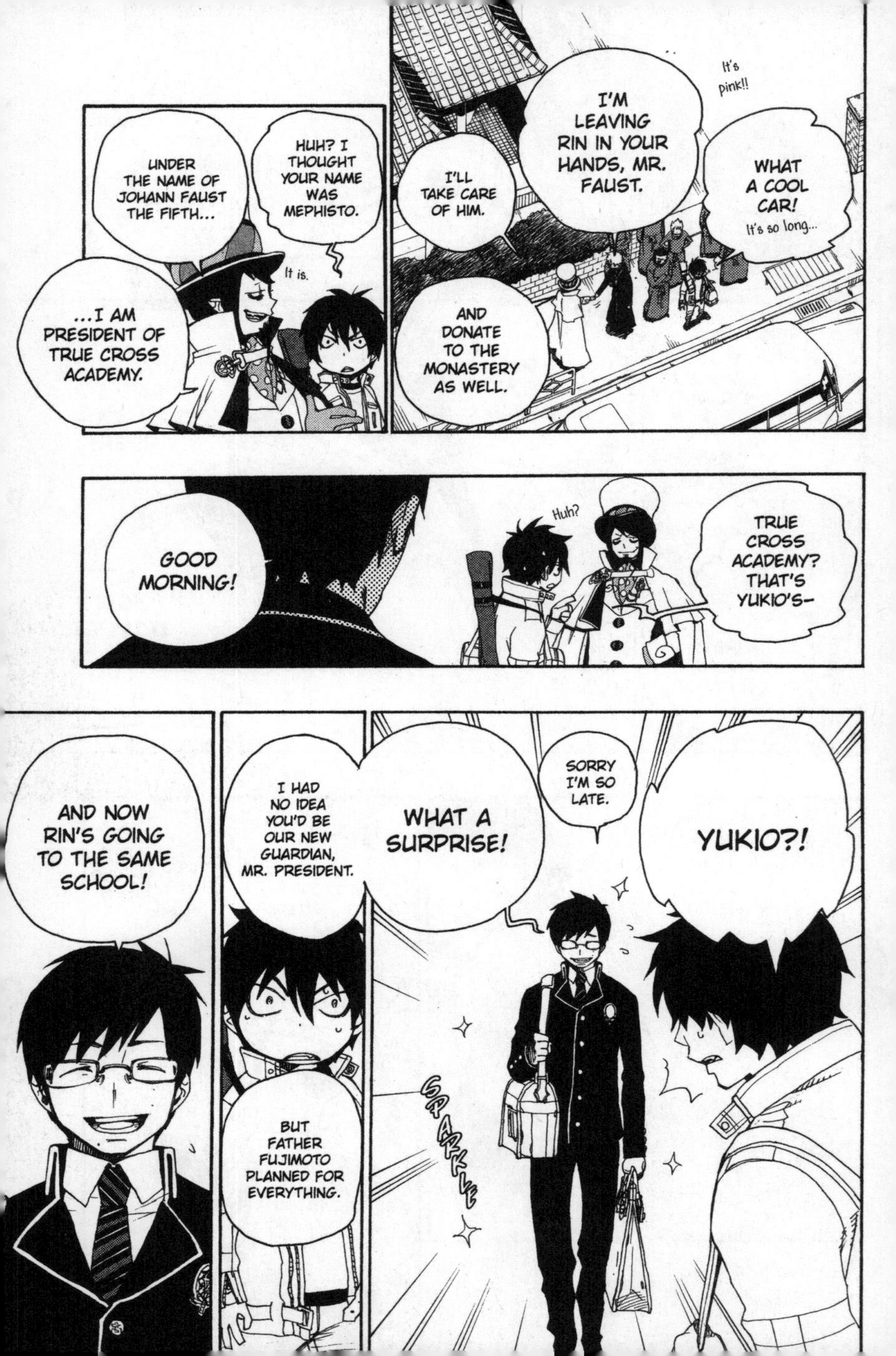
It's pink!!
WHAT A COOL CAR!
It's so long...
I'M LEAVING RIN IN YOUR HANDS, MR. FAUST.
I'LL TAKE CARE OF HIM.
AND DONATE TO THE MONASTERY AS WELL.
HUH? I THOUGHT YOUR NAME WAS MEPHISTO.
UNDER THE NAME OF JOHANN FAUST THE FIFTH...
It is.
...I AM PRESIDENT OF TRUE CROSS ACADEMY.
TRUE CROSS ACADEMY? THAT'S YUKIO'S-
Huh?
GOOD MORNING!
YUKIO?!
SORRY I'M SO LATE.
WHAT A SURPRISE!
SPARKLE
I HAD NO IDEA YOU'D BE OUR NEW GUARDIAN, MR. PRESIDENT.
BUT FATHER FUJIMOTO PLANNED FOR EVERYTHING.
AND NOW RIN'S GOING TO THE SAME SCHOOL!

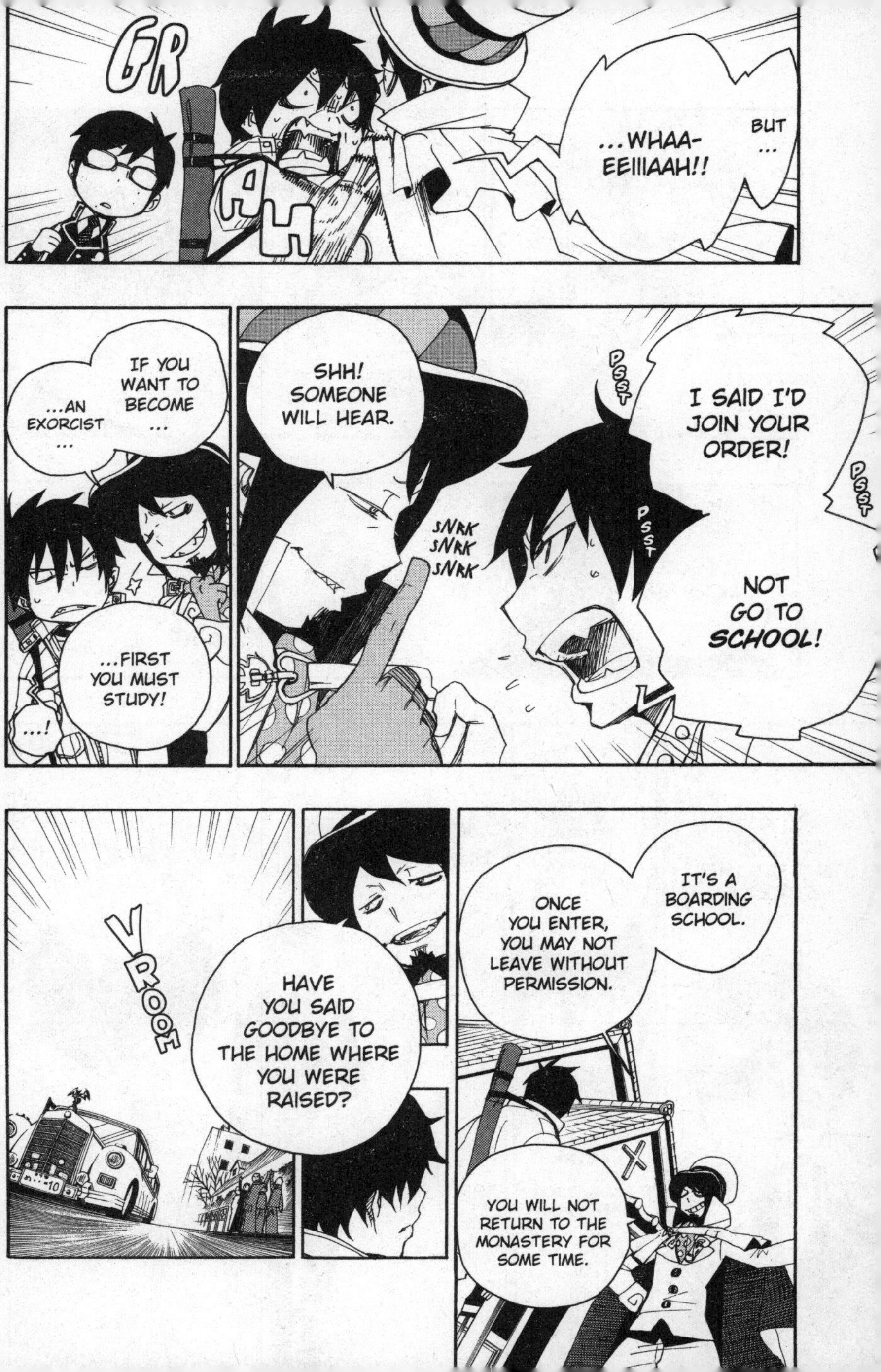
BUT ...
...WHAA-EEIIIAAH!!
GRAH
PSST
I SAID I'D JOIN YOUR ORDER!
PSST
PSST
NOT GO TO SCHOOL!
SNRK SNRK SNRK
SHH! SOMEONE WILL HEAR.
IF YOU WANT TO BECOME ...
...AN EXORCIST ...
...FIRST YOU MUST STUDY!
...!
IT'S A BOARDING SCHOOL.
ONCE YOU ENTER, YOU MAY NOT LEAVE WITHOUT PERMISSION.
YOU WILL NOT RETURN TO THE MONASTERY FOR SOME TIME.
HAVE YOU SAID GOODBYE TO THE HOME WHERE YOU WERE RAISED?
VROOM

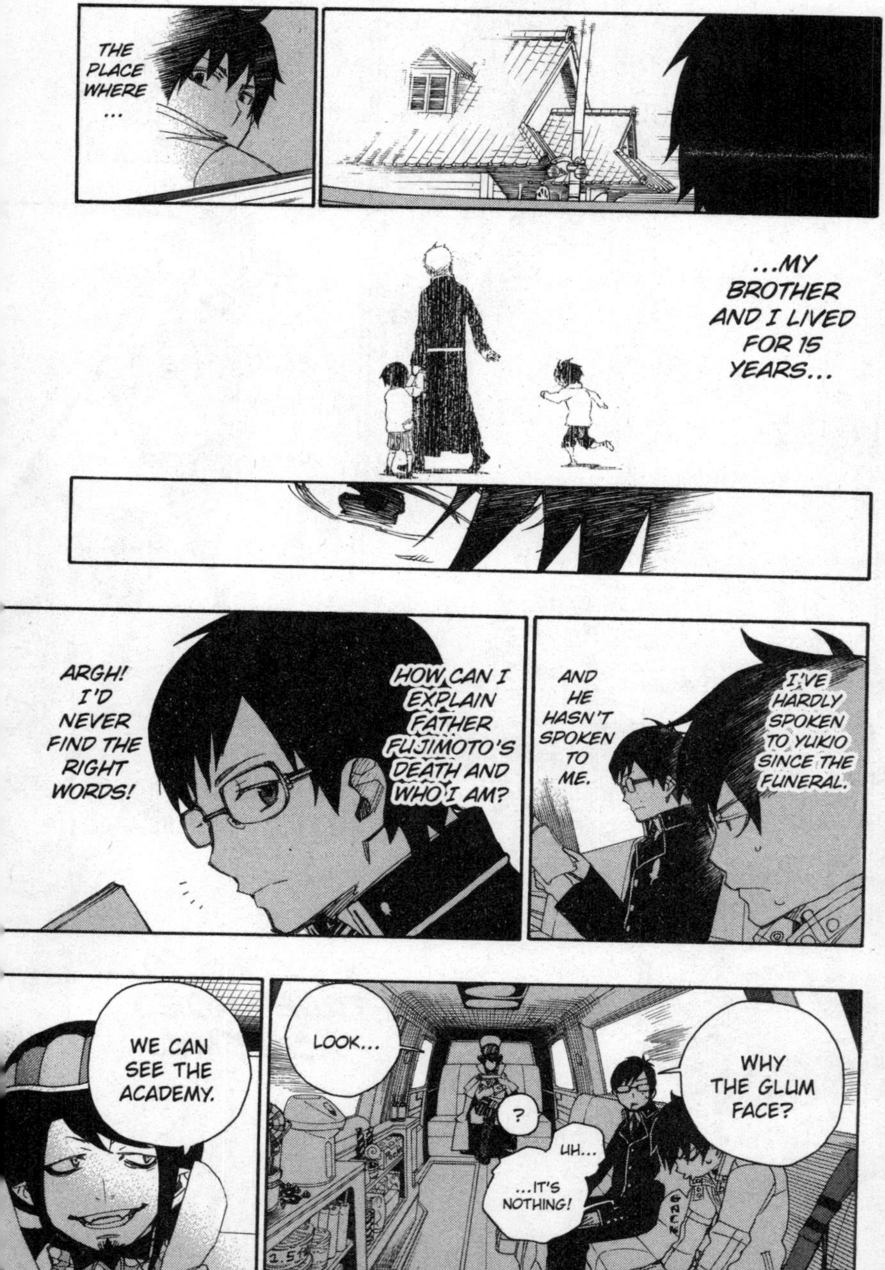
THE PLACE WHERE ...
...MY BROTHER AND I LIVED FOR 15 YEARS...
I'VE HARDLY SPOKEN TO YUKIO SINCE THE FUNERAL.
AND HE HASN'T SPOKEN TO ME.
HOW CAN I EXPLAIN FATHER FUJIMOTO'S DEATH AND WHO I AM?
ARGH! I'D NEVER FIND THE RIGHT WORDS!
WHY THE GLUM FACE?
?
UH...
...IT'S NOTHING!
LOOK...
WE CAN SEE THE ACADEMY.

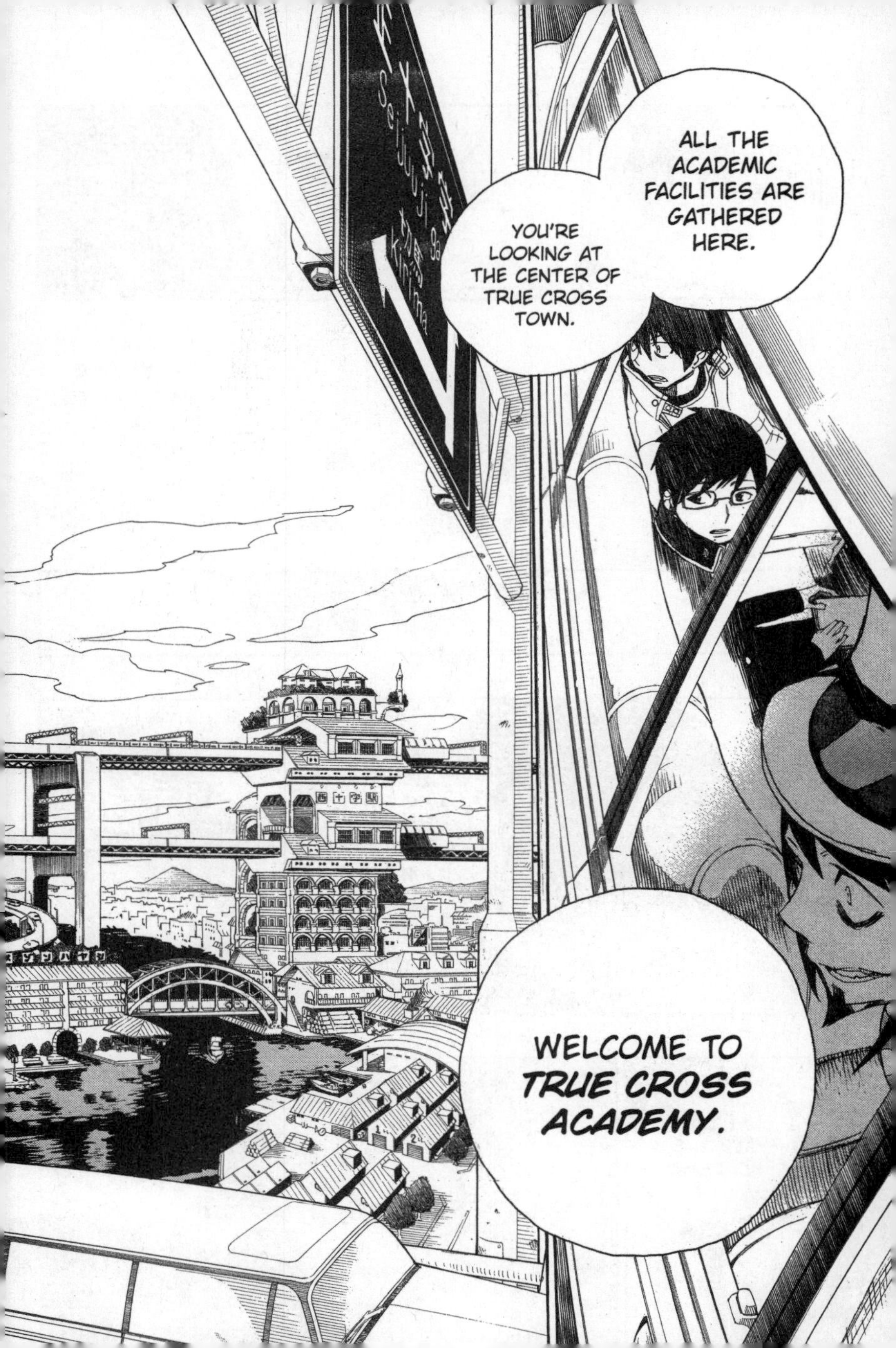
ALL THE ACADEMIC FACILITIES ARE GATHERED HERE.
YOU'RE LOOKING AT THE CENTER OF TRUE CROSS TOWN.
WELCOME TO *TRUE CROSS ACADEMY*.

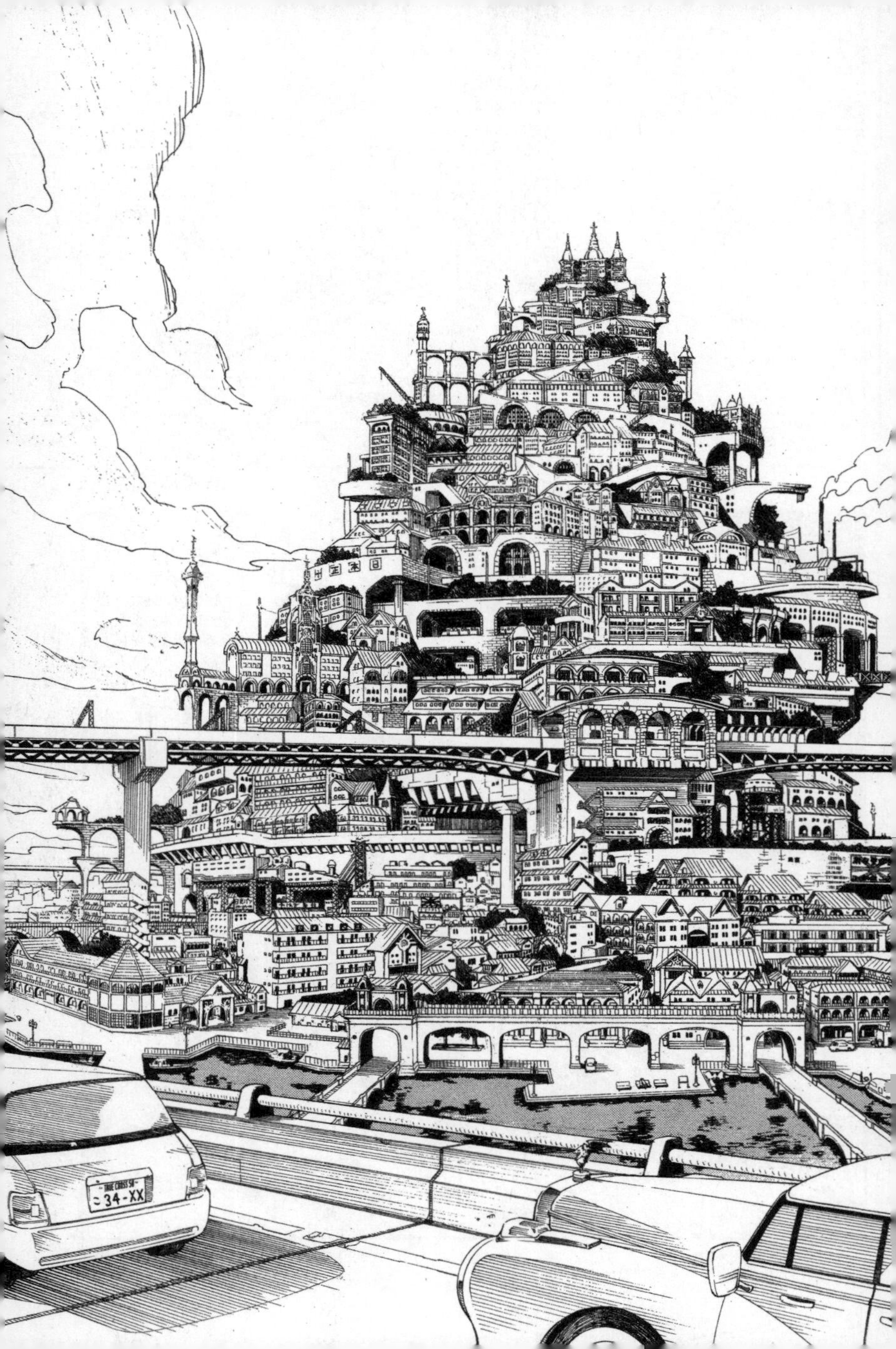
TRUE CROSS 58
こ 34-XX

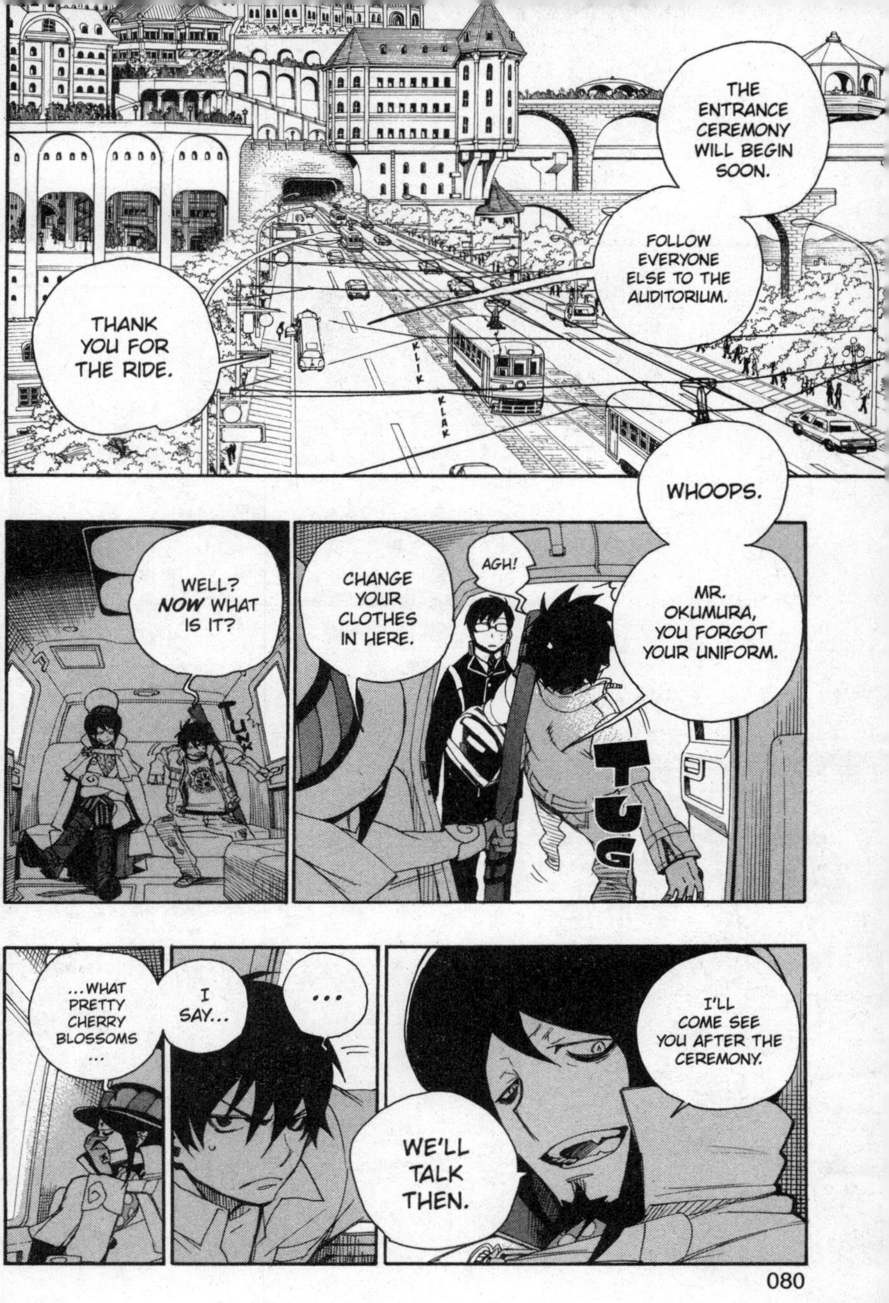
THE ENTRANCE CEREMONY WILL BEGIN SOON.
FOLLOW EVERYONE ELSE TO THE AUDITORIUM.
KLIK
KLAK
THANK YOU FOR THE RIDE.
WHOOPS.
MR. OKUMURA, YOU FORGOT YOUR UNIFORM.
TUG
AGH!
CHANGE YOUR CLOTHES IN HERE.
WELL? *NOW* WHAT IS IT?
I'LL COME SEE YOU AFTER THE CEREMONY.
WE'LL TALK THEN.
...
I SAY...
...WHAT PRETTY CHERRY BLOSSOMS ...

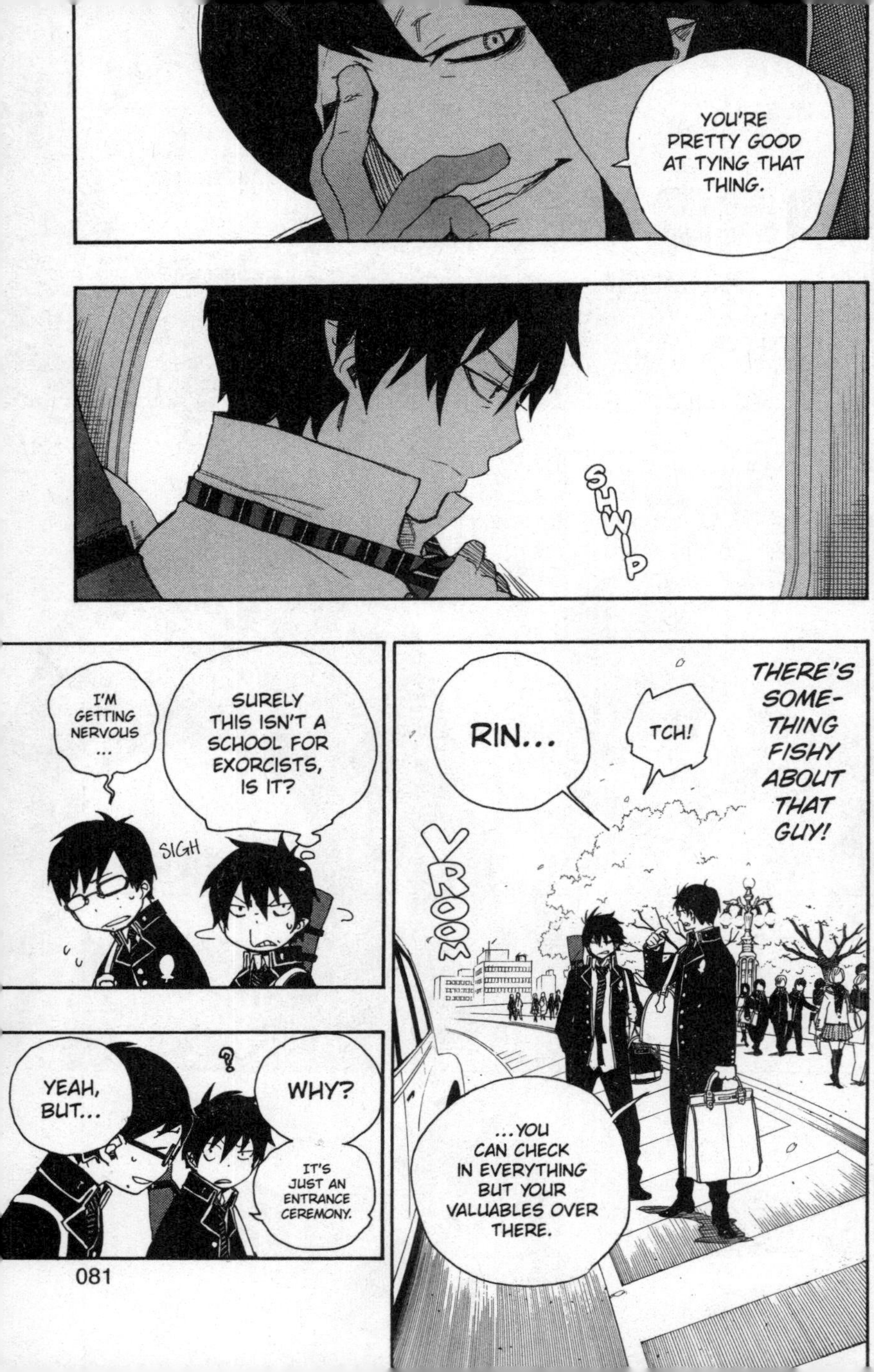
YOU'RE PRETTY GOOD AT TYING THAT THING.
SHWIP
THERE'S SOMETHING FISHY ABOUT THAT GUY!
TCH!
RIN...
VROOM
...YOU CAN CHECK IN EVERYTHING BUT YOUR VALUABLES OVER THERE.
SURELY THIS ISN'T A SCHOOL FOR EXORCISTS, IS IT?
SIGH
I'M GETTING NERVOUS ...
WHY?
?
IT'S JUST AN ENTRANCE CEREMONY.
YEAH, BUT...

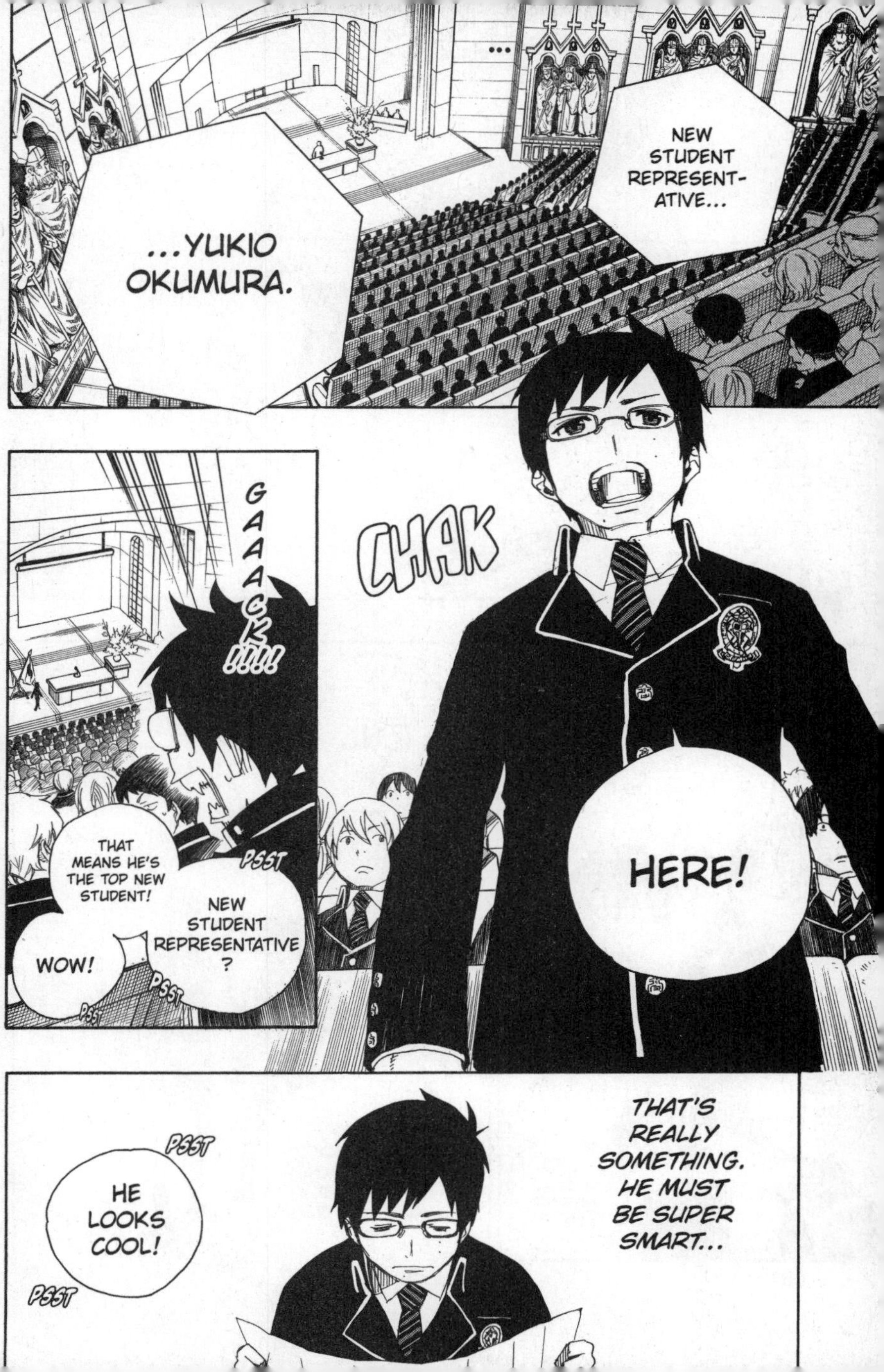
...
NEW STUDENT REPRESENT-ATIVE...
...YUKIO OKUMURA.
CHAK
HERE!
GAAAACK!!!!
PSST
NEW STUDENT REPRESENTATIVE?
THAT MEANS HE'S THE TOP NEW STUDENT!
PSST
WOW!
PSST
THAT'S REALLY SOMETHING. HE MUST BE SUPER SMART...
PSST
HE LOOKS COOL!
PSST

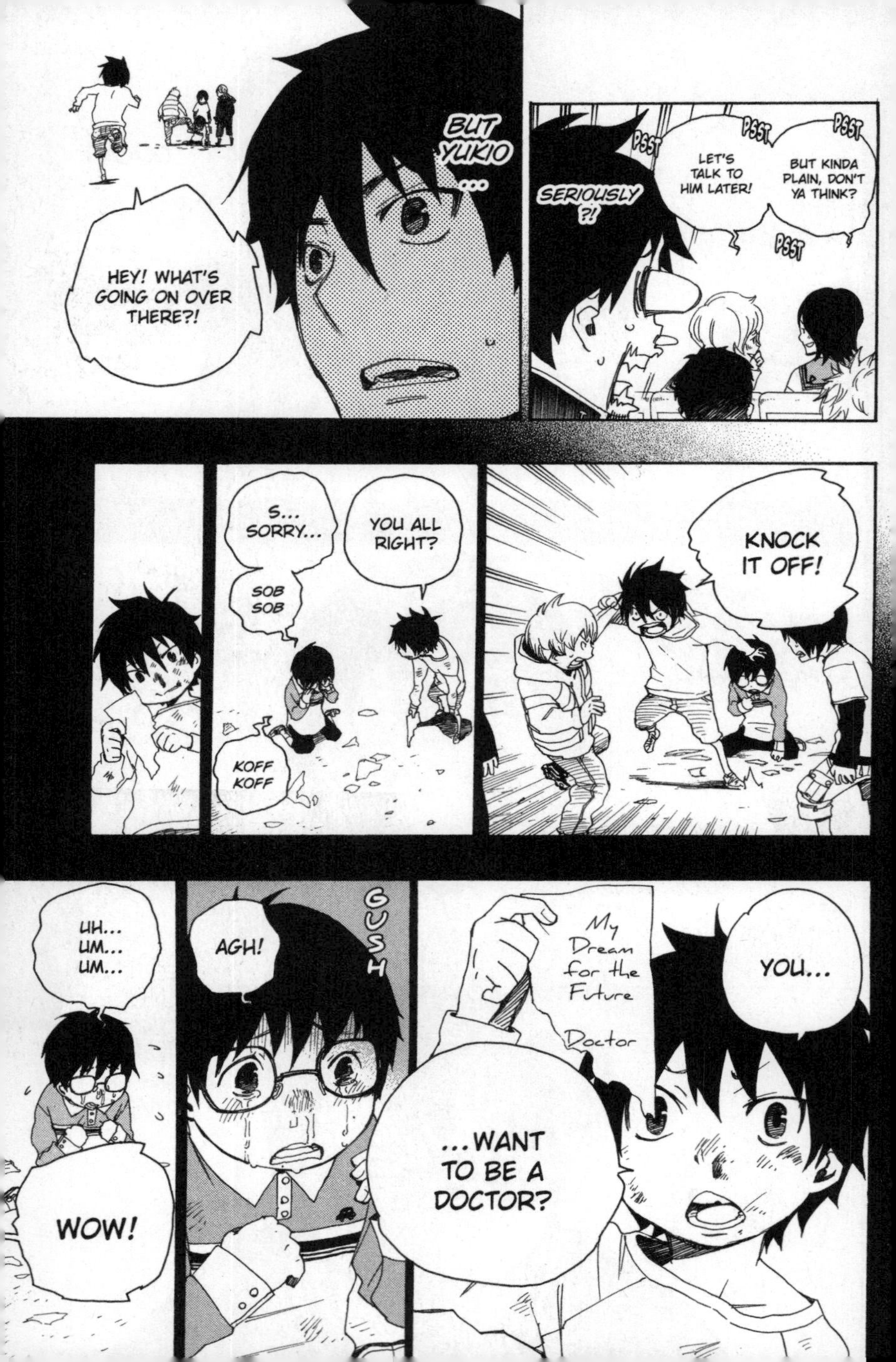
PSST
PSST
BUT KINDA PLAIN, DON'T YA THINK?
LET'S TALK TO HIM LATER!
PSST
PSST
SERIOUSLY ?!
BUT YUKIO ...
HEY! WHAT'S GOING ON OVER THERE?!
KNOCK IT OFF!
YOU ALL RIGHT?
S... SORRY...
SOB SOB
KOFF KOFF
YOU...
My Dream for the Future
Doctor
...WANT TO BE A DOCTOR?
GUSH
AGH!
UH... UM... UM...
WOW!

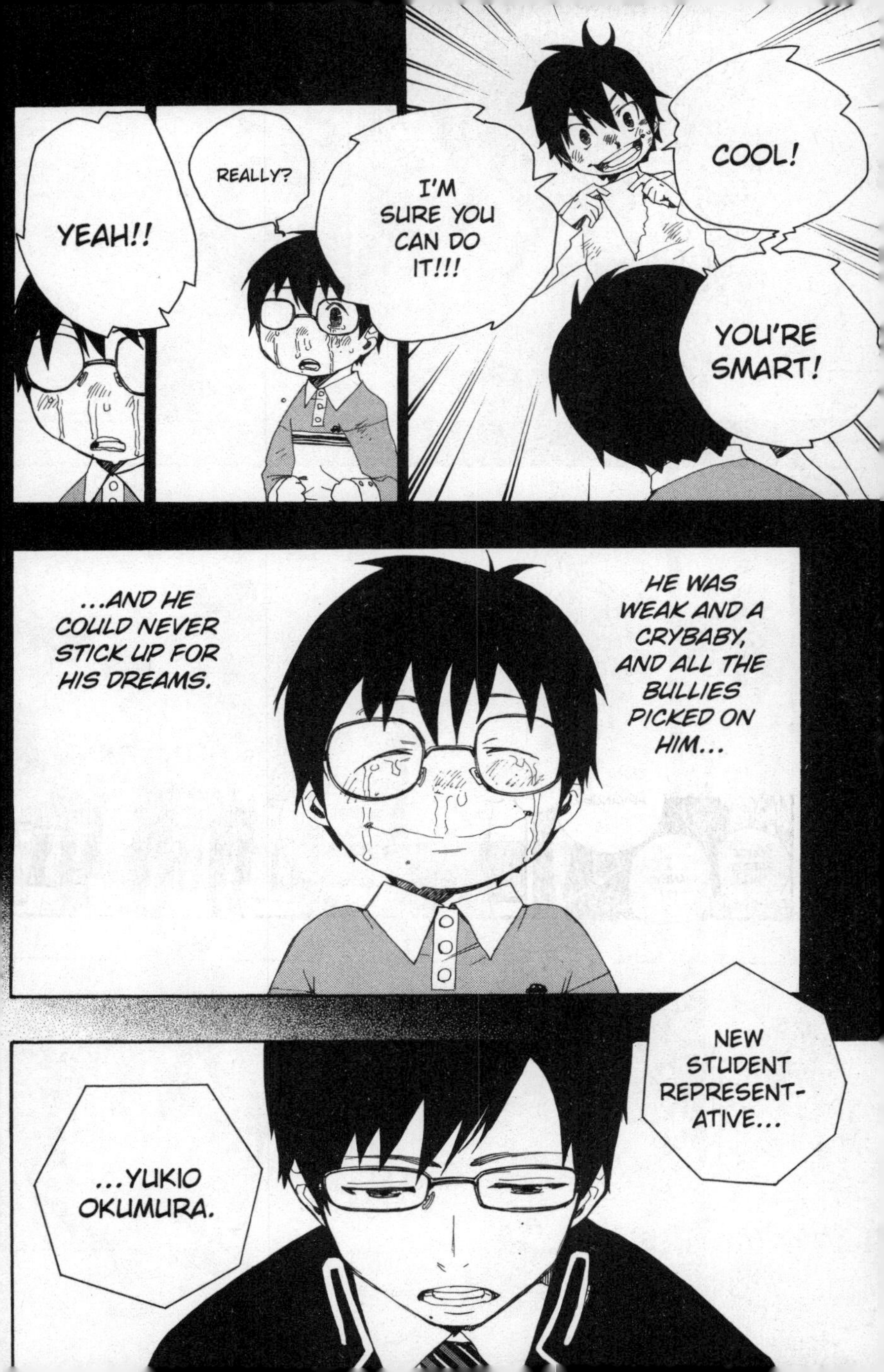
COOL!
YOU'RE SMART!
I'M SURE YOU CAN DO IT!!!
REALLY?
YEAH!!
HE WAS WEAK AND A CRYBABY, AND ALL THE BULLIES PICKED ON HIM...
...AND HE COULD NEVER STICK UP FOR HIS DREAMS.
NEW STUDENT REPRESENT-ATIVE...
...YUKIO OKUMURA.

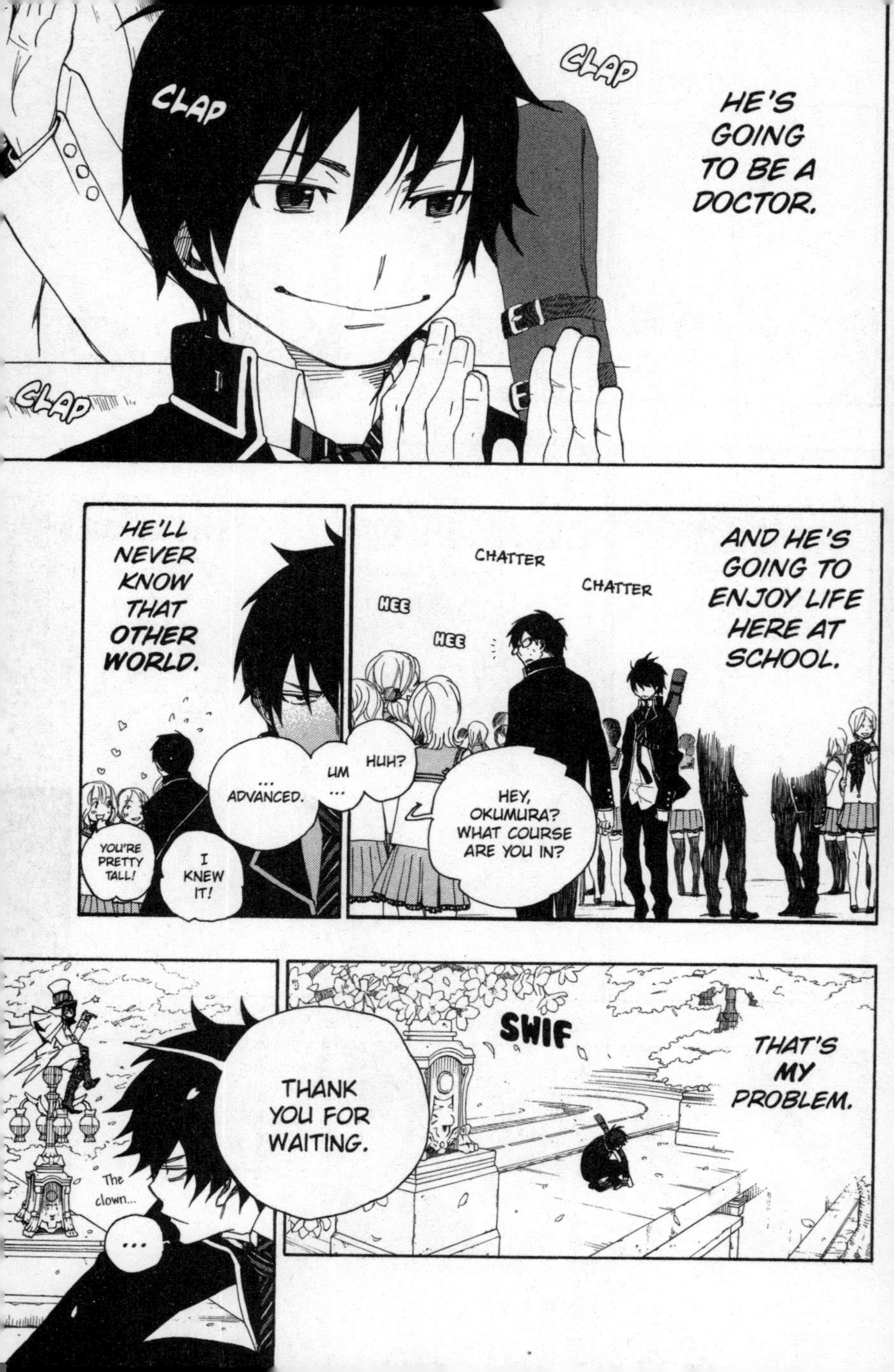
HE'S GOING TO BE A DOCTOR.
CLAP
CLAP
CLAP
AND HE'S GOING TO ENJOY LIFE HERE AT SCHOOL.
CHATTER
CHATTER
HEE
HEE
HUH?
HEY, OKUMURA? WHAT COURSE ARE YOU IN?
HE'LL NEVER KNOW THAT OTHER WORLD.
UM ...
... ADVANCED.
YOU'RE PRETTY TALL!
I KNEW IT!
THAT'S MY PROBLEM.
SWIF
THANK YOU FOR WAITING.
The clown...
...

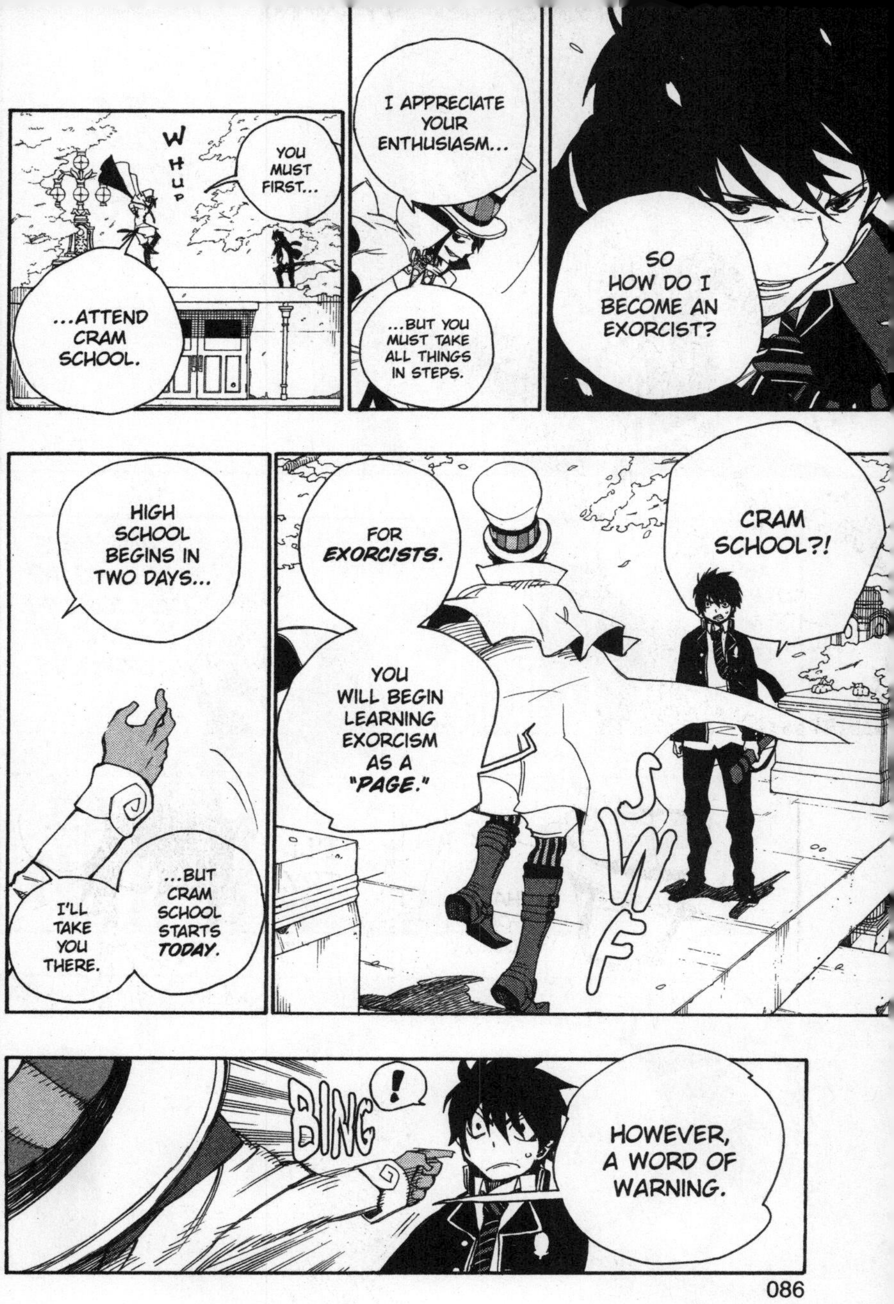
SO HOW DO I BECOME AN EXORCIST?
I APPRECIATE YOUR ENTHUSIASM...
...BUT YOU MUST TAKE ALL THINGS IN STEPS.
WHUP
YOU MUST FIRST...
...ATTEND CRAM SCHOOL.
CRAM SCHOOL?!
FOR EXORCISTS.
YOU WILL BEGIN LEARNING EXORCISM AS A "PAGE."
SWF
HIGH SCHOOL BEGINS IN TWO DAYS...
...BUT CRAM SCHOOL STARTS TODAY.
I'LL TAKE YOU THERE.
HOWEVER, A WORD OF WARNING.
!
BING

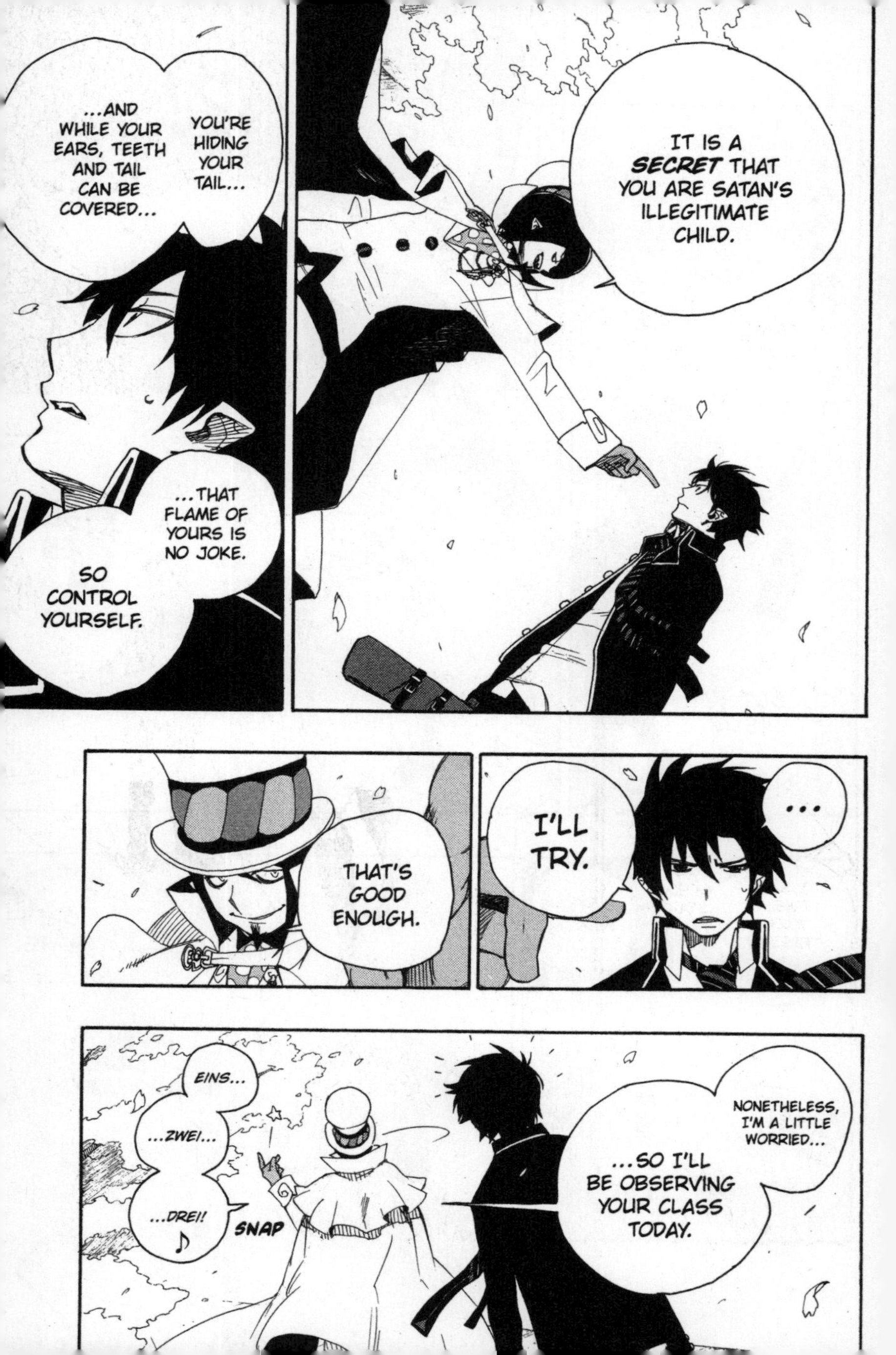
IT IS A SECRET THAT YOU ARE SATAN'S ILLEGITIMATE CHILD.
YOU'RE HIDING YOUR TAIL...
...AND WHILE YOUR EARS, TEETH AND TAIL CAN BE COVERED...
...THAT FLAME OF YOURS IS NO JOKE.
SO CONTROL YOURSELF.
...
I'LL TRY.
THAT'S GOOD ENOUGH.
NONETHELESS, I'M A LITTLE WORRIED...
...SO I'LL BE OBSERVING YOUR CLASS TODAY.
EINS...
...ZWEI...
...DREI! ♪
SNAP

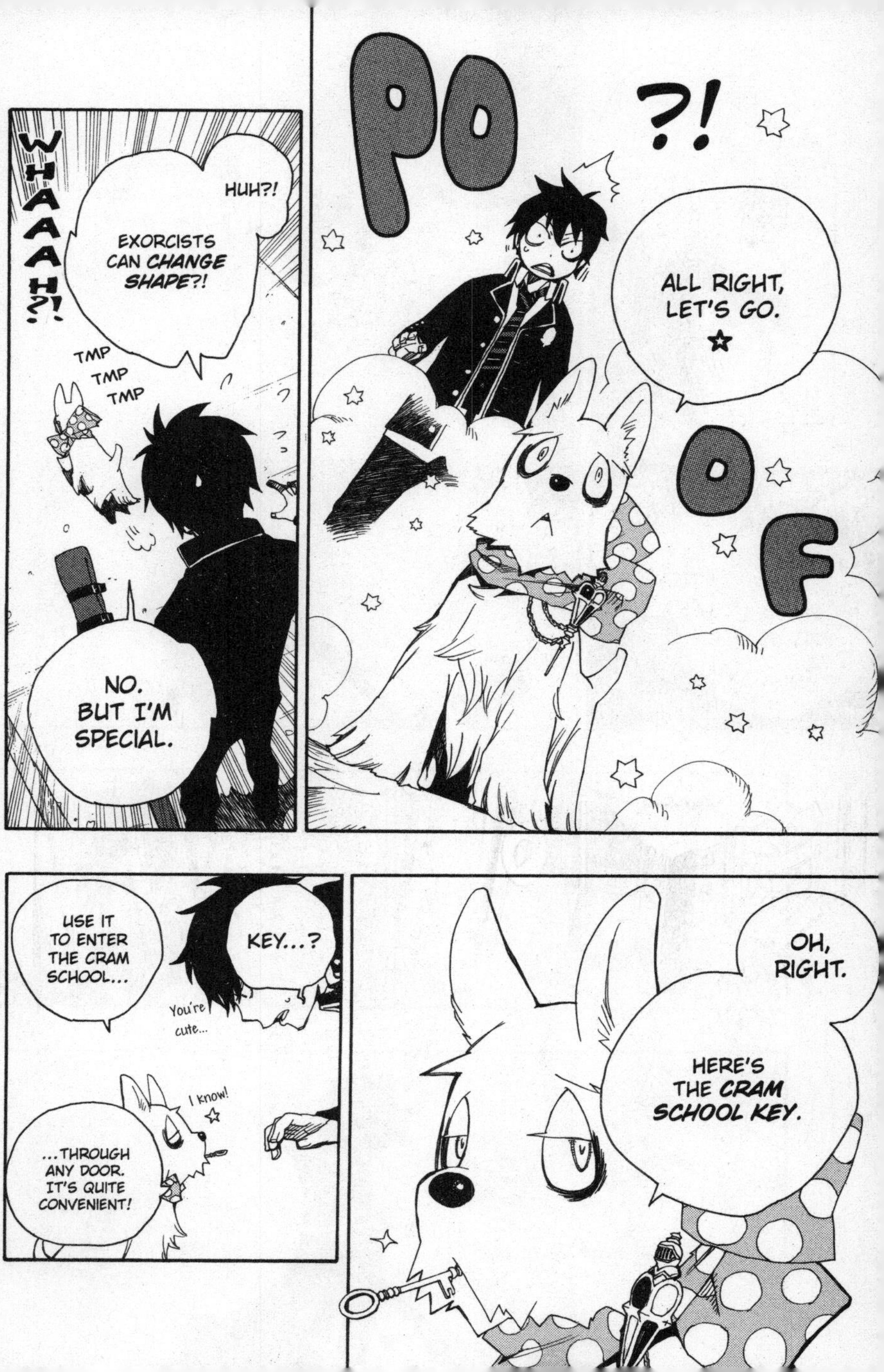
PO
?!
ALL RIGHT, LET'S GO. ☆
O
F
WHAAAAH?!
HUH?!
EXORCISTS CAN CHANGE SHAPE?!
TMP TMP TMP
NO. BUT I'M SPECIAL.
OH, RIGHT.
HERE'S THE CRAM SCHOOL KEY.
KEY...?
USE IT TO ENTER THE CRAM SCHOOL...
You're cute...
I know!
...THROUGH ANY DOOR. IT'S QUITE CONVENIENT!

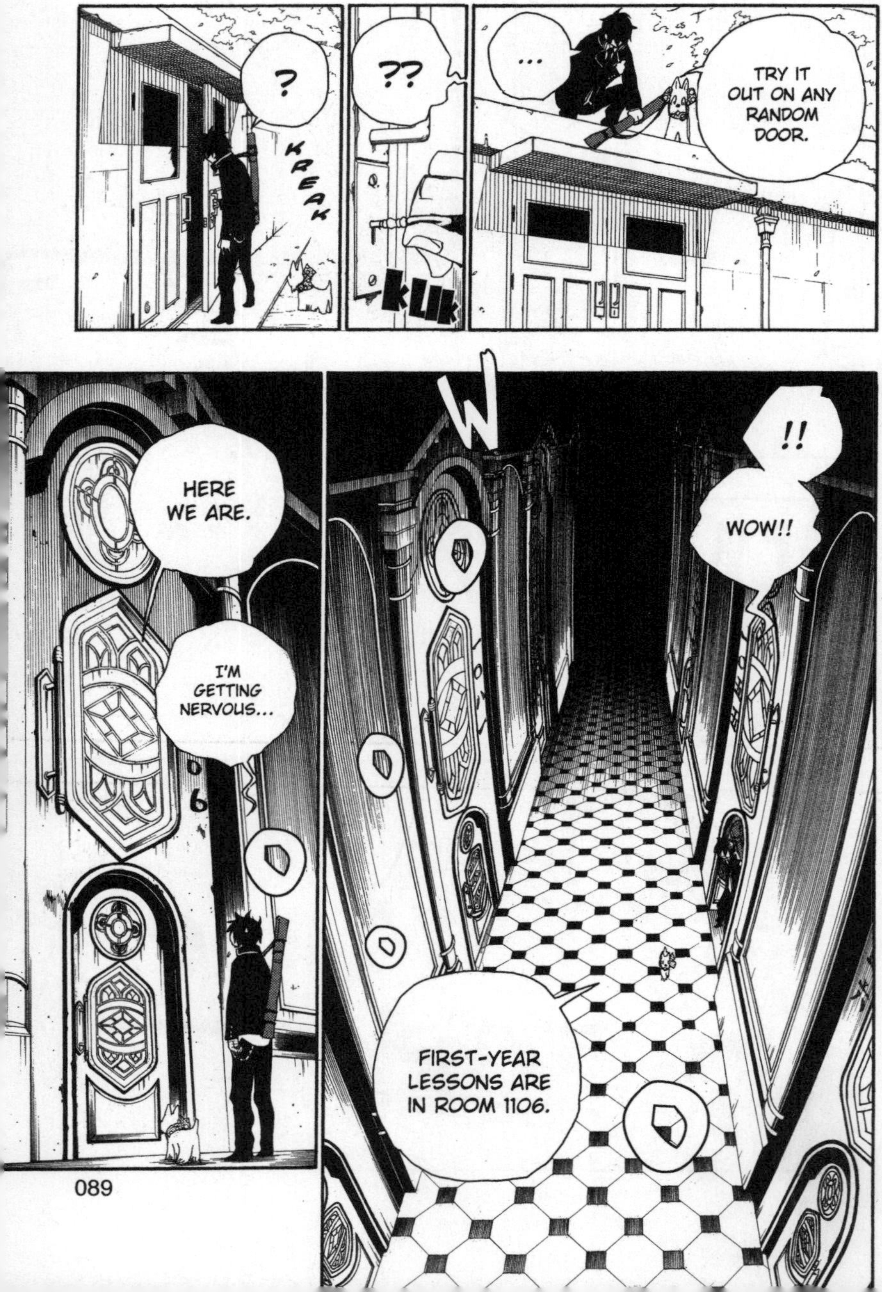
TRY IT OUT ON ANY RANDOM DOOR.
...
??
KLIK
?
KREAK
!!
W
WOW!!
FIRST-YEAR LESSONS ARE IN ROOM 1106.
HERE WE ARE.
I'M GETTING NERVOUS...

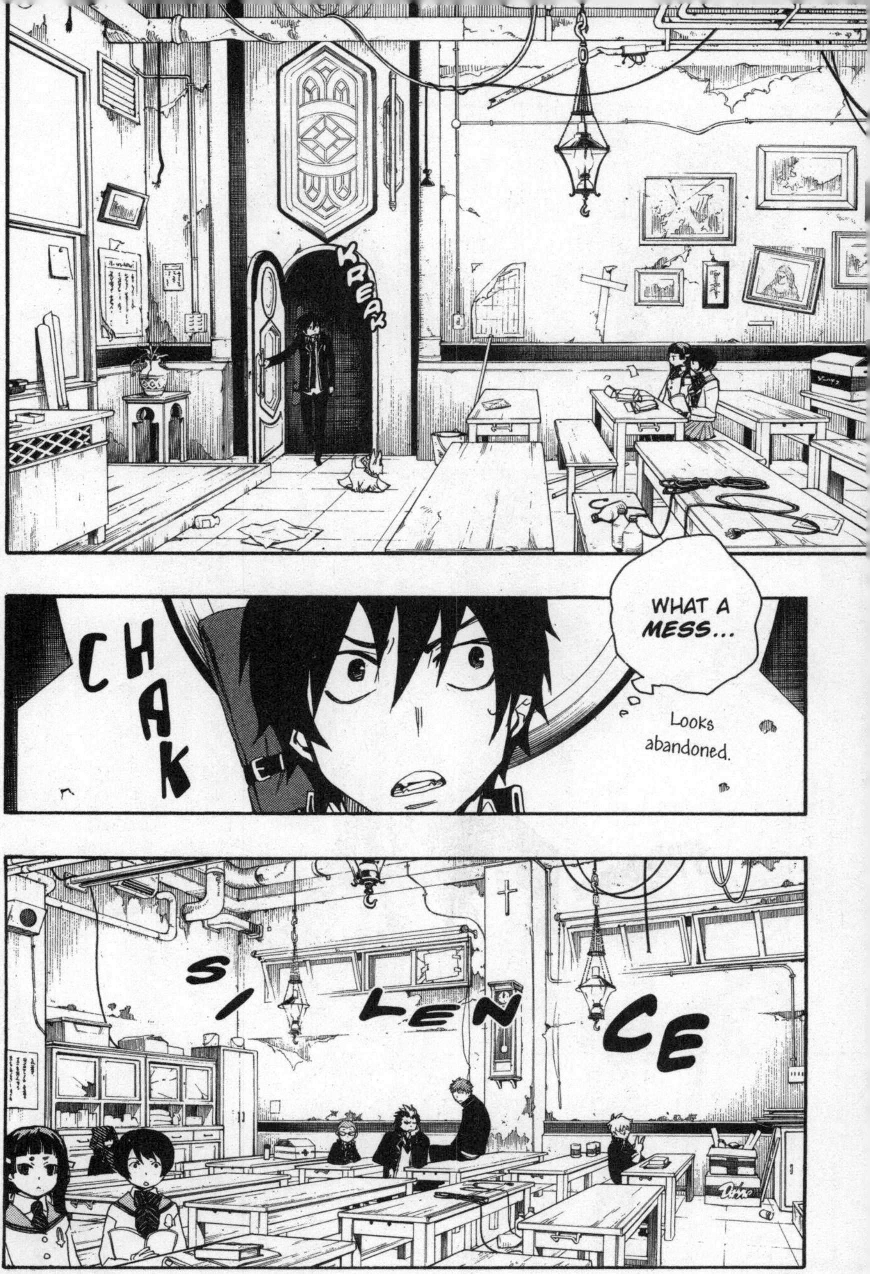
KREAK
WHAT A MESS...
Looks abandoned.
CHAK
SI LEN CE

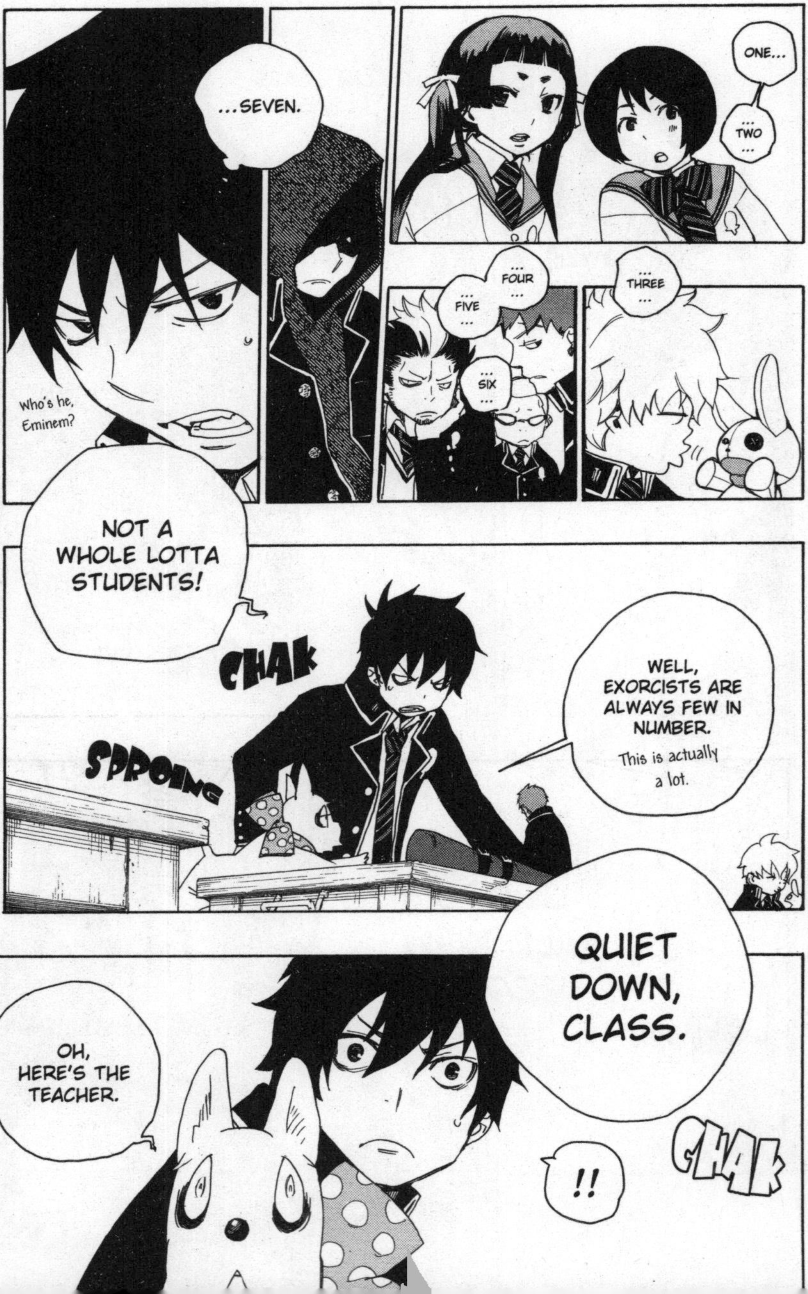
ONE...
...TWO...
...THREE...
...FOUR...
...FIVE...
...SIX...
...SEVEN.
Who's he, Eminem?
NOT A WHOLE LOTTA STUDENTS!
CHAK
SPROING
WELL, EXORCISTS ARE ALWAYS FEW IN NUMBER.
This is actually a lot.
QUIET DOWN, CLASS.
OH, HERE'S THE TEACHER.
!!
CHAK

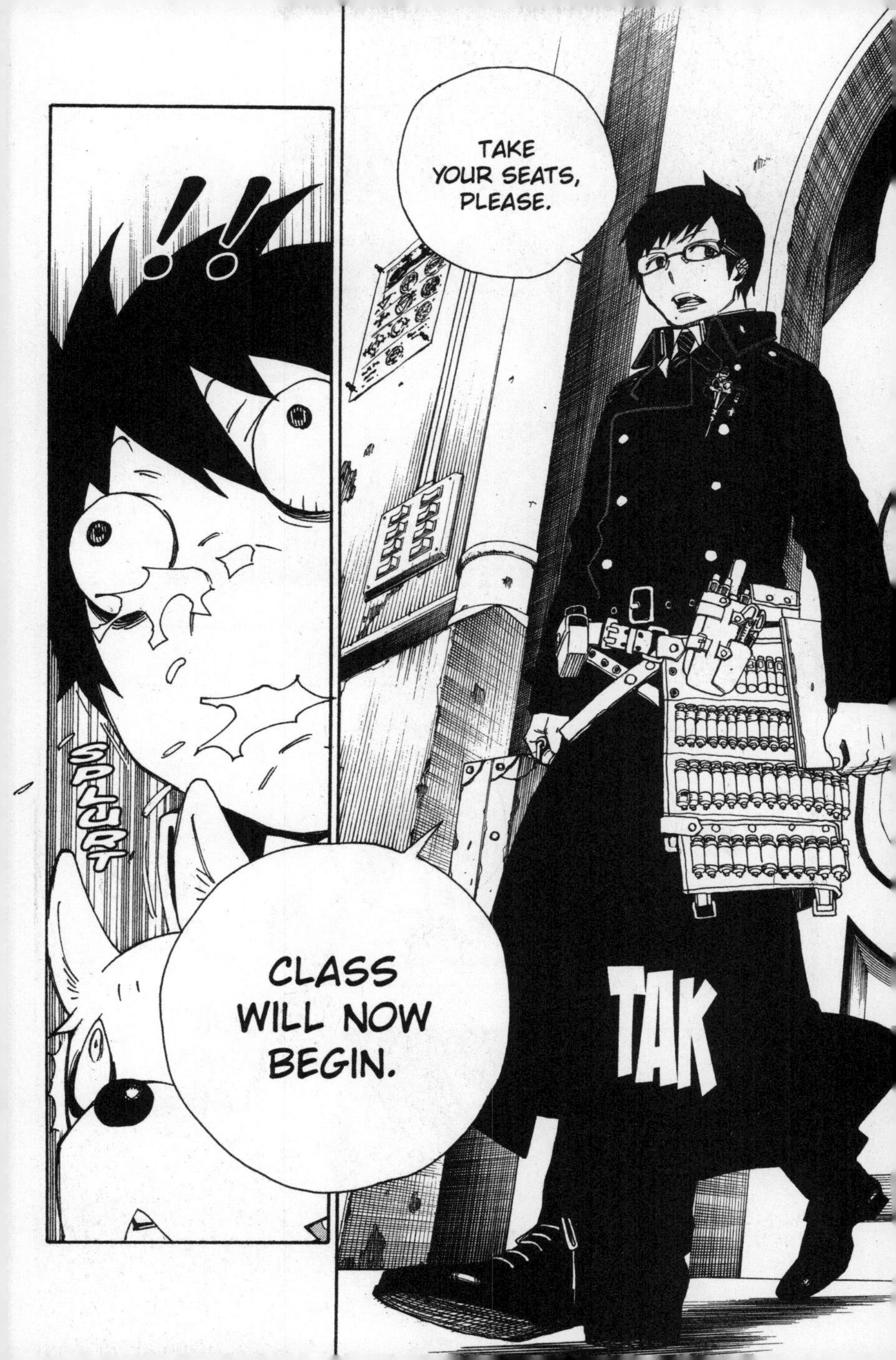
TAKE YOUR SEATS, PLEASE.
TAK
!!
SPLURT
CLASS WILL NOW BEGIN.

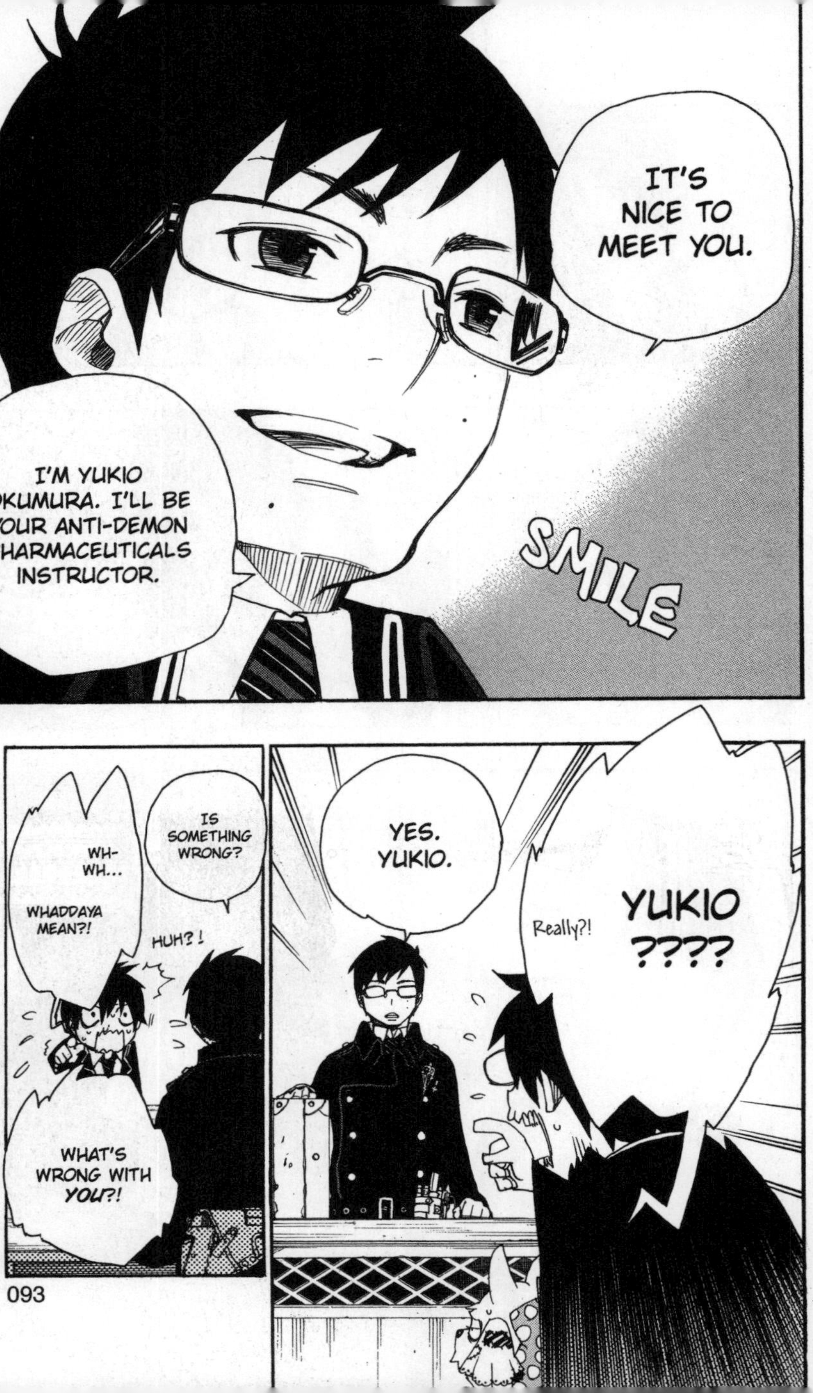
IT'S NICE TO MEET YOU.
I'M YUKIO OKUMURA. I'LL BE YOUR ANTI-DEMON PHARMACEUTICALS INSTRUCTOR.
SMILE
YUKIO ????
Really?!
YES. YUKIO.
IS SOMETHING WRONG?
HUH?!
WH- WH... WHADDAYA MEAN?!
WHAT'S WRONG WITH *YOU*?!

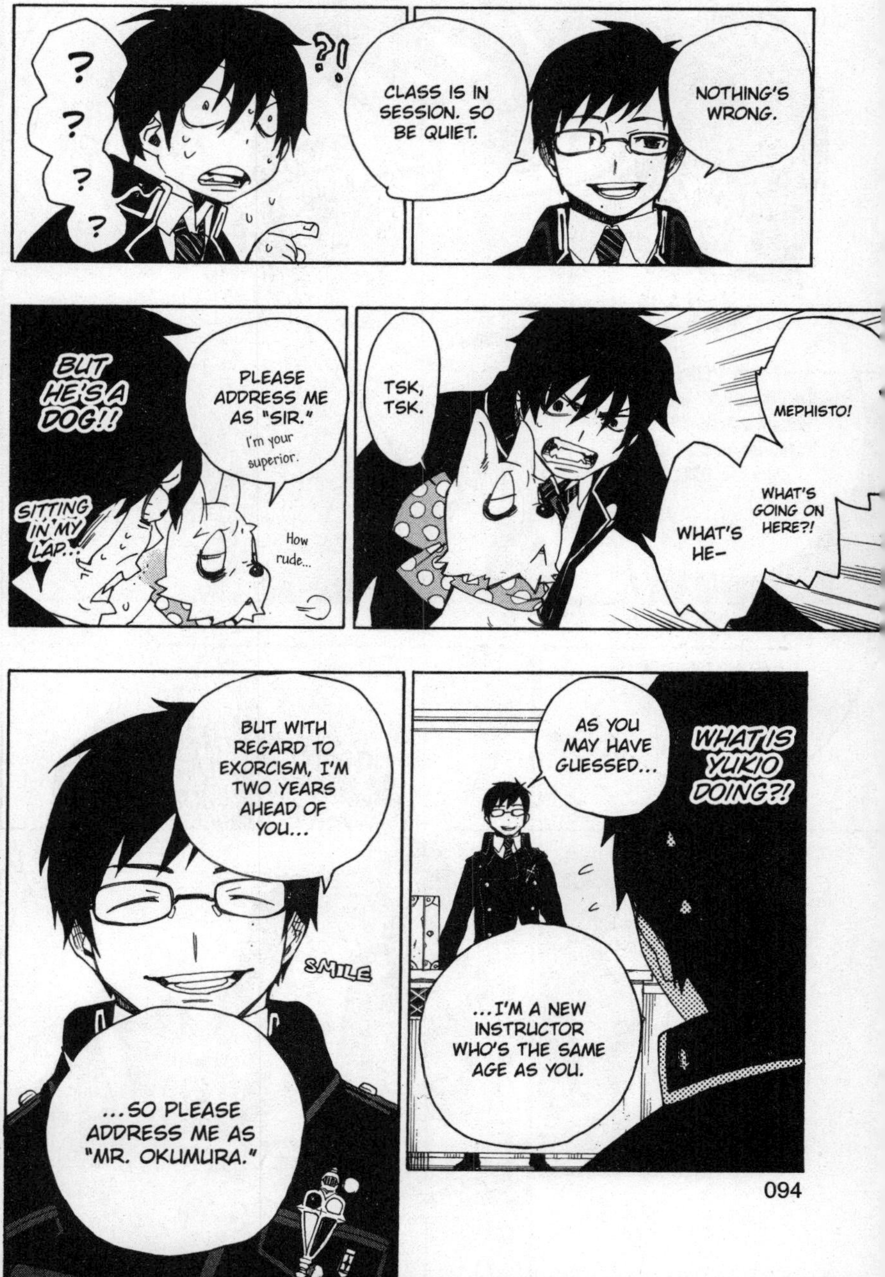
NOTHING'S WRONG.
CLASS IS IN SESSION. SO BE QUIET.
?!
? ? ? ?
MEPHISTO!
WHAT'S GOING ON HERE?!
WHAT'S HE-
TSK, TSK.
PLEASE ADDRESS ME AS "SIR." I'm your superior.
BUT HE'S A DOG!!
SITTING IN MY LAP...
How rude...
AS YOU MAY HAVE GUESSED...
WHAT IS YUKIO DOING?!
...I'M A NEW INSTRUCTOR WHO'S THE SAME AGE AS YOU.
BUT WITH REGARD TO EXORCISM, I'M TWO YEARS AHEAD OF YOU...
SMILE
...SO PLEASE ADDRESS ME AS "MR. OKUMURA."

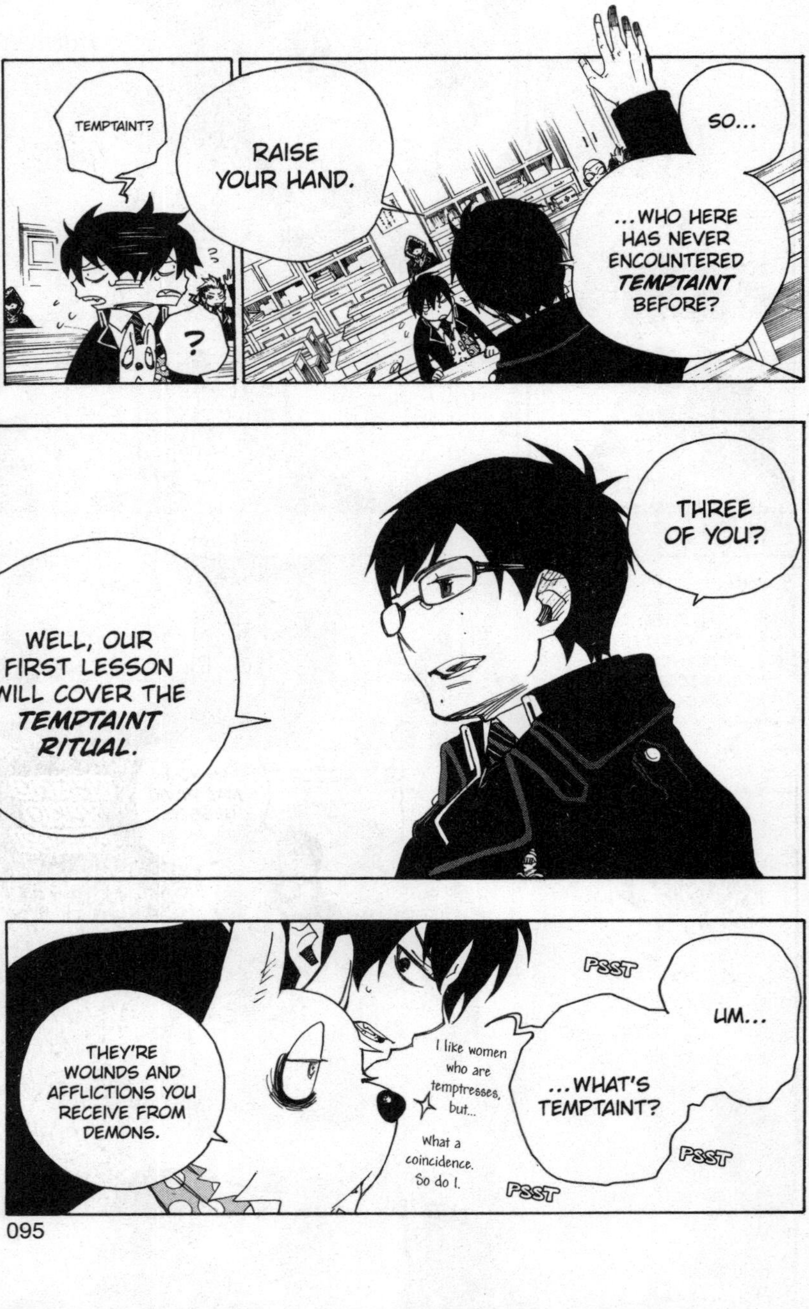
SO...
...WHO HERE HAS NEVER ENCOUNTERED *TEMPTAINT* BEFORE?
RAISE YOUR HAND.
TEMPTAINT?
?
THREE OF YOU?
WELL, OUR FIRST LESSON WILL COVER THE *TEMPTAINT RITUAL*.
PSST
UM...
...WHAT'S TEMPTAINT?
PSST
PSST
I like women who are temptresses, but...
What a coincidence. So do I.
THEY'RE WOUNDS AND AFFLICTIONS YOU RECEIVE FROM DEMONS.

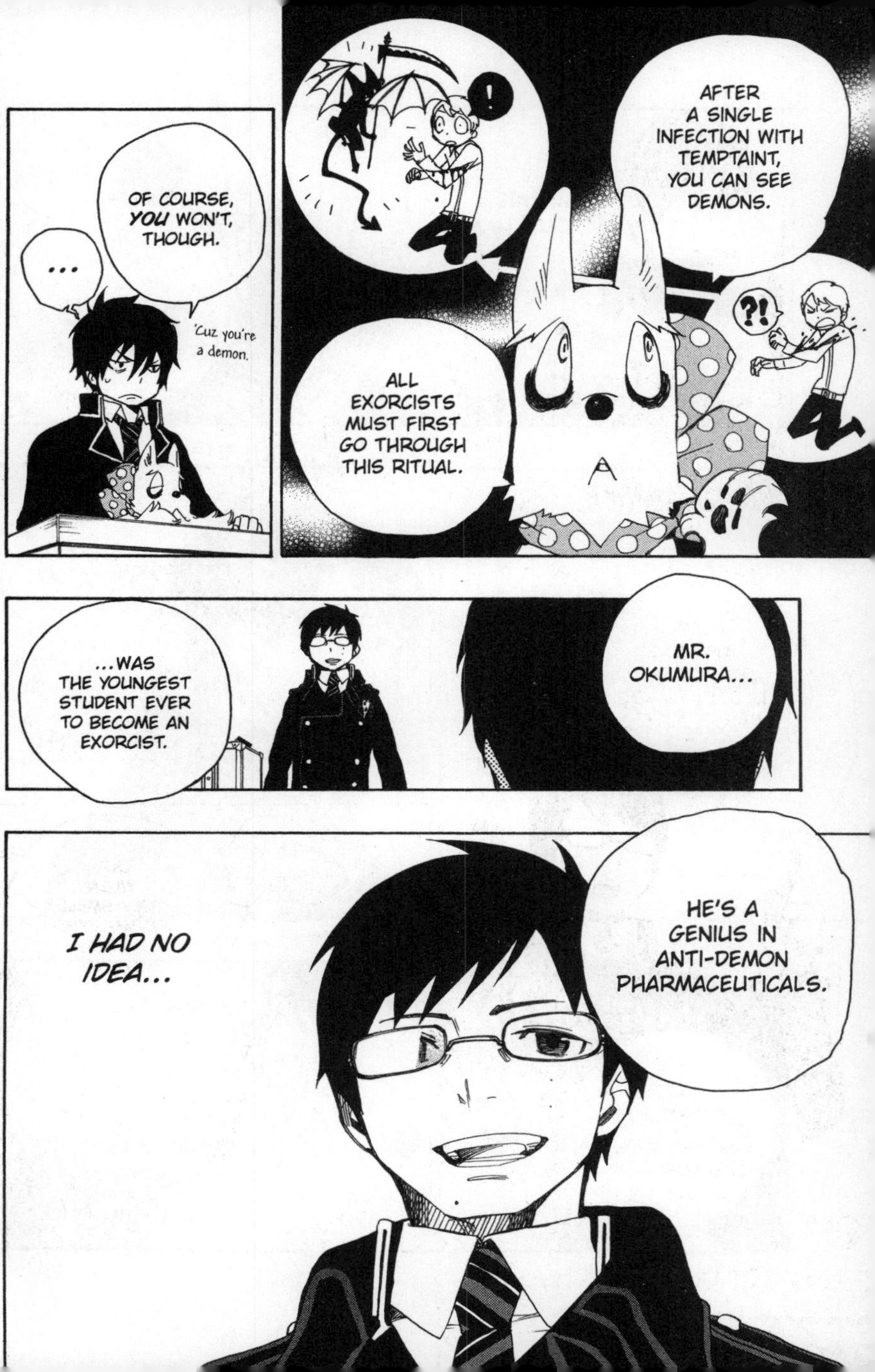
AFTER A SINGLE INFECTION WITH TEMPTAINT, YOU CAN SEE DEMONS.
?!
!
ALL EXORCISTS MUST FIRST GO THROUGH THIS RITUAL.
OF COURSE, *YOU* WON'T, THOUGH.
'Cuz you're a demon.
...
MR. OKUMURA...
...WAS THE YOUNGEST STUDENT EVER TO BECOME AN EXORCIST.
HE'S A GENIUS IN ANTI-DEMON PHARMACEUTICALS.
I HAD NO IDEA...

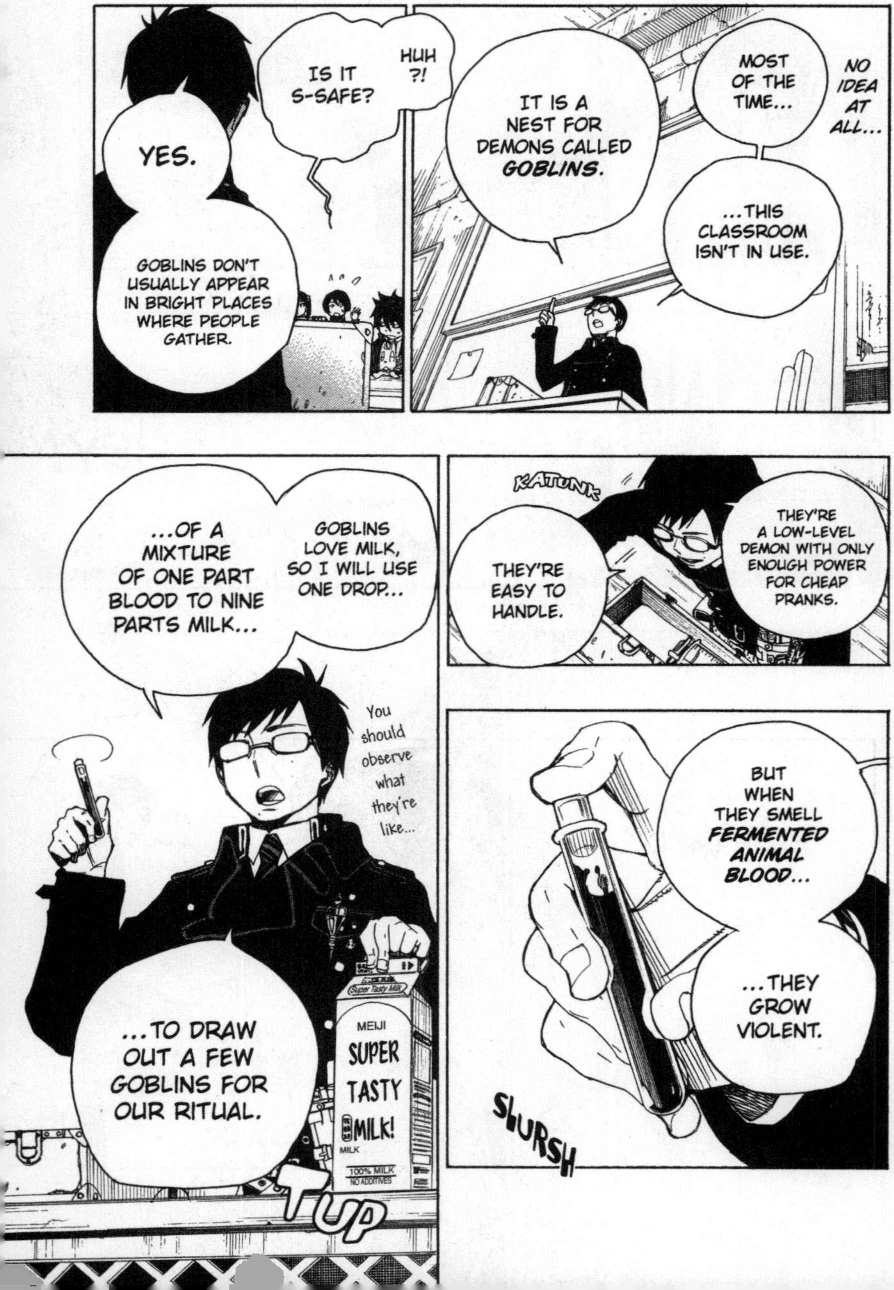
NO IDEA AT ALL...
MOST OF THE TIME...
...THIS CLASSROOM ISN'T IN USE.
IT IS A NEST FOR DEMONS CALLED GOBLINS.
HUH ?!
IS IT S-SAFE?
YES.
GOBLINS DON'T USUALLY APPEAR IN BRIGHT PLACES WHERE PEOPLE GATHER.
KATUNK
THEY'RE A LOW-LEVEL DEMON WITH ONLY ENOUGH POWER FOR CHEAP PRANKS.
THEY'RE EASY TO HANDLE.
BUT WHEN THEY SMELL FERMENTED ANIMAL BLOOD...
...THEY GROW VIOLENT.
SLURSH
GOBLINS LOVE MILK, SO I WILL USE ONE DROP...
...OF A MIXTURE OF ONE PART BLOOD TO NINE PARTS MILK...
You should observe what they're like...
...TO DRAW OUT A FEW GOBLINS FOR OUR RITUAL.
Super Tasty Milk
MEIJI
SUPER TASTY MILK!
MILK
100% MILK
NO ADDITIVES
TUP

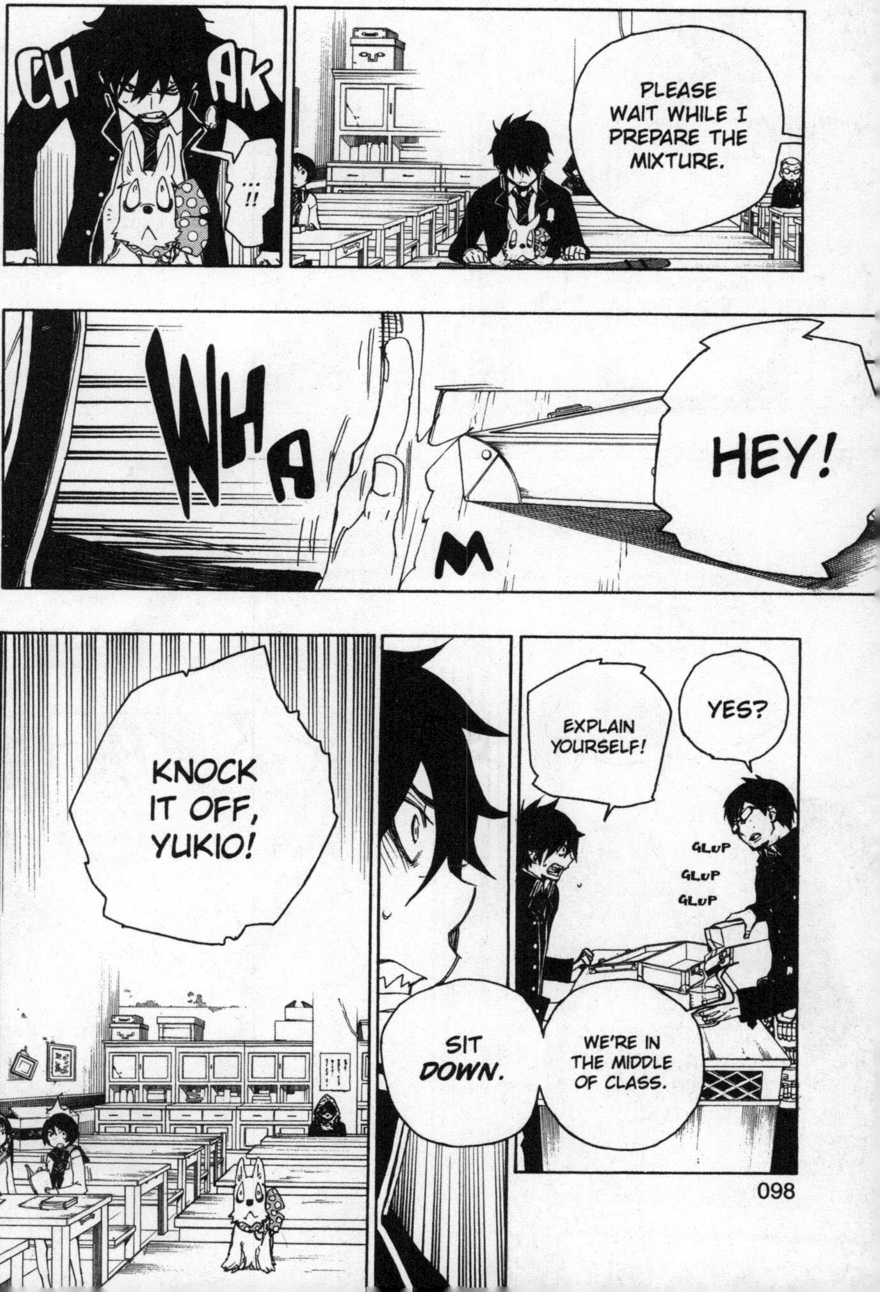
PLEASE WAIT WHILE I PREPARE THE MIXTURE.
CH AK
...
!!
HEY!
WHAM
YES?
EXPLAIN YOURSELF!
GLUP
GLUP
GLUP
WE'RE IN THE MIDDLE OF CLASS.
SIT DOWN.
KNOCK IT OFF, YUKIO!

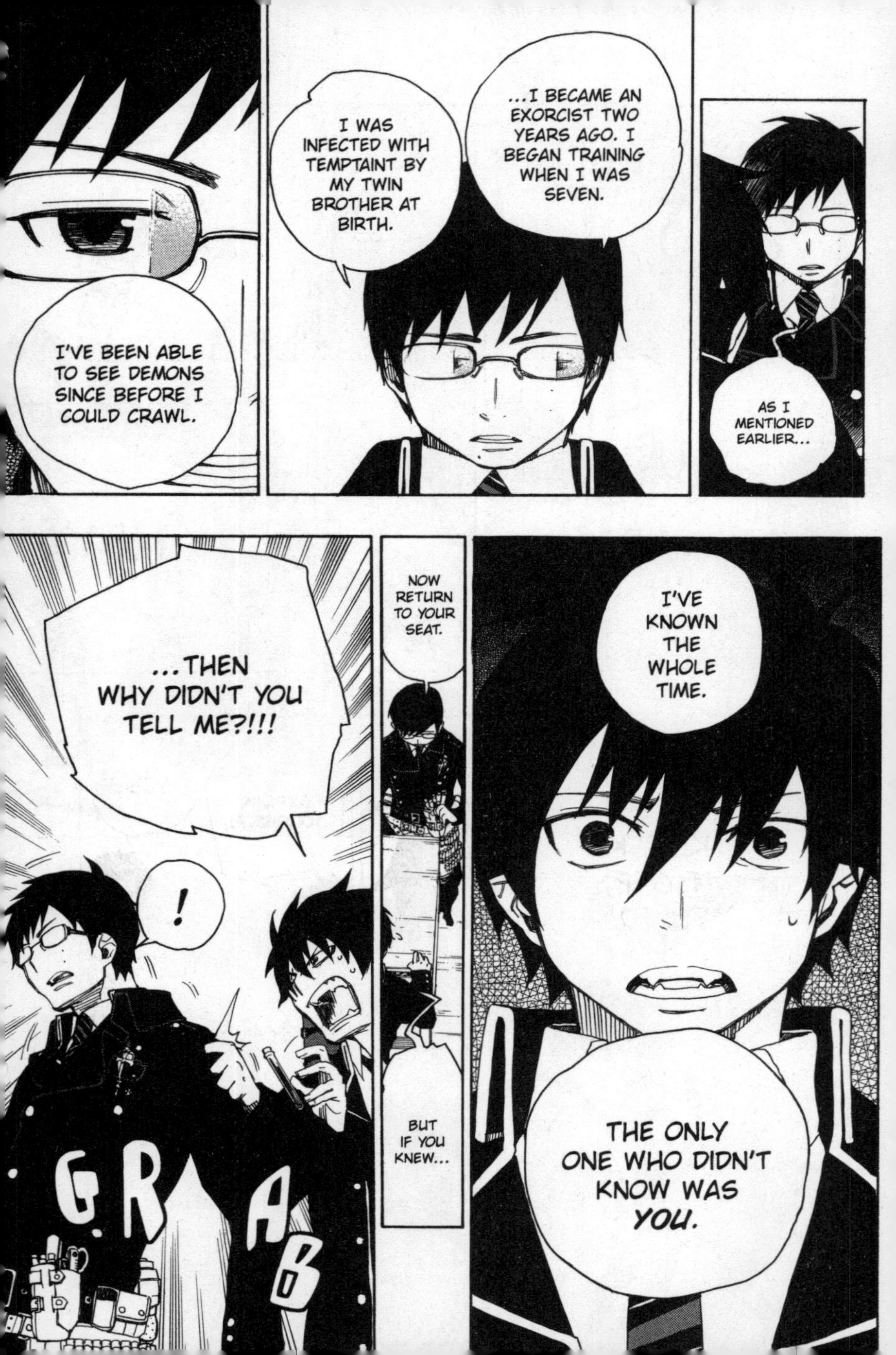
AS I MENTIONED EARLIER...
...I BECAME AN EXORCIST TWO YEARS AGO. I BEGAN TRAINING WHEN I WAS SEVEN.
I WAS INFECTED WITH TEMPTAINT BY MY TWIN BROTHER AT BIRTH.
I'VE BEEN ABLE TO SEE DEMONS SINCE BEFORE I COULD CRAWL.
I'VE KNOWN THE WHOLE TIME.
THE ONLY ONE WHO DIDN'T KNOW WAS *YOU*.
NOW RETURN TO YOUR SEAT.
BUT IF YOU KNEW...
...THEN WHY DIDN'T YOU TELL ME?!!!
!
GRAB

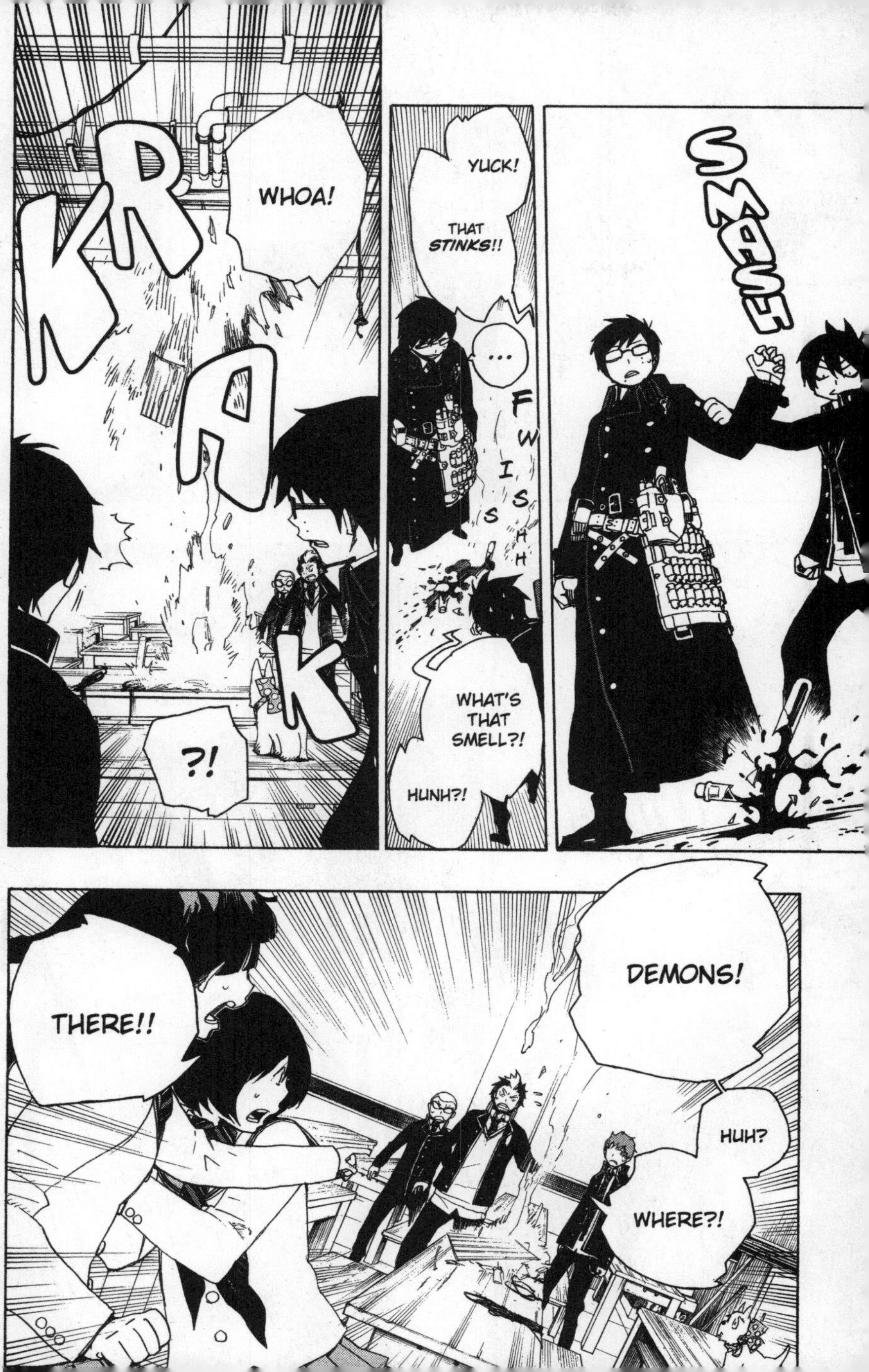

SMASH
YUCK!
THAT STINKS!!
...
FWISSHH
WHAT'S THAT SMELL?!
HUNH?!
WHOA!
KRAK
?!
DEMONS!
HUH?
WHERE?!
THERE!!

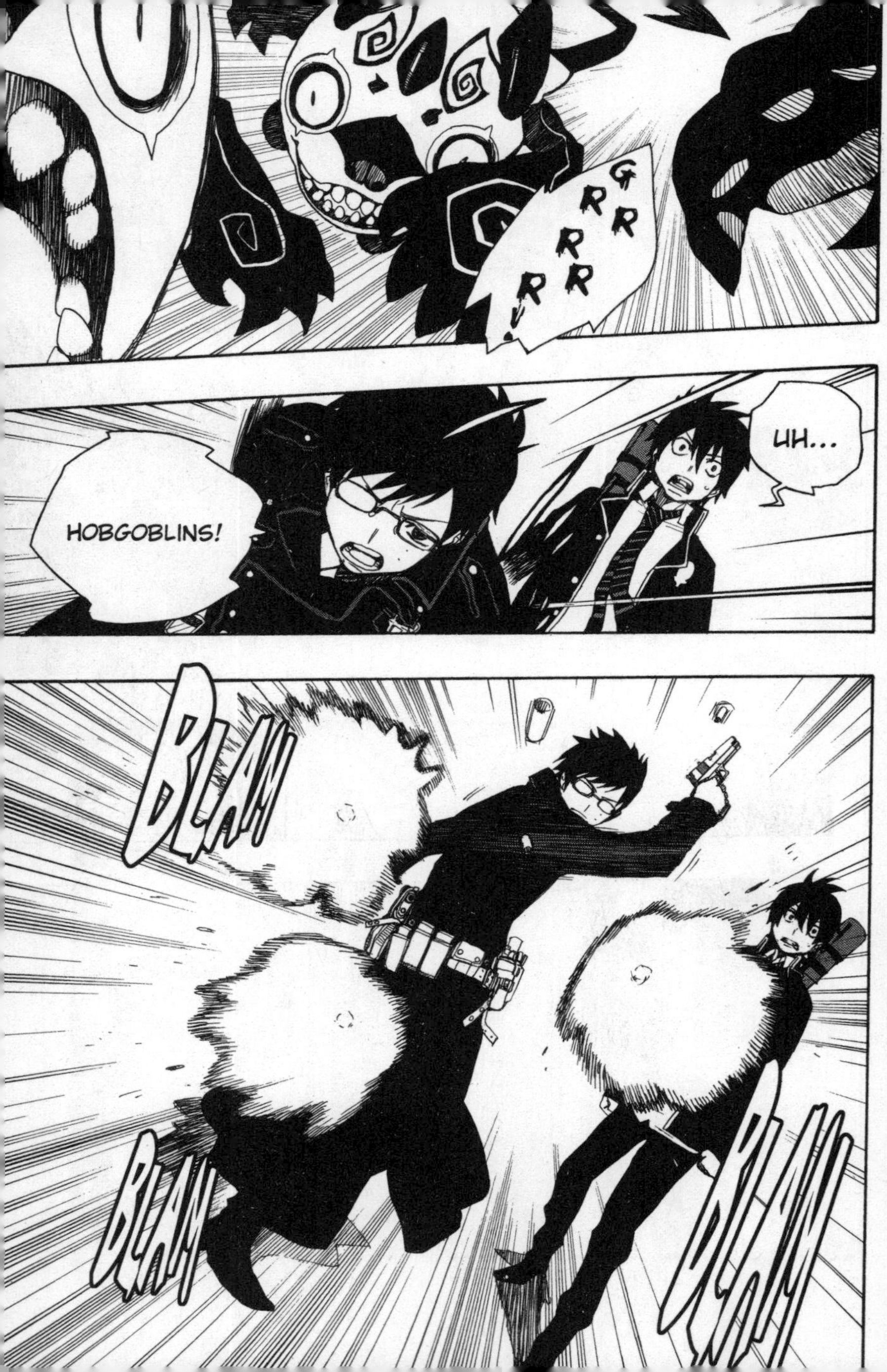
GRRRRR!
UH...
HOBGOBLINS!
BLAM
BLAM
BLAM

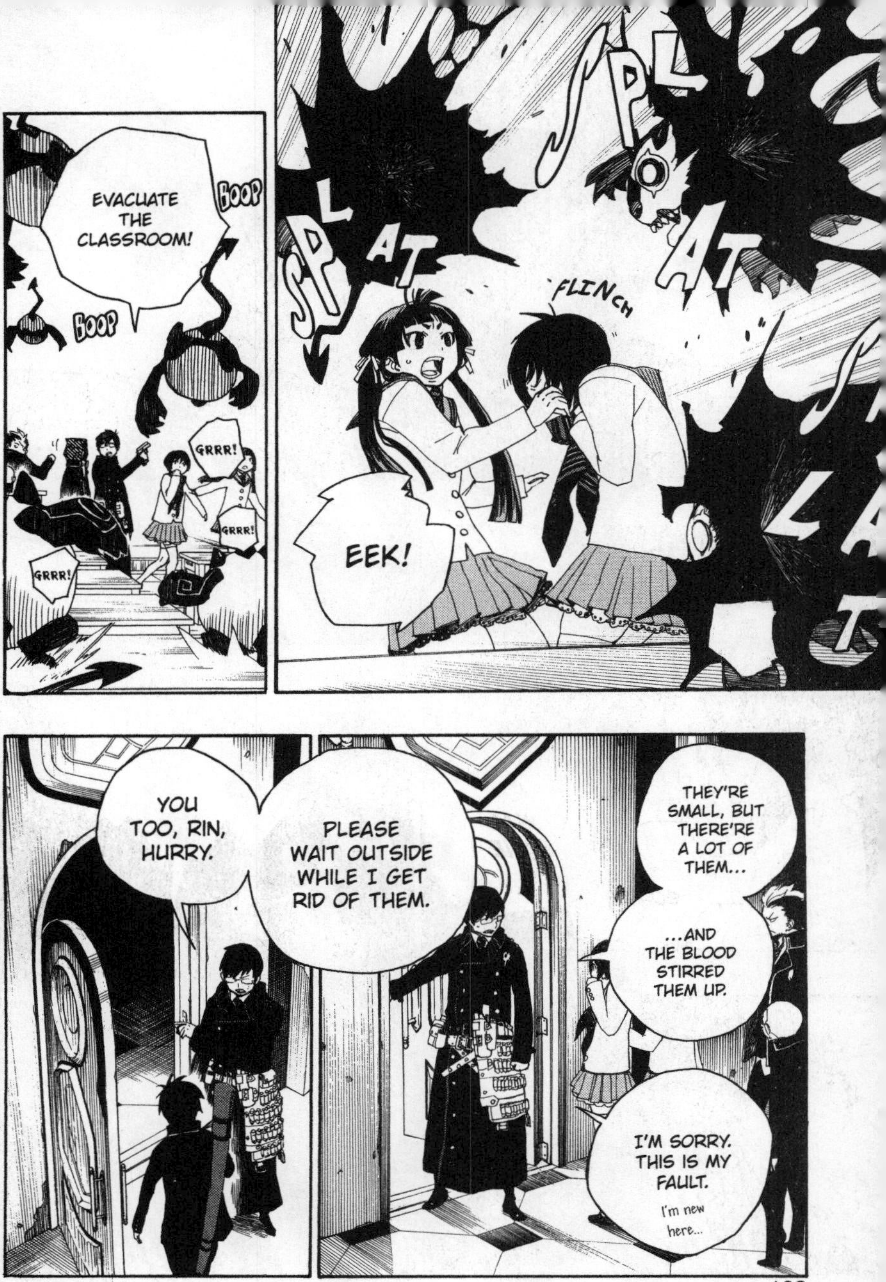
SPLAT
SPLAT
FLINCH
EEK!
EVACUATE THE CLASSROOM!
BOOP
BOOP
GRRR!
GRRR!
GRRR!
THEY'RE SMALL, BUT THERE'RE A LOT OF THEM...
...AND THE BLOOD STIRRED THEM UP.
I'M SORRY. THIS IS MY FAULT.
I'm new here...
PLEASE WAIT OUTSIDE WHILE I GET RID OF THEM.
YOU TOO, RIN, HURRY.

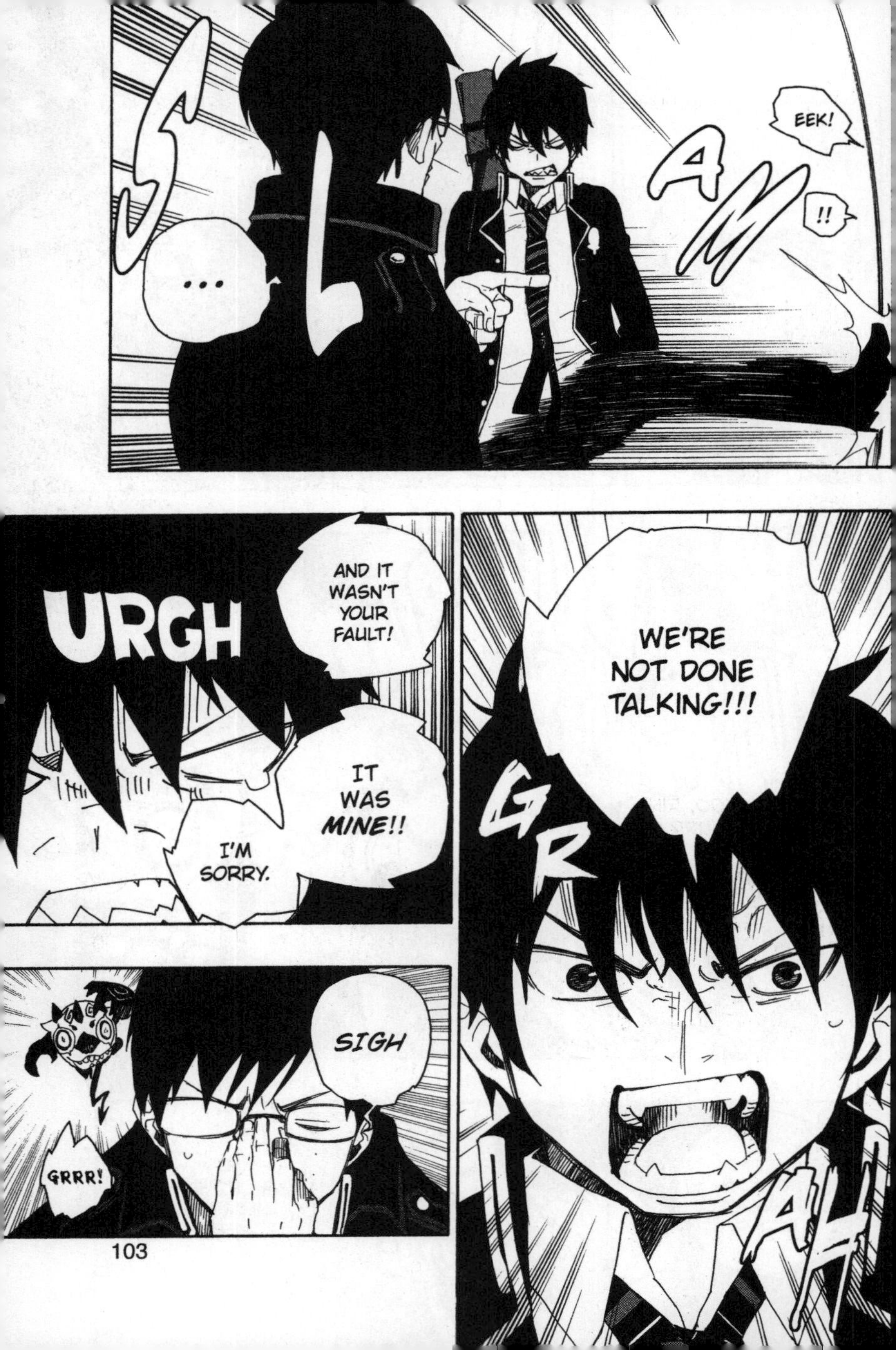
EEK!
AN
!!
...
S
WE'RE NOT DONE TALKING!!!
GR
AH
AND IT WASN'T YOUR FAULT!
IT WAS MINE!!
I'M SORRY.
URGH
SIGH
GRRR!

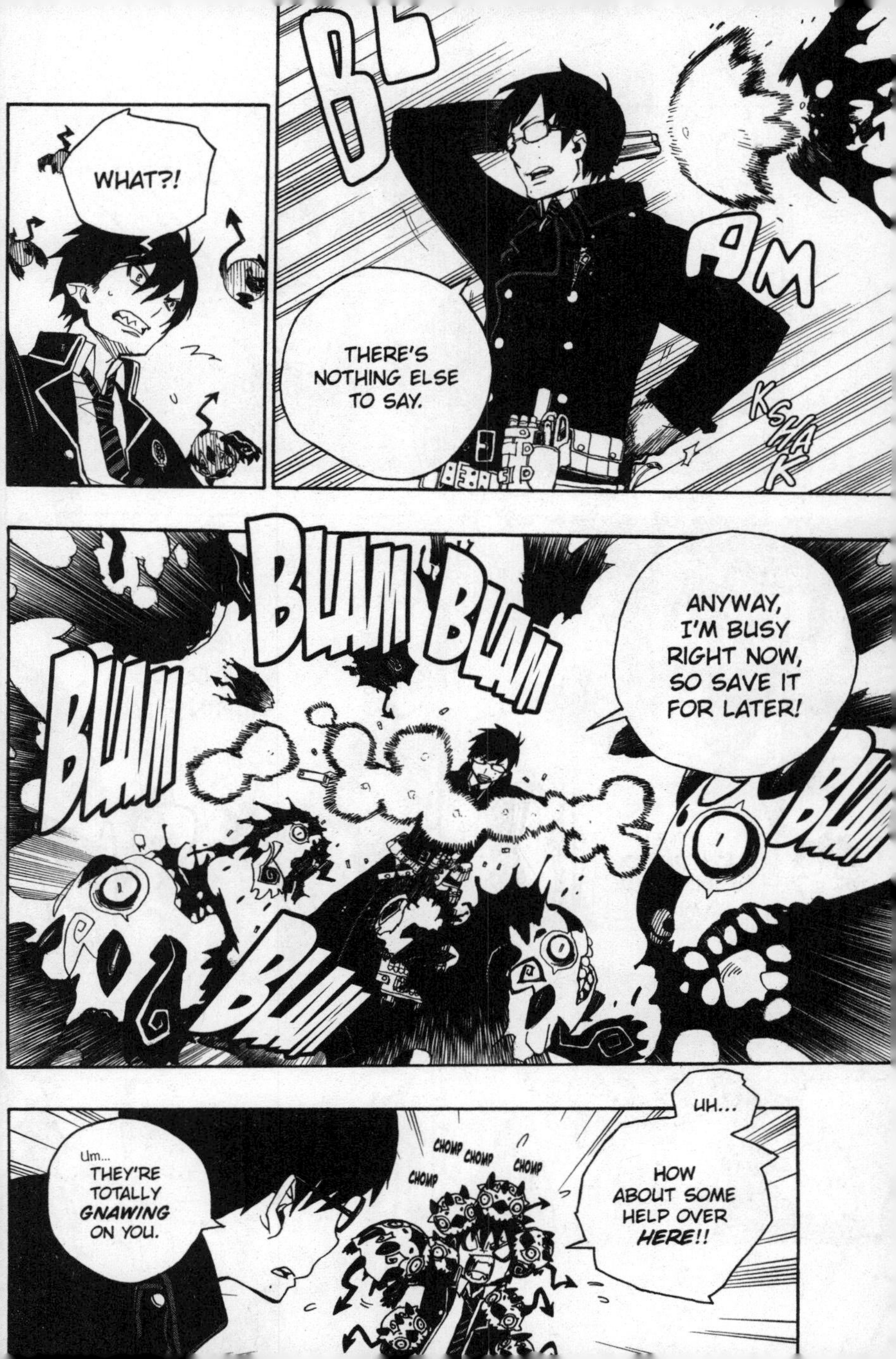
B
AM
THERE'S NOTHING ELSE TO SAY.
KSHAK
WHAT?!
ANYWAY, I'M BUSY RIGHT NOW, SO SAVE IT FOR LATER!
BLA
BLAM
BLAM
BLAM
BLAM
UH...
HOW ABOUT SOME HELP OVER *HERE*!!
CHOMP
CHOMP
CHOMP
CHOMP
Um... THEY'RE TOTALLY *GNAWING* ON YOU.

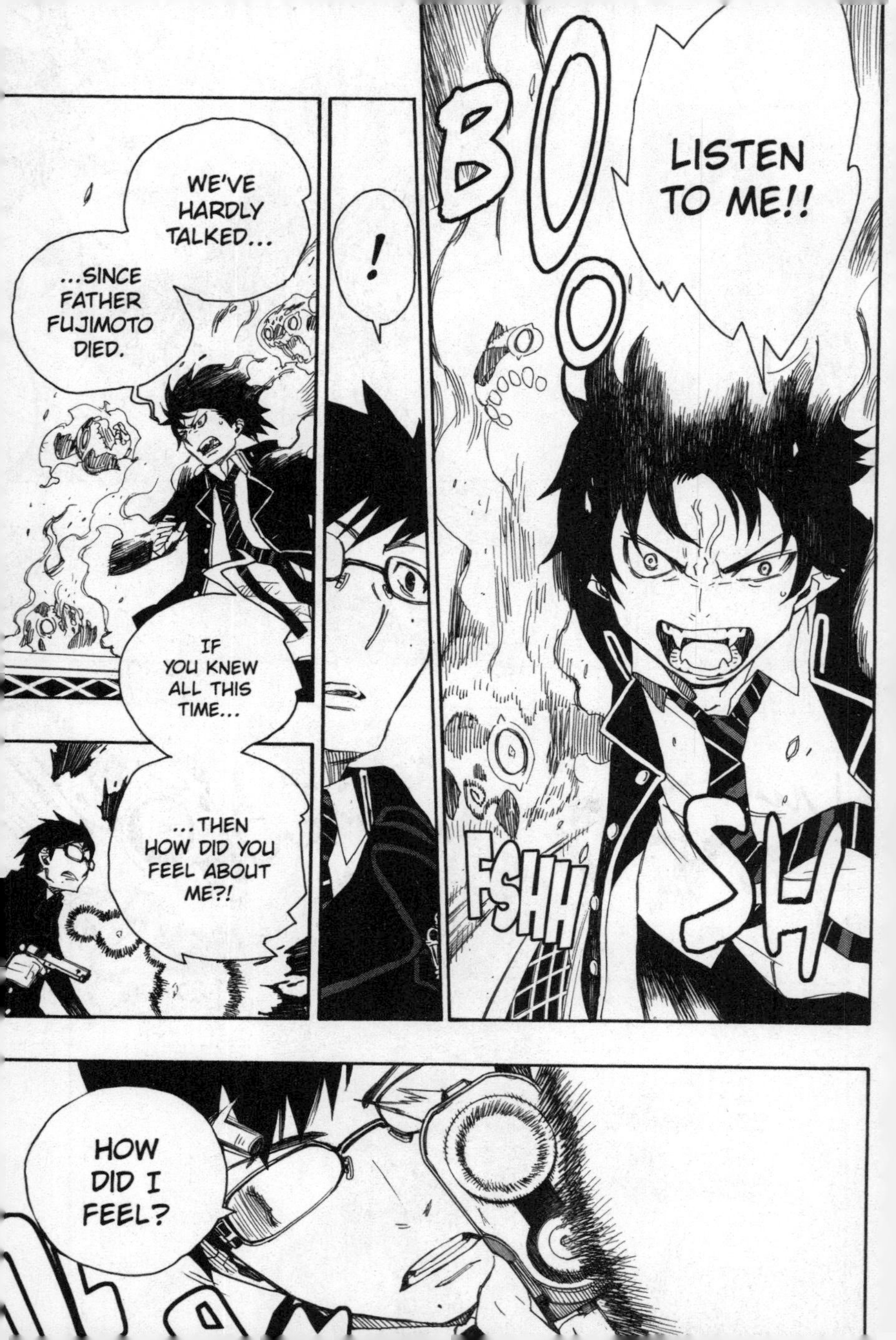
LISTEN TO ME!!
BOO
FSHH
SH
!
WE'VE HARDLY TALKED...
...SINCE FATHER FUJIMOTO DIED.
IF YOU KNEW ALL THIS TIME...
...THEN HOW DID YOU FEEL ABOUT ME?!
HOW DID I FEEL?

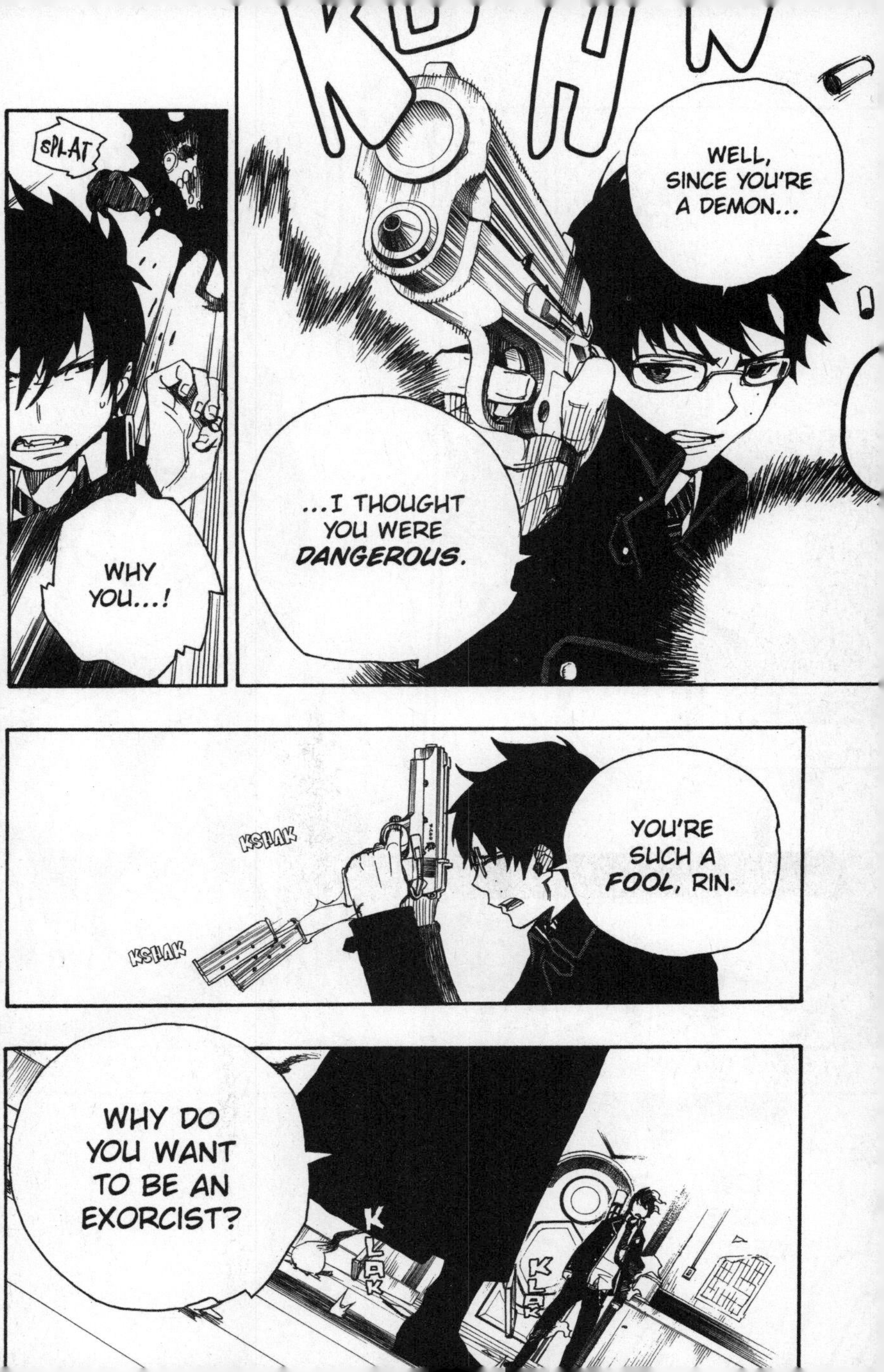
WELL, SINCE YOU'RE A DEMON...
...I THOUGHT YOU WERE DANGEROUS.
SPLAT
WHY YOU...!
YOU'RE SUCH A FOOL, RIN.
KSHAK
KSHAK
KLAK
KLAK
WHY DO YOU WANT TO BE AN EXORCIST?

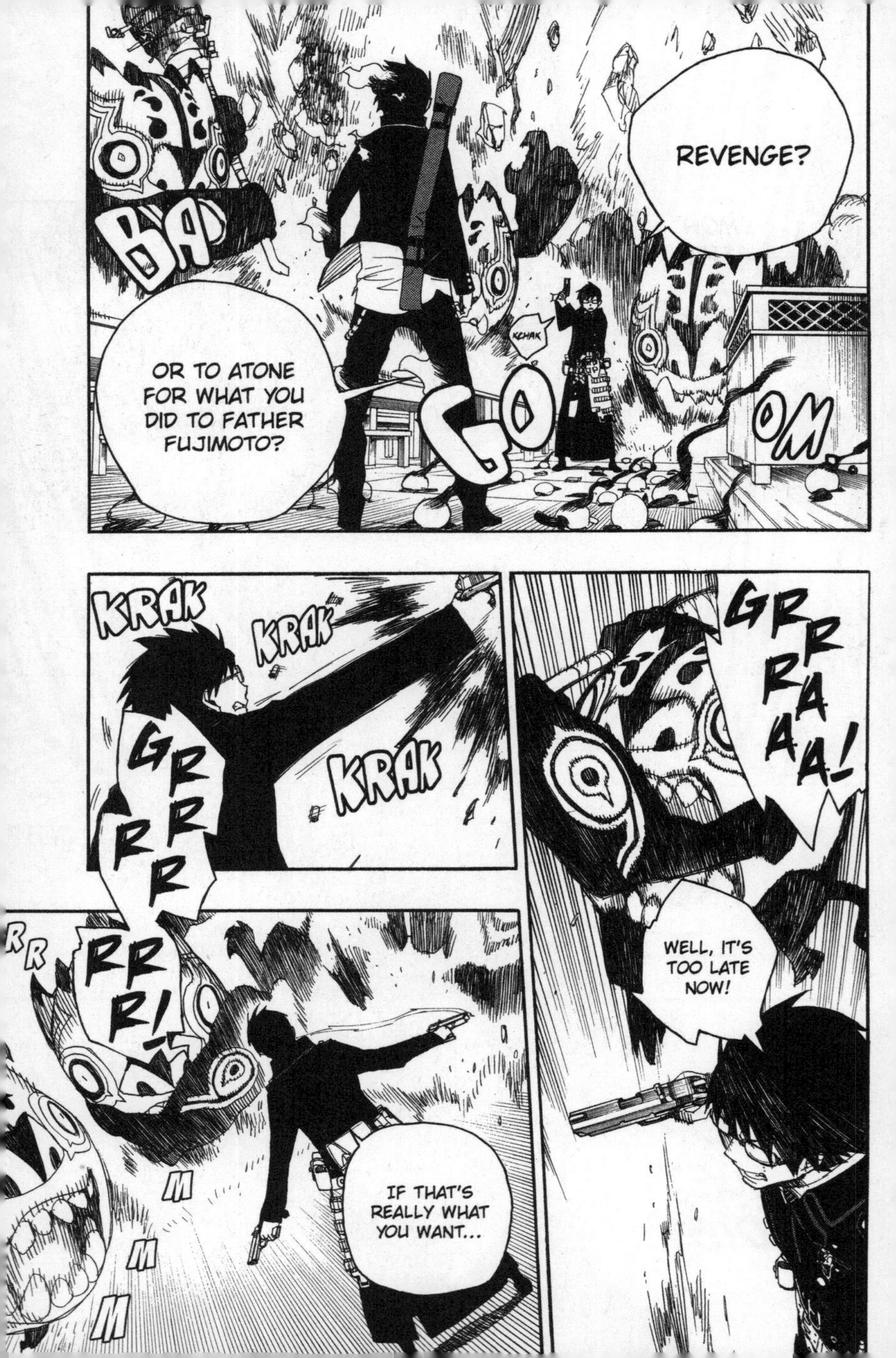
REVENGE?
OR TO ATONE FOR WHAT YOU DID TO FATHER FUJIMOTO?
KCHAK
BA
GO
OM
GRRRAAA!
WELL, IT'S TOO LATE NOW!
KRAK
KRAK
KRAK
GRRRRRRRR!
RR
IF THAT'S REALLY WHAT YOU WANT...
M
M
M

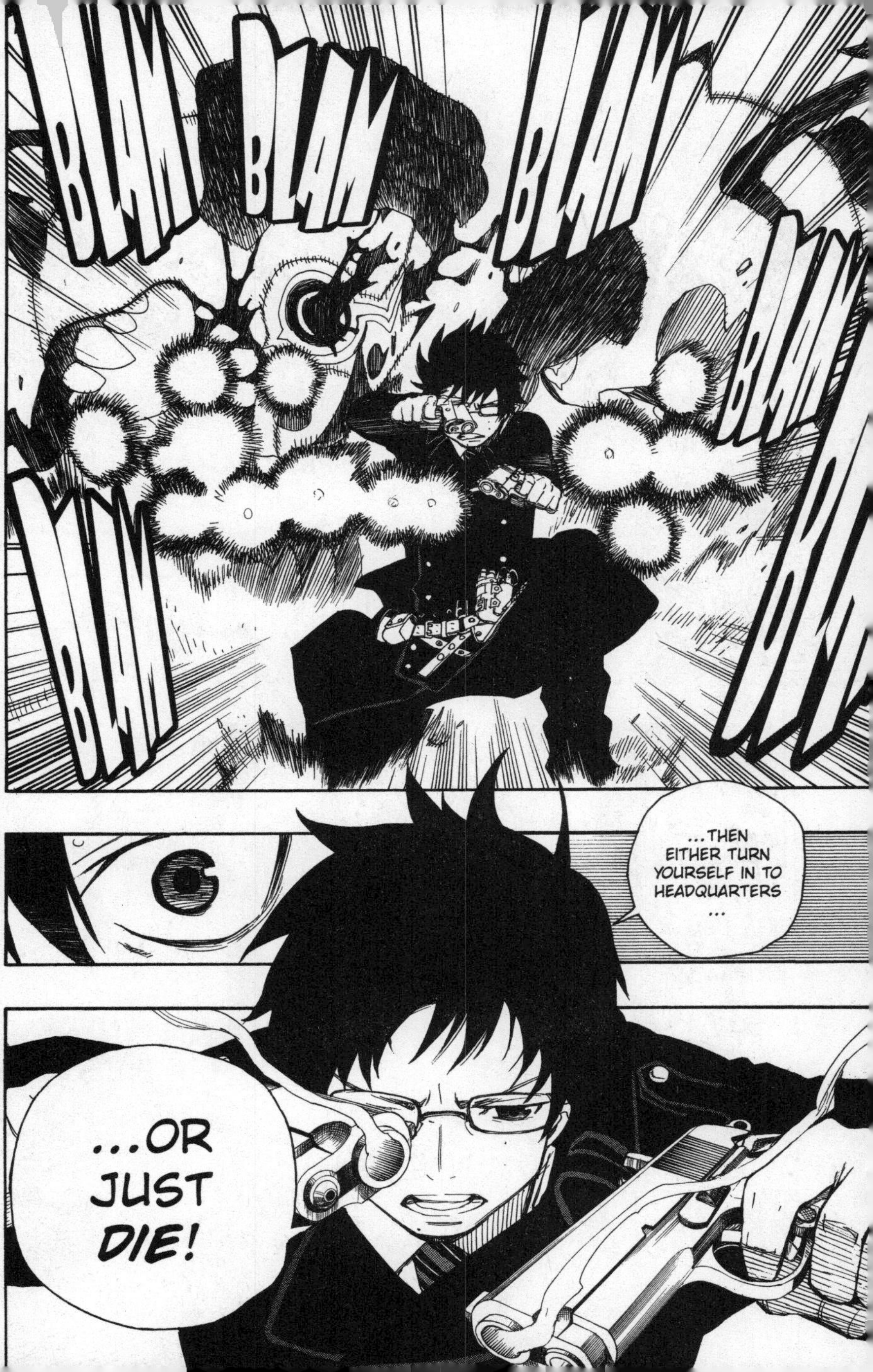
BLAM BLAM BLAM BLAM
BLAM BLAM
BLAM
...THEN EITHER TURN YOURSELF IN TO HEADQUARTERS ...
...OR JUST DIE!

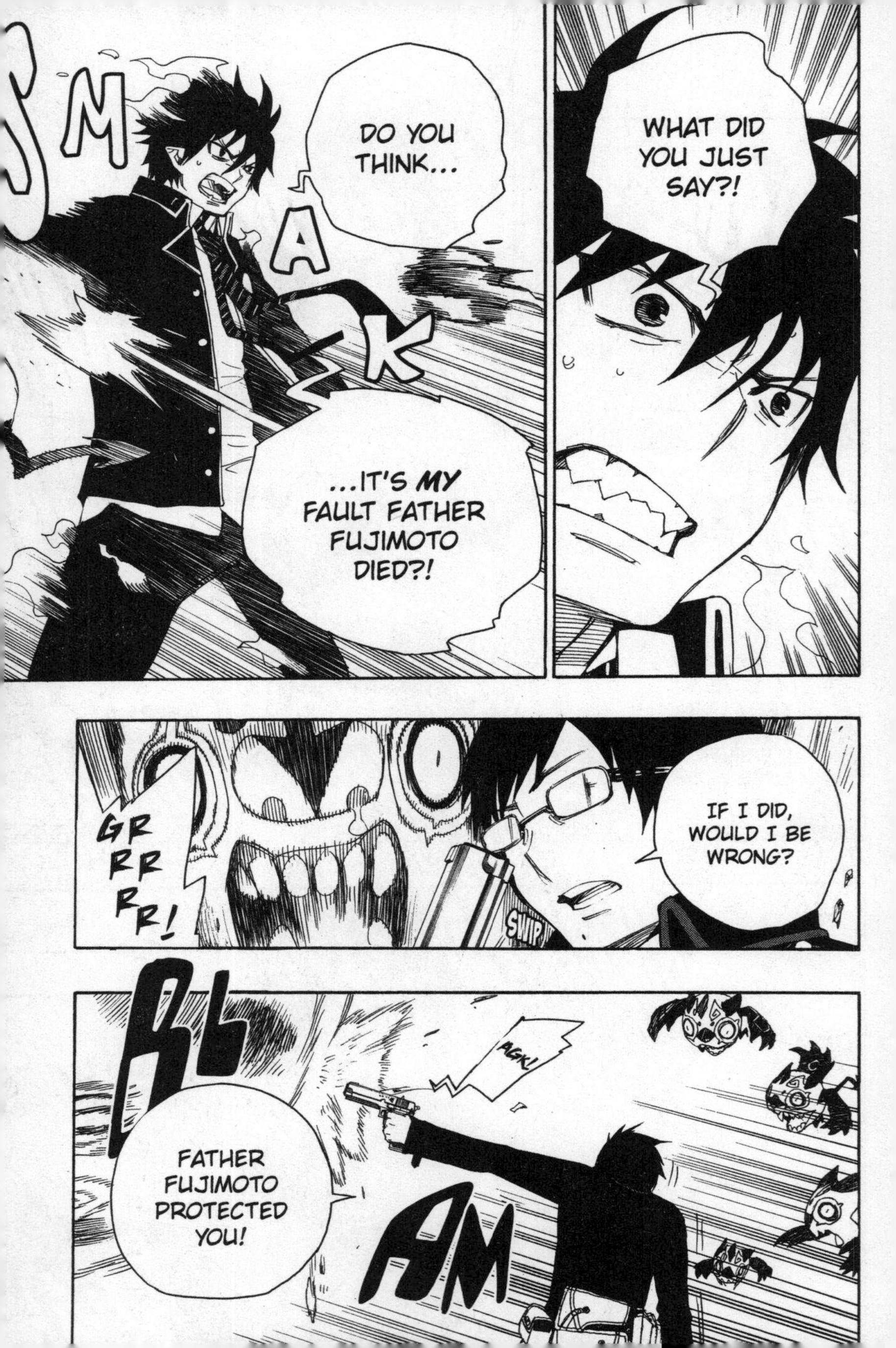
WHAT DID YOU JUST SAY?!
SMACK
DO YOU THINK...
...IT'S *MY* FAULT FATHER FUJIMOTO DIED?!
IF I DID, WOULD I BE WRONG?
SWIP
GRRRRR!
AGK!
BLAM
FATHER FUJIMOTO PROTECTED YOU!

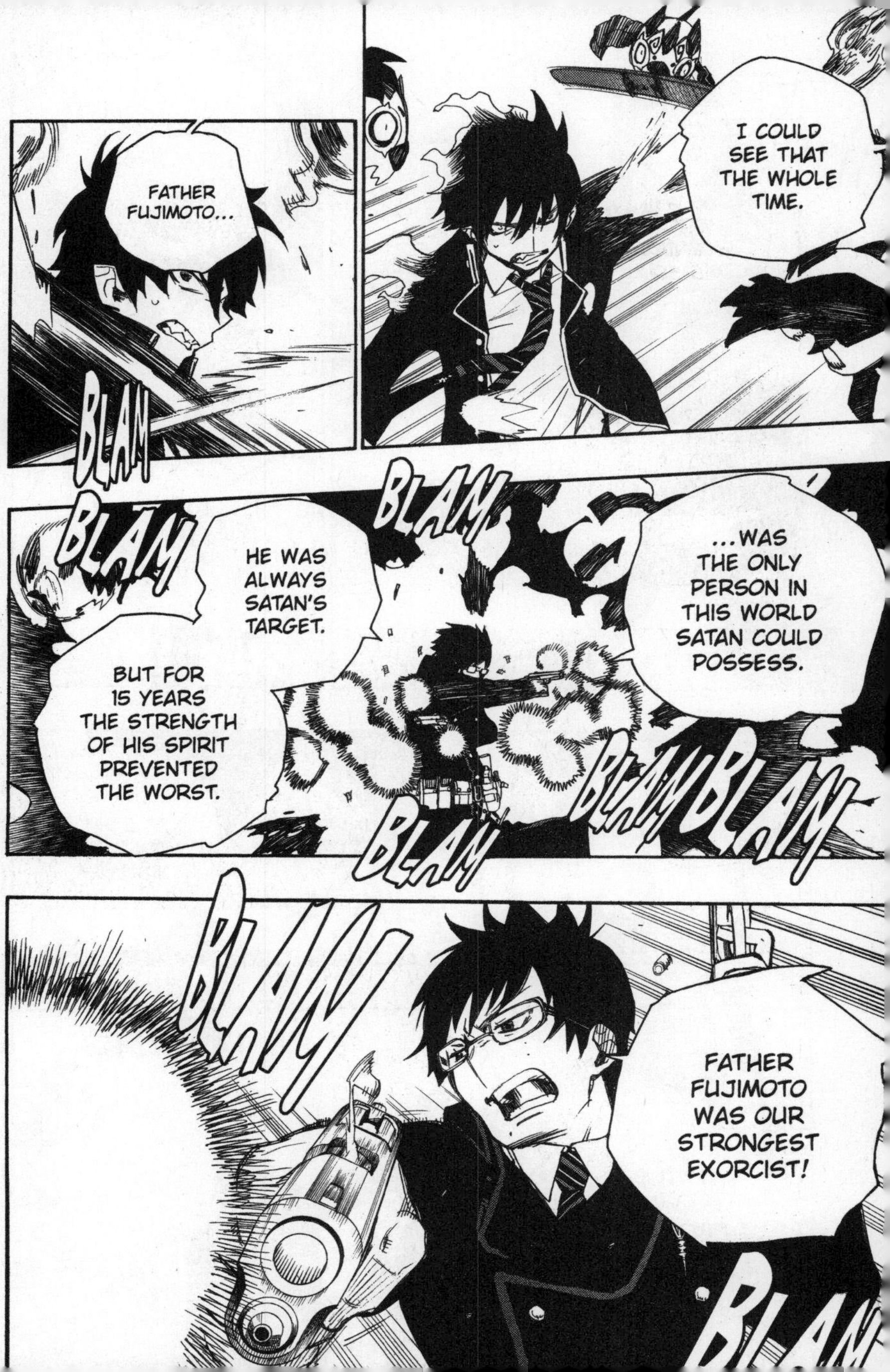
I COULD SEE THAT THE WHOLE TIME.
FATHER FUJIMOTO...
BLAM
BLAM
...WAS THE ONLY PERSON IN THIS WORLD SATAN COULD POSSESS.
HE WAS ALWAYS SATAN'S TARGET.
BLAM
BUT FOR 15 YEARS THE STRENGTH OF HIS SPIRIT PREVENTED THE WORST.
BLAM BLAM
BLAM
FATHER FUJIMOTO WAS OUR STRONGEST EXORCIST!
BLAM

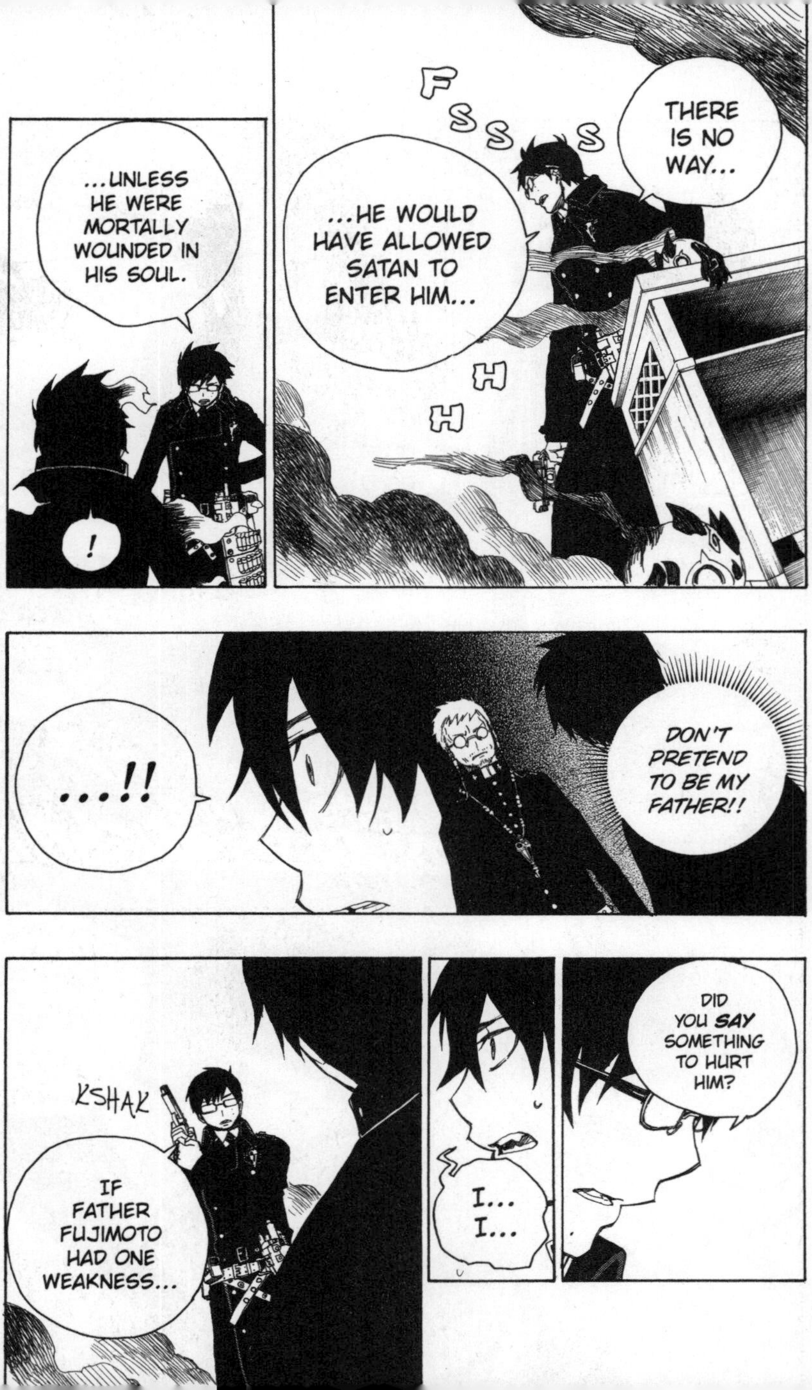
THERE IS NO WAY...
FSSS
S
...HE WOULD HAVE ALLOWED SATAN TO ENTER HIM...
H
H
...UNLESS HE WERE MORTALLY WOUNDED IN HIS SOUL.
!
DON'T PRETEND TO BE MY FATHER!!
...!!
DID YOU SAY SOMETHING TO HURT HIM?
I... I...
KSHAK
IF FATHER FUJIMOTO HAD ONE WEAKNESS...

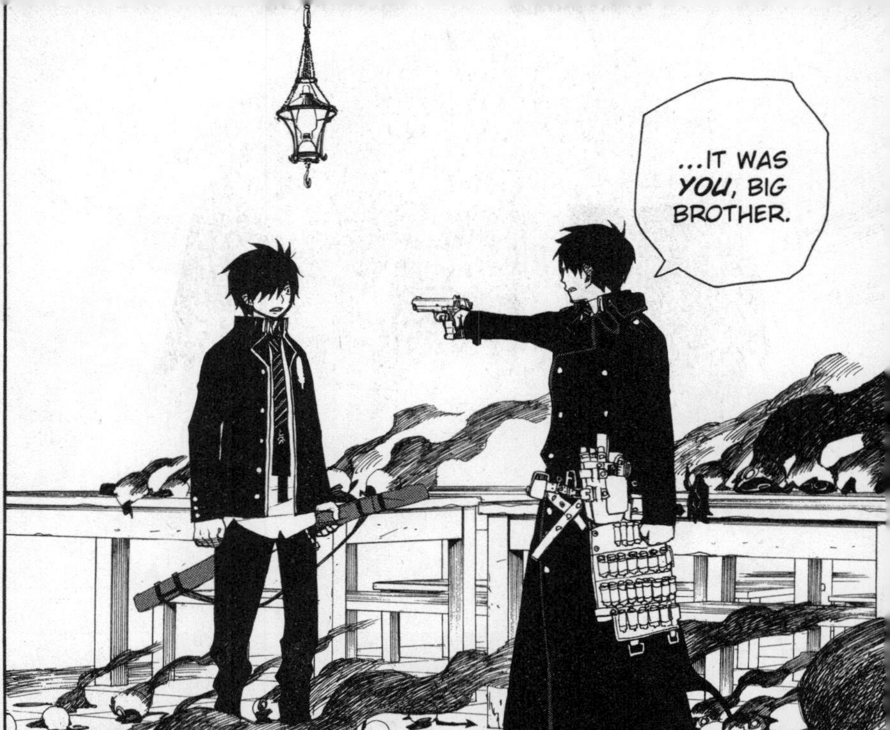
...IT WAS YOU, BIG BROTHER.
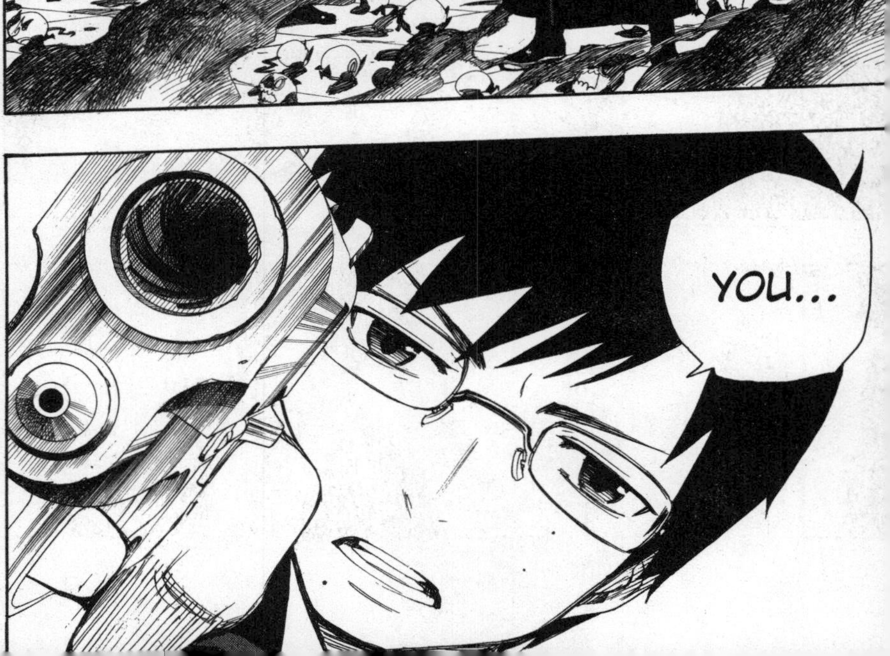
YOU...

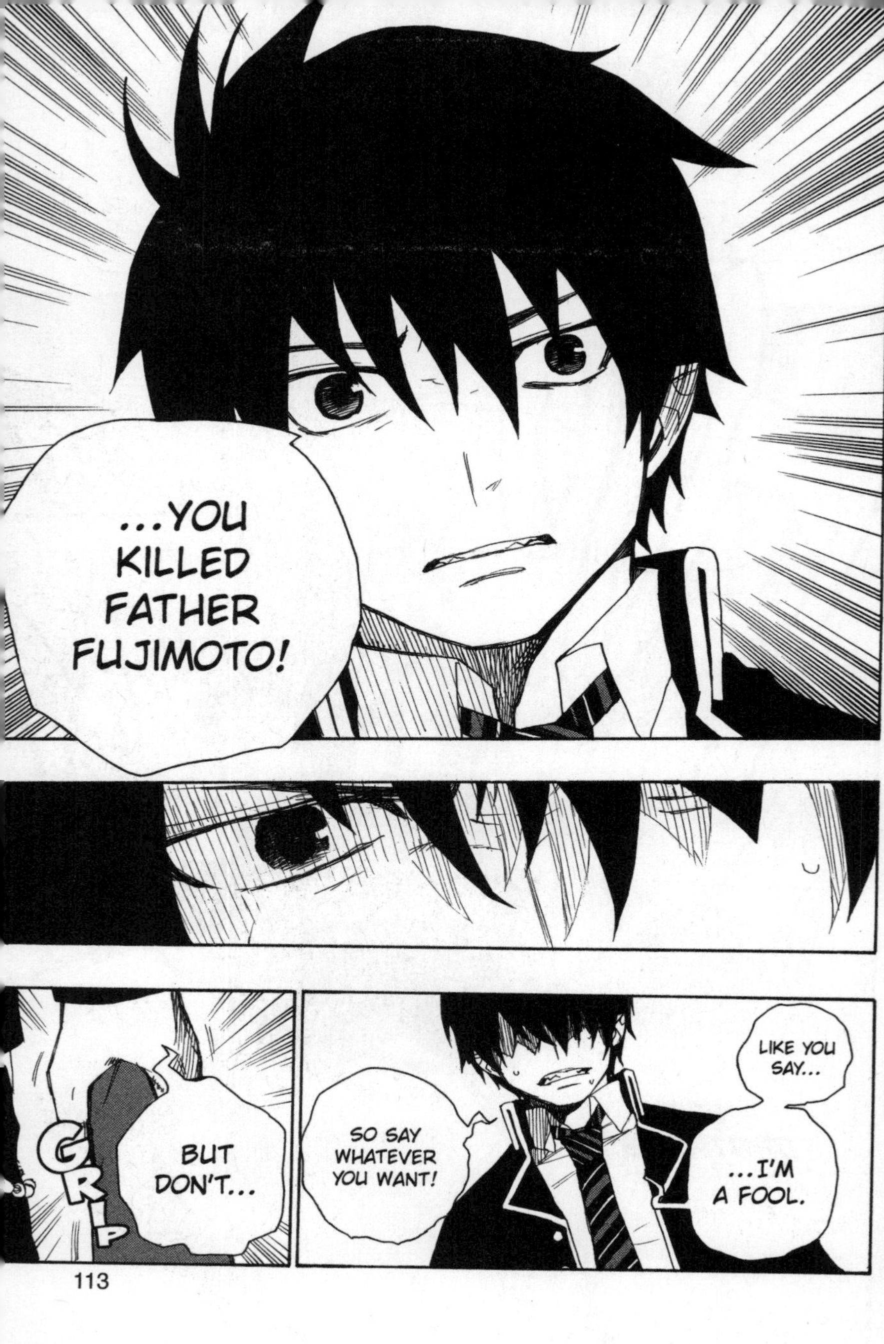
...YOU KILLED FATHER FUJIMOTO!
LIKE YOU SAY...
...I'M A FOOL.
SO SAY WHATEVER YOU WANT!
GRIP
BUT DON'T...

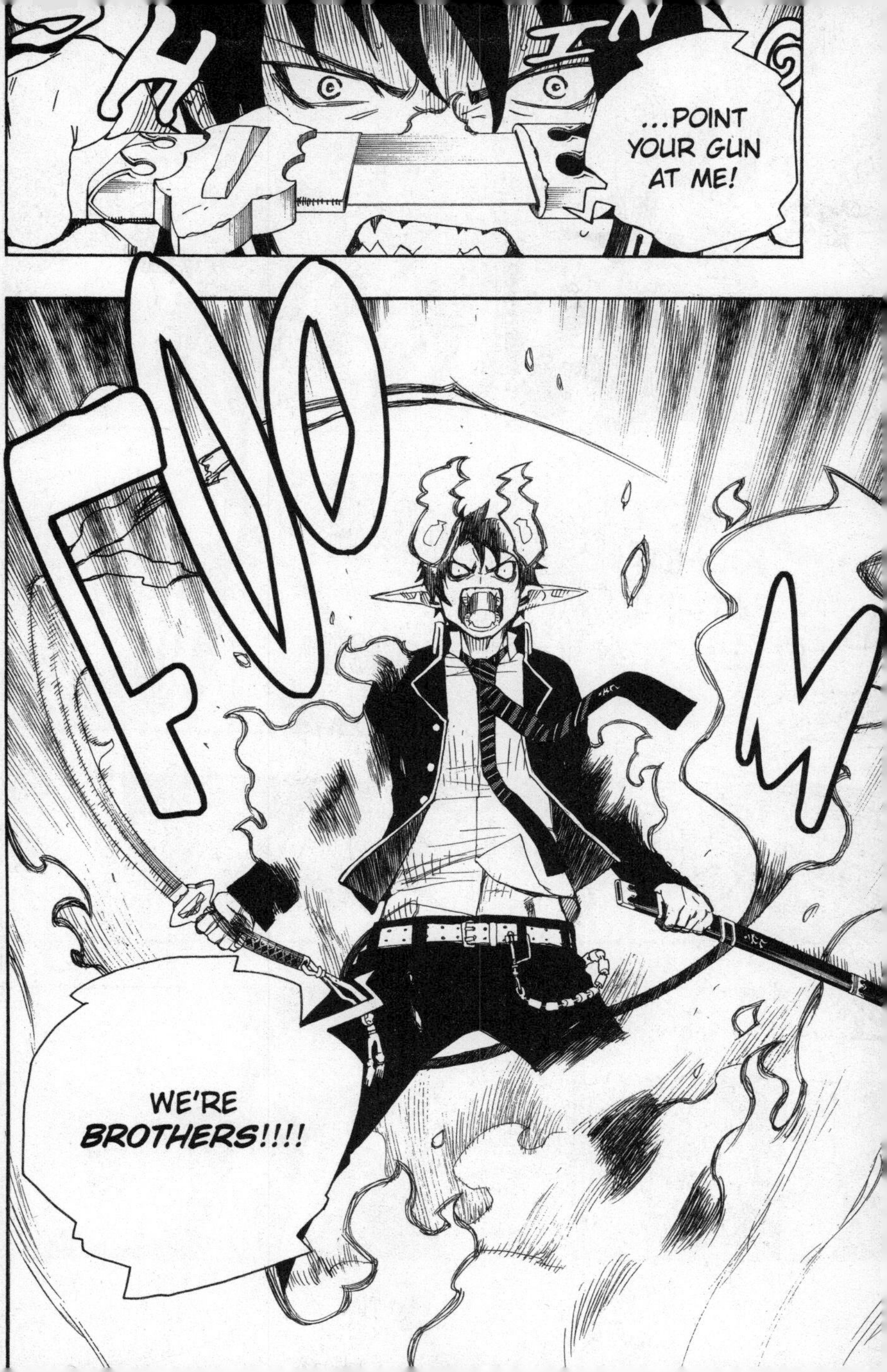
...POINT YOUR GUN AT ME!
FOOM
WE'RE BROTHERS!!!!

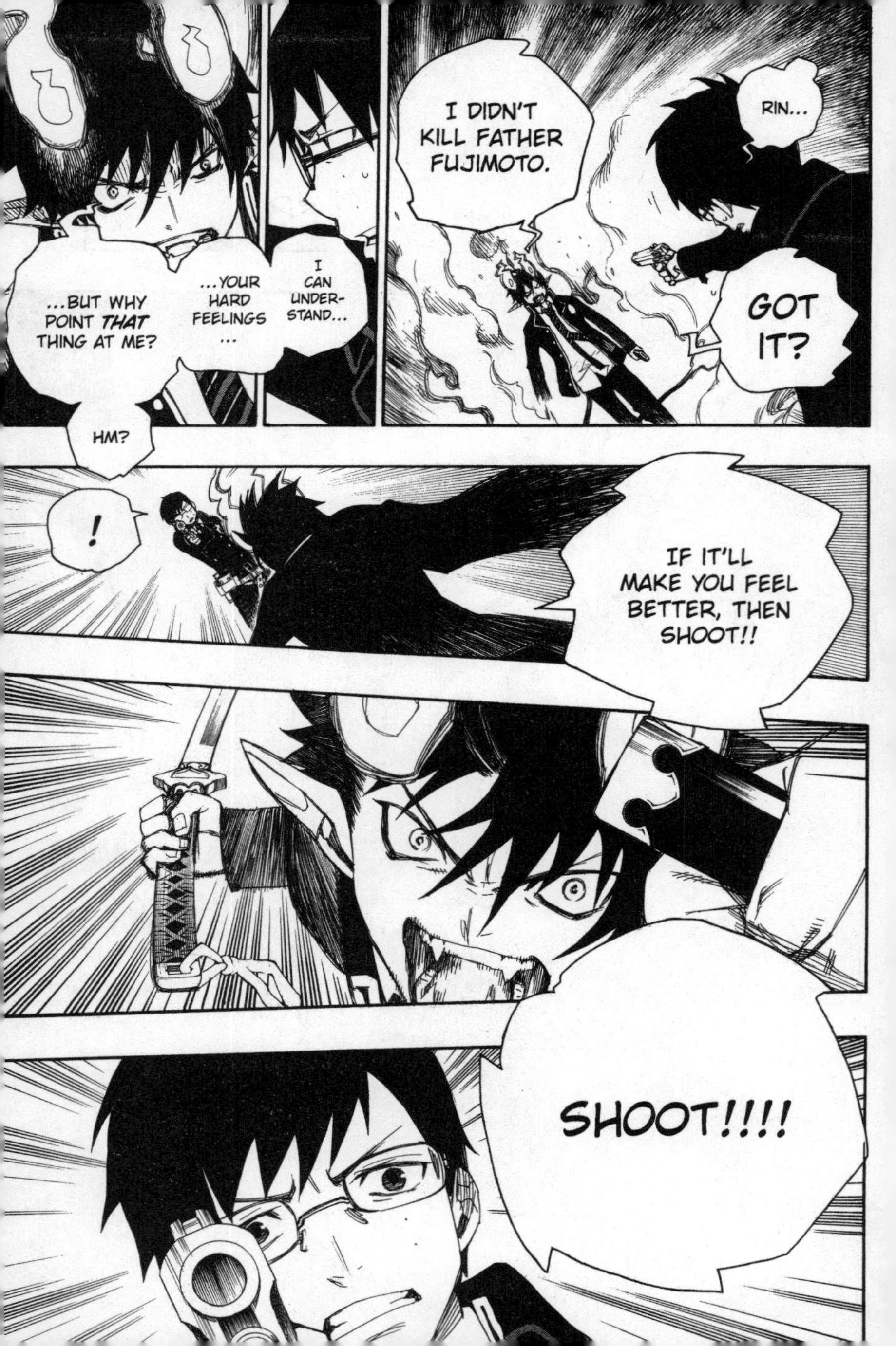
RIN...
I DIDN'T KILL FATHER FUJIMOTO.
GOT IT?
I CAN UNDER-STAND...
...YOUR HARD FEELINGS...
...BUT WHY POINT *THAT* THING AT ME?
HM?
IF IT'LL MAKE YOU FEEL BETTER, THEN SHOOT!!
!
SHOOT!!!!

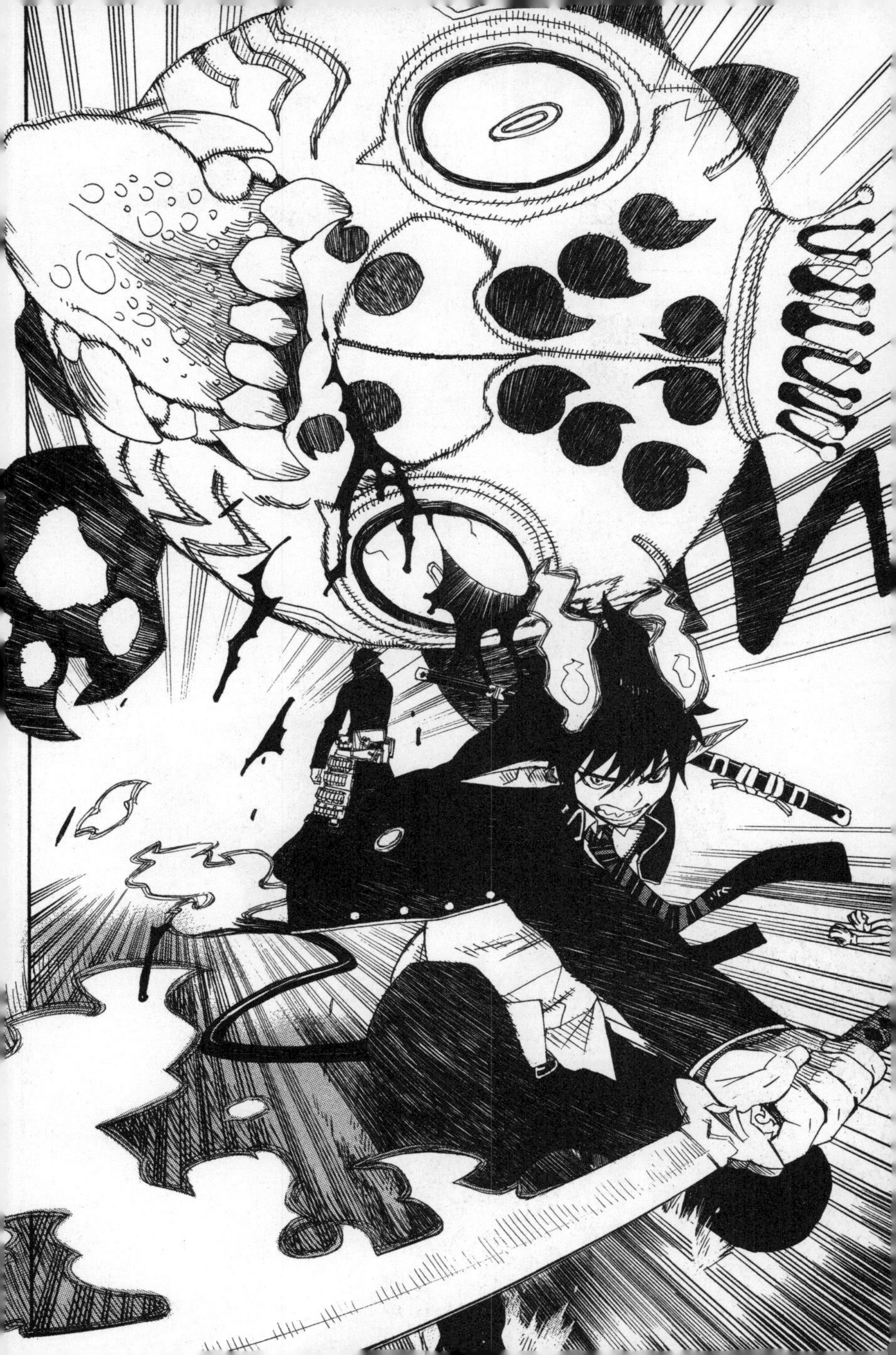

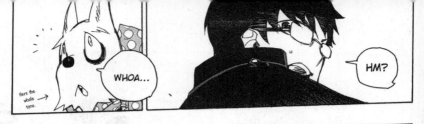

WHOA...

HM?

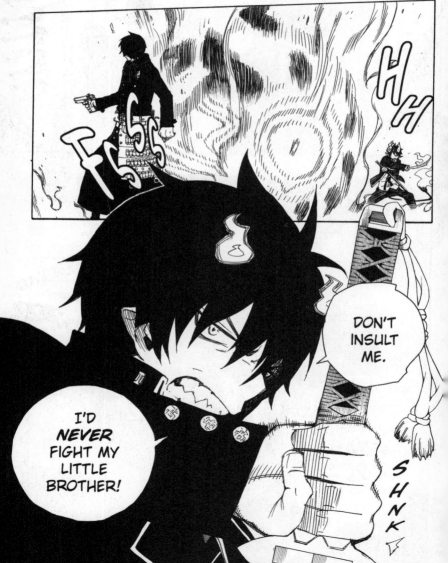

Here the whole time.

HH

FS55

DON'T INSULT ME.

I'D *NEVER* FIGHT MY LITTLE BROTHER!

SHNK

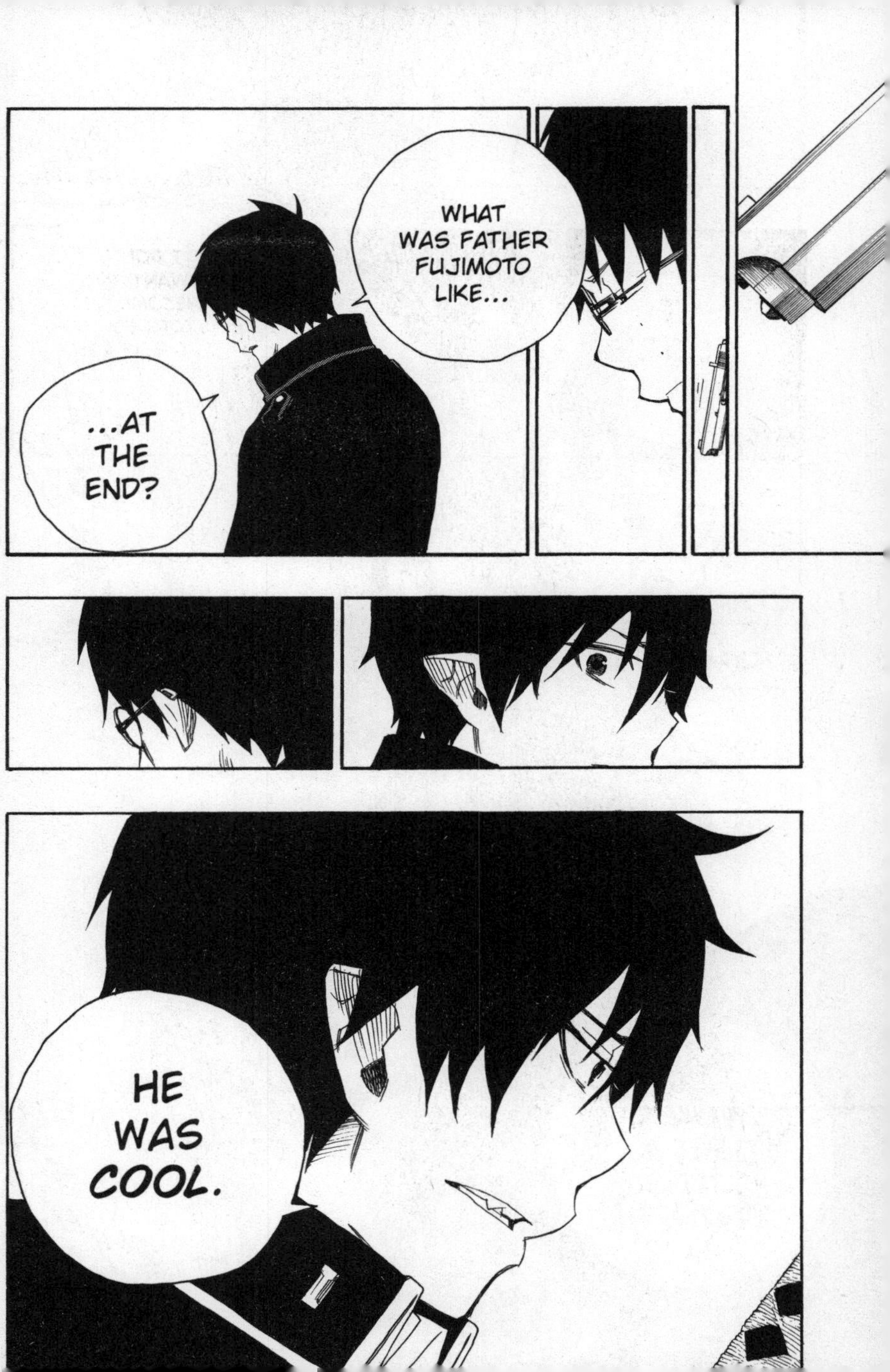
WHAT WAS FATHER FUJIMOTO LIKE...
...AT THE END?
HE WAS COOL.

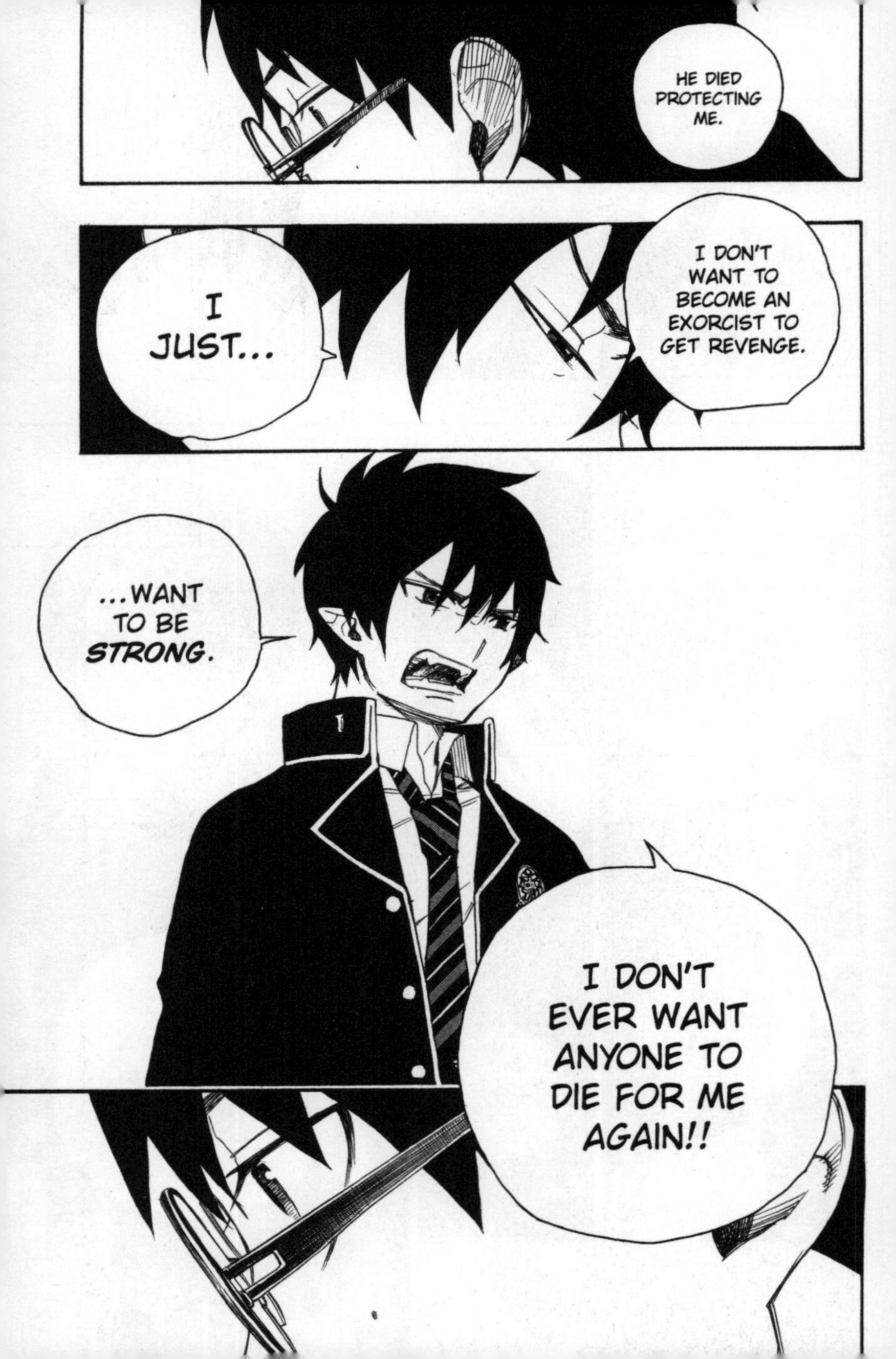
HE DIED PROTECTING ME.
I DON'T WANT TO BECOME AN EXORCIST TO GET REVENGE.
I JUST...
...WANT TO BE *STRONG*.
I DON'T EVER WANT ANYONE TO DIE FOR ME AGAIN!!

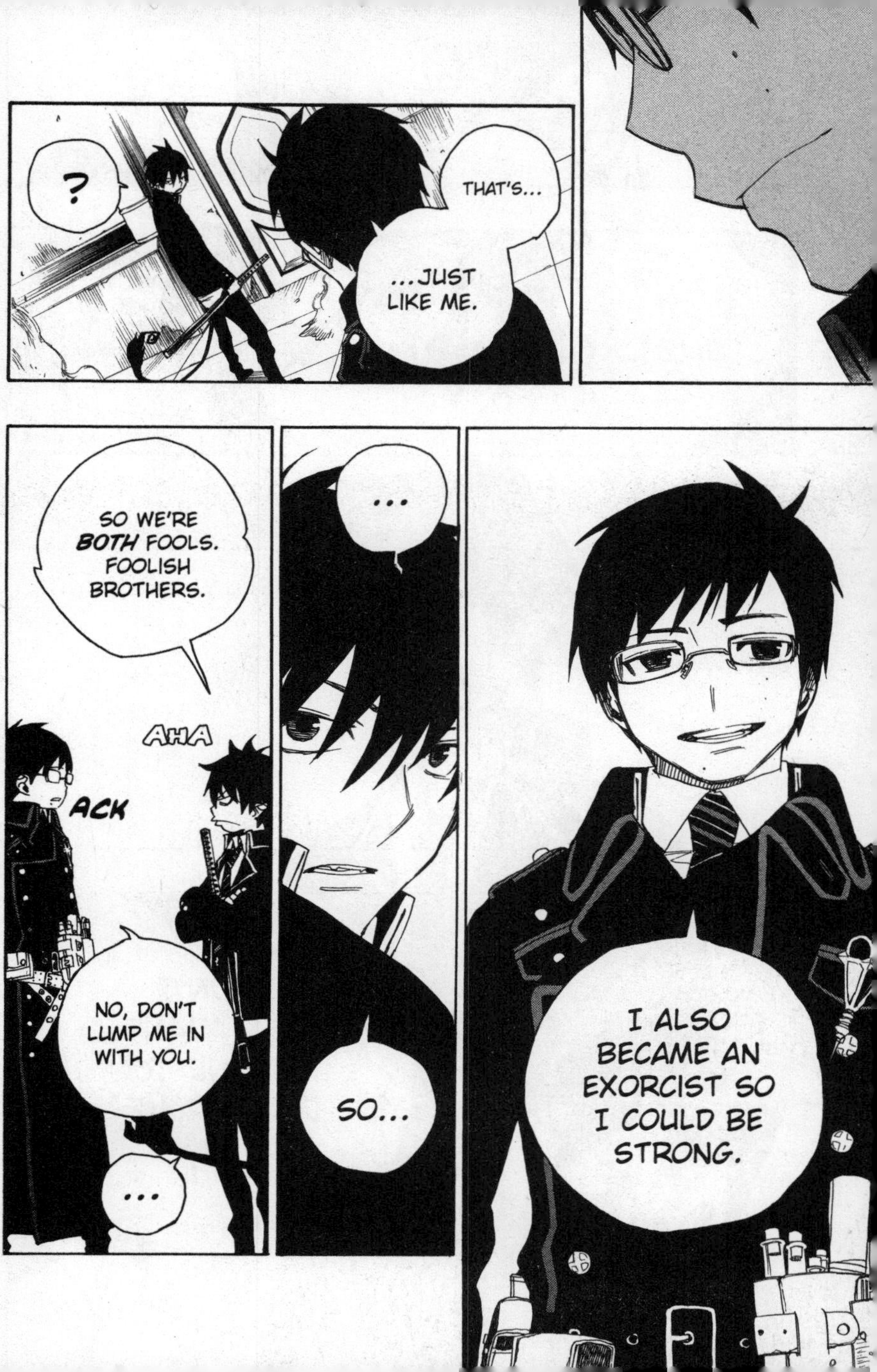
THAT'S...
...JUST LIKE ME.
?
I ALSO BECAME AN EXORCIST SO I COULD BE STRONG.
...
SO...
SO WE'RE BOTH FOOLS. FOOLISH BROTHERS.
AHA
ACK
NO, DON'T LUMP ME IN WITH YOU.
...

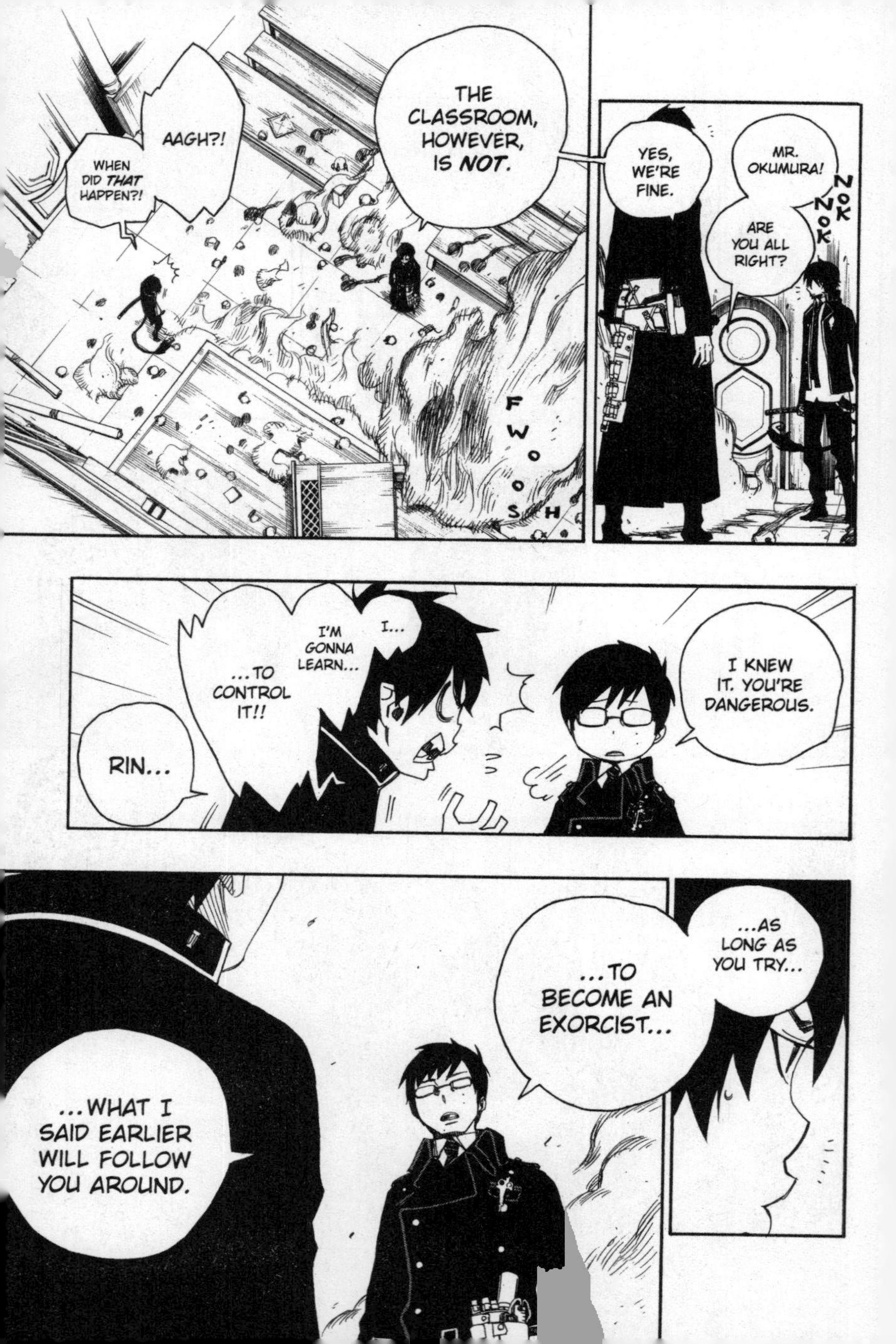
NOK NOK
MR. OKUMURA!
ARE YOU ALL RIGHT?
YES, WE'RE FINE.
THE CLASSROOM, HOWEVER, IS *NOT*.
AAGH?!
WHEN DID *THAT* HAPPEN?!
FWOOSH
I KNEW IT. YOU'RE DANGEROUS.
I...
I'M GONNA LEARN...
...TO CONTROL IT!!
RIN...
...AS LONG AS YOU TRY...
...TO BECOME AN EXORCIST...
...WHAT I SAID EARLIER WILL FOLLOW YOU AROUND.

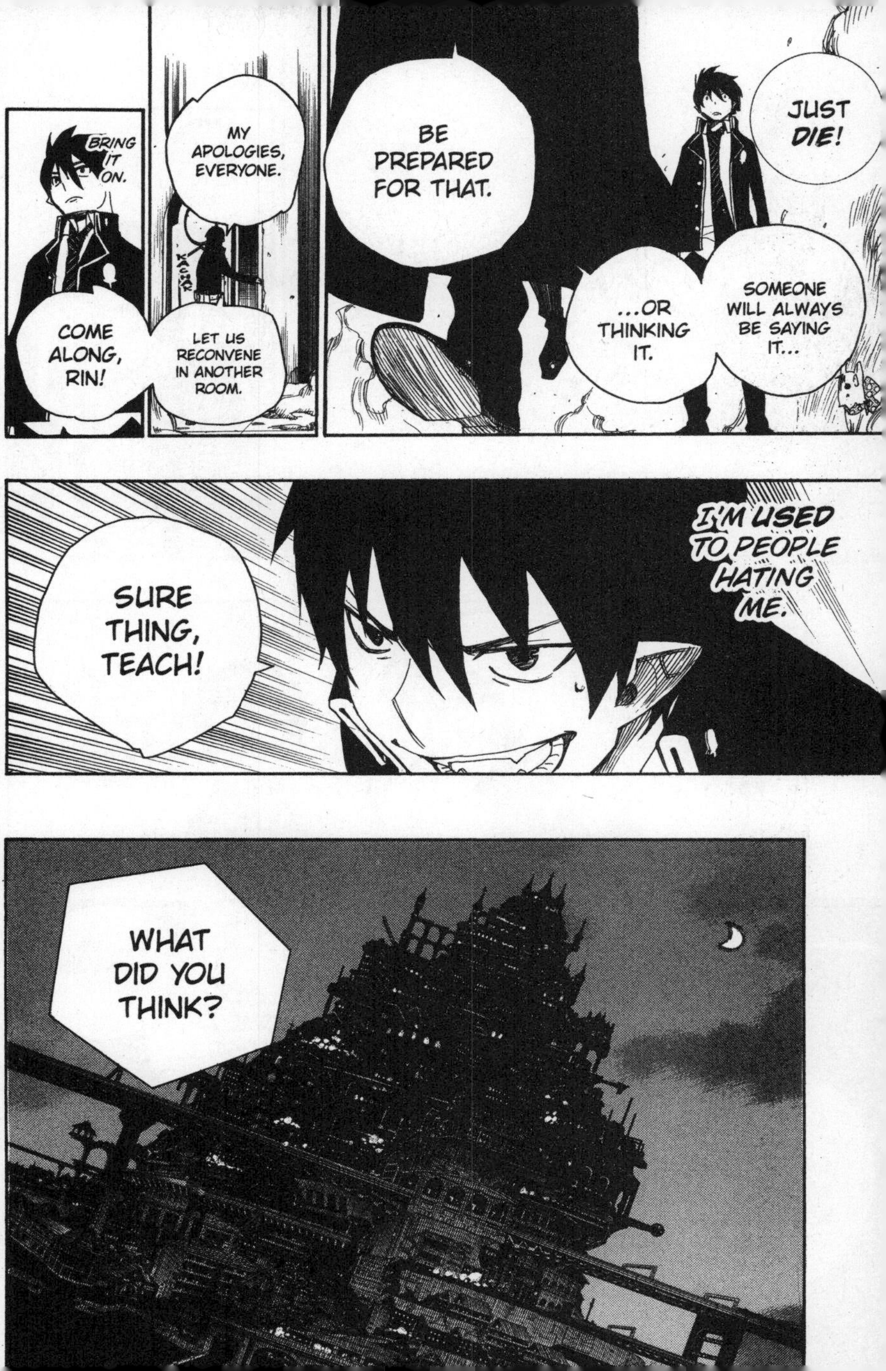
JUST DIE!
SOMEONE WILL ALWAYS BE SAYING IT...
...OR THINKING IT.
BE PREPARED FOR THAT.
MY APOLOGIES, EVERYONE.
KACHAK
LET US RECONVENE IN ANOTHER ROOM.
BRING IT ON.
COME ALONG, RIN!
I'M USED TO PEOPLE HATING ME.
SURE THING, TEACH!
WHAT DID YOU THINK?

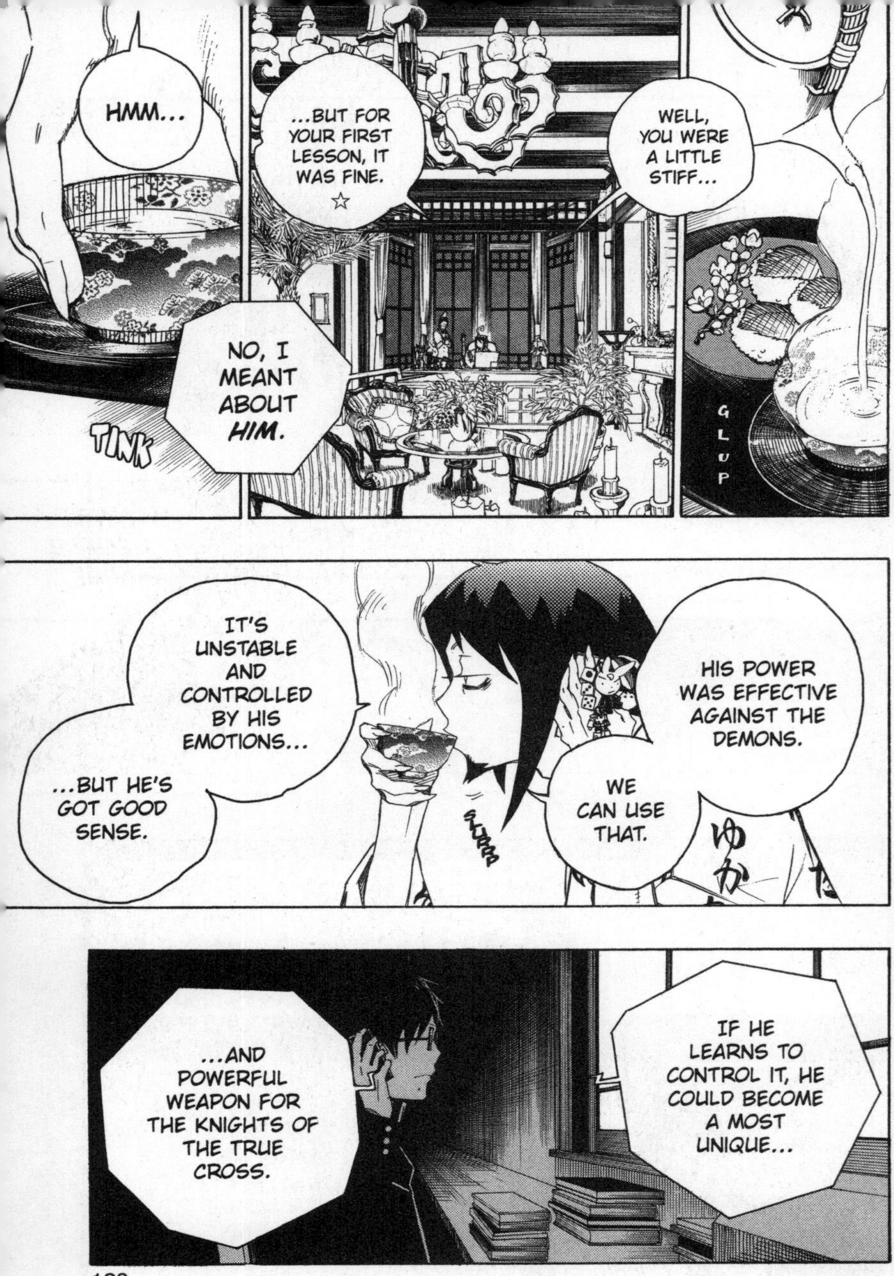
WELL, YOU WERE A LITTLE STIFF...
GLUP
...BUT FOR YOUR FIRST LESSON, IT WAS FINE. ☆
NO, I MEANT ABOUT *HIM.*
HMM...
TINK
HIS POWER WAS EFFECTIVE AGAINST THE DEMONS.
WE CAN USE THAT.
SLURP
IT'S UNSTABLE AND CONTROLLED BY HIS EMOTIONS...
...BUT HE'S GOT GOOD SENSE.
IF HE LEARNS TO CONTROL IT, HE COULD BECOME A MOST UNIQUE...
...AND POWERFUL WEAPON FOR THE KNIGHTS OF THE TRUE CROSS.

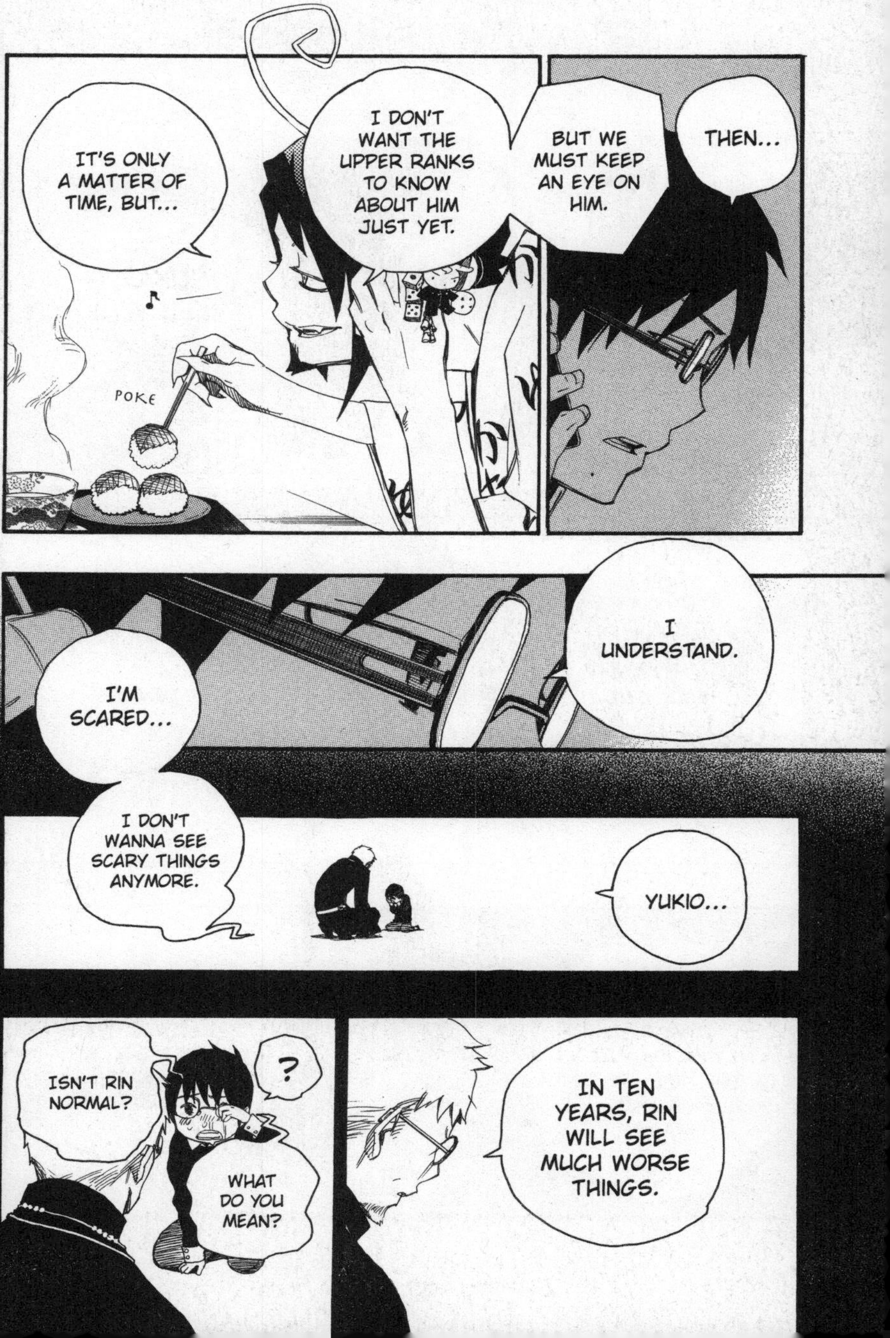
THEN...
BUT WE MUST KEEP AN EYE ON HIM.
I DON'T WANT THE UPPER RANKS TO KNOW ABOUT HIM JUST YET.
IT'S ONLY A MATTER OF TIME, BUT...
POKE
I UNDERSTAND.
I'M SCARED...
YUKIO...
I DON'T WANNA SEE SCARY THINGS ANYMORE.
IN TEN YEARS, RIN WILL SEE MUCH WORSE THINGS.
?
ISN'T RIN NORMAL?
WHAT DO YOU MEAN?

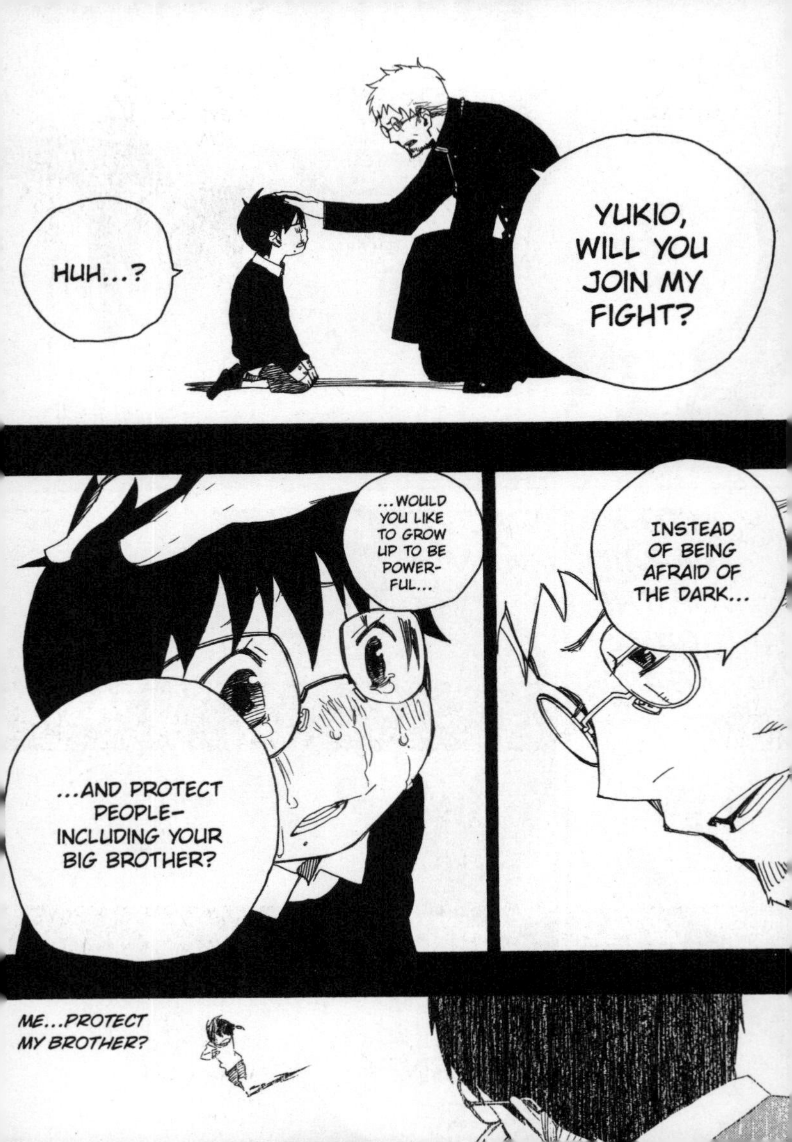
YUKIO, WILL YOU JOIN MY FIGHT?
HUH...?
INSTEAD OF BEING AFRAID OF THE DARK...
...WOULD YOU LIKE TO GROW UP TO BE POWER-FUL...
...AND PROTECT PEOPLE-INCLUDING YOUR BIG BROTHER?
ME...PROTECT MY BROTHER?

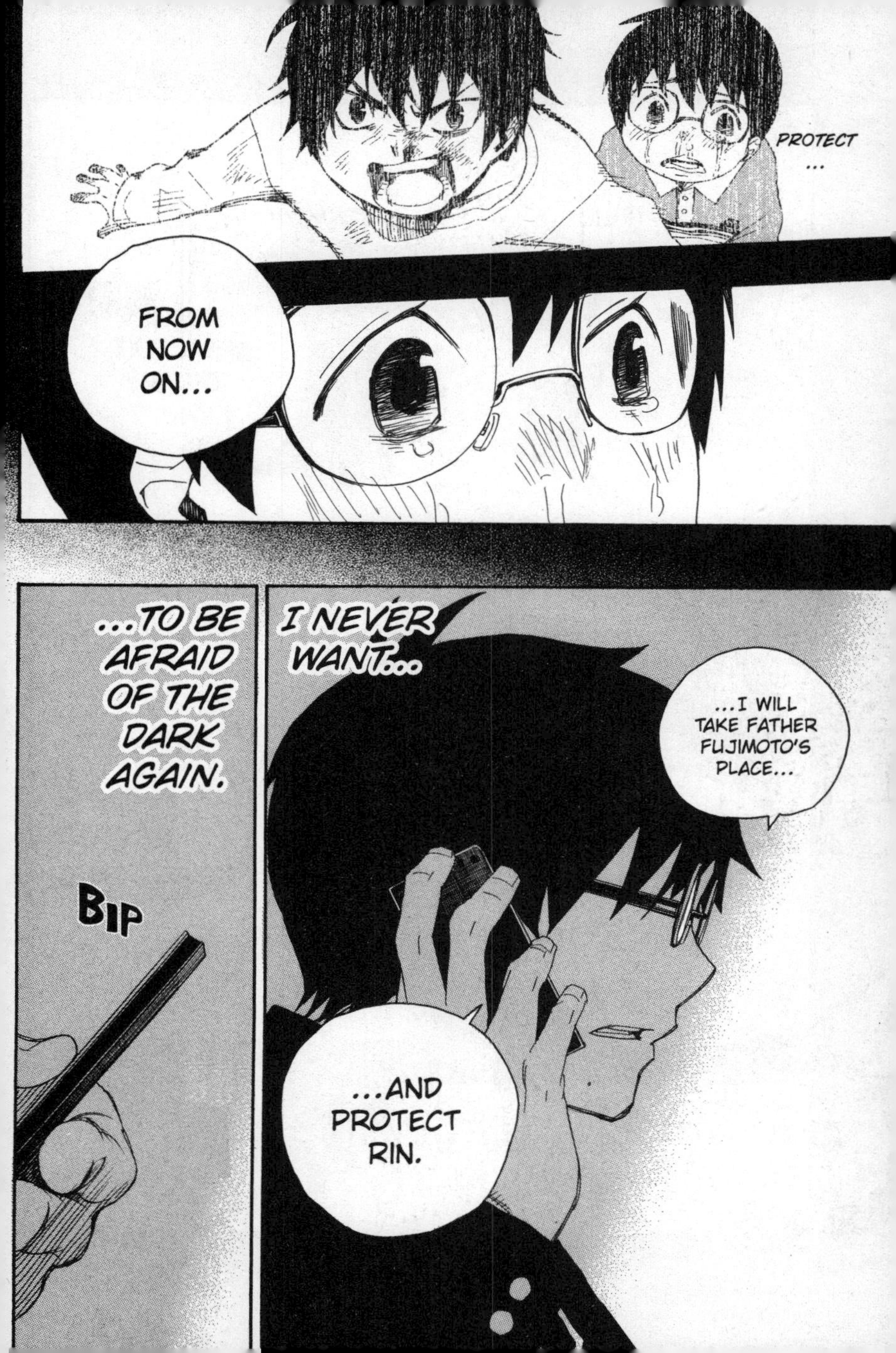
PROTECT ...
FROM NOW ON...
...I WILL TAKE FATHER FUJIMOTO'S PLACE...
...AND PROTECT RIN.
I NEVER WANT...
...TO BE AFRAID OF THE DARK AGAIN.
BIP

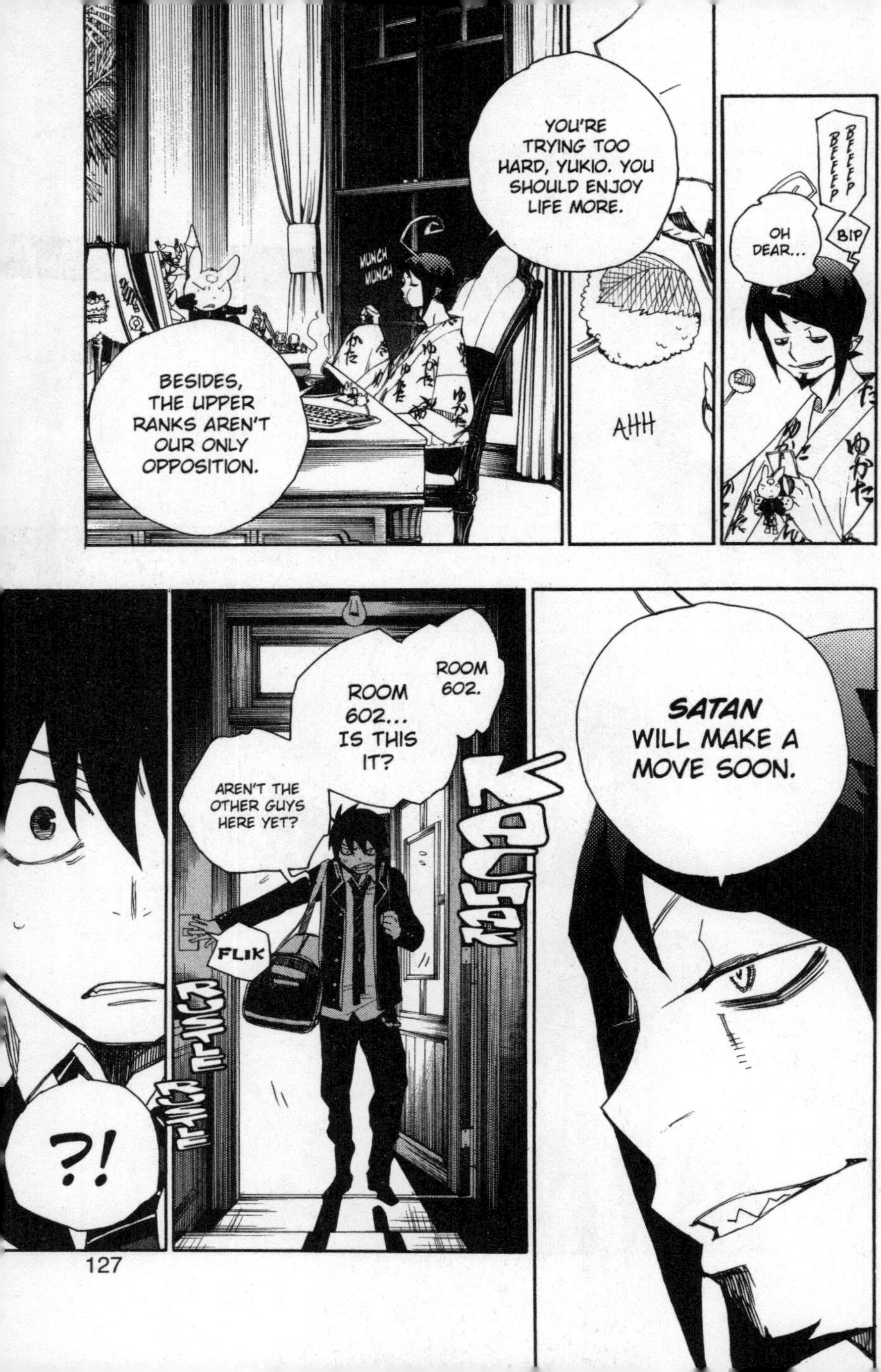
BEEEP BEEEP
BIP
OH DEAR...
YOU'RE TRYING TOO HARD, YUKIO. YOU SHOULD ENJOY LIFE MORE.
AHH
MUNCH MUNCH
BESIDES, THE UPPER RANKS AREN'T OUR ONLY OPPOSITION.
SATAN WILL MAKE A MOVE SOON.
ROOM 602.
ROOM 602... IS THIS IT?
KACHAK
AREN'T THE OTHER GUYS HERE YET?
FLIK
RUSTLE
RUSTLE
?!

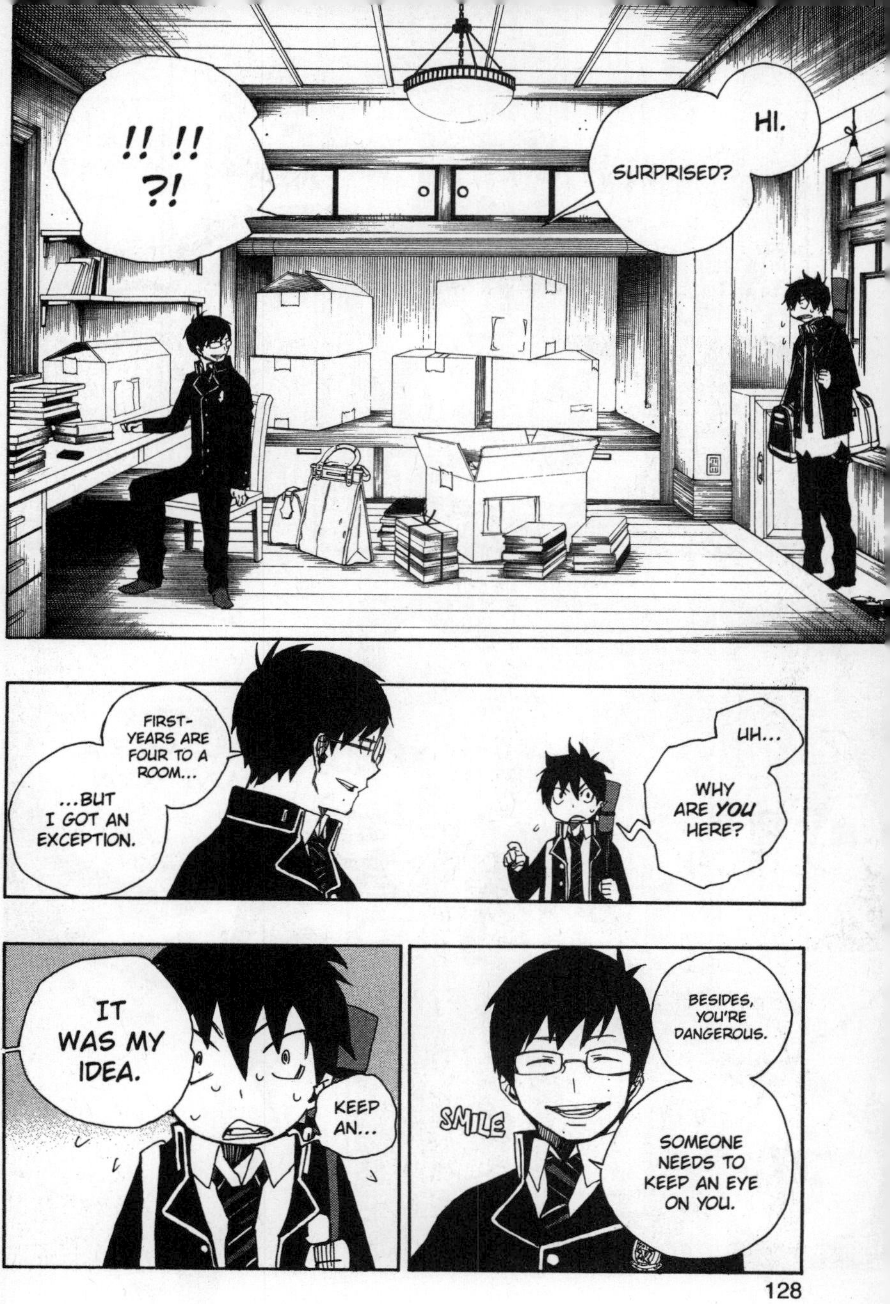
HI.
SURPRISED?
!! !! ?!
UH...
WHY ARE *YOU* HERE?
FIRST-YEARS ARE FOUR TO A ROOM...
...BUT I GOT AN EXCEPTION.
BESIDES, YOU'RE DANGEROUS.
SMILE
SOMEONE NEEDS TO KEEP AN EYE ON YOU.
KEEP AN...
IT WAS MY IDEA.

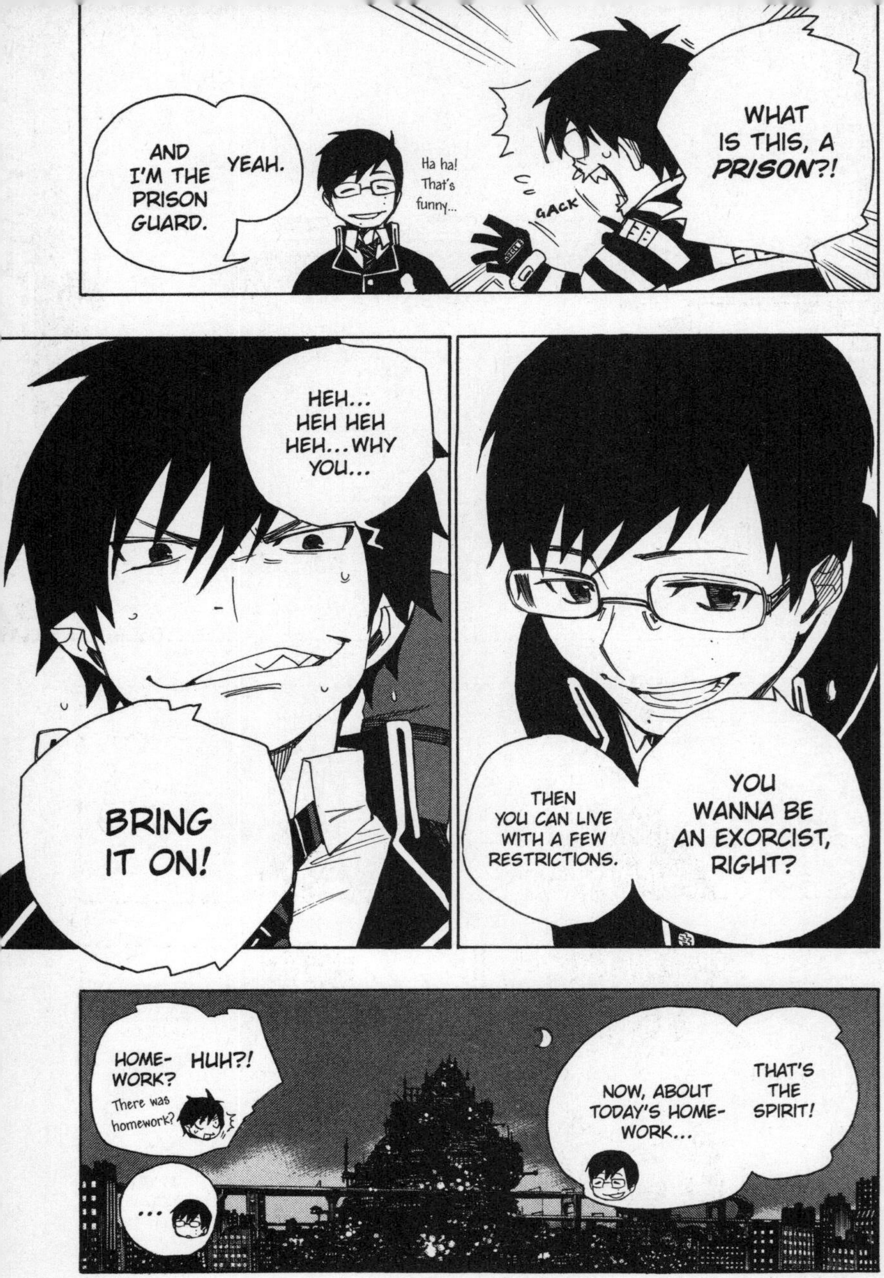
WHAT IS THIS, A PRISON?!
GACK
Ha ha! That's funny...
YEAH.
AND I'M THE PRISON GUARD.
YOU WANNA BE AN EXORCIST, RIGHT?
THEN YOU CAN LIVE WITH A FEW RESTRICTIONS.
HEH... HEH HEH HEH...WHY YOU...
BRING IT ON!
THAT'S THE SPIRIT!
NOW, ABOUT TODAY'S HOME-WORK...
HUH?!
HOME-WORK?
There was homework?
...

Blue Exorcist Chapter 2 Big Brother, Little Brother

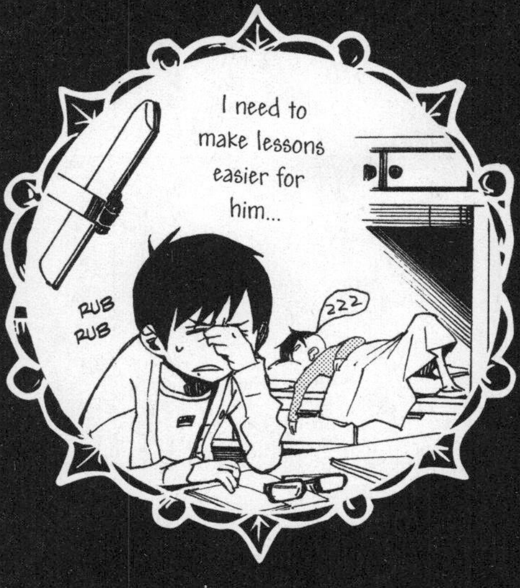
I need to make lessons easier for him...
RUB RUB
ZZZ

Chapter 3
The Garden of Amahara

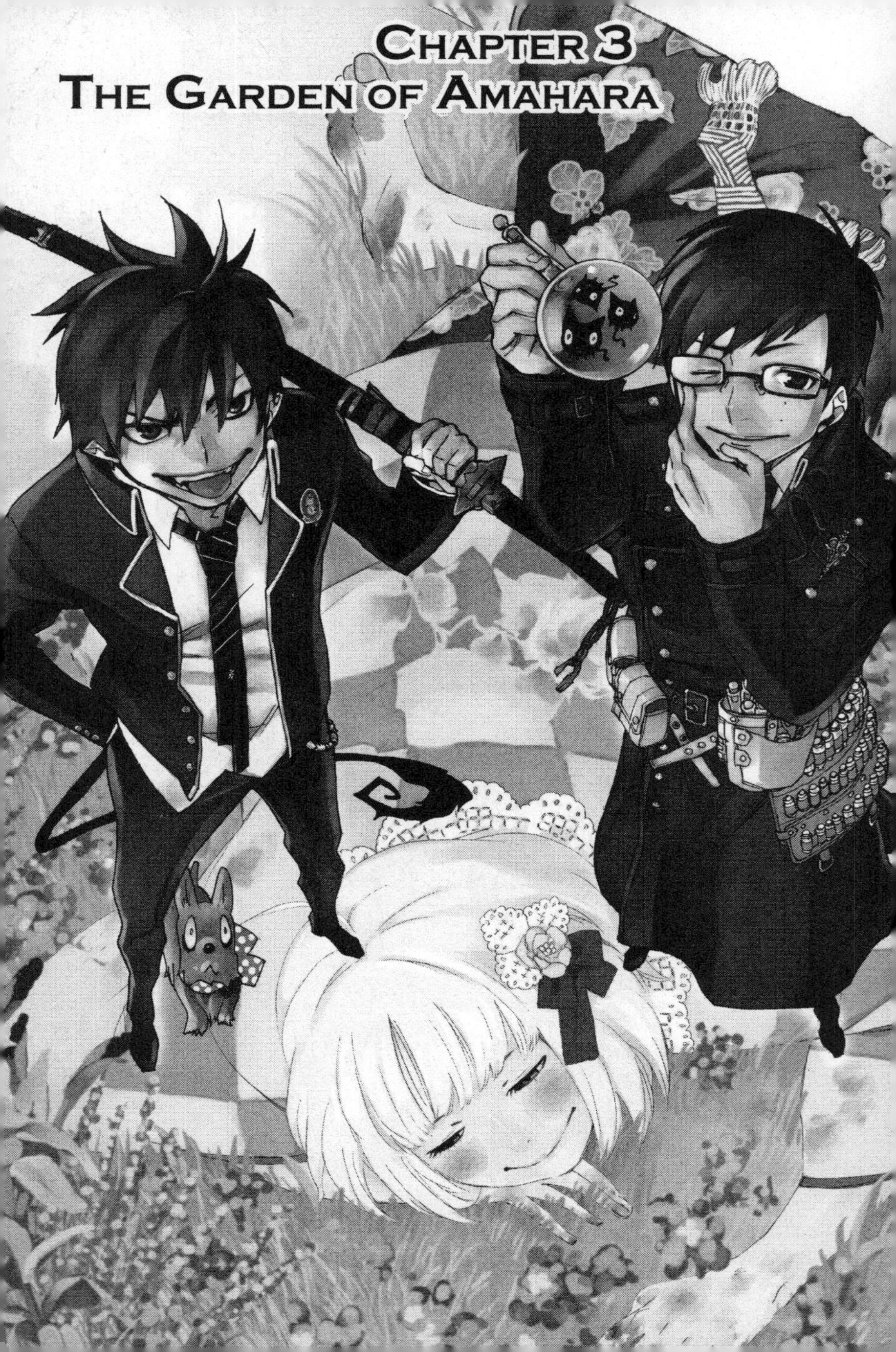

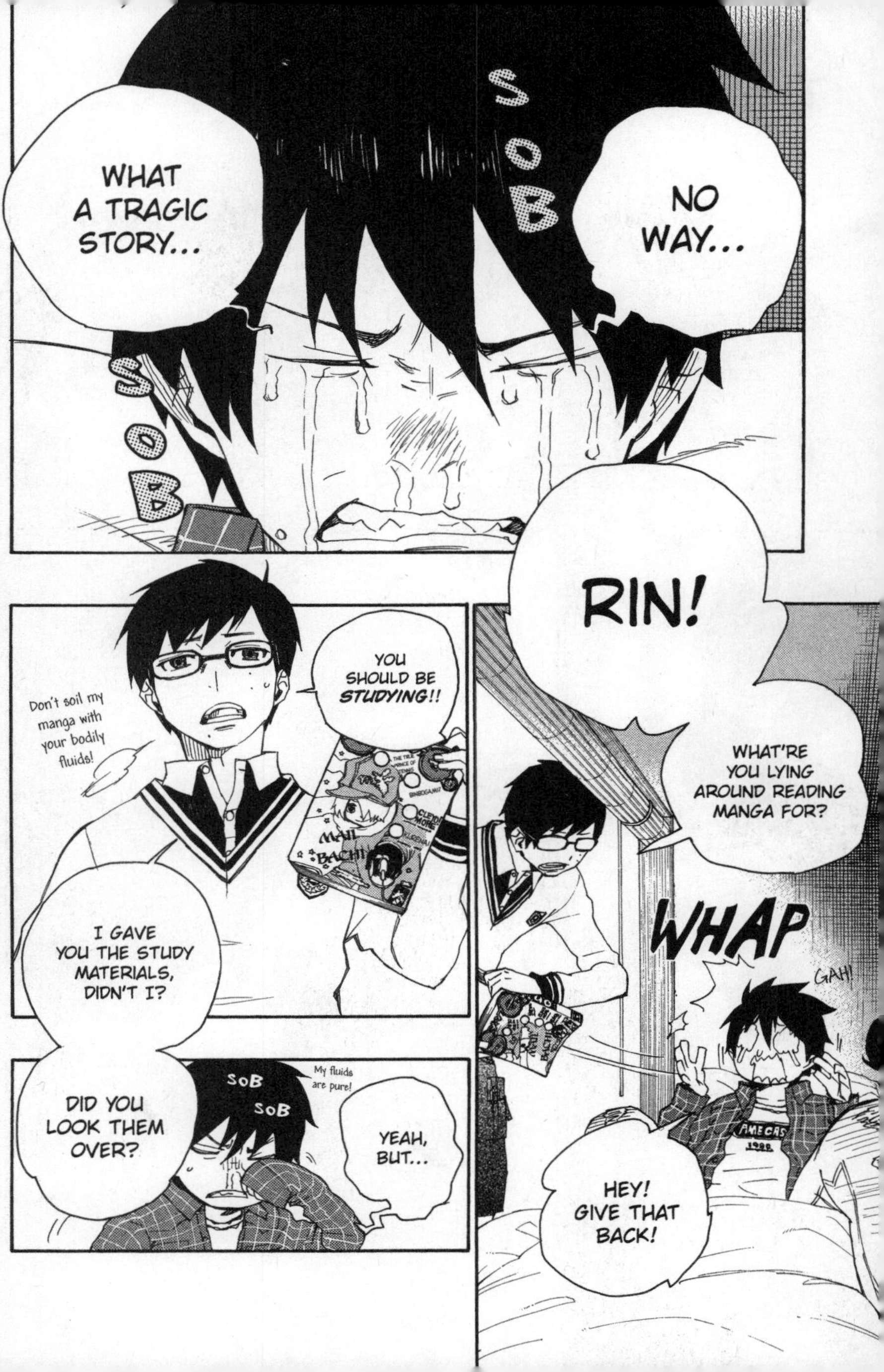
NO WAY...
SOB
WHAT A TRAGIC STORY...
SOB
RIN!
WHAT'RE YOU LYING AROUND READING MANGA FOR?
WHAP
GAH!
HEY! GIVE THAT BACK!
YOU SHOULD BE STUDYING!!
Don't soil my manga with your bodily fluids!
I GAVE YOU THE STUDY MATERIALS, DIDN'T I?
DID YOU LOOK THEM OVER?
YEAH, BUT...
My fluids are pure!
SOB
SOB

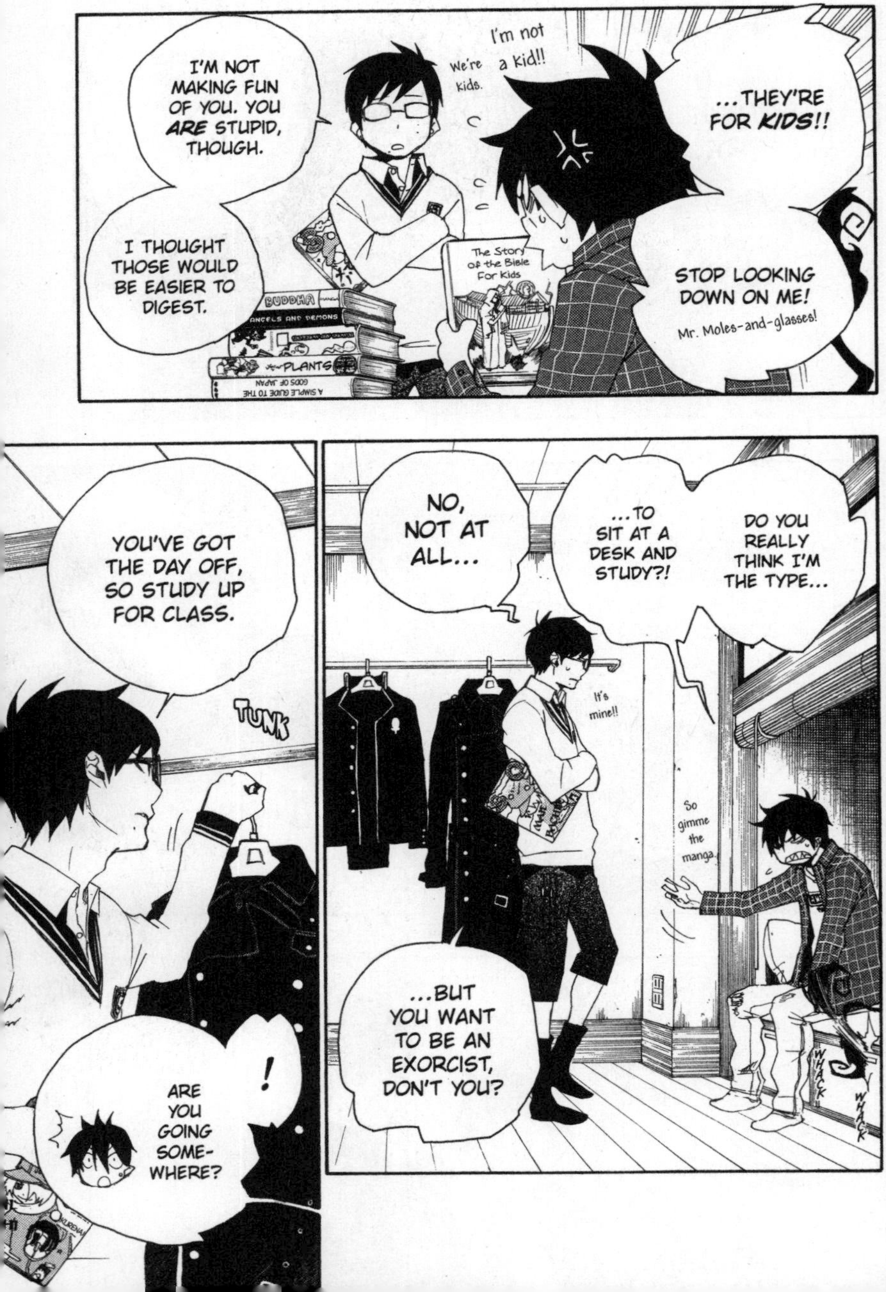
...THEY'RE FOR *KIDS*!!
STOP LOOKING DOWN ON ME!
Mr. Moles-and-glasses!
I'm not a kid!!
We're kids.
The Story of the Bible For Kids
I'M NOT MAKING FUN OF YOU. YOU *ARE* STUPID, THOUGH.
I THOUGHT THOSE WOULD BE EASIER TO DIGEST.
BUDDHA
ANGELS AND DEMONS
PLANTS
A SIMPLE GUIDE TO THE GODS OF JAPAN
DO YOU REALLY THINK I'M THE TYPE...
...TO SIT AT A DESK AND STUDY?!
NO, NOT AT ALL...
It's mine!!
So gimme the manga.
...BUT YOU WANT TO BE AN EXORCIST, DON'T YOU?
WHACK
WHACK
YOU'VE GOT THE DAY OFF, SO STUDY UP FOR CLASS.
TUNK
!
ARE YOU GOING SOME-WHERE?

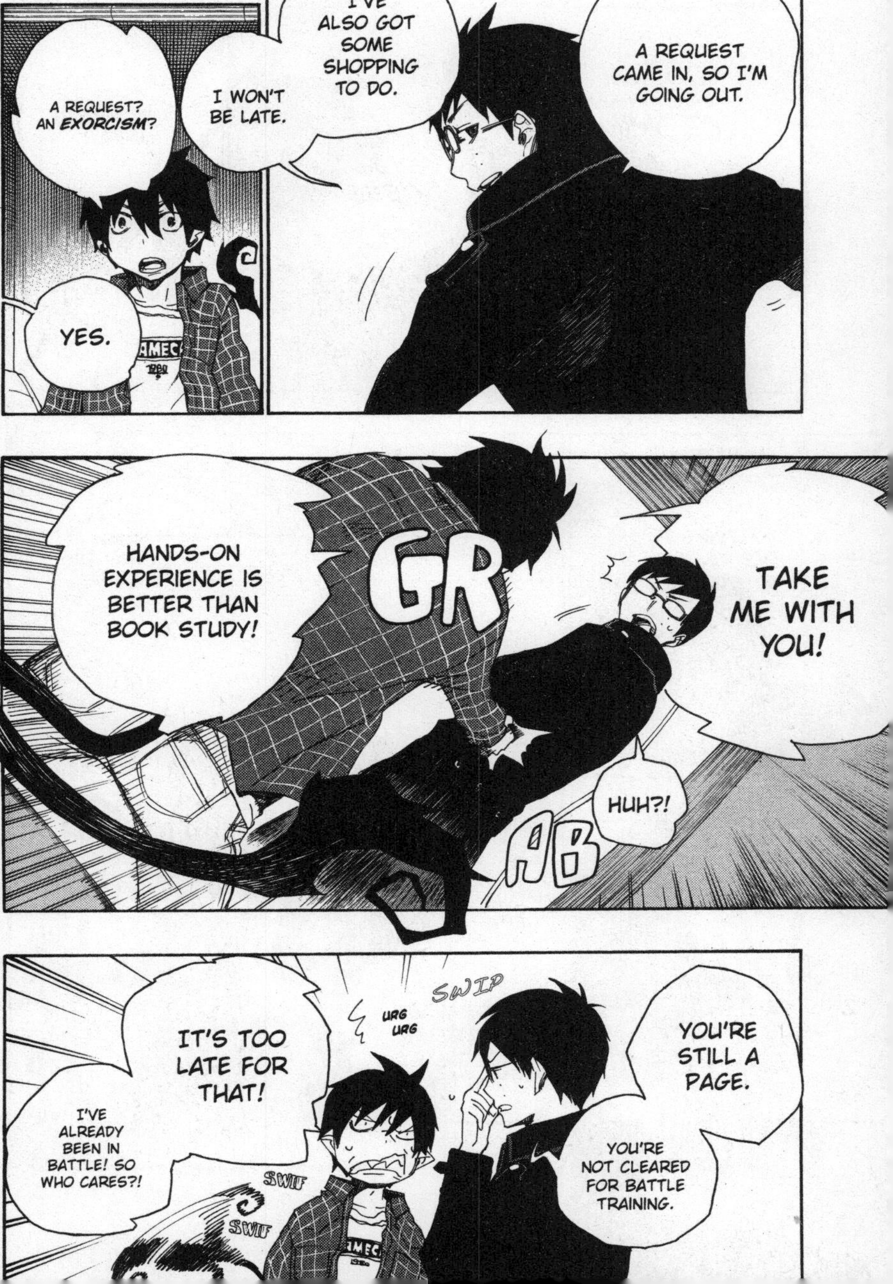
A REQUEST CAME IN, SO I'M GOING OUT.
I'VE ALSO GOT SOME SHOPPING TO DO.
I WON'T BE LATE.
A REQUEST? AN *EXORCISM*?
YES.
TAKE ME WITH YOU!
HUH?!
AB
GR
HANDS-ON EXPERIENCE IS BETTER THAN BOOK STUDY!
SWIP
YOU'RE STILL A PAGE.
YOU'RE NOT CLEARED FOR BATTLE TRAINING.
URG URG
IT'S TOO LATE FOR THAT!
I'VE ALREADY BEEN IN BATTLE! SO WHO CARES?!
SWIF
SWIF

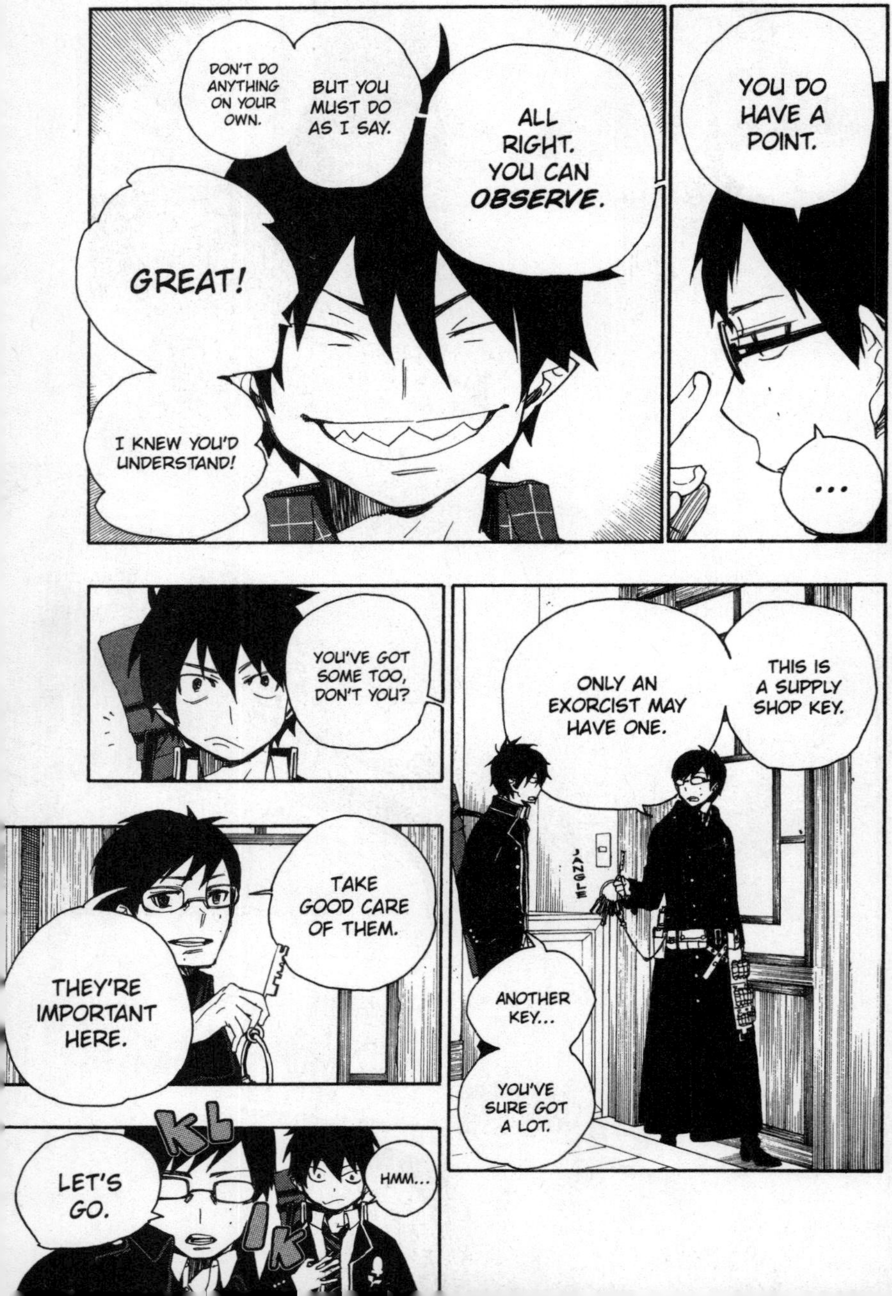
YOU DO HAVE A POINT.
...
ALL RIGHT. YOU CAN OBSERVE.
BUT YOU MUST DO AS I SAY.
DON'T DO ANYTHING ON YOUR OWN.
GREAT!
I KNEW YOU'D UNDERSTAND!
THIS IS A SUPPLY SHOP KEY.
ONLY AN EXORCIST MAY HAVE ONE.
JANGLE
ANOTHER KEY...
YOU'VE SURE GOT A LOT.
YOU'VE GOT SOME TOO, DON'T YOU?
TAKE GOOD CARE OF THEM.
THEY'RE IMPORTANT HERE.
HMM...
KLIK
LET'S GO.

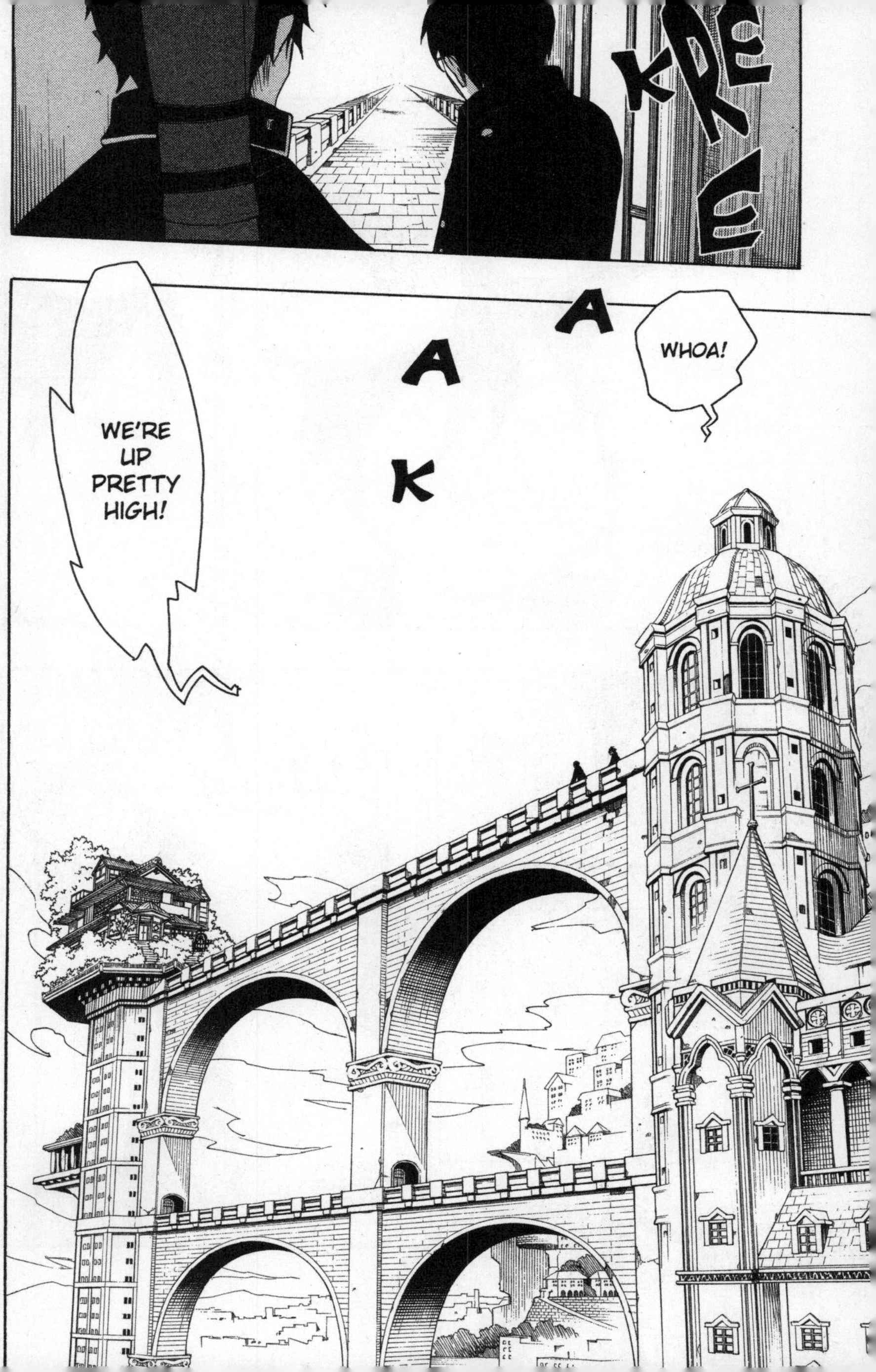
KREE
AAK
WHOA!
WE'RE UP PRETTY HIGH!

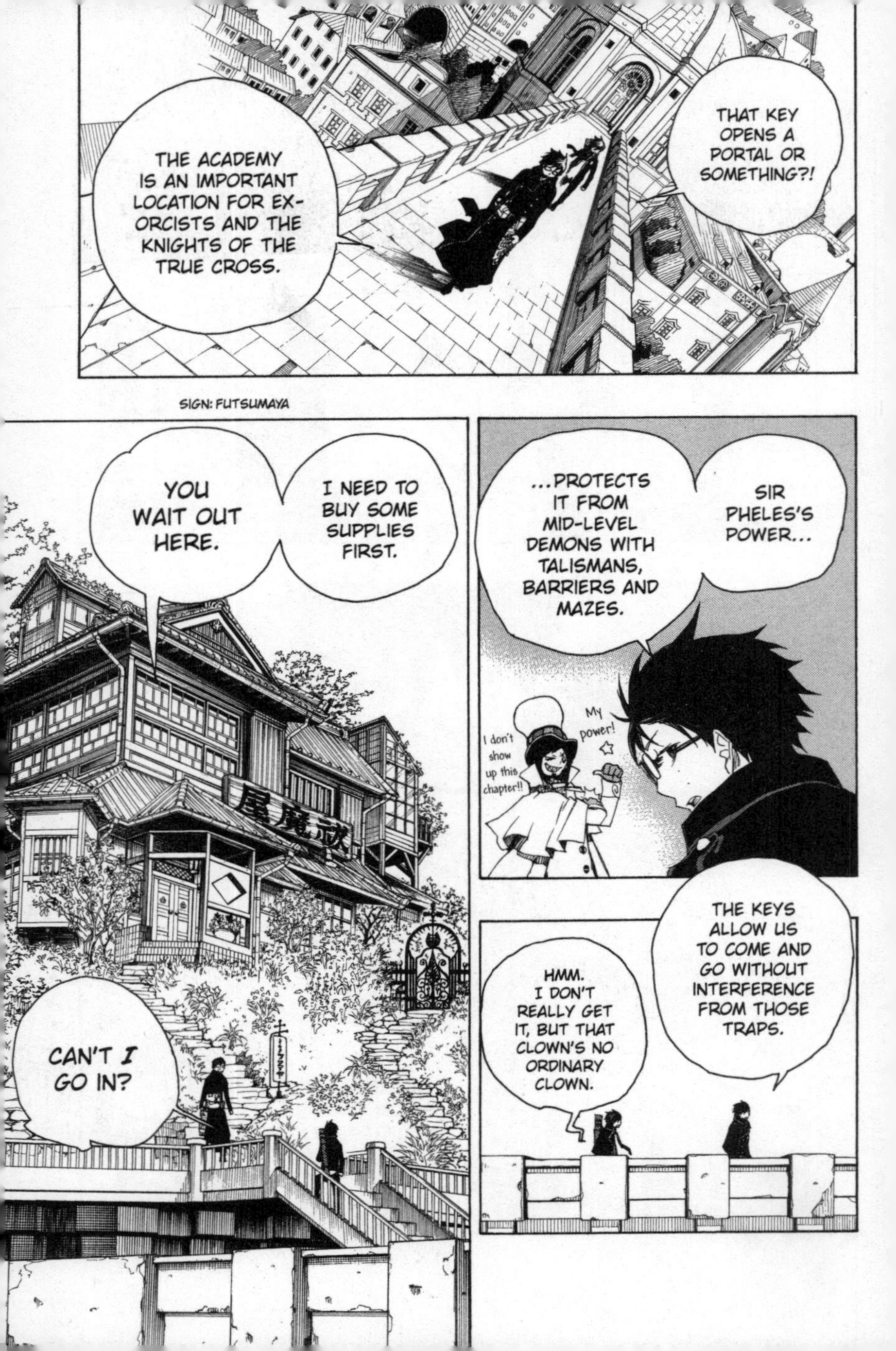
THAT KEY OPENS A PORTAL OR SOMETHING?!
THE ACADEMY IS AN IMPORTANT LOCATION FOR EX-ORCISTS AND THE KNIGHTS OF THE TRUE CROSS.
SIR PHELES'S POWER...
...PROTECTS IT FROM MID-LEVEL DEMONS WITH TALISMANS, BARRIERS AND MAZES.
My power!
I don't show up this chapter!!
THE KEYS ALLOW US TO COME AND GO WITHOUT INTERFERENCE FROM THOSE TRAPS.
HMM. I DON'T REALLY GET IT, BUT THAT CLOWN'S NO ORDINARY CLOWN.
SIGN: FUTSUMAYA
I NEED TO BUY SOME SUPPLIES FIRST.
YOU WAIT OUT HERE.
CAN'T I GO IN?

SIGN: EXORCISM SUPPLY SHOP FUTSUMAYA

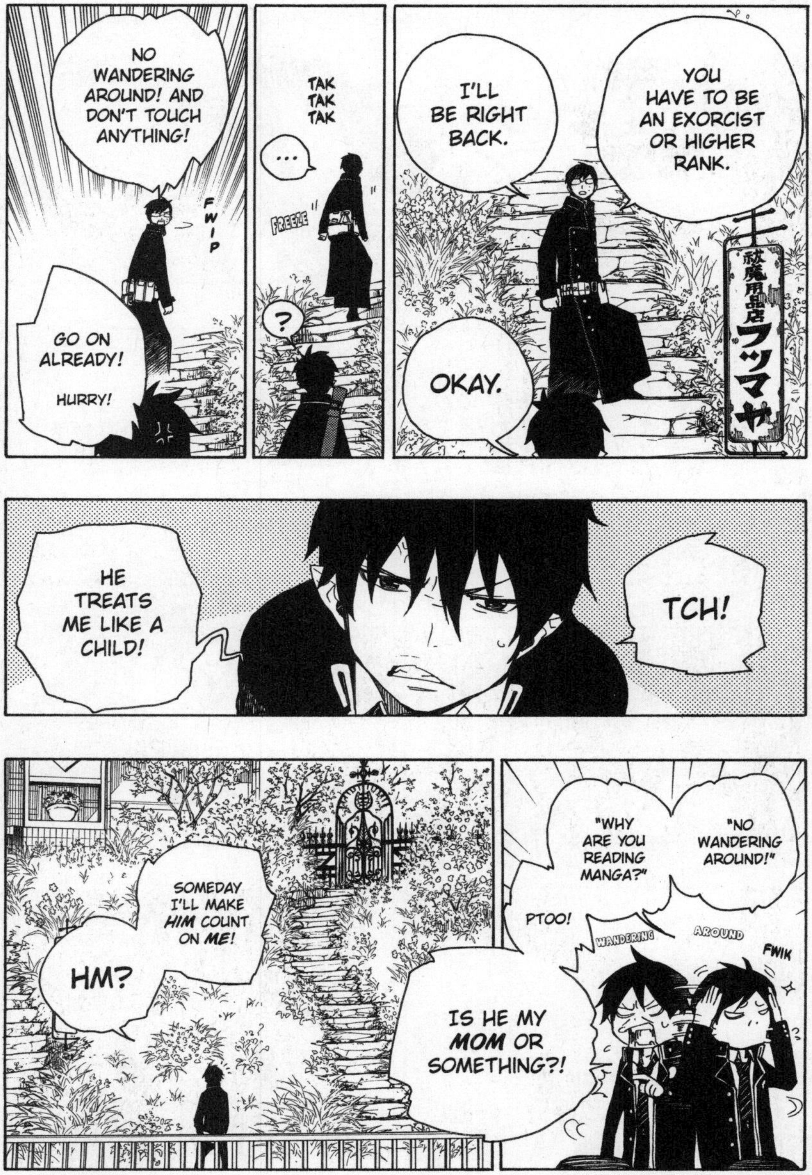
YOU HAVE TO BE AN EXORCIST OR HIGHER RANK.
I'LL BE RIGHT BACK.
祓魔用品店 フツマヤ
OKAY.
TAK TAK TAK
...
FREEZE
?
NO WANDERING AROUND! AND DON'T TOUCH ANYTHING!
FWIP
GO ON ALREADY!
HURRY!
TCH!
HE TREATS ME LIKE A CHILD!
"NO WANDERING AROUND!"
"WHY ARE YOU READING MANGA?"
AROUND
WANDERING
FWIK
PTOO!
IS HE MY *MOM* OR SOMETHING?!
SOMEDAY I'LL MAKE *HIM* COUNT ON *ME*!
HM?

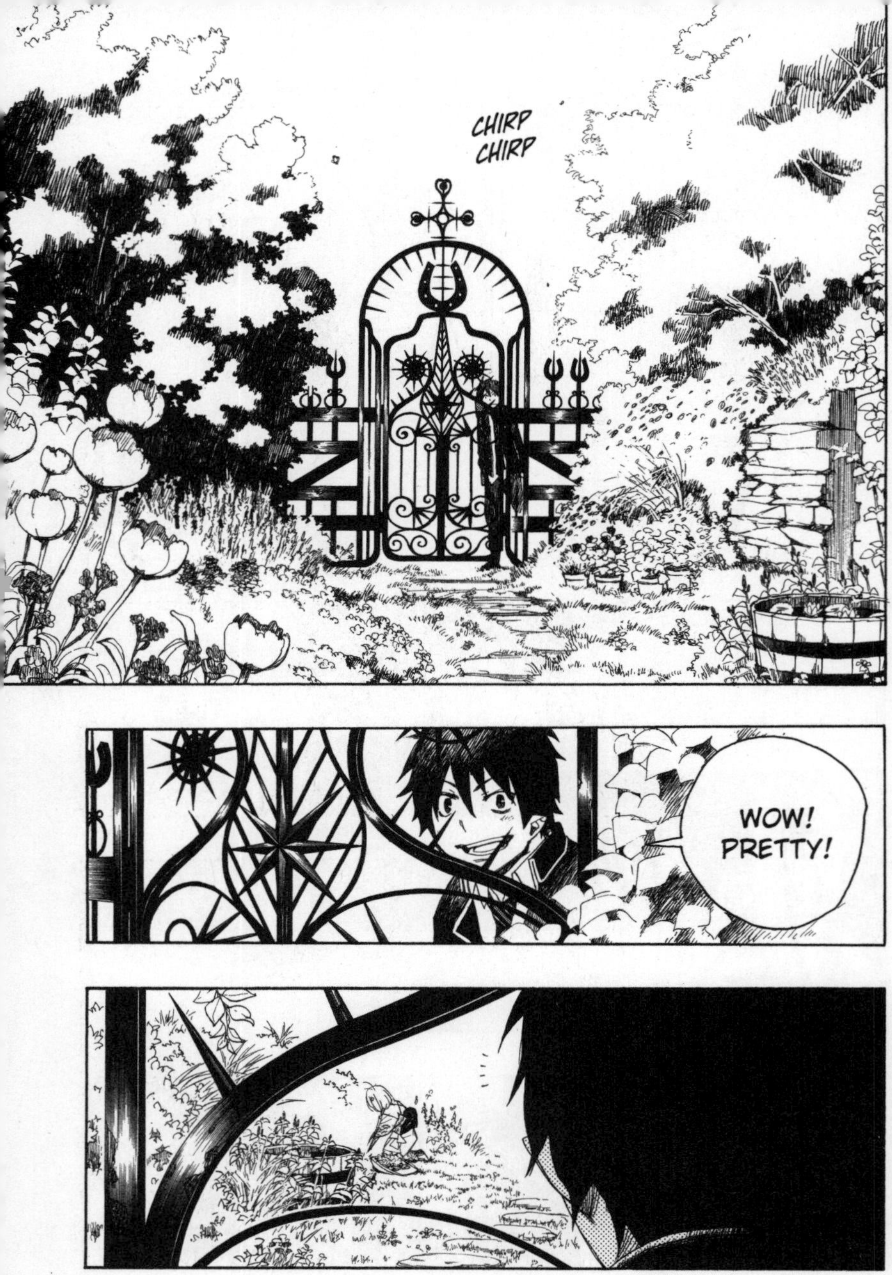
CHIRP CHIRP
WOW! PRETTY!

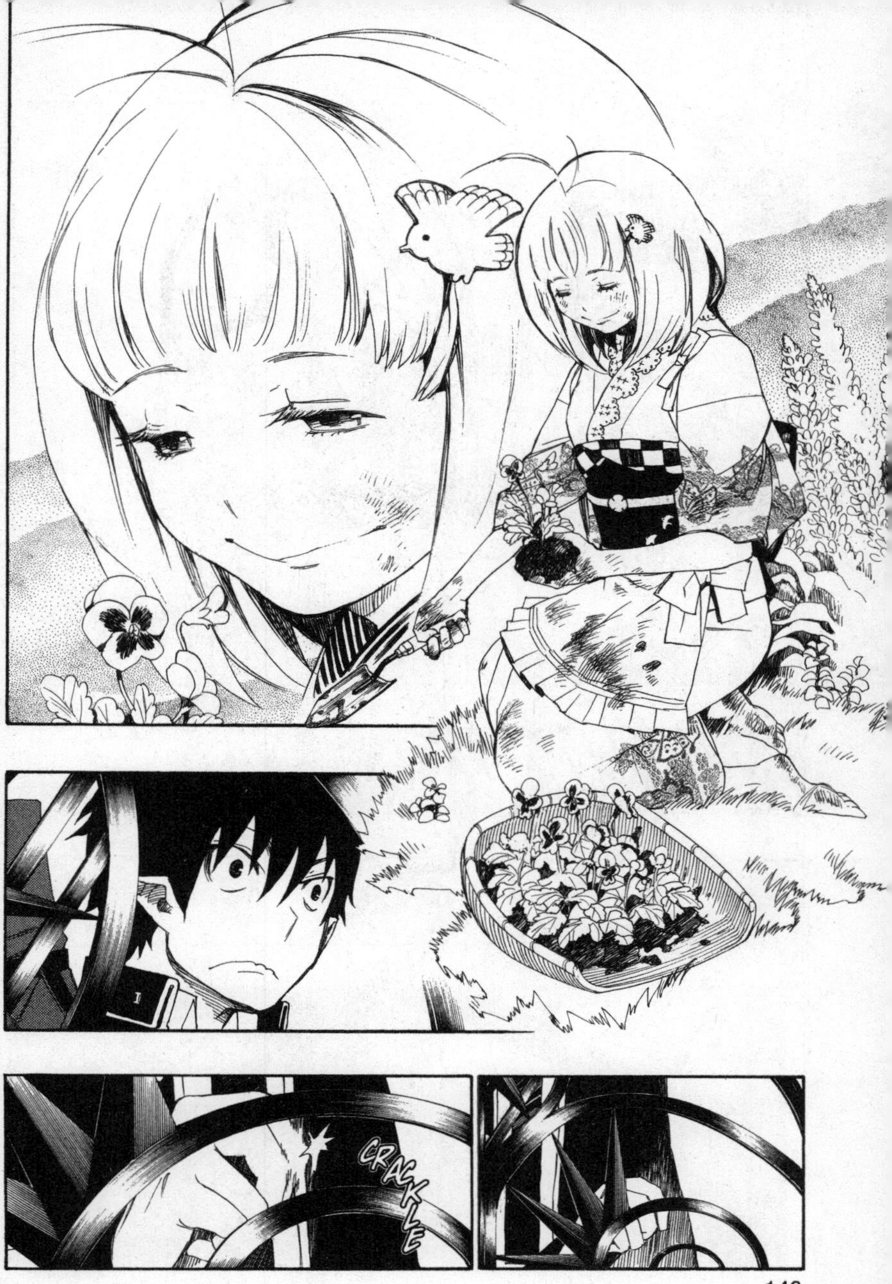
CRACKLE

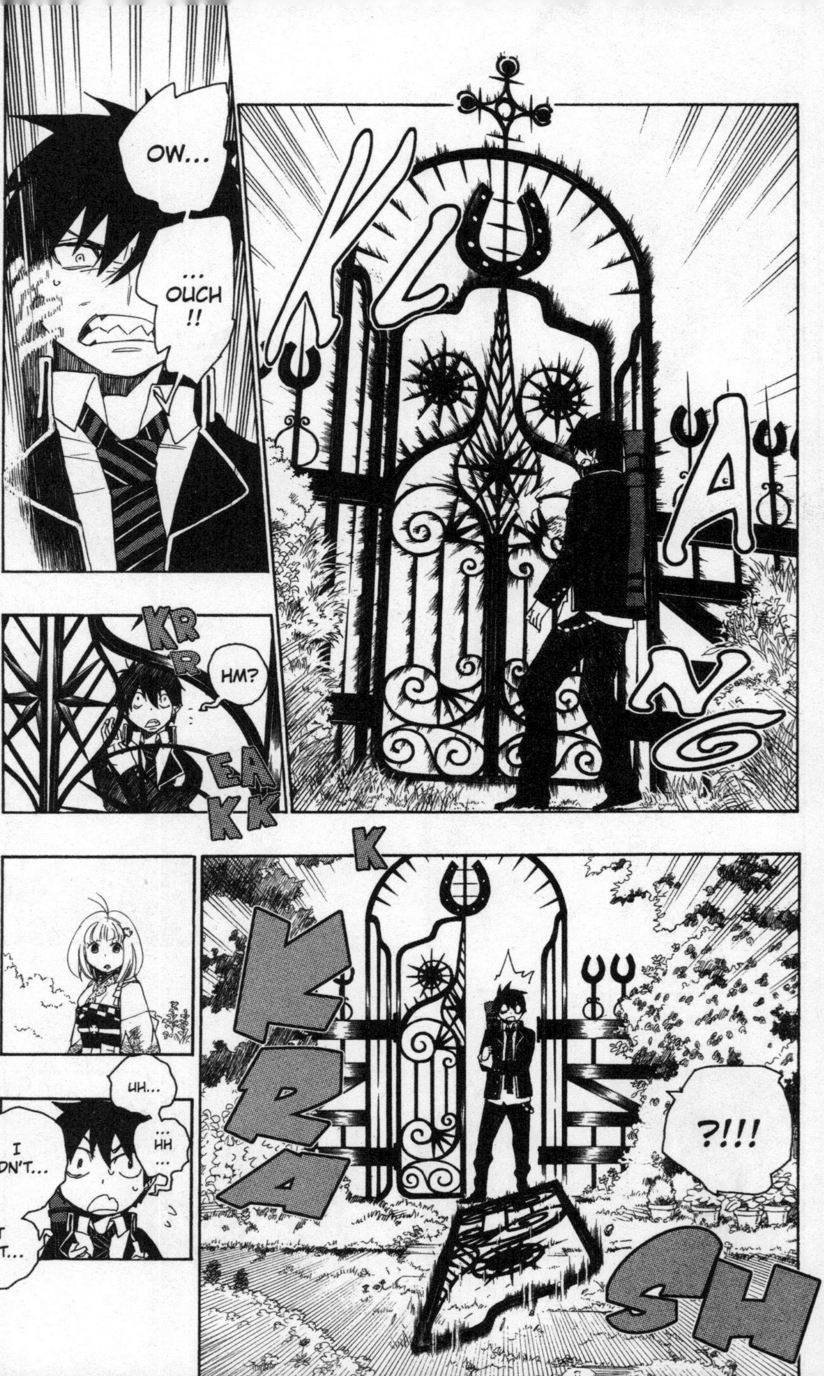
KLUANG
OW...
...OUCH!!
KRR
HM?
EAKK
KKRASH
?!!!
UH...
...HH...
I DIDN'T...
IT JUST...

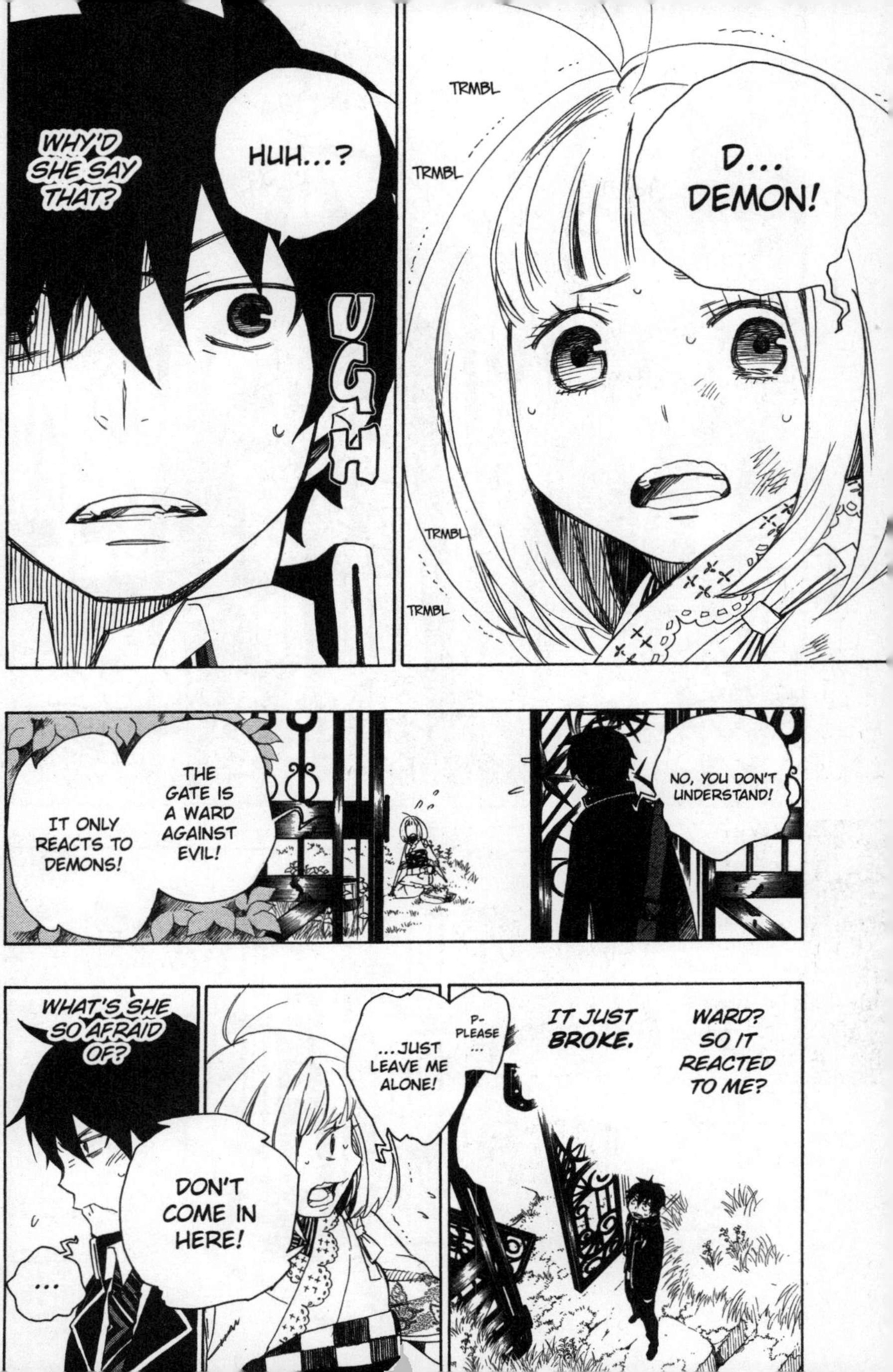

TRMBL
D... DEMON!
TRMBL
TRMBL
TRMBL
HUH...?
WHY'D SHE SAY THAT?
UGH
NO, YOU DON'T UNDERSTAND!
THE GATE IS A WARD AGAINST EVIL!
IT ONLY REACTS TO DEMONS!
WARD? SO IT REACTED TO ME?
IT JUST BROKE.
P-PLEASE ...
...JUST LEAVE ME ALONE!
DON'T COME IN HERE!
WHAT'S SHE SO AFRAID OF?
...

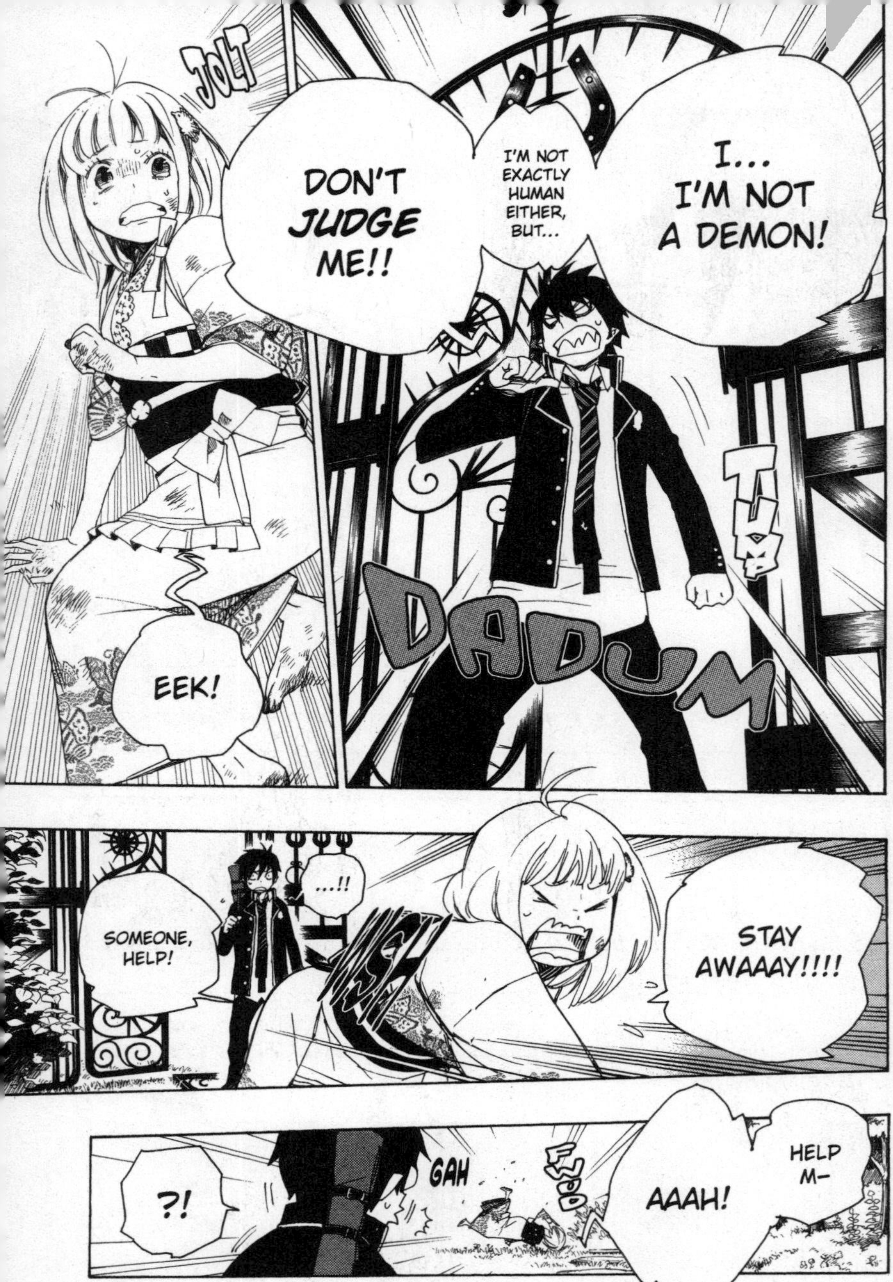
I... I'M NOT A DEMON!
I'M NOT EXACTLY HUMAN EITHER, BUT...
DON'T JUDGE ME!!
TUMP
DADUM
JOLT
EEK!
STAY AWAAAY!!!!
...!!
SOMEONE, HELP!
HELP M—
AAAH!
FWOO
GAH
?!

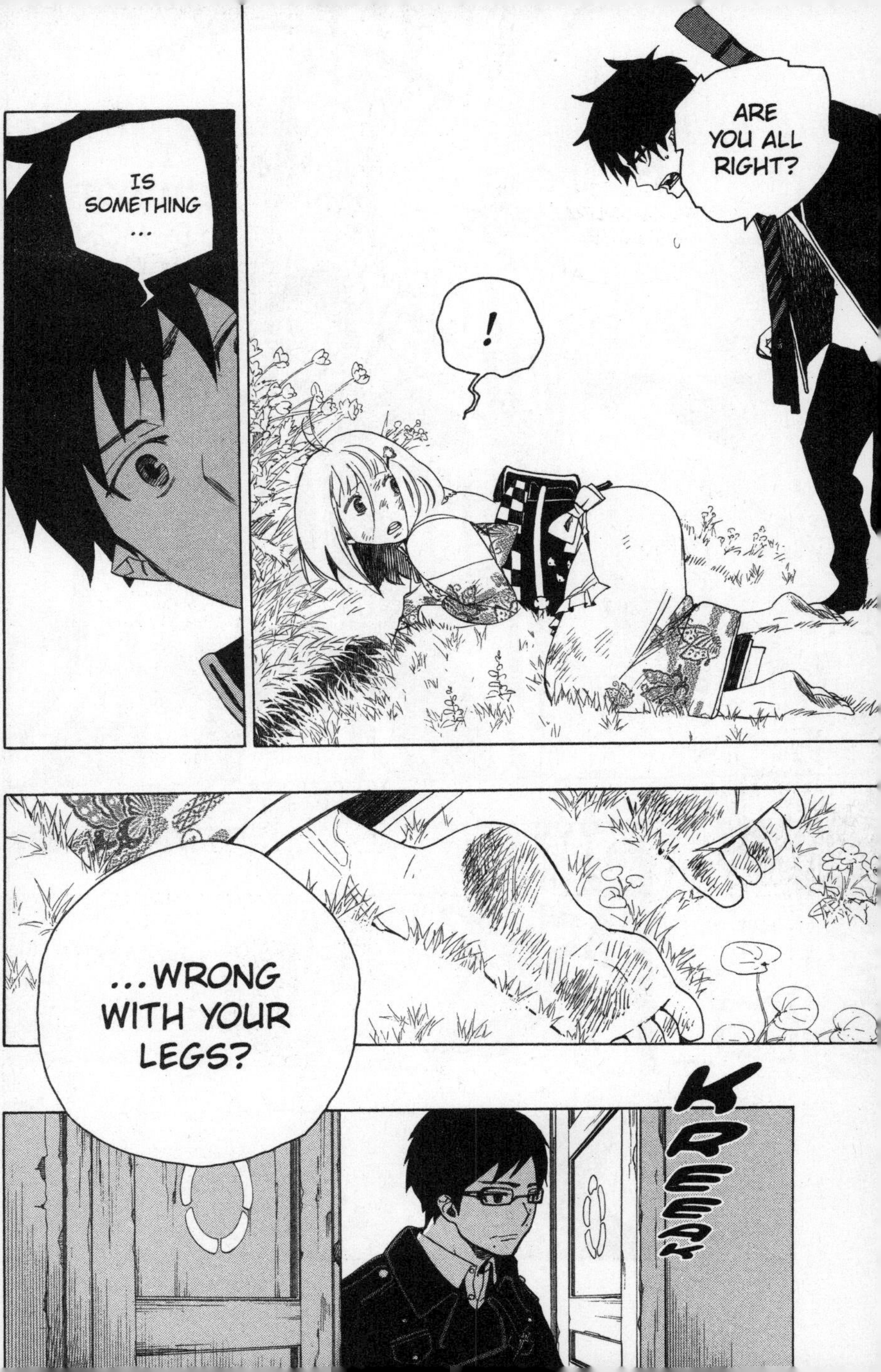
ARE YOU ALL RIGHT?
!
IS SOMETHING ...
...WRONG WITH YOUR LEGS?
KREEAK

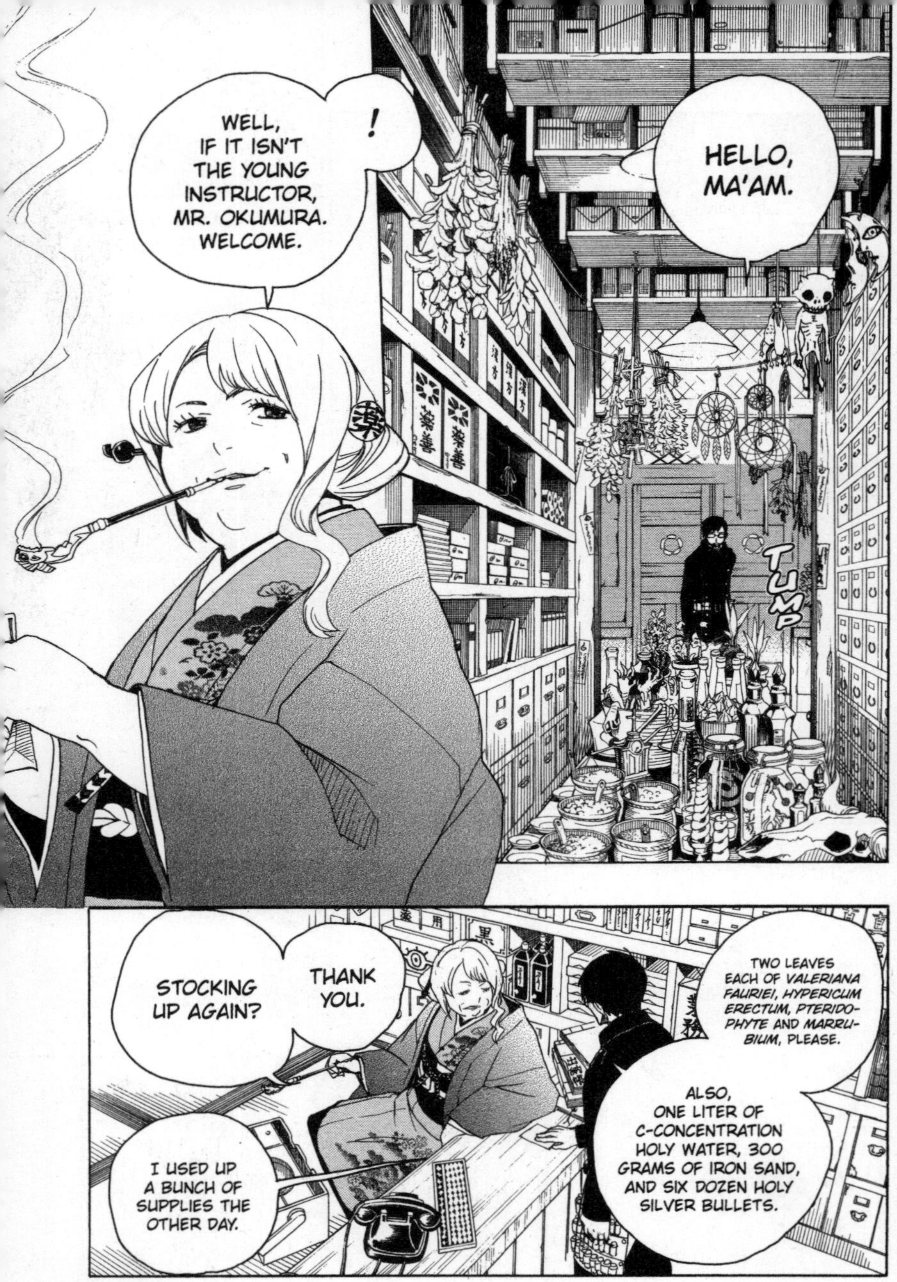
HELLO, MA'AM.
!
WELL, IF IT ISN'T THE YOUNG INSTRUCTOR, MR. OKUMURA. WELCOME.
TUMP
TWO LEAVES EACH OF *VALERIANA FAURIEI, HYPERICUM ERECTUM, PTERIDOPHYTE* AND *MARRUBIUM*, PLEASE.
ALSO, ONE LITER OF C-CONCENTRATION HOLY WATER, 300 GRAMS OF IRON SAND, AND SIX DOZEN HOLY SILVER BULLETS.
THANK YOU.
STOCKING UP AGAIN?
I USED UP A BUNCH OF SUPPLIES THE OTHER DAY.

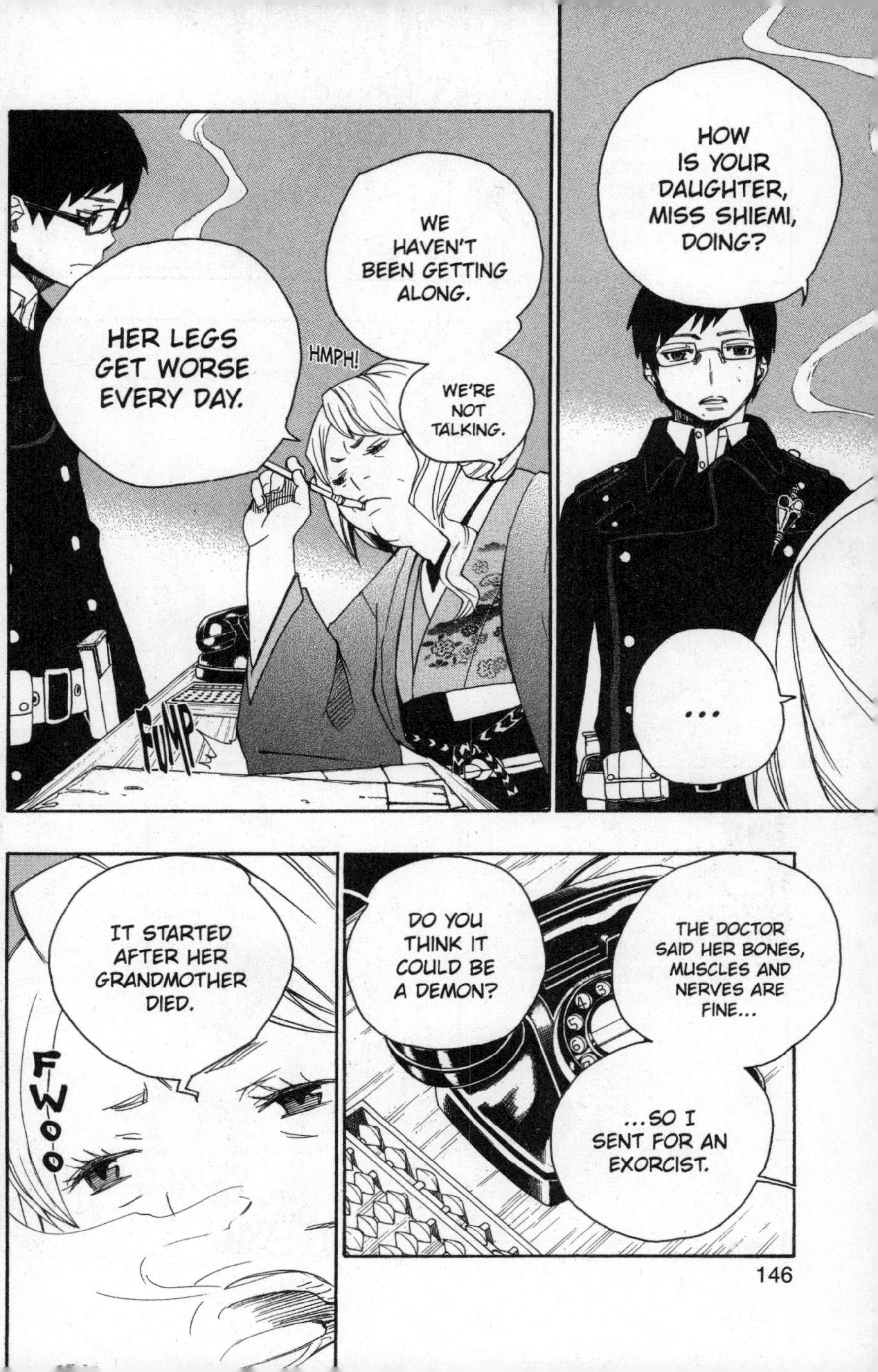
HOW IS YOUR DAUGHTER, MISS SHIEMI, DOING?
...
WE HAVEN'T BEEN GETTING ALONG.
WE'RE NOT TALKING.
HMPH!
HER LEGS GET WORSE EVERY DAY.
FUMP
THE DOCTOR SAID HER BONES, MUSCLES AND NERVES ARE FINE...
...SO I SENT FOR AN EXORCIST.
DO YOU THINK IT COULD BE A DEMON?
IT STARTED AFTER HER GRANDMOTHER DIED.
FWOO

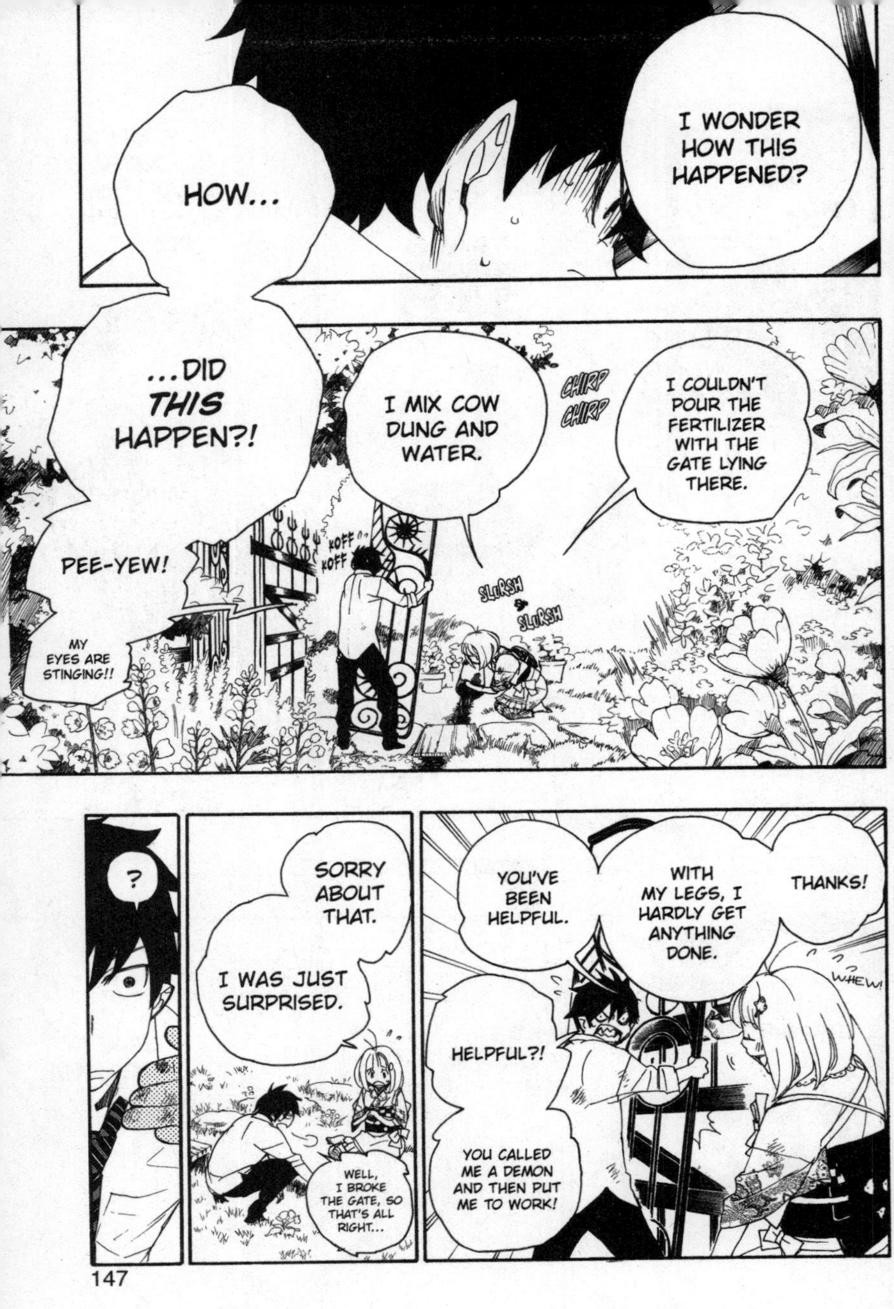
I WONDER HOW THIS HAPPENED?
HOW...
I COULDN'T POUR THE FERTILIZER WITH THE GATE LYING THERE.
CHIRP CHIRP
I MIX COW DUNG AND WATER.
SLURSH SLURSH
KOFF KOFF
...DID *THIS* HAPPEN?!
PEE-YEW!
MY EYES ARE STINGING!!
THANKS!
WITH MY LEGS, I HARDLY GET ANYTHING DONE.
YOU'VE BEEN HELPFUL.
WHEW!
HELPFUL?!
YOU CALLED ME A DEMON AND THEN PUT ME TO WORK!
SORRY ABOUT THAT.
I WAS JUST SURPRISED.
WELL, I BROKE THE GATE, SO THAT'S ALL RIGHT...
?

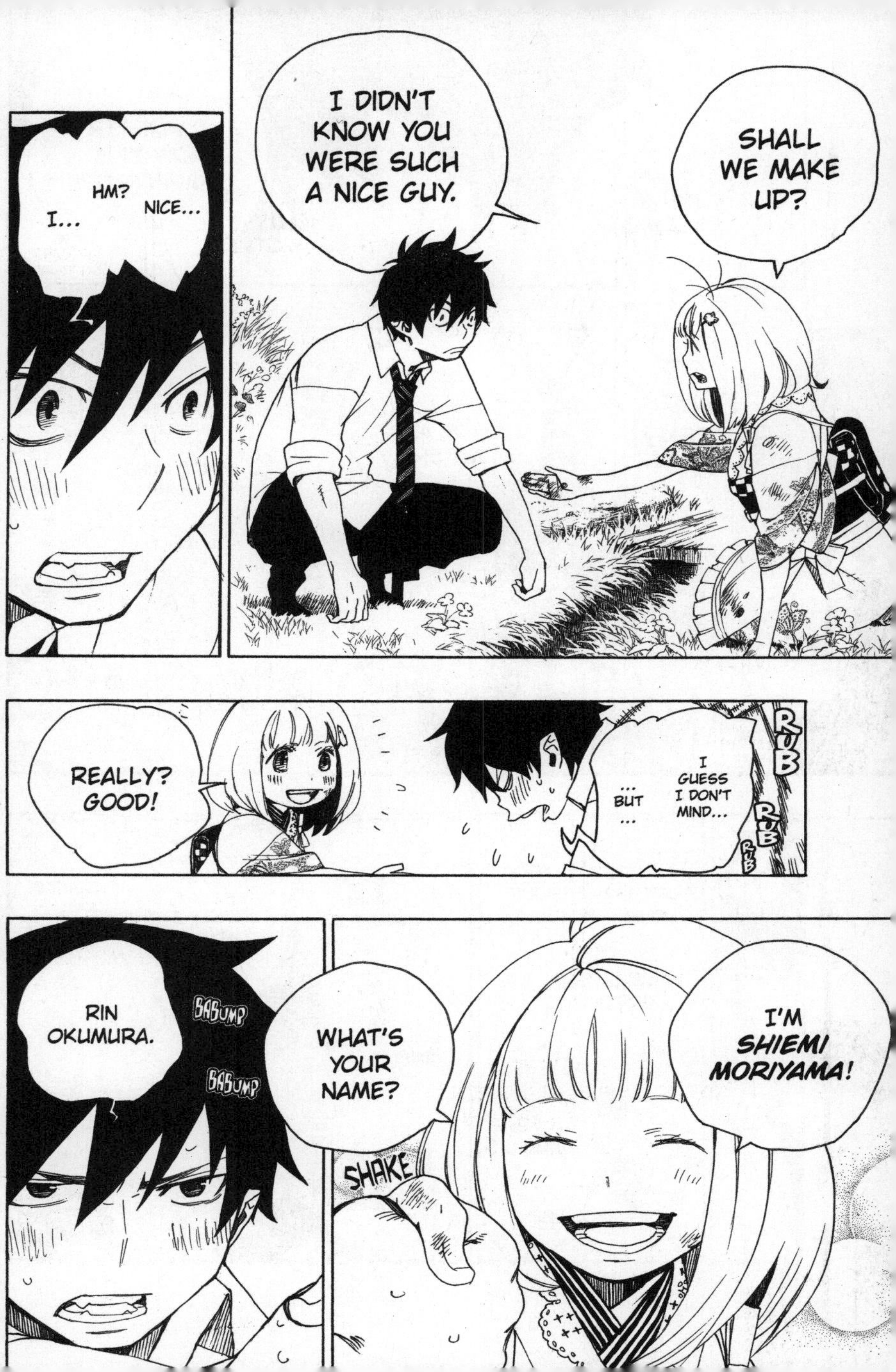
SHALL WE MAKE UP?
I DIDN'T KNOW YOU WERE SUCH A NICE GUY.
HM? I... NICE...
RUB RUB RUB
I GUESS I DON'T MIND...
...BUT...
REALLY? GOOD!
I'M SHIEMI MORIYAMA!
WHAT'S YOUR NAME?
SHAKE
BABUMP BABUMP
RIN OKUMURA.

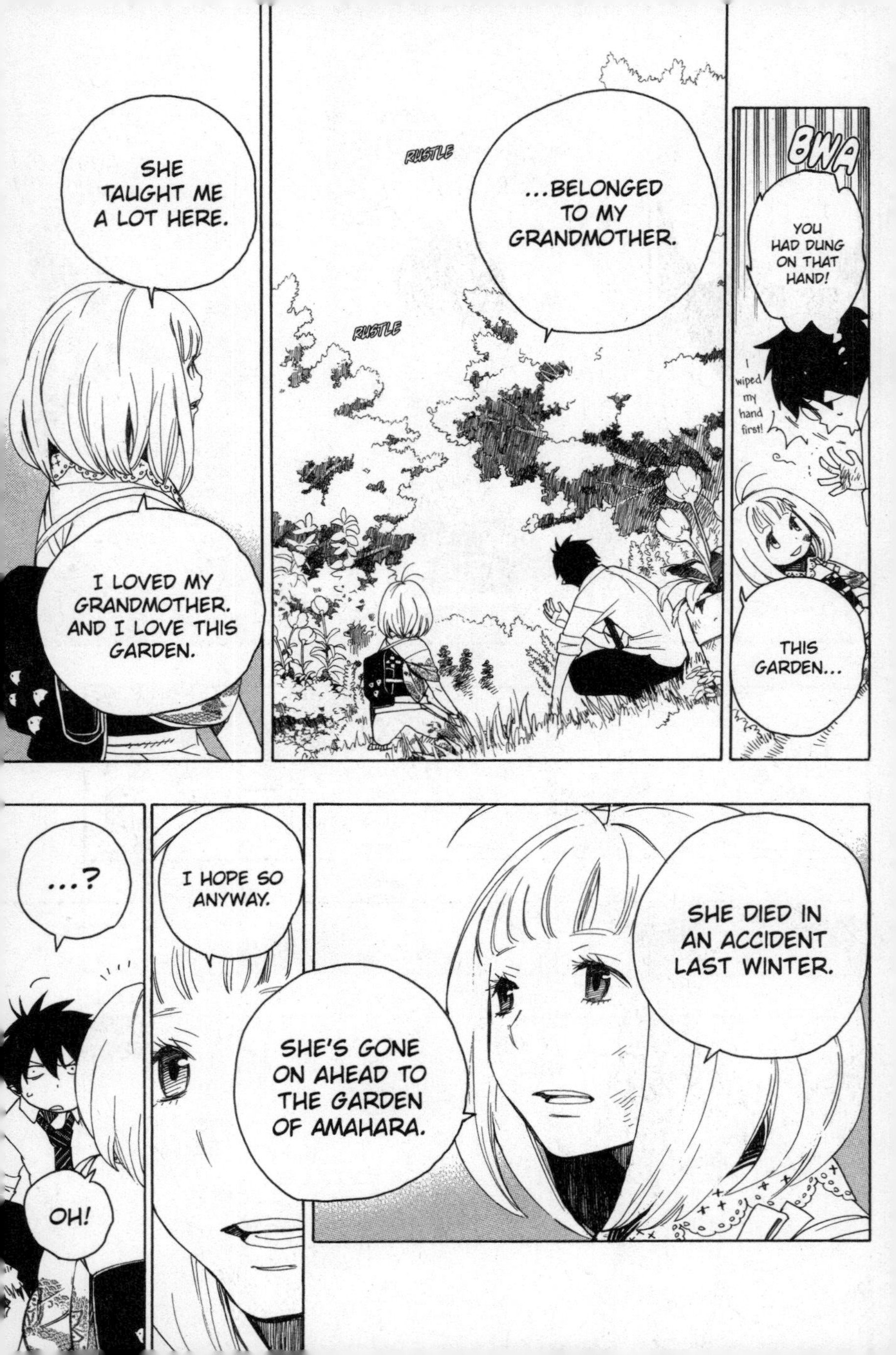

BWA
YOU HAD DUNG ON THAT HAND!
I wiped my hand first!
THIS GARDEN...
RUSTLE
RUSTLE
...BELONGED TO MY GRANDMOTHER.
SHE TAUGHT ME A LOT HERE.
I LOVED MY GRANDMOTHER. AND I LOVE THIS GARDEN.
SHE DIED IN AN ACCIDENT LAST WINTER.
SHE'S GONE ON AHEAD TO THE GARDEN OF AMAHARA.
I HOPE SO ANYWAY.
...?
OH!

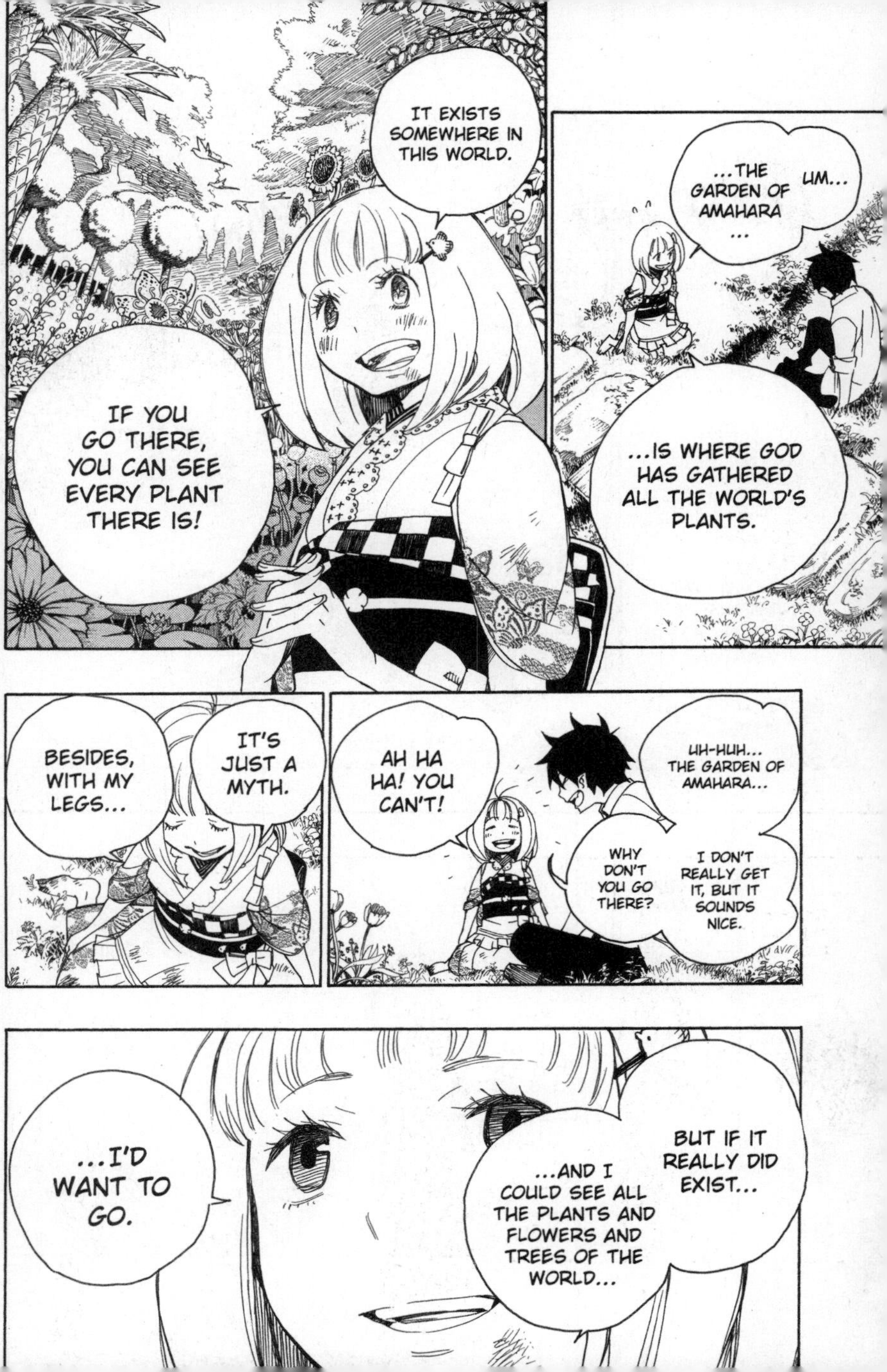
UM...
...THE GARDEN OF AMAHARA...
...IS WHERE GOD HAS GATHERED ALL THE WORLD'S PLANTS.
IT EXISTS SOMEWHERE IN THIS WORLD.
IF YOU GO THERE, YOU CAN SEE EVERY PLANT THERE IS!
UH-HUH... THE GARDEN OF AMAHARA...
I DON'T REALLY GET IT, BUT IT SOUNDS NICE.
WHY DON'T YOU GO THERE?
AH HA HA! YOU CAN'T!
IT'S JUST A MYTH.
BESIDES, WITH MY LEGS...
BUT IF IT REALLY DID EXIST...
...AND I COULD SEE ALL THE PLANTS AND FLOWERS AND TREES OF THE WORLD...
...I'D WANT TO GO.

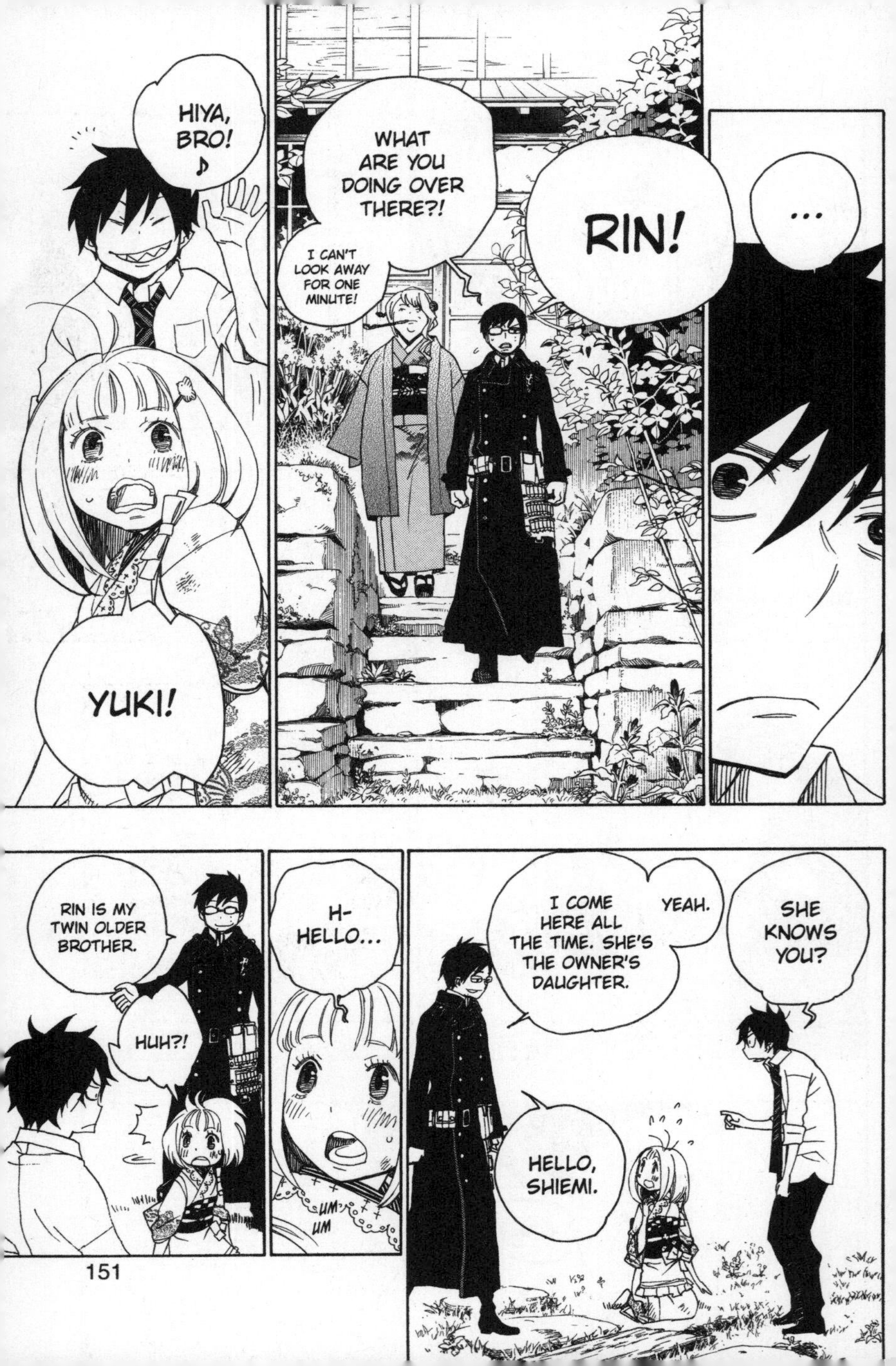
...
RIN!
WHAT ARE YOU DOING OVER THERE?!
I CAN'T LOOK AWAY FOR ONE MINUTE!
HIYA, BRO! ♪
YUKI!
SHE KNOWS YOU?
YEAH.
I COME HERE ALL THE TIME. SHE'S THE OWNER'S DAUGHTER.
HELLO, SHIEMI.
H- HELLO...
UM UM
RIN IS MY TWIN OLDER BROTHER.
HUH?!

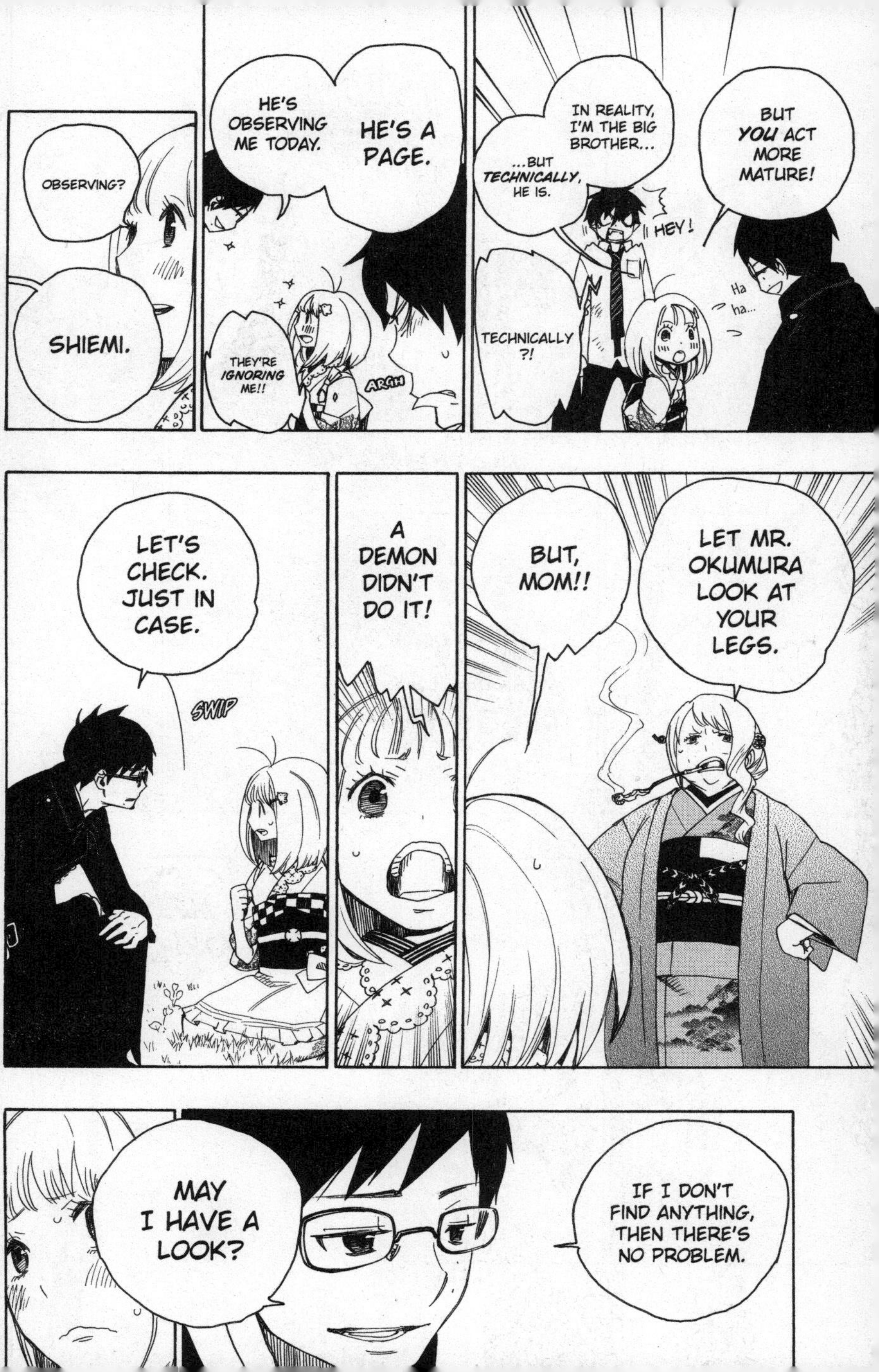
BUT YOU ACT MORE MATURE!
IN REALITY, I'M THE BIG BROTHER...
...BUT TECHNICALLY, HE IS.
HEY!
Ha ha...
TECHNICALLY ?!
HE'S A PAGE.
HE'S OBSERVING ME TODAY.
THEY'RE IGNORING ME!!
ARGH
OBSERVING?
SHIEMI.
LET MR. OKUMURA LOOK AT YOUR LEGS.
BUT, MOM!!
A DEMON DIDN'T DO IT!
LET'S CHECK. JUST IN CASE.
SWIP
IF I DON'T FIND ANYTHING, THEN THERE'S NO PROBLEM.
MAY I HAVE A LOOK?

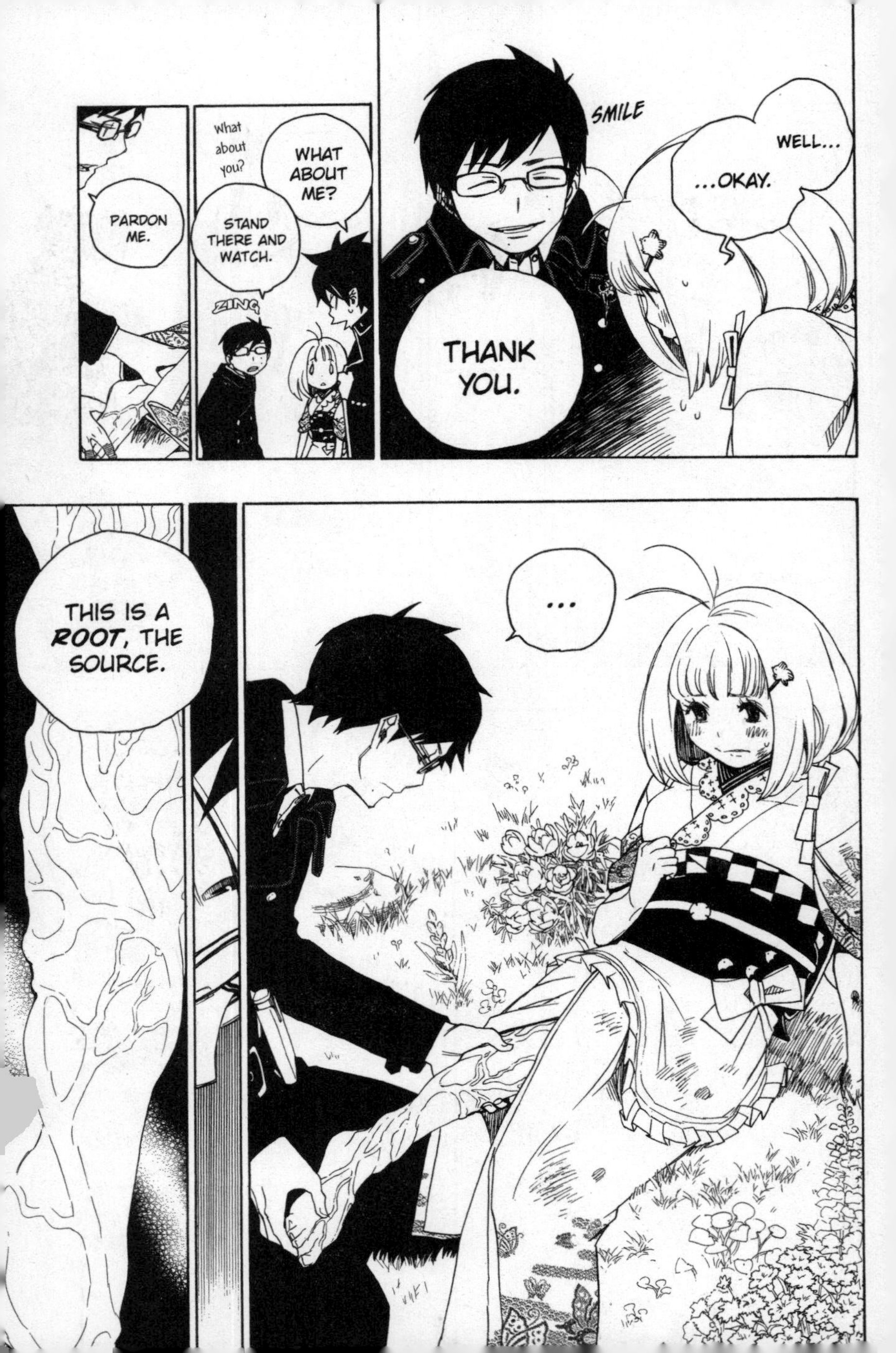
WELL...
...OKAY.
SMILE
THANK YOU.
WHAT ABOUT ME?
What about you?
STAND THERE AND WATCH.
ZING
PARDON ME.
...
THIS IS A *ROOT*, THE SOURCE.

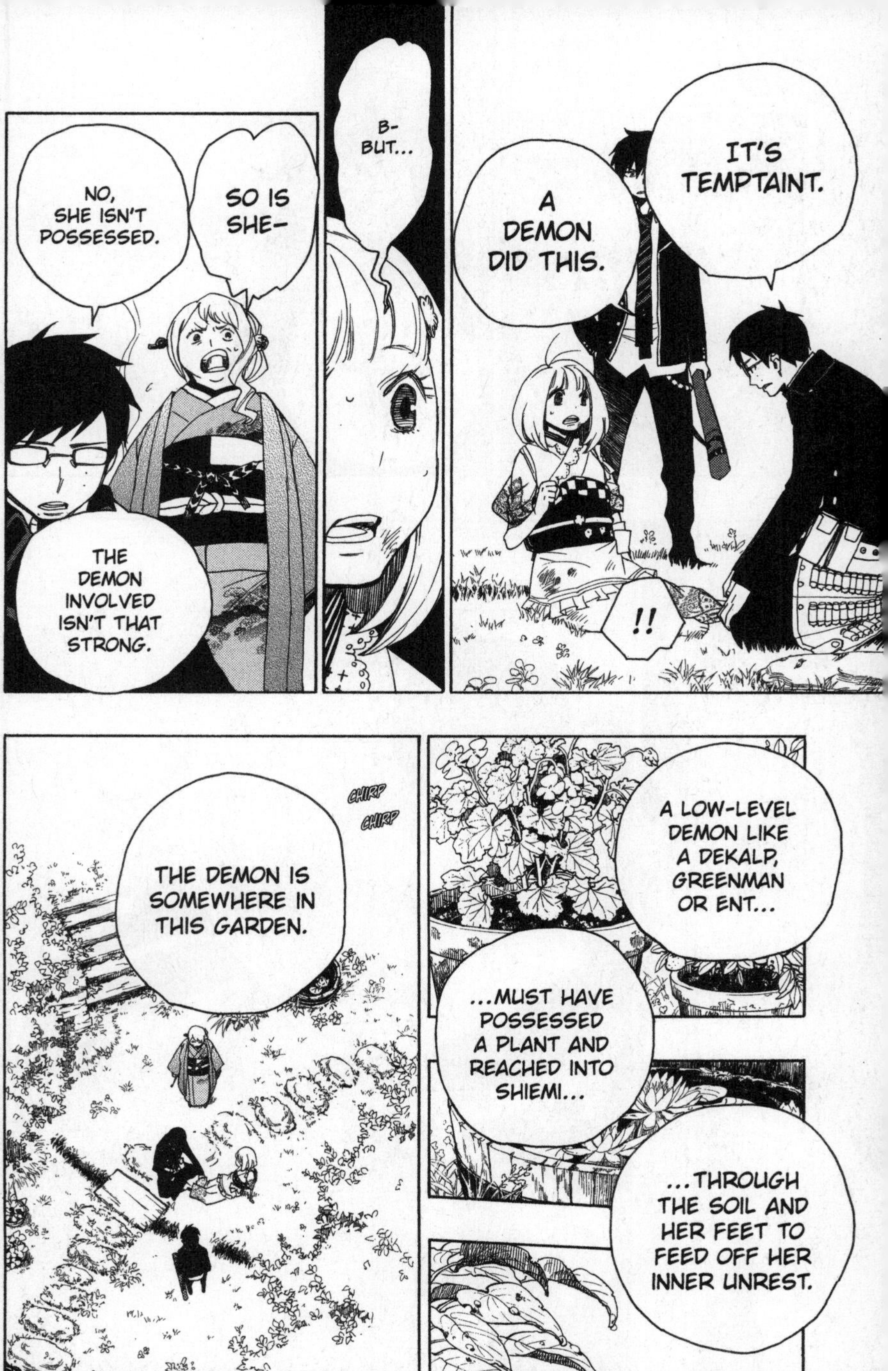
IT'S TEMPTAINT.
A DEMON DID THIS.
!!
B- BUT...
SO IS SHE-
NO, SHE ISN'T POSSESSED.
THE DEMON INVOLVED ISN'T THAT STRONG.
A LOW-LEVEL DEMON LIKE A DEKALP, GREENMAN OR ENT...
...MUST HAVE POSSESSED A PLANT AND REACHED INTO SHIEMI...
...THROUGH THE SOIL AND HER FEET TO FEED OFF HER INNER UNREST.
CHIRP CHIRP
THE DEMON IS SOMEWHERE IN THIS GARDEN.

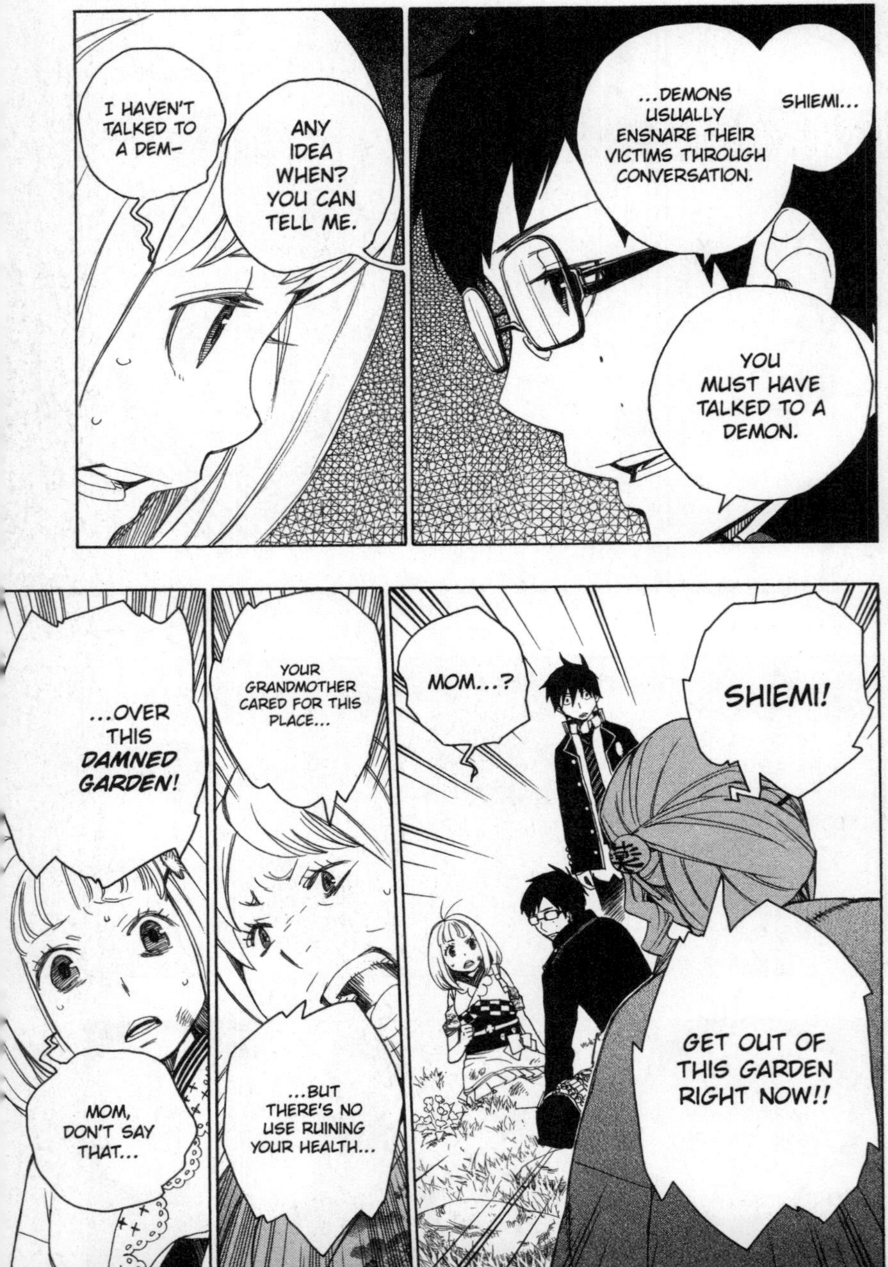
SHIEMI...
...DEMONS USUALLY ENSNARE THEIR VICTIMS THROUGH CONVERSATION.
YOU MUST HAVE TALKED TO A DEMON.
I HAVEN'T TALKED TO A DEM-
ANY IDEA WHEN? YOU CAN TELL ME.
SHIEMI!
MOM...?
GET OUT OF THIS GARDEN RIGHT NOW!!
YOUR GRANDMOTHER CARED FOR THIS PLACE...
...BUT THERE'S NO USE RUINING YOUR HEALTH...
...OVER THIS *DAMNED GARDEN!*
MOM, DON'T SAY THAT...

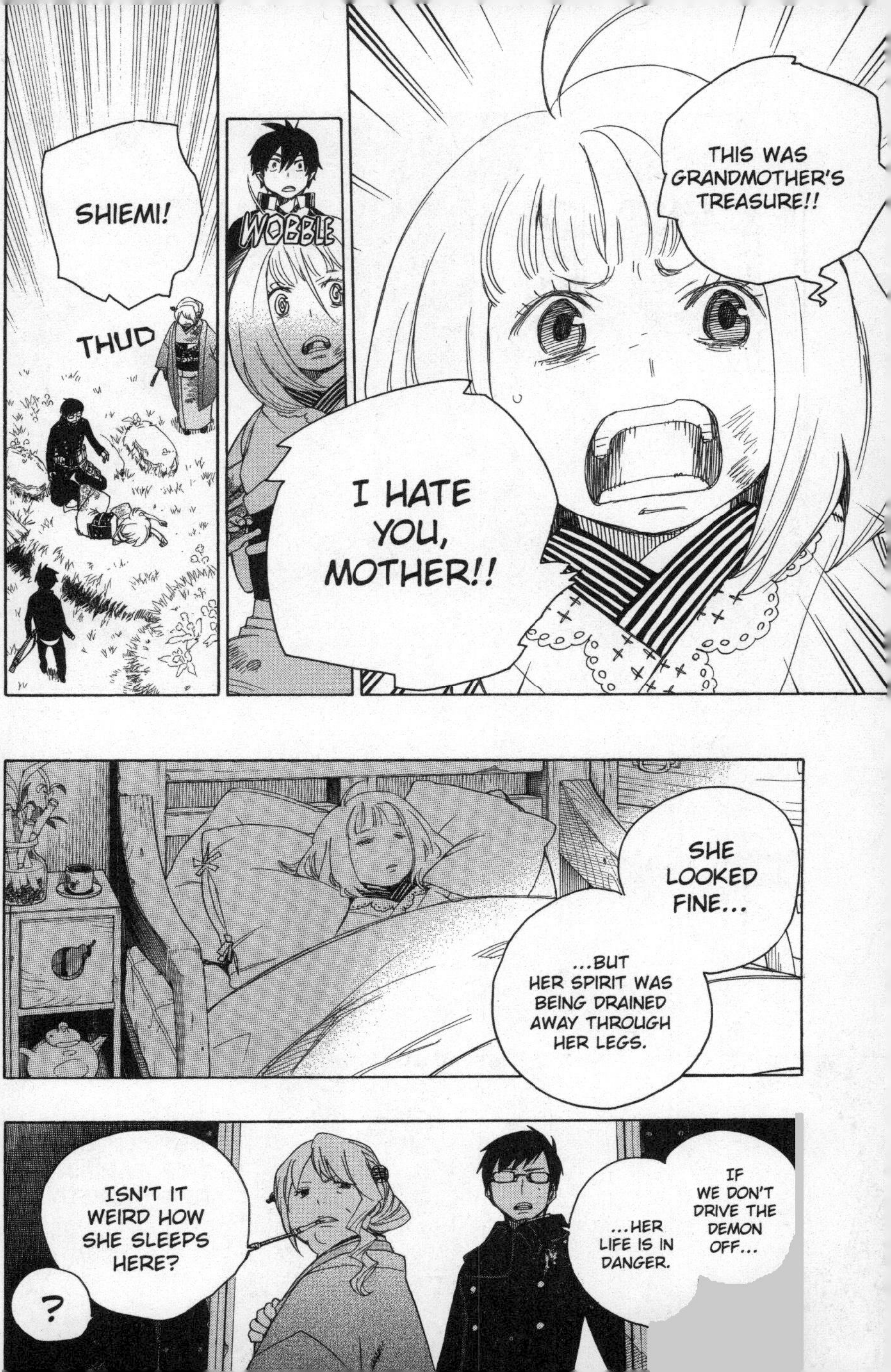
THIS WAS GRANDMOTHER'S TREASURE!!
I HATE YOU, MOTHER!!
WOBBLE
SHIEMI!
THUD
SHE LOOKED FINE...
...BUT HER SPIRIT WAS BEING DRAINED AWAY THROUGH HER LEGS.
IF WE DON'T DRIVE THE DEMON OFF...
...HER LIFE IS IN DANGER.
ISN'T IT WEIRD HOW SHE SLEEPS HERE?
?

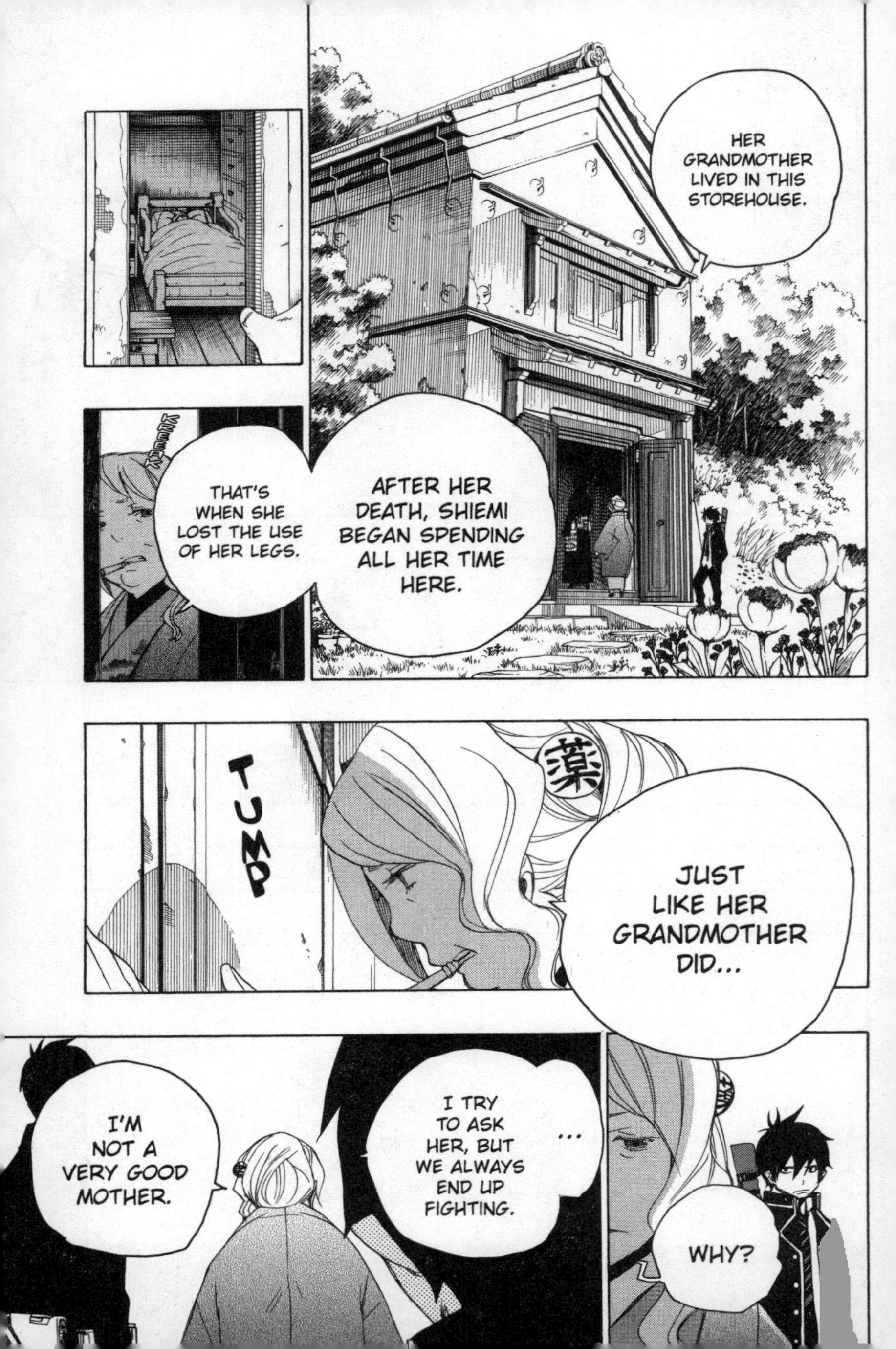
HER GRANDMOTHER LIVED IN THIS STOREHOUSE.
AFTER HER DEATH, SHIEMI BEGAN SPENDING ALL HER TIME HERE.
THAT'S WHEN SHE LOST THE USE OF HER LEGS.
JUST LIKE HER GRANDMOTHER DID...
TUMP
WHY?
...
I TRY TO ASK HER, BUT WE ALWAYS END UP FIGHTING.
I'M NOT A VERY GOOD MOTHER.

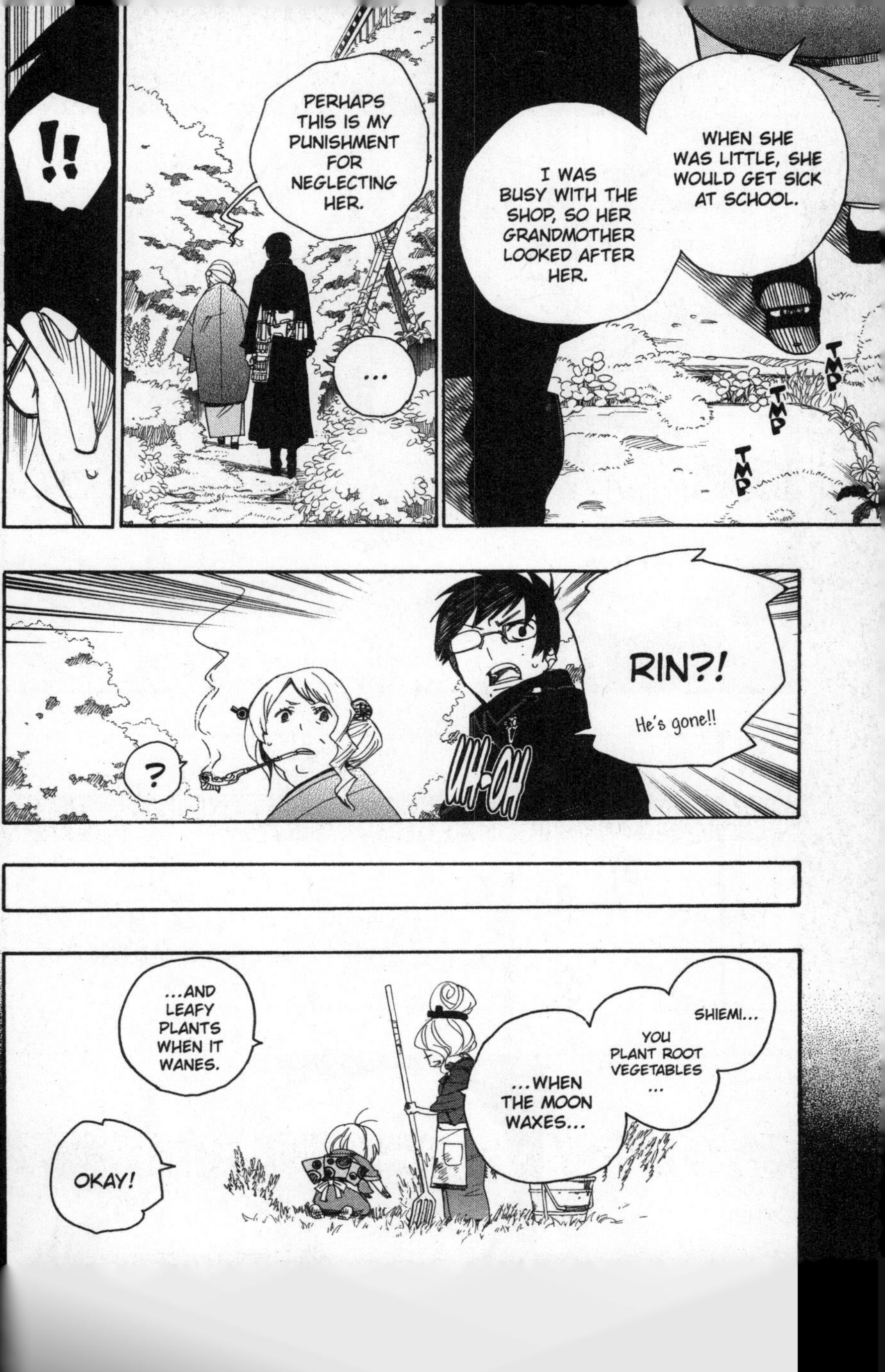
WHEN SHE WAS LITTLE, SHE WOULD GET SICK AT SCHOOL.
I WAS BUSY WITH THE SHOP, SO HER GRANDMOTHER LOOKED AFTER HER.
TMP
TMP
TMP
PERHAPS THIS IS MY PUNISHMENT FOR NEGLECTING HER.
...
!!
RIN?!
He's gone!!
UH-OH
?
SHIEMI...
YOU PLANT ROOT VEGETABLES ...
...WHEN THE MOON WAXES...
...AND LEAFY PLANTS WHEN IT WANES.
OKAY!

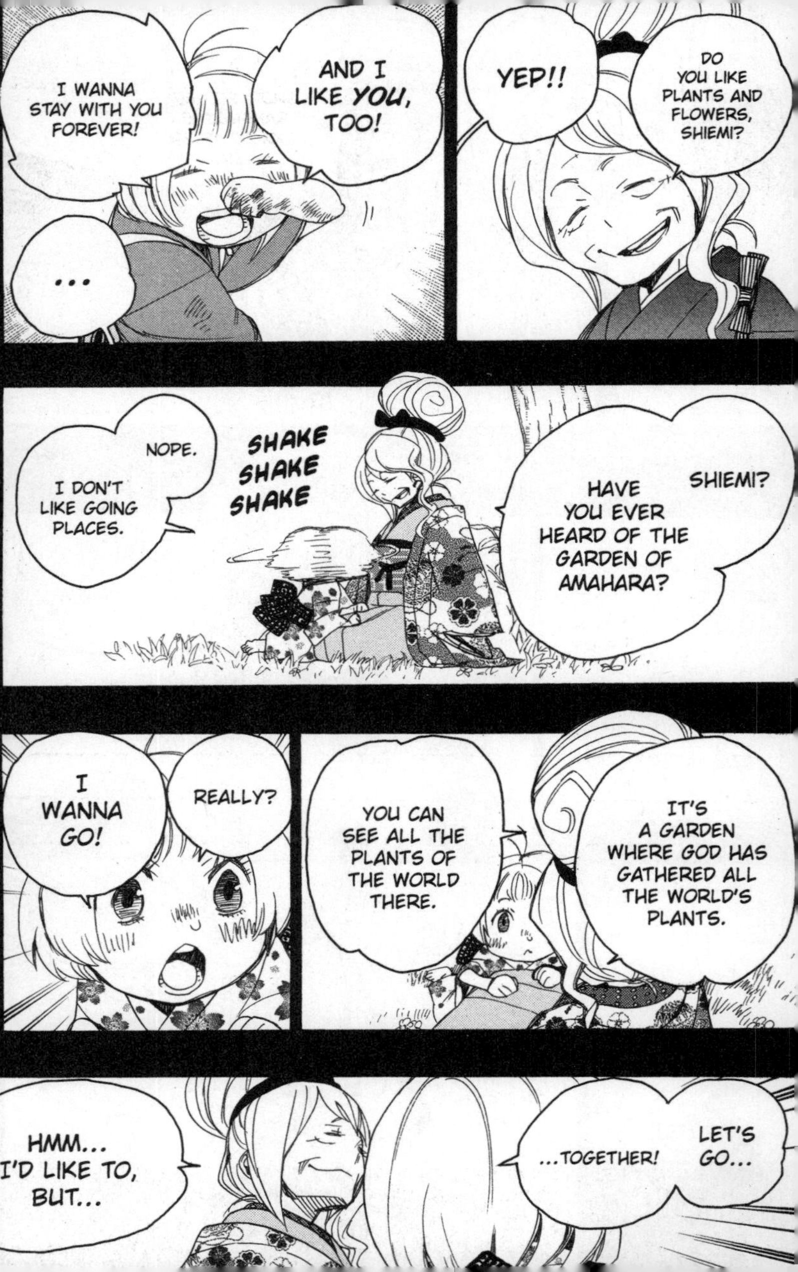
DO YOU LIKE PLANTS AND FLOWERS, SHIEMI?
YEP!!
AND I LIKE YOU, TOO!
I WANNA STAY WITH YOU FOREVER!
...
SHIEMI?
HAVE YOU EVER HEARD OF THE GARDEN OF AMAHARA?
SHAKE SHAKE SHAKE
NOPE.
I DON'T LIKE GOING PLACES.
IT'S A GARDEN WHERE GOD HAS GATHERED ALL THE WORLD'S PLANTS.
YOU CAN SEE ALL THE PLANTS OF THE WORLD THERE.
REALLY?
I WANNA GO!
LET'S GO...
...TOGETHER!
HMM... I'D LIKE TO, BUT...

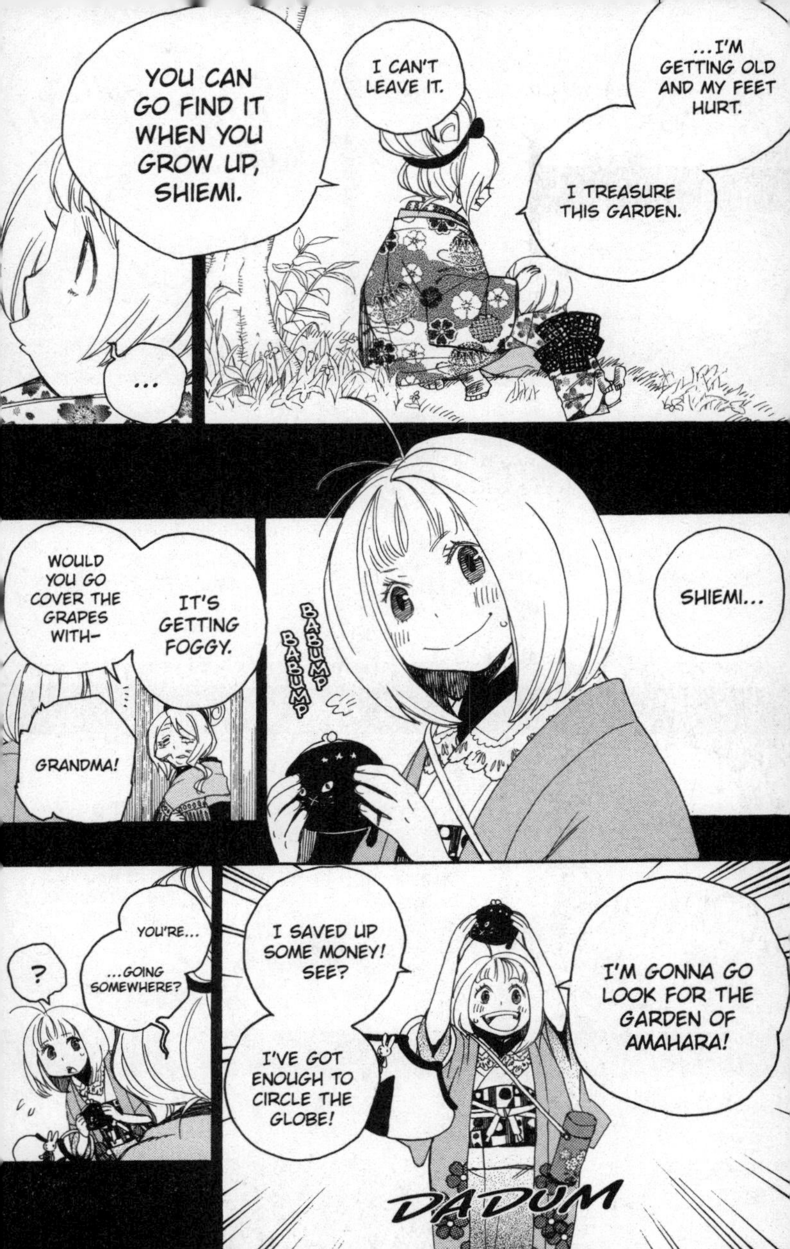
...I'M GETTING OLD AND MY FEET HURT.
I TREASURE THIS GARDEN.
I CAN'T LEAVE IT.
YOU CAN GO FIND IT WHEN YOU GROW UP, SHIEMI.
...
SHIEMI...
BABUMP BABUMP
IT'S GETTING FOGGY.
WOULD YOU GO COVER THE GRAPES WITH-
GRANDMA!
I'M GONNA GO LOOK FOR THE GARDEN OF AMAHARA!
I SAVED UP SOME MONEY! SEE?
I'VE GOT ENOUGH TO CIRCLE THE GLOBE!
DADUM
YOU'RE...
...GOING SOMEWHERE?
?

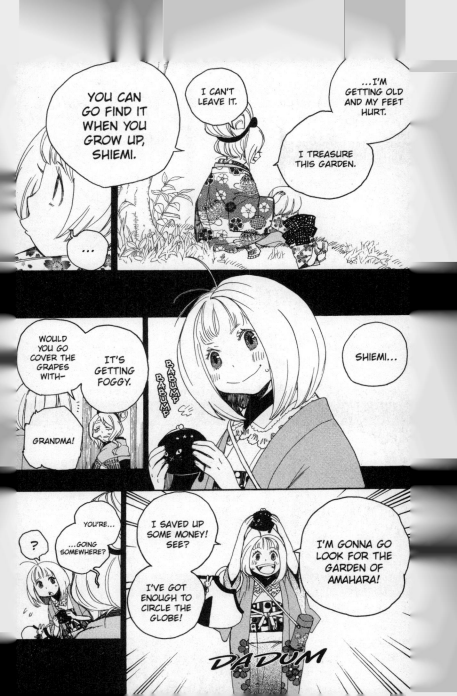

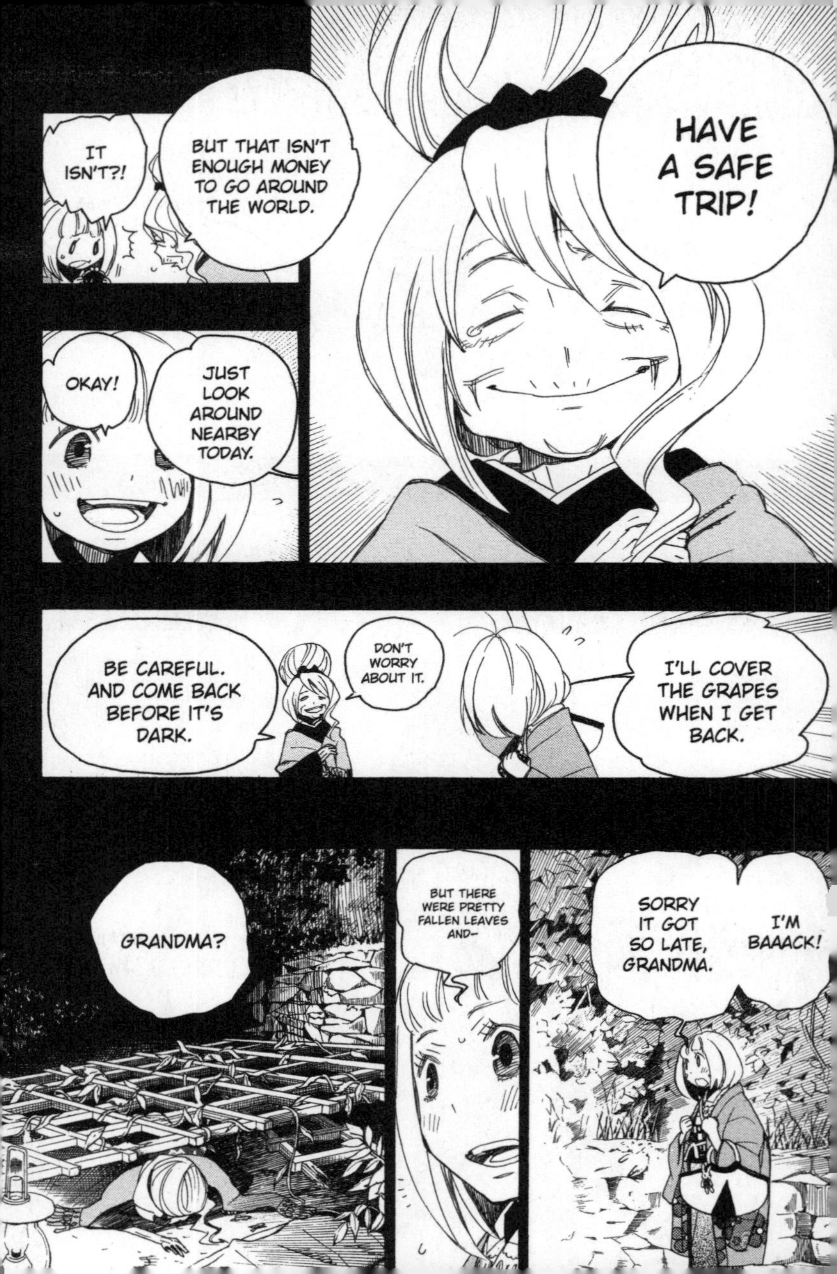
HAVE A SAFE TRIP!
BUT THAT ISN'T ENOUGH MONEY TO GO AROUND THE WORLD.
IT ISN'T?!
JUST LOOK AROUND NEARBY TODAY.
OKAY!
I'LL COVER THE GRAPES WHEN I GET BACK.
DON'T WORRY ABOUT IT.
BE CAREFUL. AND COME BACK BEFORE IT'S DARK.
I'M BAAACK!
SORRY IT GOT SO LATE, GRANDMA.
BUT THERE WERE PRETTY FALLEN LEAVES AND–
GRANDMA?

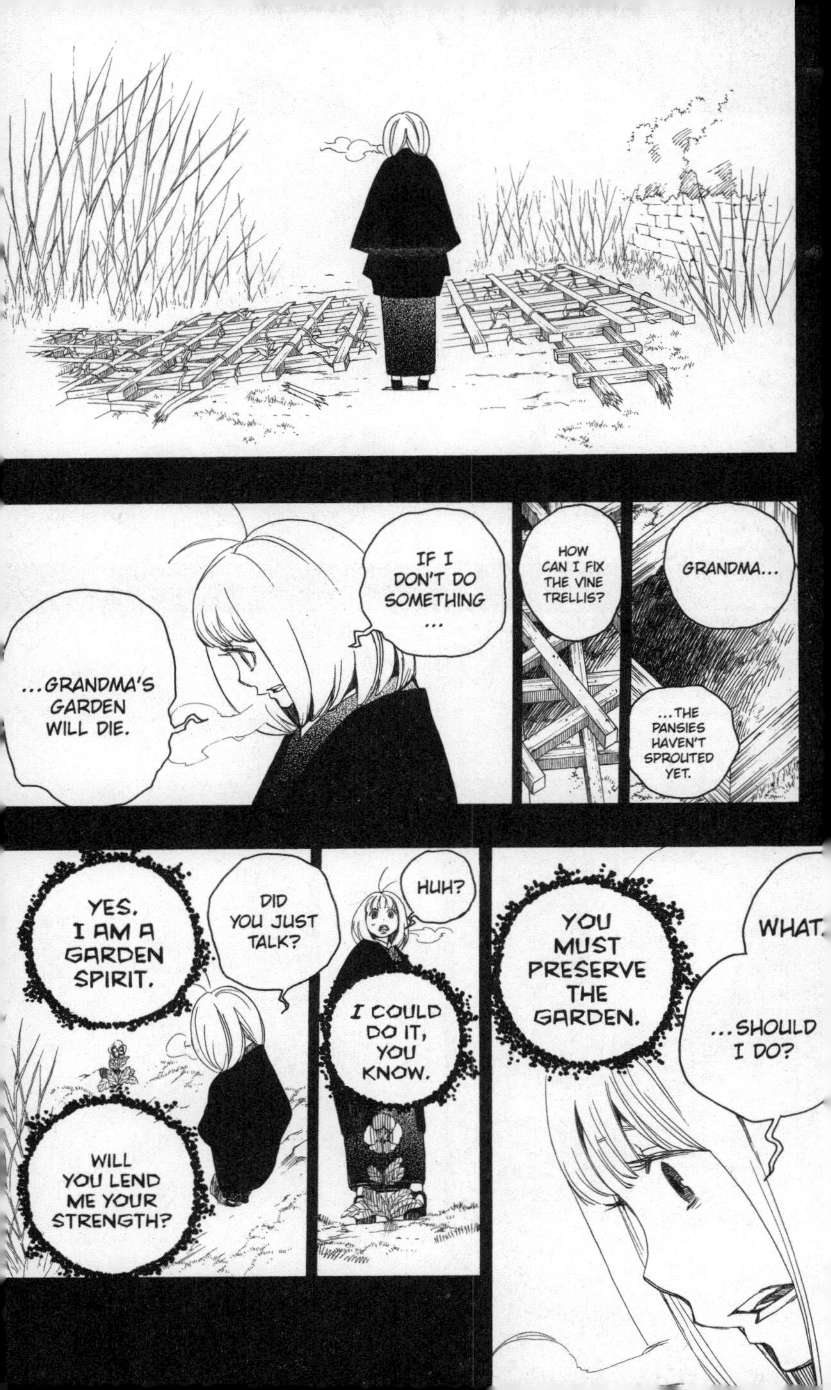
GRANDMA...
...THE PANSIES HAVEN'T SPROUTED YET.
HOW CAN I FIX THE VINE TRELLIS?
IF I DON'T DO SOMETHING...
...GRANDMA'S GARDEN WILL DIE.
WHAT
...SHOULD I DO?
YOU MUST PRESERVE THE GARDEN.
HUH?
I COULD DO IT, YOU KNOW.
DID YOU JUST TALK?
YES. I AM A GARDEN SPIRIT.
WILL YOU LEND ME YOUR STRENGTH?

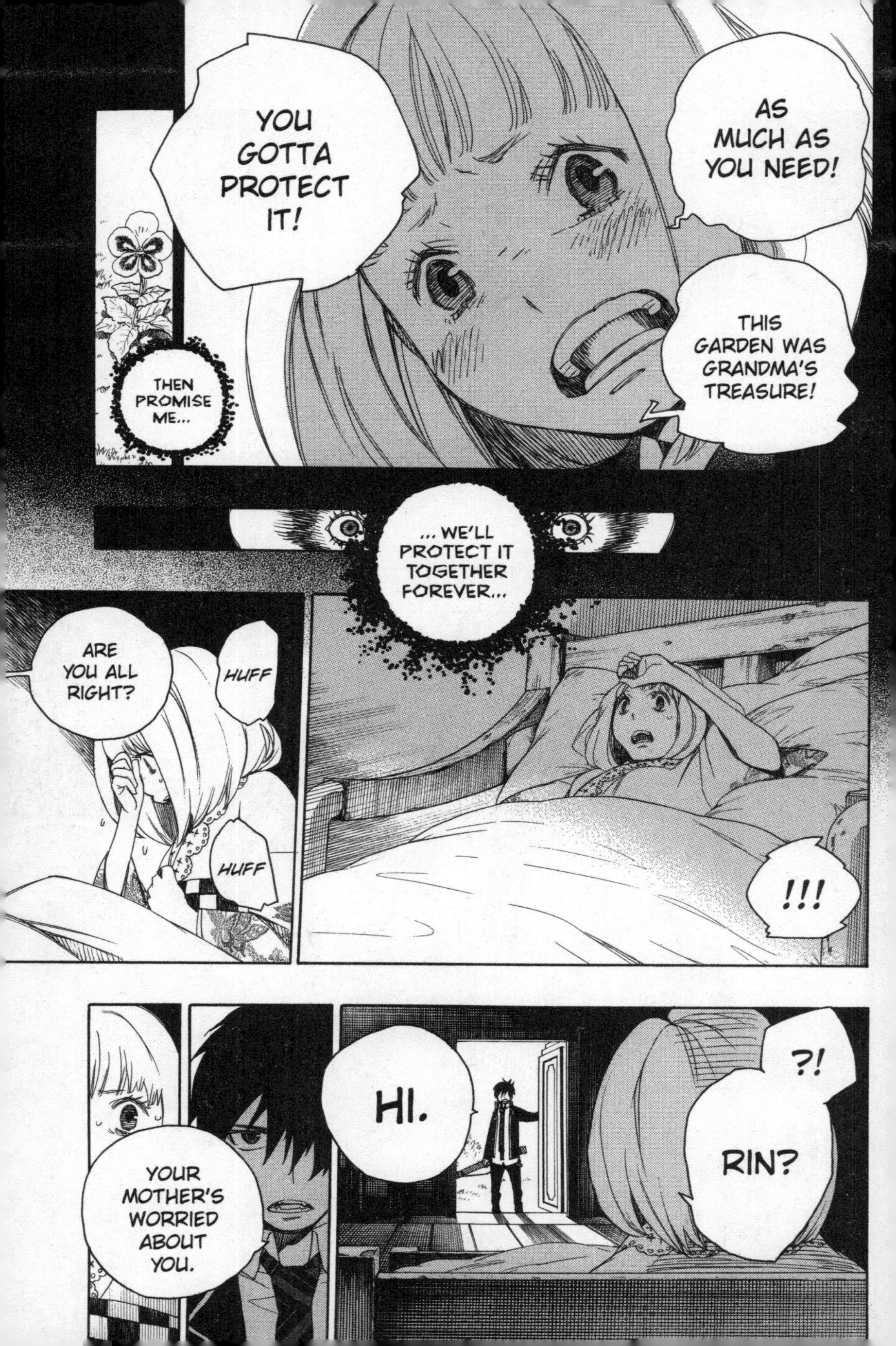
AS MUCH AS YOU NEED!
YOU GOTTA PROTECT IT!
THIS GARDEN WAS GRANDMA'S TREASURE!
THEN PROMISE ME...
... WE'LL PROTECT IT TOGETHER FOREVER...
!!!
HUFF
ARE YOU ALL RIGHT?
HUFF
?!
RIN?
HI.
YOUR MOTHER'S WORRIED ABOUT YOU.

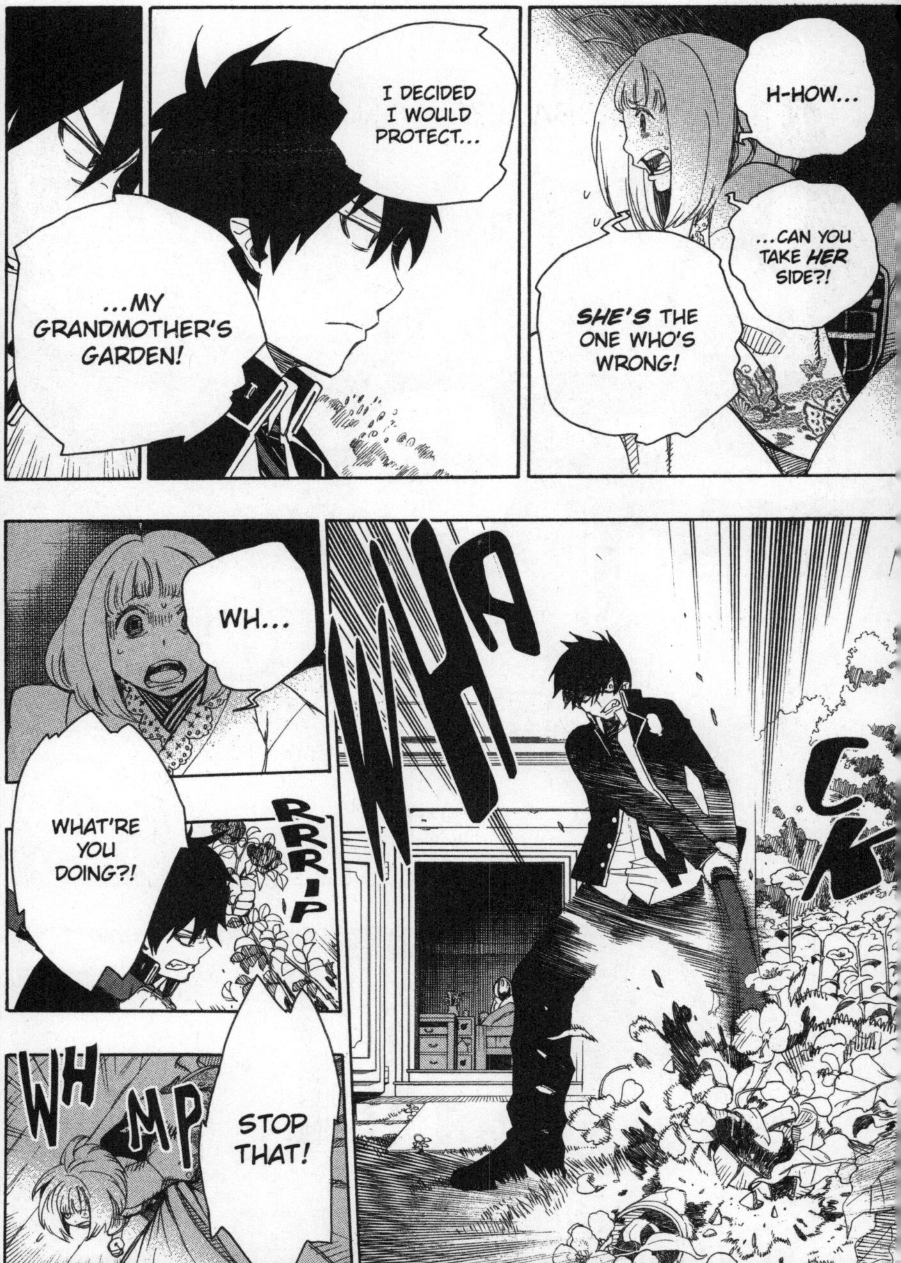
H-HOW...
...CAN YOU TAKE HER SIDE?!
SHE'S THE ONE WHO'S WRONG!
I DECIDED I WOULD PROTECT...
...MY GRANDMOTHER'S GARDEN!
WHA
CK
WH...
WHAT'RE YOU DOING?!
RRRIP
WHMP
STOP THAT!

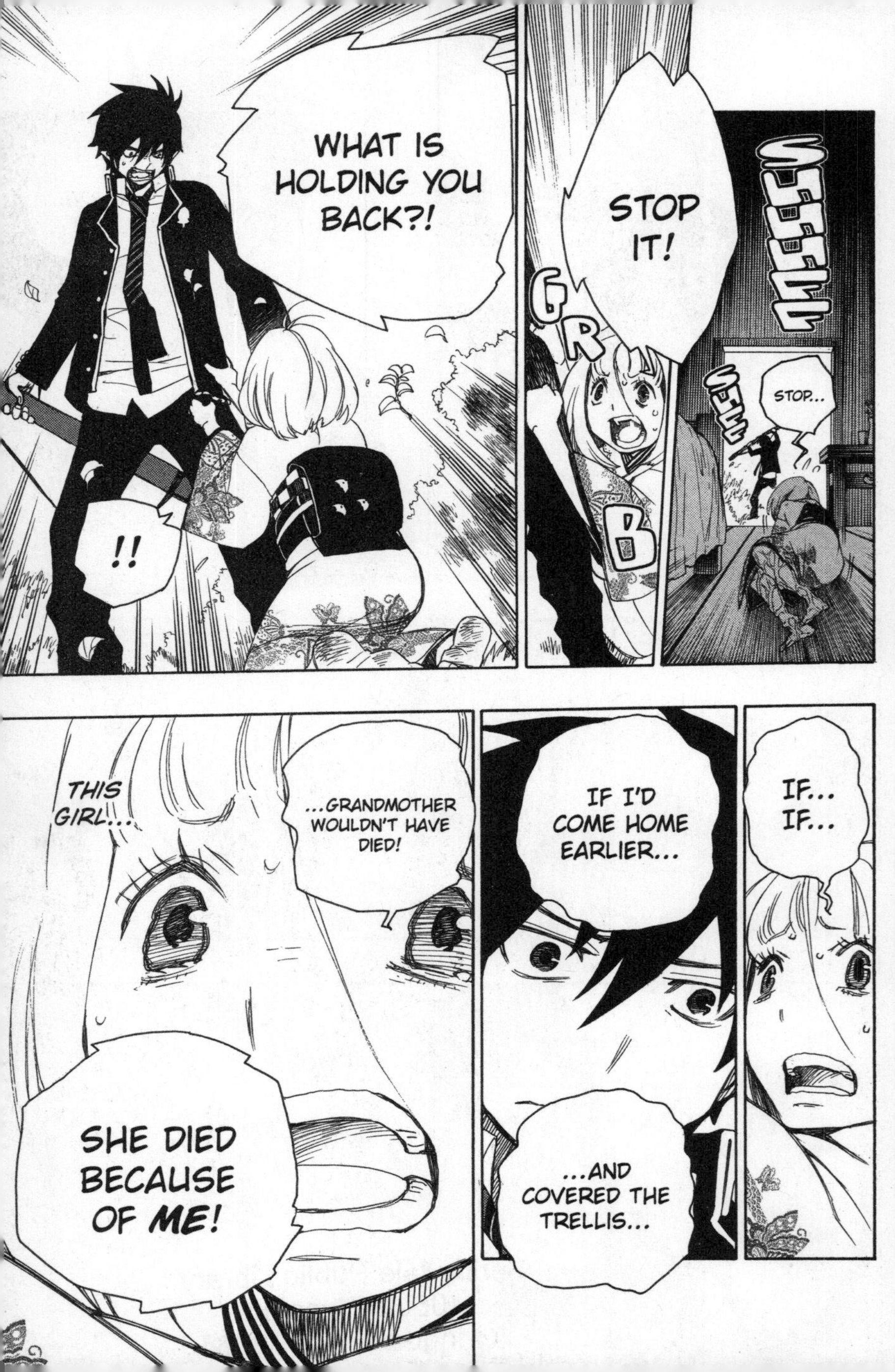
STOP...
STOP IT!
GRB
WHAT IS HOLDING YOU BACK?!
!!
IF... IF...
IF I'D COME HOME EARLIER...
...AND COVERED THE TRELLIS...
THIS GIRL...
...GRANDMOTHER WOULDN'T HAVE DIED!
SHE DIED BECAUSE OF ME!

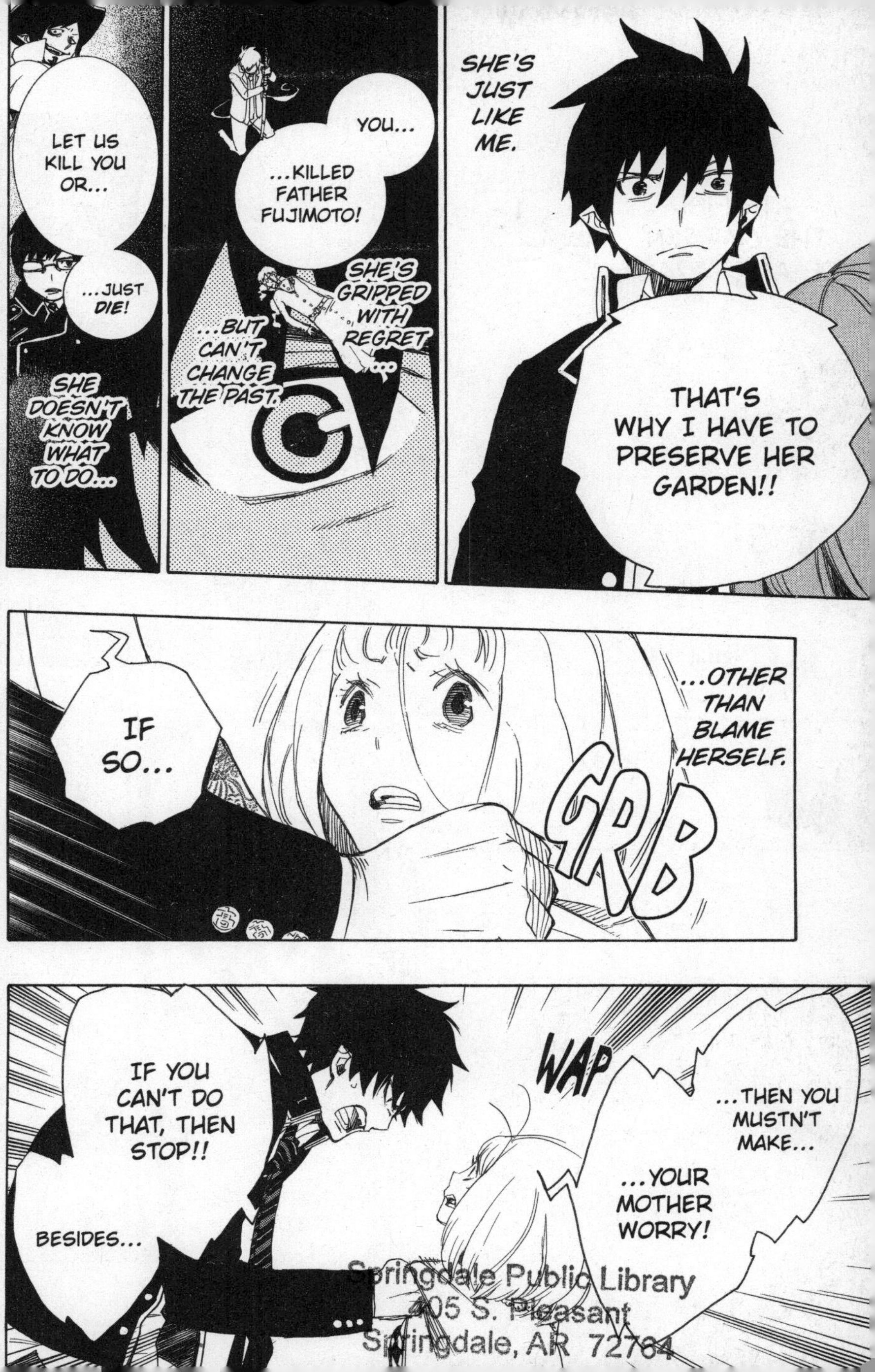
SHE'S JUST LIKE ME.
THAT'S WHY I HAVE TO PRESERVE HER GARDEN!!
YOU...
...KILLED FATHER FUJIMOTO!
SHE'S GRIPPED WITH REGRET...
...BUT CAN'T CHANGE THE PAST.
LET US KILL YOU OR...
...JUST DIE!
SHE DOESN'T KNOW WHAT TO DO...
...OTHER THAN BLAME HERSELF.
GRB
IF SO...
...THEN YOU MUSTN'T MAKE...
...YOUR MOTHER WORRY!
WAP
IF YOU CAN'T DO THAT, THEN STOP!!
BESIDES...

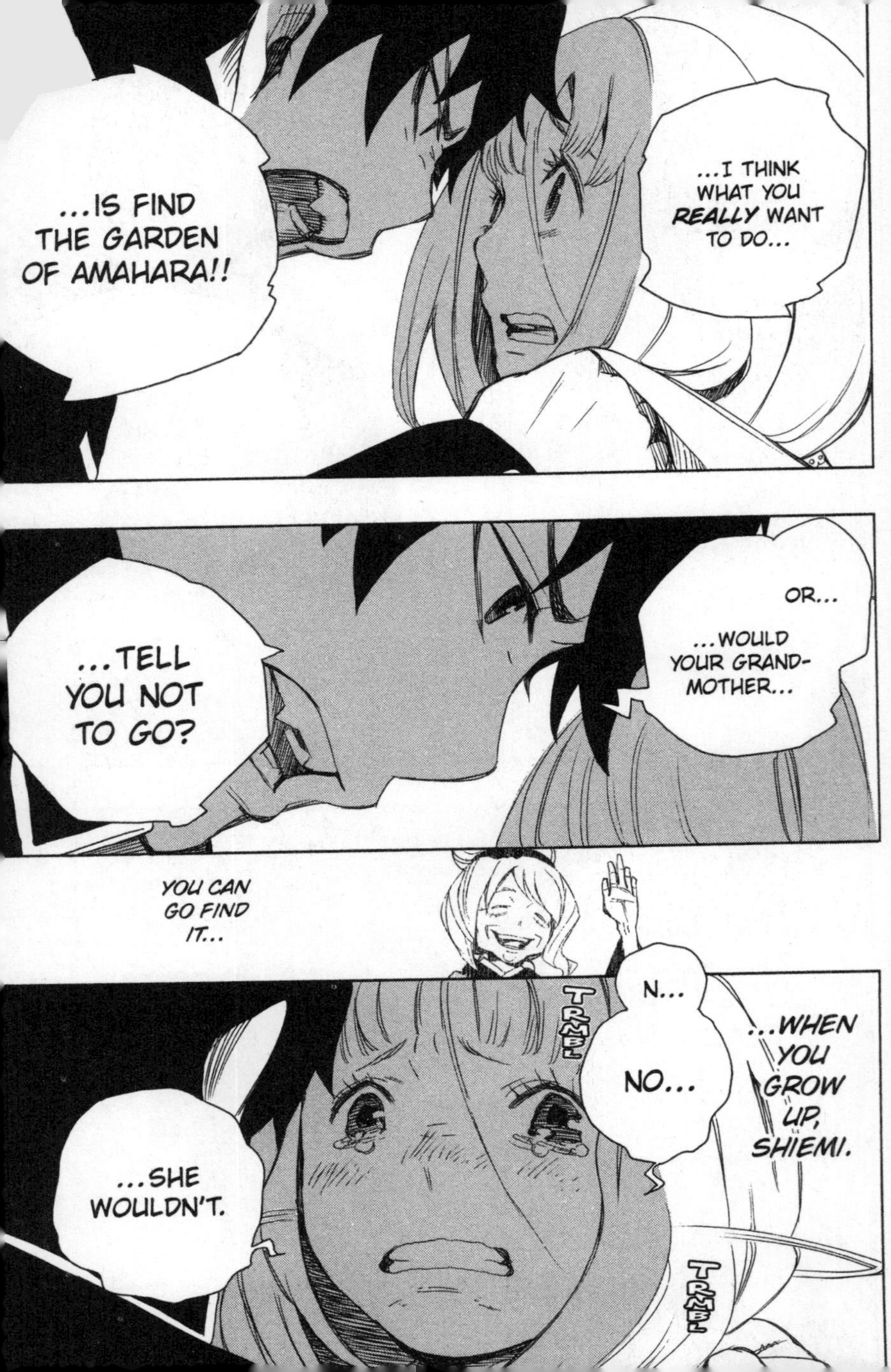
...I THINK WHAT YOU REALLY WANT TO DO...
...IS FIND THE GARDEN OF AMAHARA!!
OR...
...WOULD YOUR GRAND-MOTHER...
...TELL YOU NOT TO GO?
YOU CAN GO FIND IT...
...WHEN YOU GROW UP, SHIEMI.
TRMBL
N...
NO...
TRMBL
...SHE WOULDN'T.

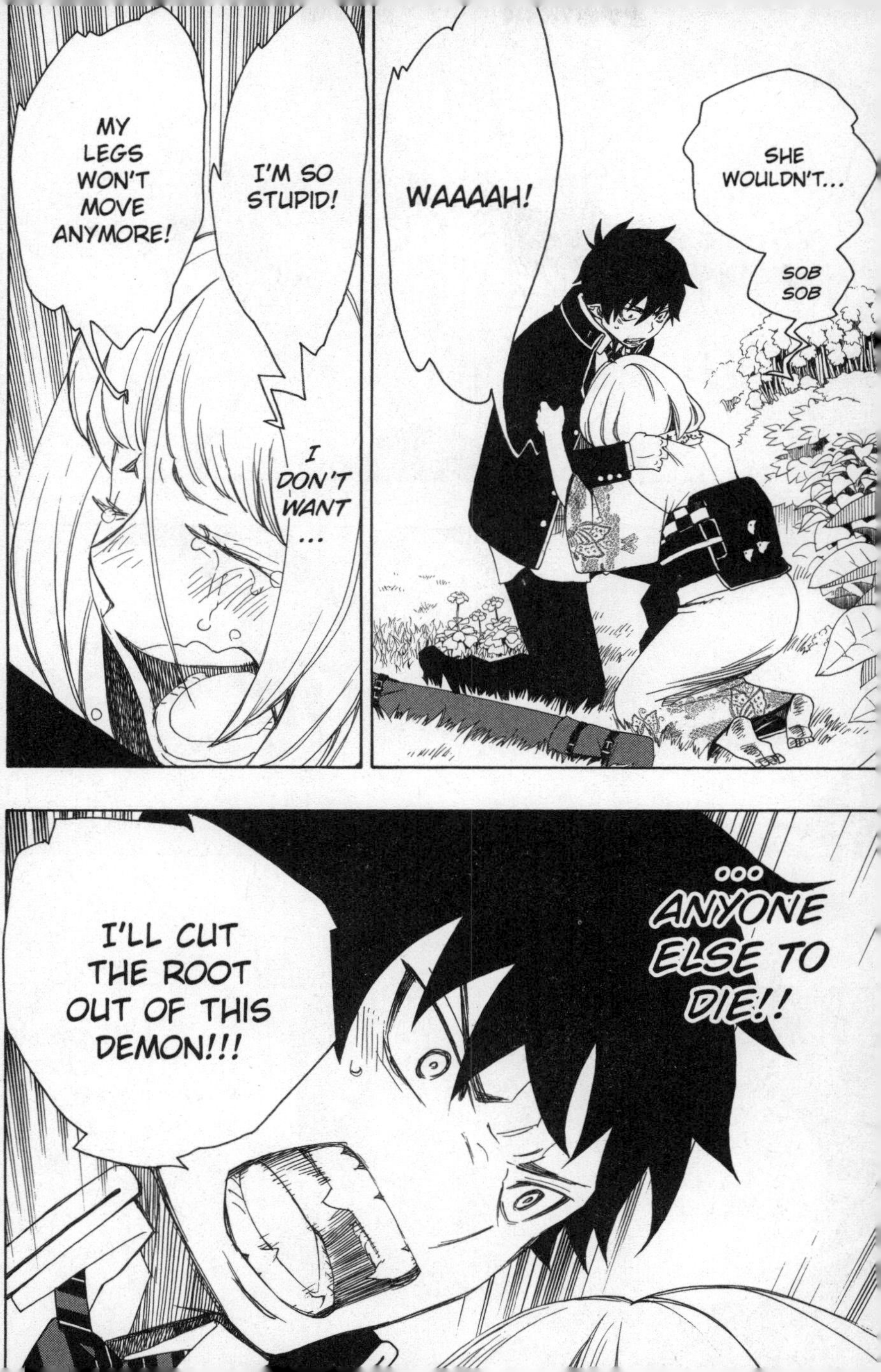
SHE WOULDN'T...
SOB SOB
WAAAAH!
I'M SO STUPID!
MY LEGS WON'T MOVE ANYMORE!
I DON'T WANT ...
...ANYONE ELSE TO DIE!!
I'LL CUT THE ROOT OUT OF THIS DEMON!!!

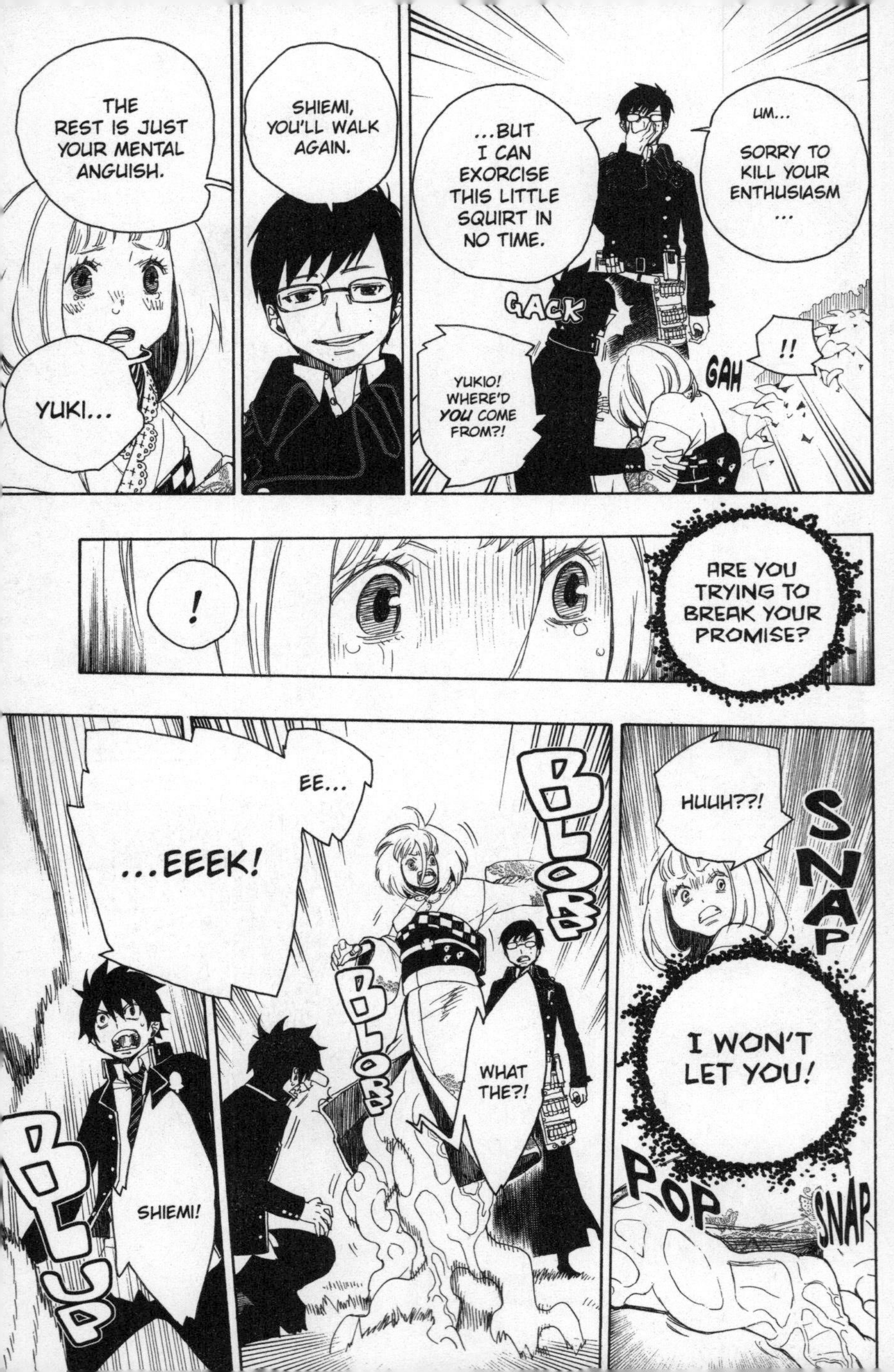
UM...
SORRY TO KILL YOUR ENTHUSIASM ...
...BUT I CAN EXORCISE THIS LITTLE SQUIRT IN NO TIME.
GACK
!!
GAH
YUKIO! WHERE'D *YOU* COME FROM?!
SHIEMI, YOU'LL WALK AGAIN.
THE REST IS JUST YOUR MENTAL ANGUISH.
YUKI...
ARE YOU TRYING TO BREAK YOUR PROMISE?
!
HUUH??!
SNAP
I WON'T LET YOU!
POP
SNAP
EE...
...EEEK!
BLORP
BLORP
WHAT THE?!
BLUP
SHIEMI!

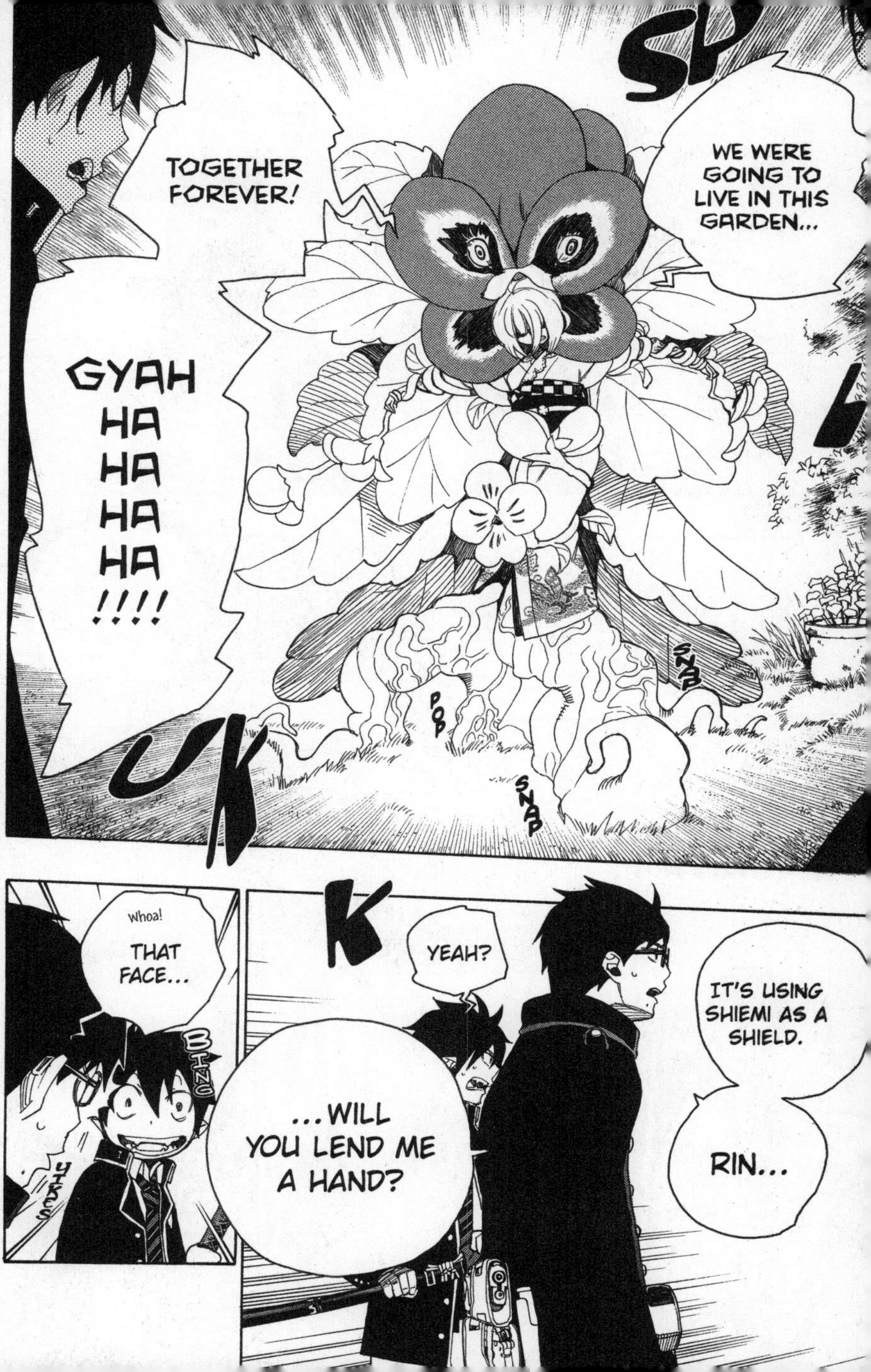
SP
WE WERE GOING TO LIVE IN THIS GARDEN...
TOGETHER FOREVER!
GYAH HA HA HA HA!!!!
SNAP
POP
SNAP
UK
K
IT'S USING SHIEMI AS A SHIELD.
RIN...
...WILL YOU LEND ME A HAND?
YEAH?
Whoa!
THAT FACE...
BING
YIKES

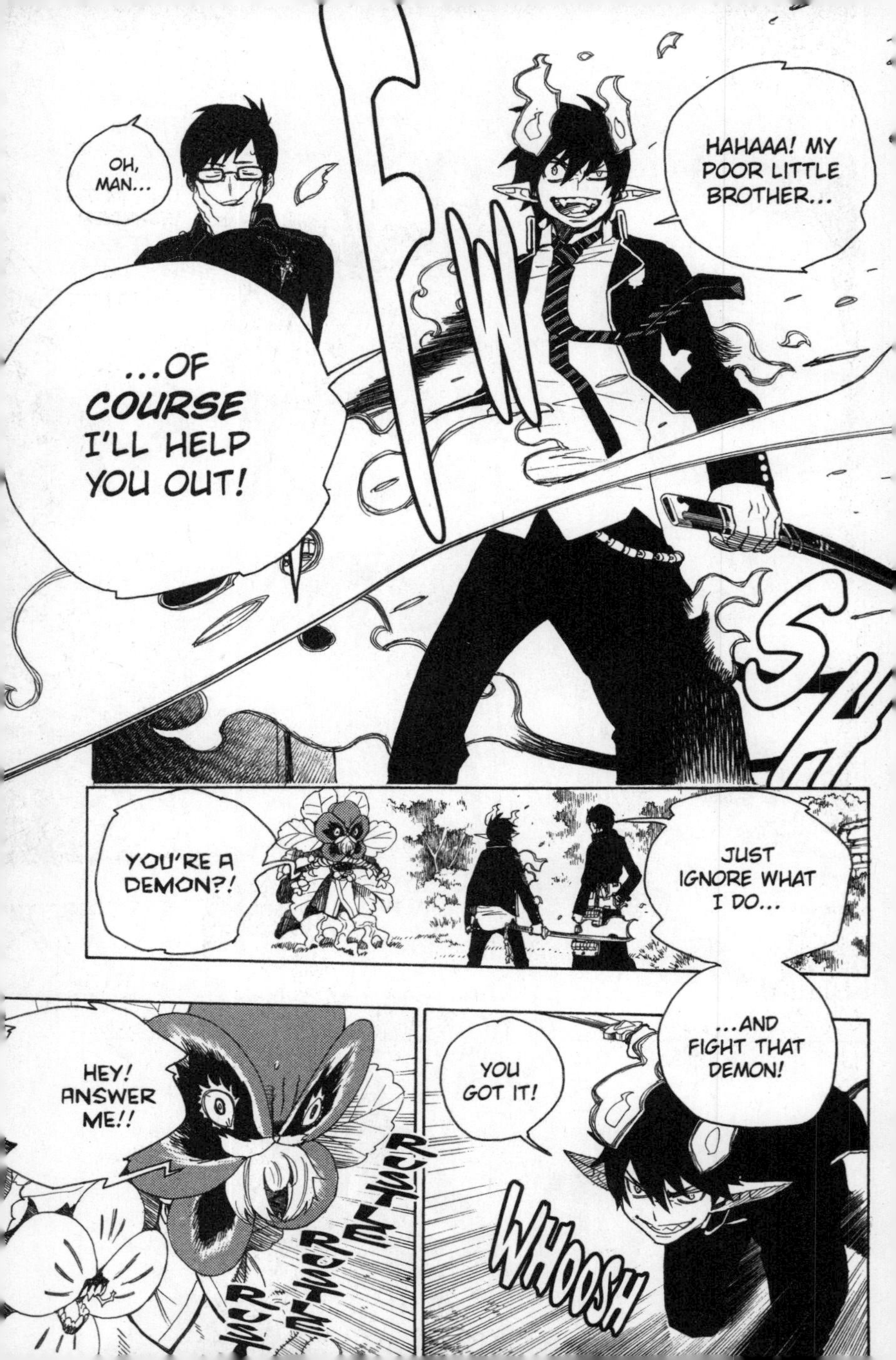
HAHAAA! MY POOR LITTLE BROTHER...
OH, MAN...
...OF **COURSE** I'LL HELP YOU OUT!
JUST IGNORE WHAT I DO...
YOU'RE A DEMON?!
...AND FIGHT THAT DEMON!
YOU GOT IT!
WHOOSH
HEY! ANSWER ME!!
RUSTLE RUSTLE RUST

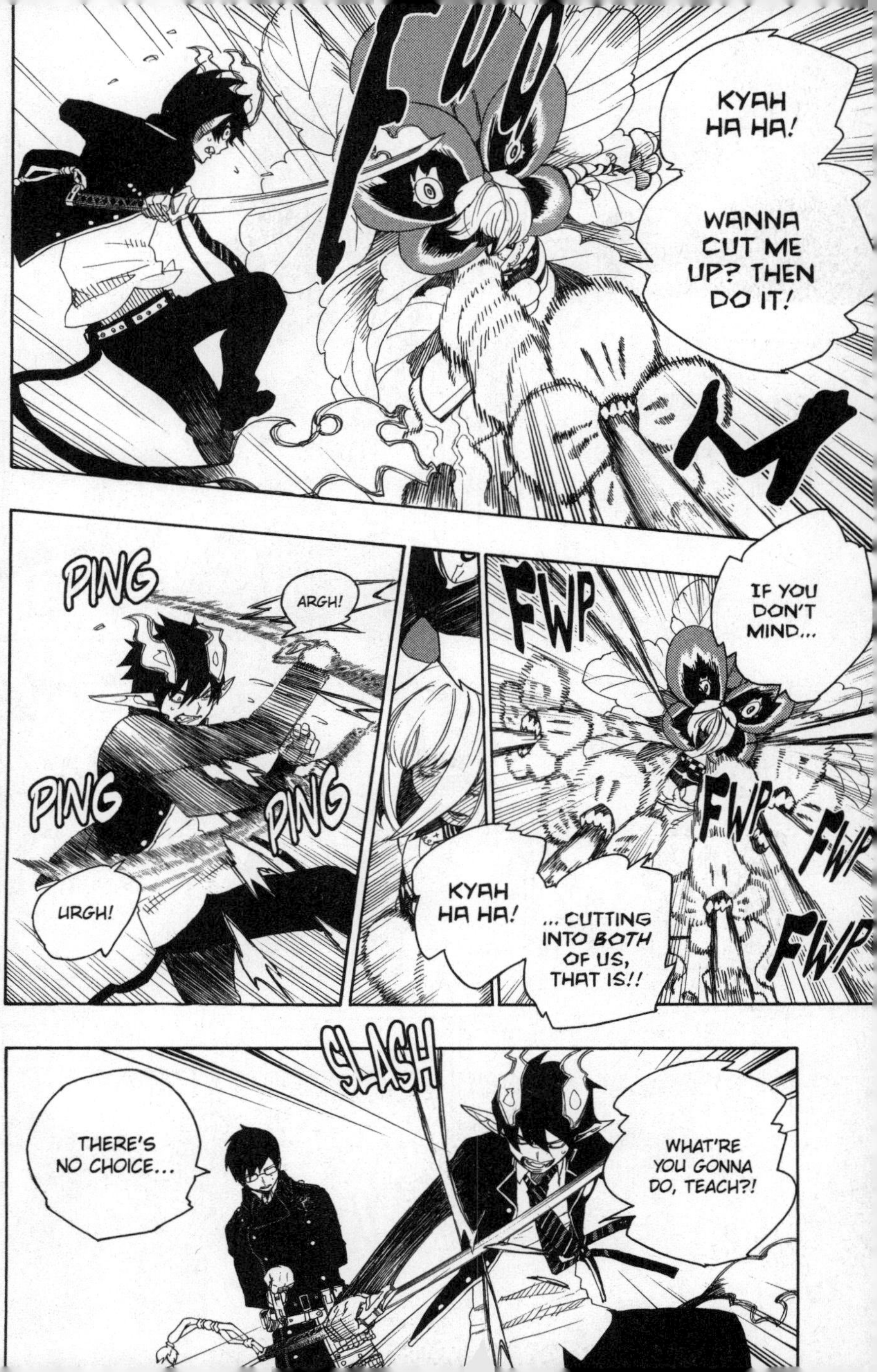
KYAH HA HA!
WANNA CUT ME UP? THEN DO IT!
IF YOU DON'T MIND...
FWP
FWP
FWP
FWP
KYAH HA HA!
... CUTTING INTO BOTH OF US, THAT IS!!
PING
ARGH!
PING
PING
URGH!
SLASH
WHAT'RE YOU GONNA DO, TEACH?!
THERE'S NO CHOICE...

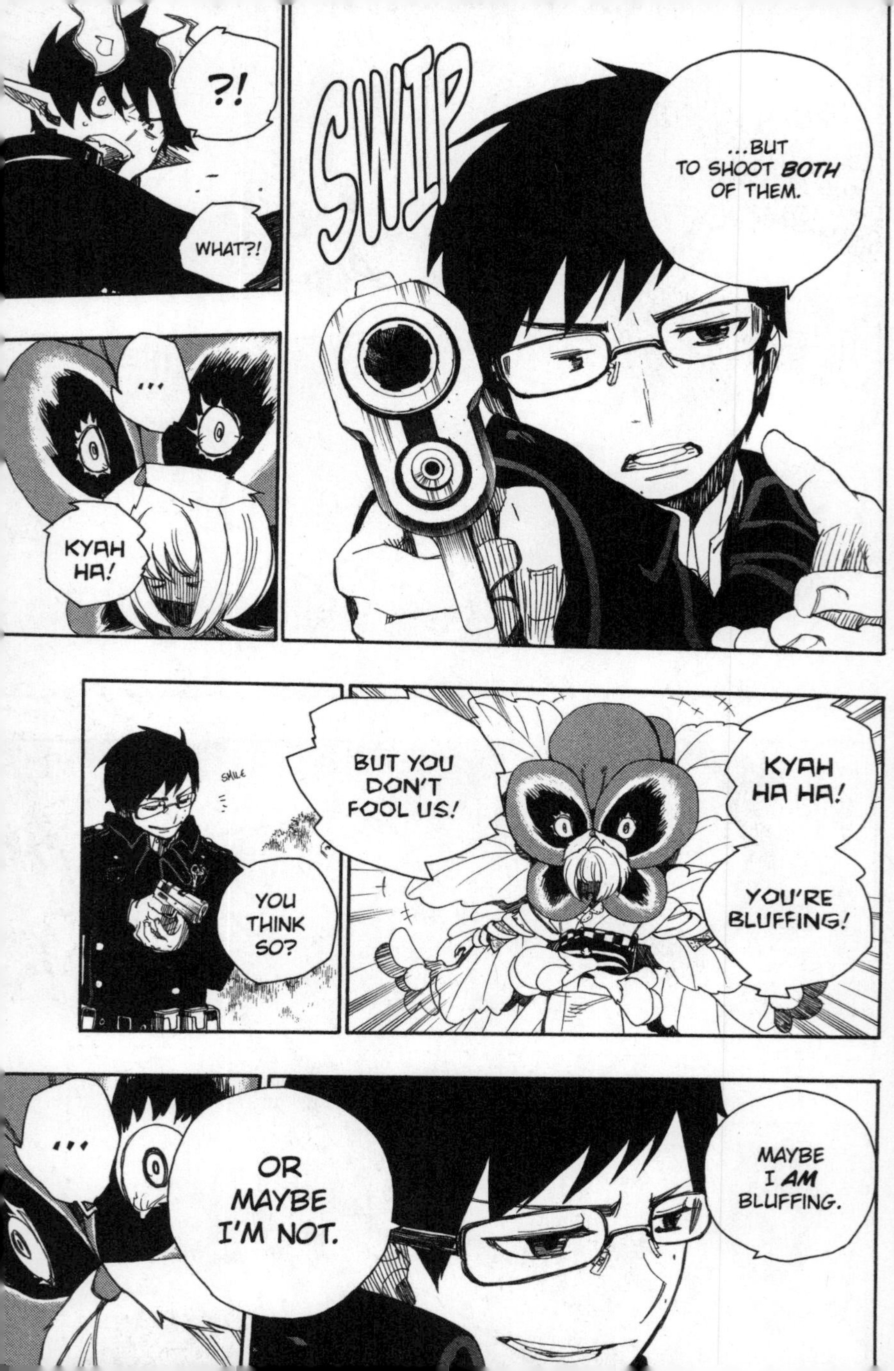
...BUT TO SHOOT BOTH OF THEM.
SWIP
?!
WHAT?!
...
KYAH HA!
KYAH HA HA!
YOU'RE BLUFFING!
BUT YOU DON'T FOOL US!
SMILE
YOU THINK SO?
MAYBE I AM BLUFFING.
OR MAYBE I'M NOT.
...

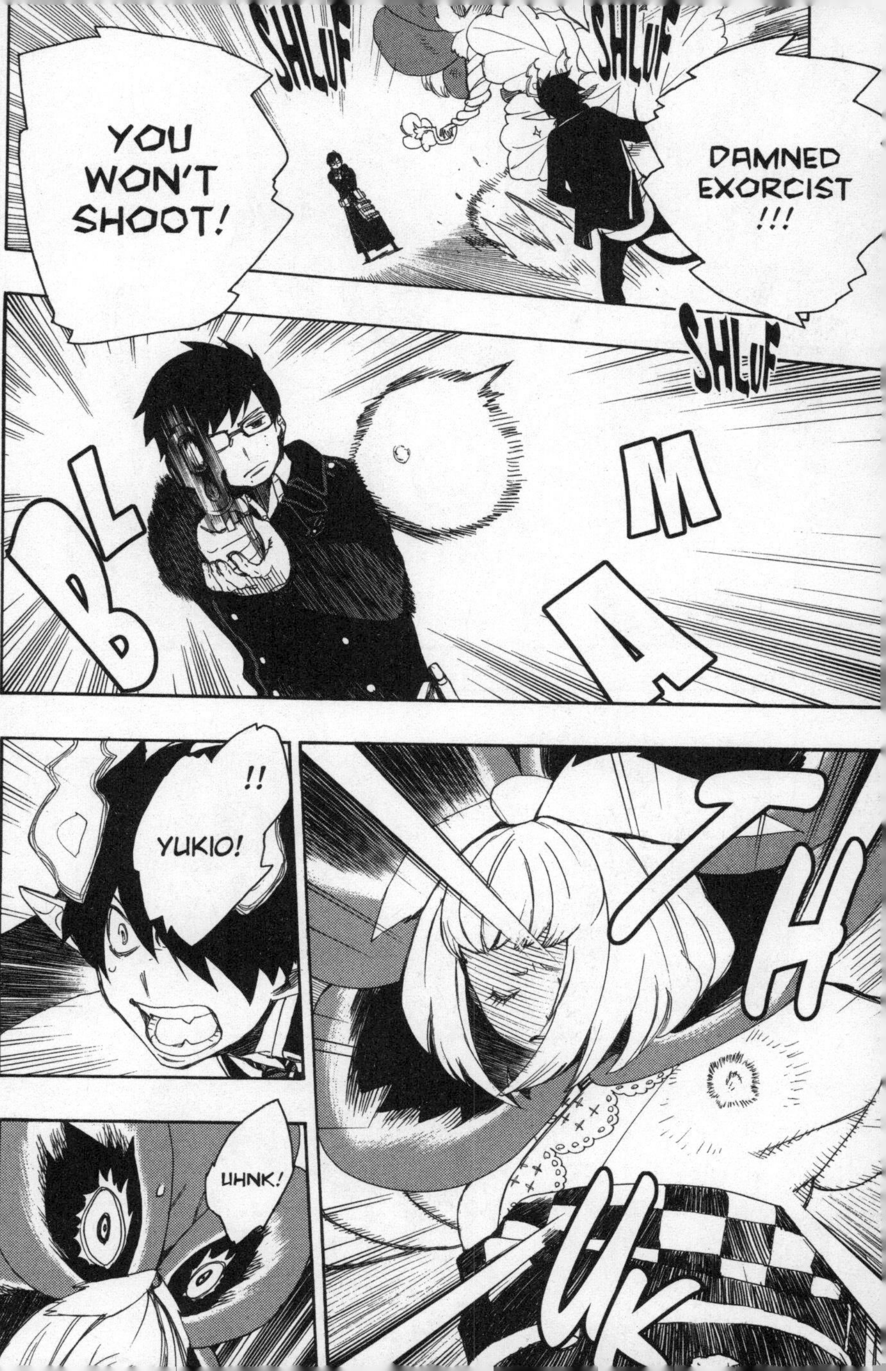
SHLUF
DAMNED EXORCIST !!!
SHLUF
YOU WON'T SHOOT!
SHLUF
BLAM
THUK
!! YUKIO!
UHNK!

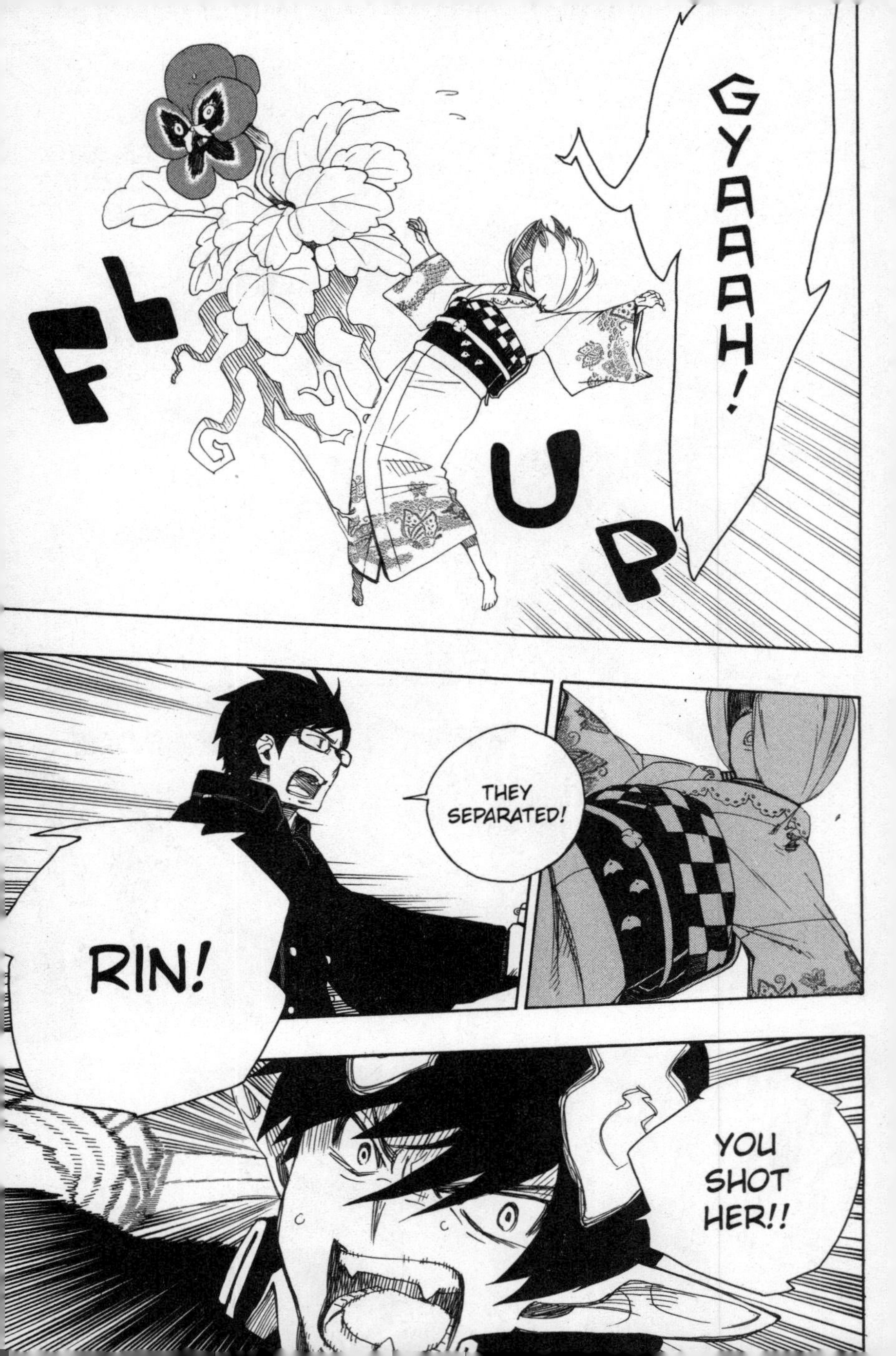
GYAAAH!
FLUP
THEY SEPARATED!
RIN!
YOU SHOT HER!!

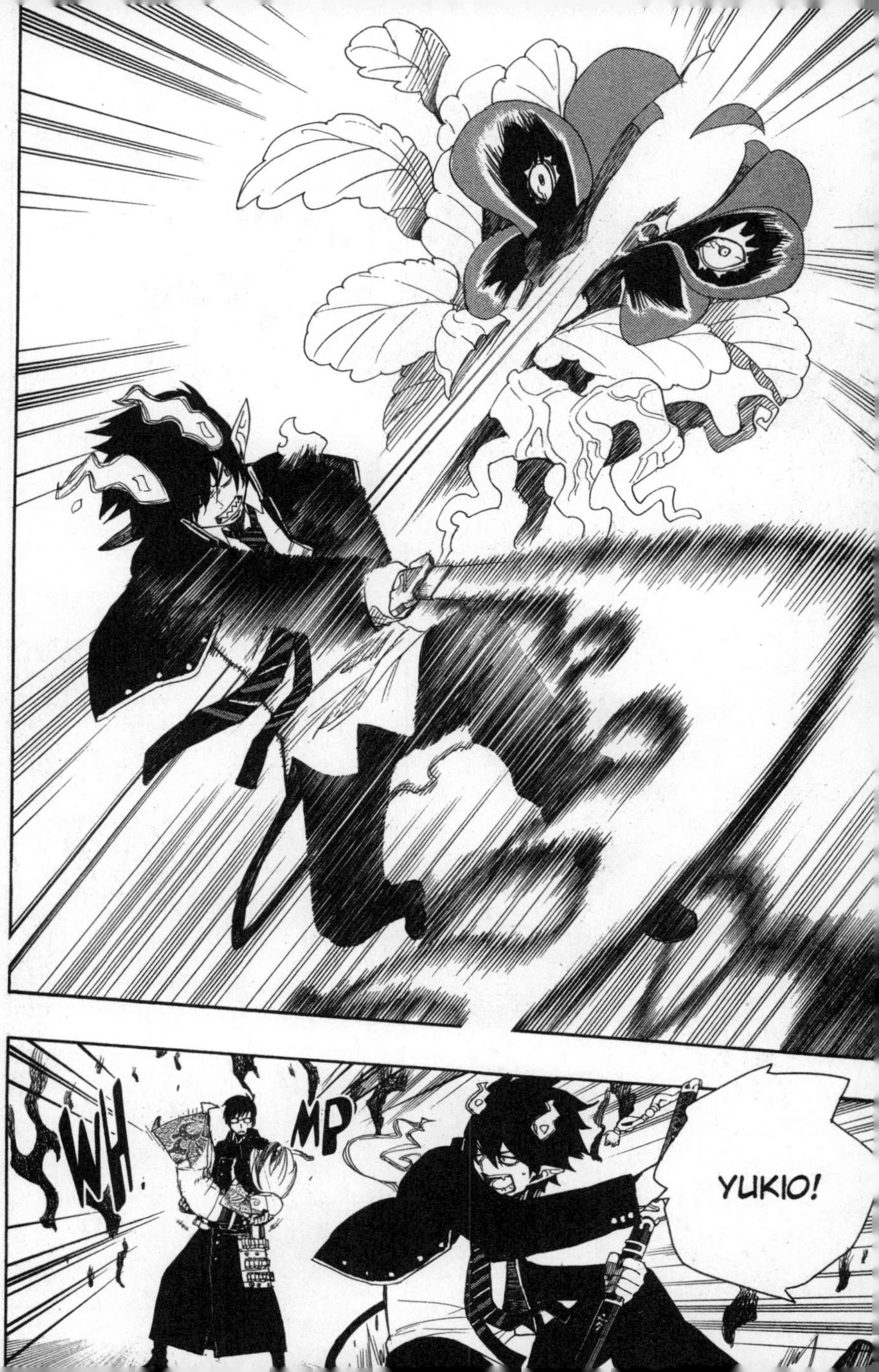
YUKIO!
WH MP

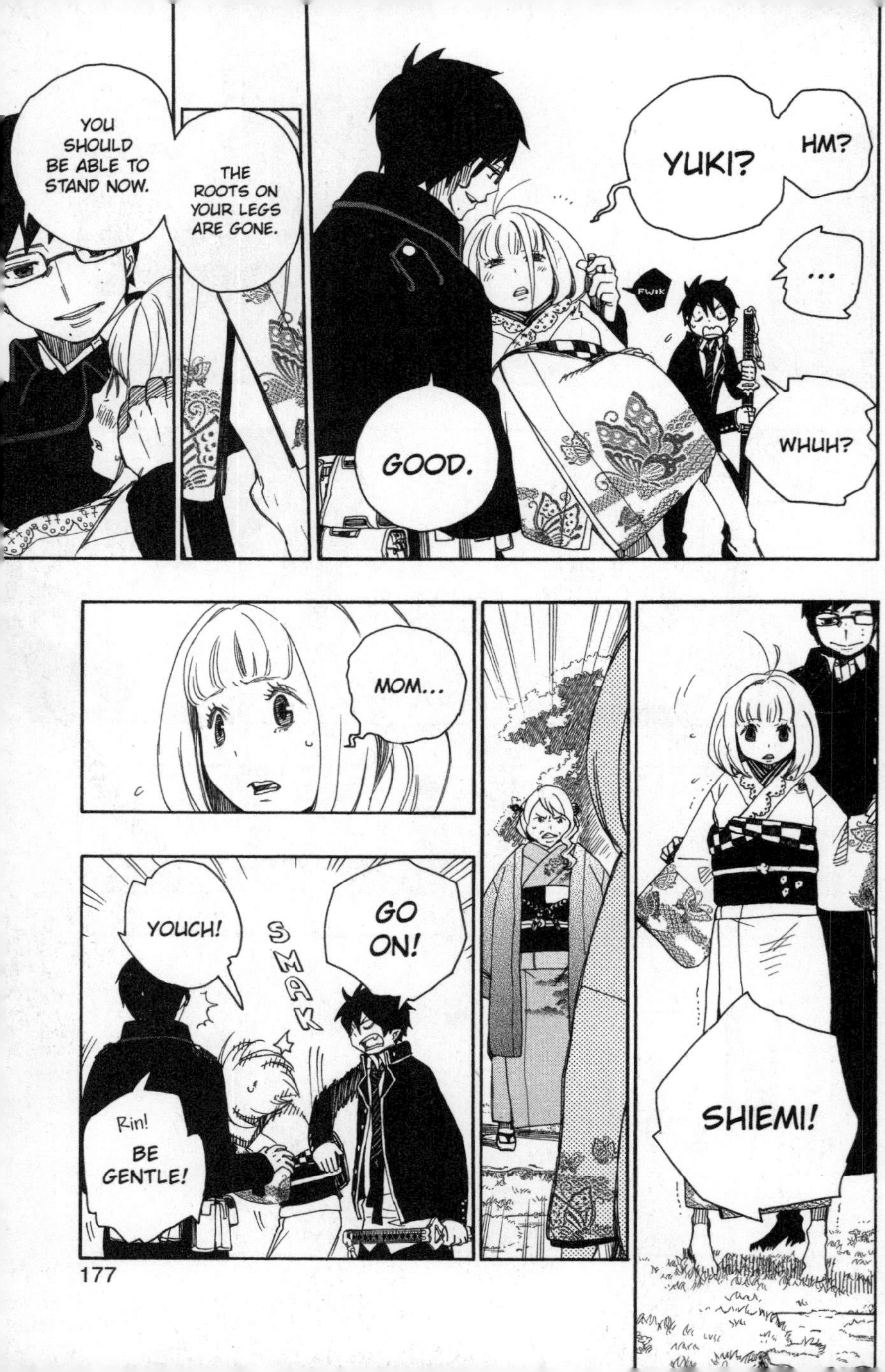
HM?
YUKI?
FWIK
...
WHUH?
GOOD.
THE ROOTS ON YOUR LEGS ARE GONE.
YOU SHOULD BE ABLE TO STAND NOW.
SHIEMI!
MOM...
GO ON!
SMAK
YOUCH!
Rin! BE GENTLE!

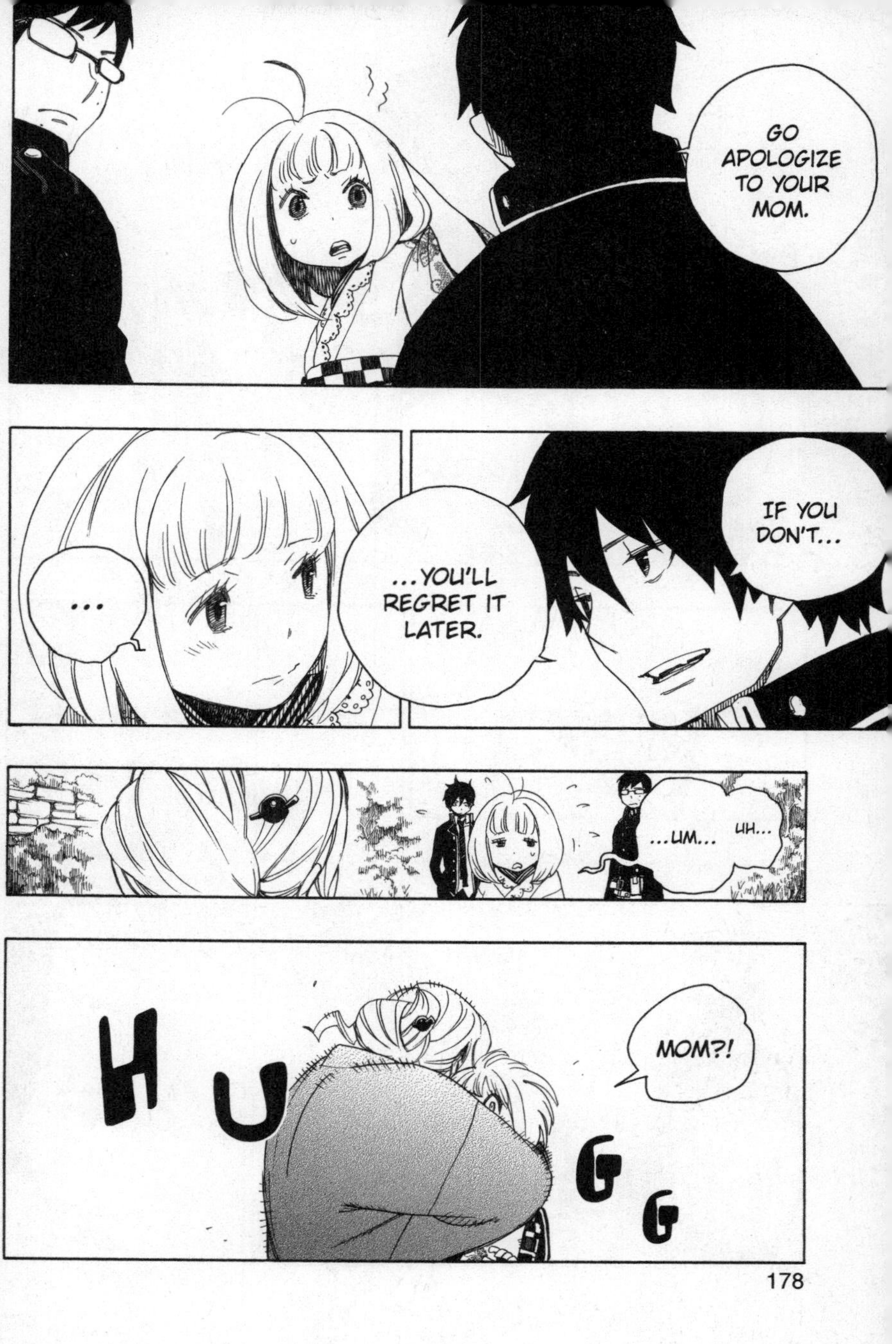
GO APOLOGIZE TO YOUR MOM.
IF YOU DON'T...
...YOU'LL REGRET IT LATER.
...
UH...
...UM...
MOM?!
HUGG

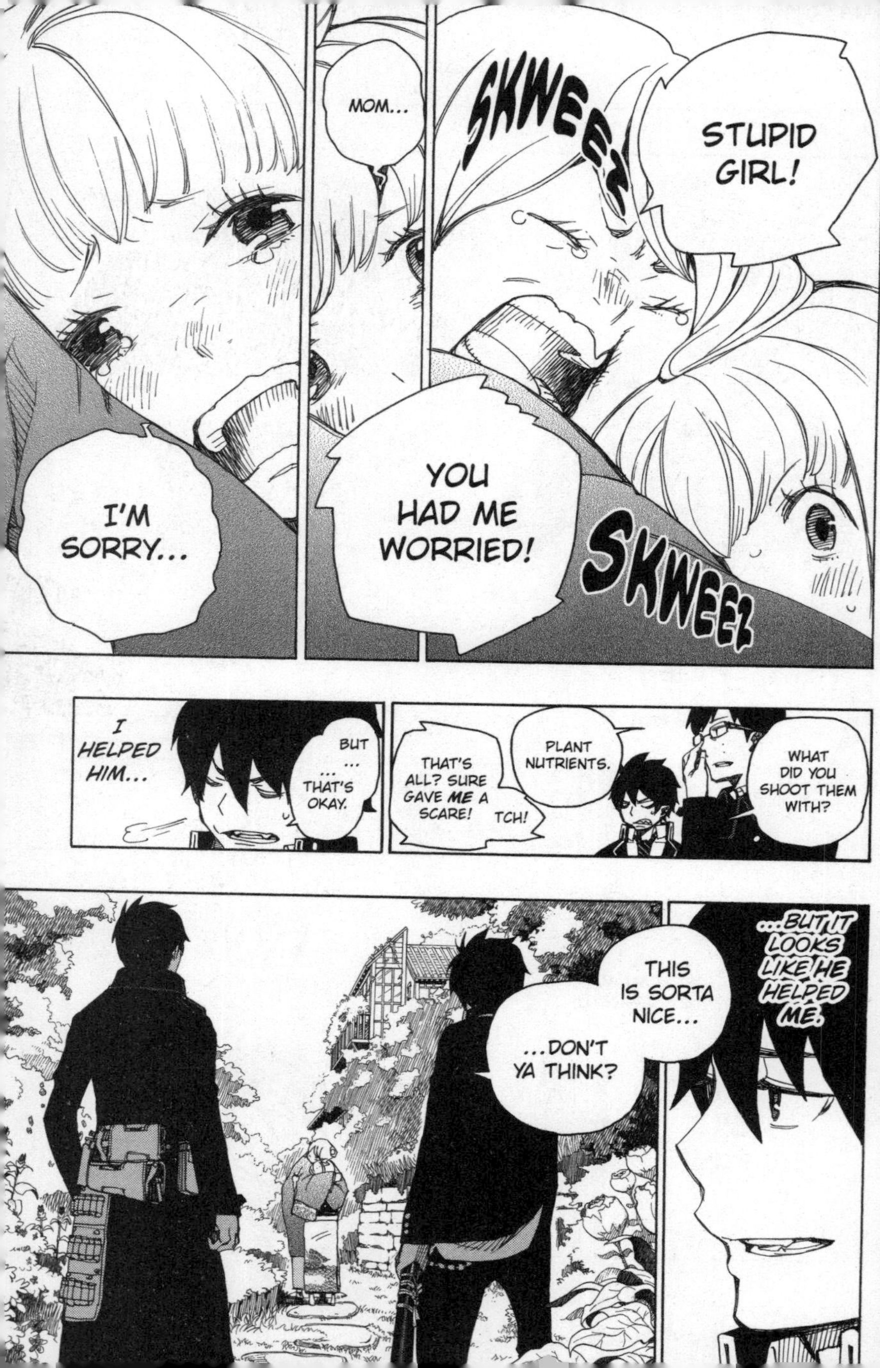
STUPID GIRL!
SKWEEZ
SKWEEZ
YOU HAD ME WORRIED!
MOM...
I'M SORRY...
WHAT DID YOU SHOOT THEM WITH?
PLANT NUTRIENTS.
THAT'S ALL? SURE GAVE *ME* A SCARE!
TCH!
BUT ... ...THAT'S OKAY.
I HELPED HIM...
...BUT IT LOOKS LIKE HE HELPED ME.
THIS IS SORTA NICE...
...DON'T YA THINK?

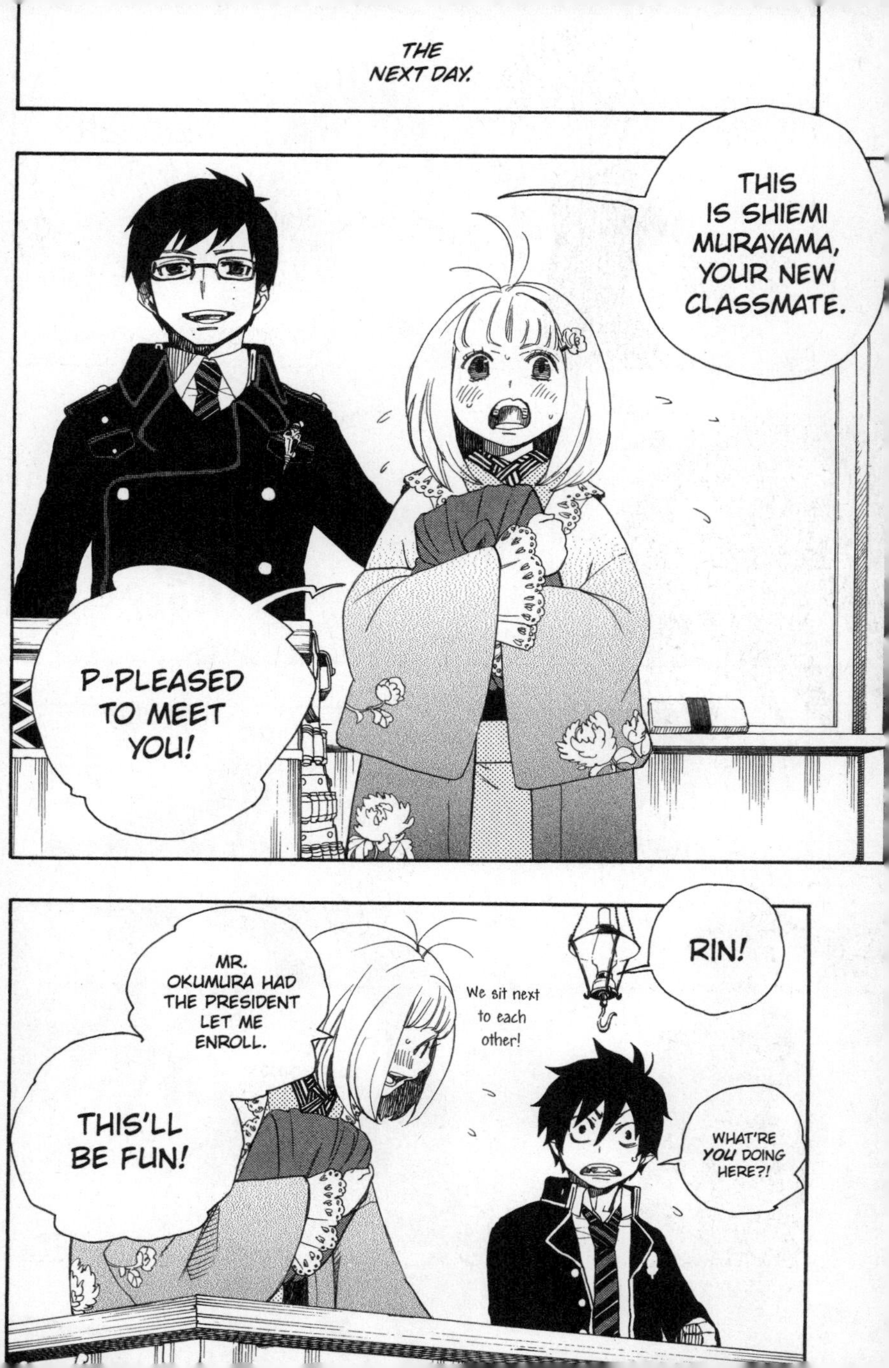
THE NEXT DAY.
THIS IS SHIEMI MURAYAMA, YOUR NEW CLASSMATE.
P-PLEASED TO MEET YOU!
RIN!
WHAT'RE *YOU* DOING HERE?!
We sit next to each other!
MR. OKUMURA HAD THE PRESIDENT LET ME ENROLL.
THIS'LL BE FUN!

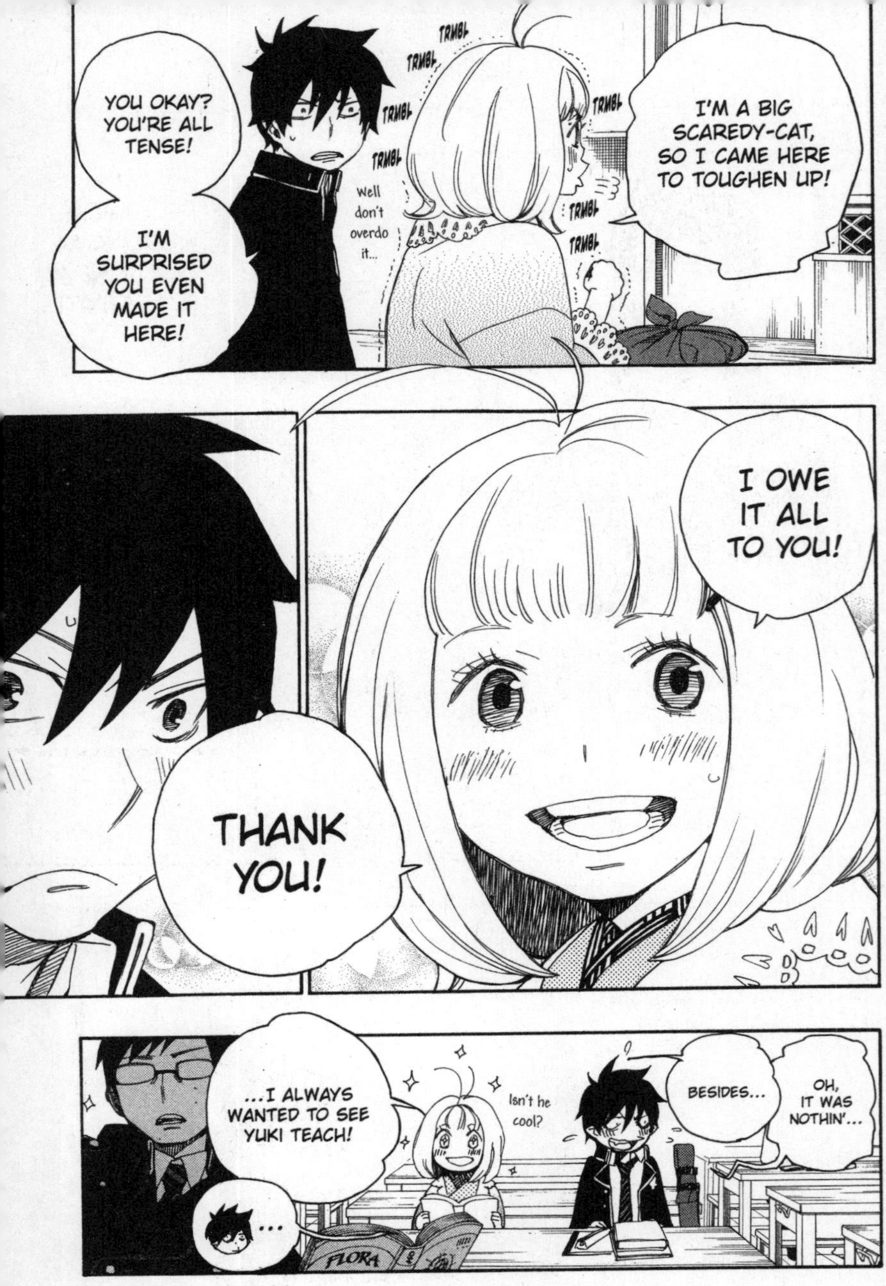
I'M A BIG SCAREDY-CAT, SO I CAME HERE TO TOUGHEN UP!
TRMBL TRMBL TRMBL TRMBL TRMBL TRMBL TRMBL
Well don't overdo it...
YOU OKAY? YOU'RE ALL TENSE!
I'M SURPRISED YOU EVEN MADE IT HERE!
I OWE IT ALL TO YOU!
THANK YOU!
OH, IT WAS NOTHIN'...
BESIDES...
Isn't he cool?
...I ALWAYS WANTED TO SEE YUKI TEACH!
...
FLORA

Blue Exorcist 1 (End)

Blue Exorcist Chapter 3 The Garden of Amahara

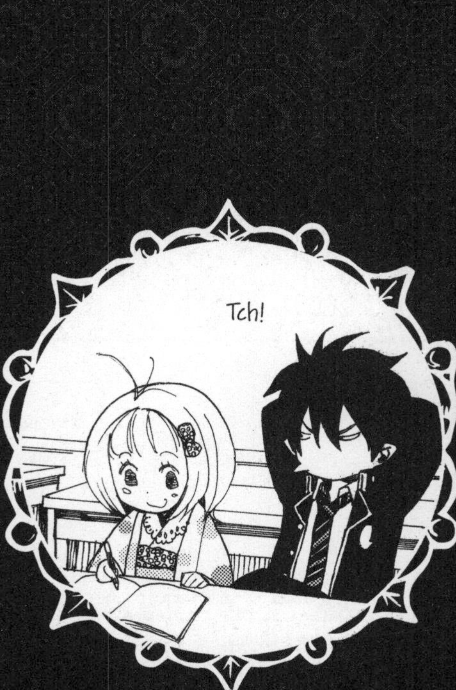
Tch!

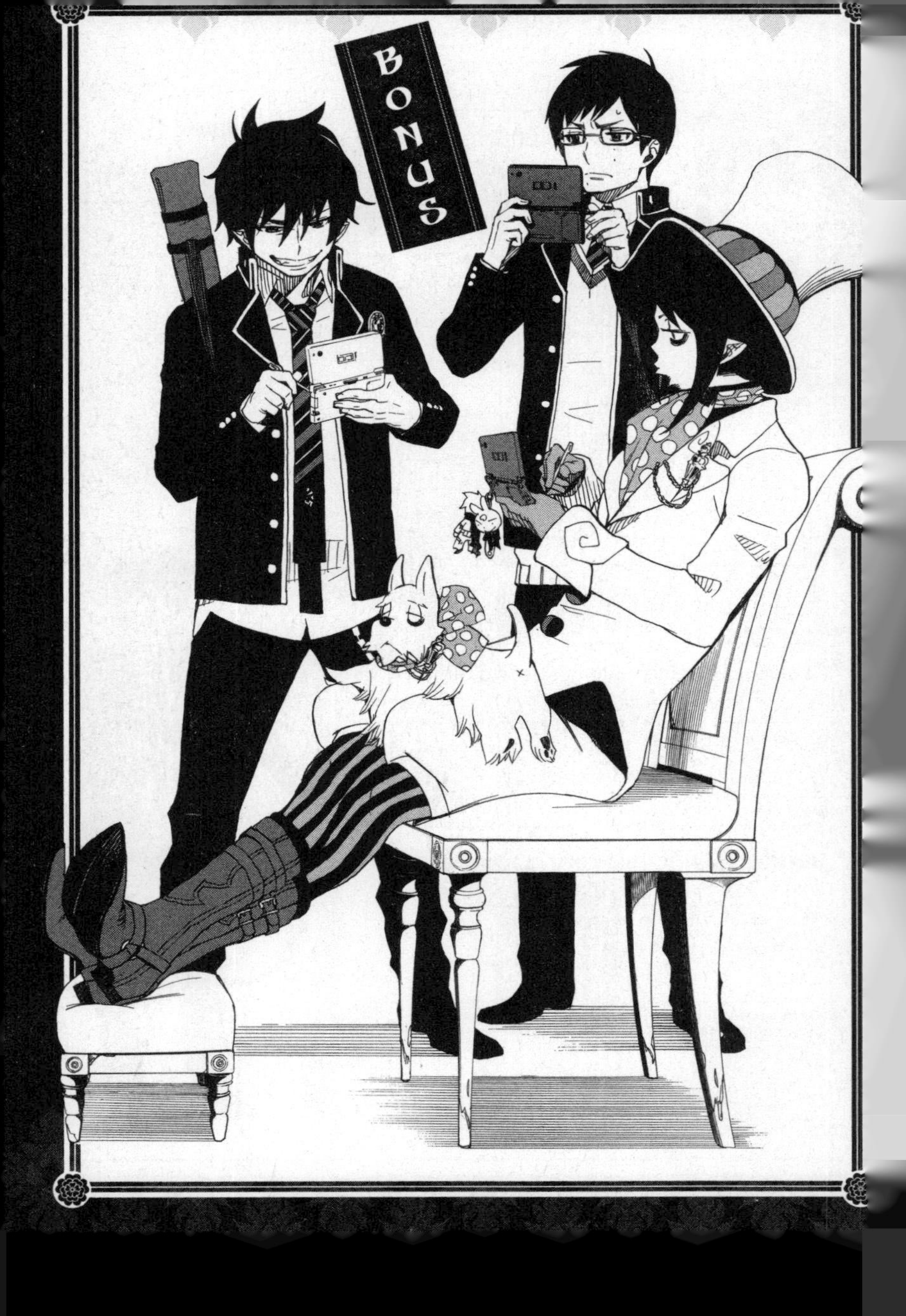
BONUS

True Cross Academy Exorcism Cram School: Exorcists and Students No. 0001

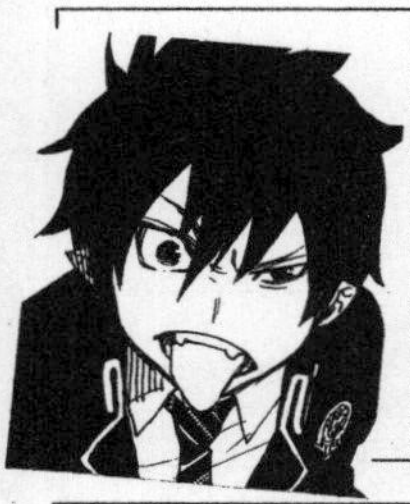

Name	Sex	Age
Rin Okumura	Male	15

Status:

First-year high school student, True Cross Academy Page, Exorcism Cram School

Date of birth	December 27
Blood type	A
Height	173 cm
Weight	63 kg
Pastimes and talents	Cooking, sleeping, eating, spacing out
Average hours of sleep per night	11
Favorite Foods	Sukiyaki (with any kind of ingredients)
Favorite manga genres (Circle all that apply.)	Battle/action Gags Comedy Romance Horror Suspense/mystery Emotional drama Social drama Other ( )
Favorite type of girl:	Hot, sexy girls

Details:

- Surprisingly good with his hands
- Cooking repertoire includes all kinds of Japanese and Western foods (home cuisine)

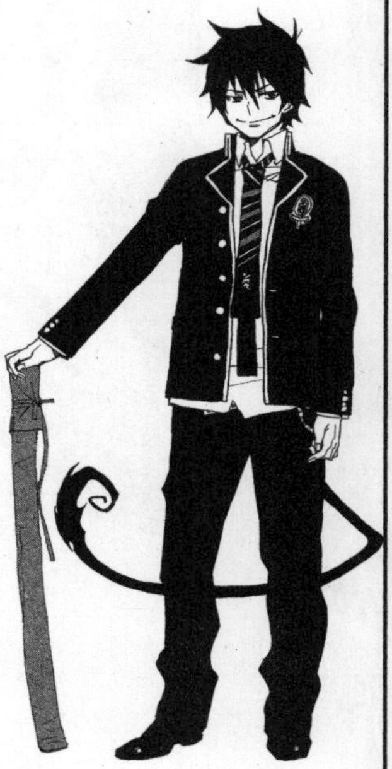

True Cross Academy Exorcism Cram School: Exorcists and Students No. 0002

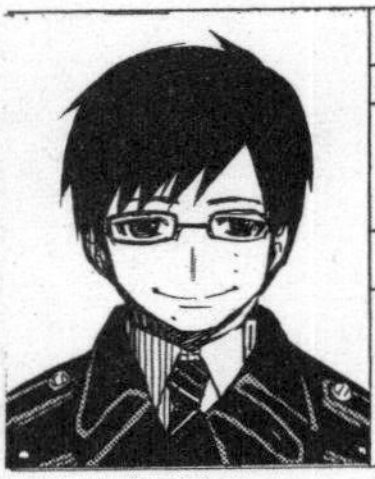

Name	Sex	Age
Yukio Okumura	Male	15

Status

First-year high-school student, True Cross Academy
Exorcism Instructor, Knights of the True Cross (Titles: Dragoon, Doctor)
Instructor of Demon Pharmaceuticals, Year One, Exorcism Cram School

Date of birth:	December 27
Blood type	O
Height	180 cm
Weight	70 kg
Pastimes and talents	Formulating plans, mixing in with a crowd, reading Jump Square every month
Average hours of sleep	4
Favorite food	Seafood (especially sashimi)
Favorite manga genres (Circle all that apply.)	Battle/action Gags Comedy Romance Horror Suspense/mystery Emotional drama Social drama Other ( )
Favorite type of girl	...

Details:
- Popular with girls
- Extremely poor eyesight
- Ambidextrous
- Embarrassed by how many moles he has

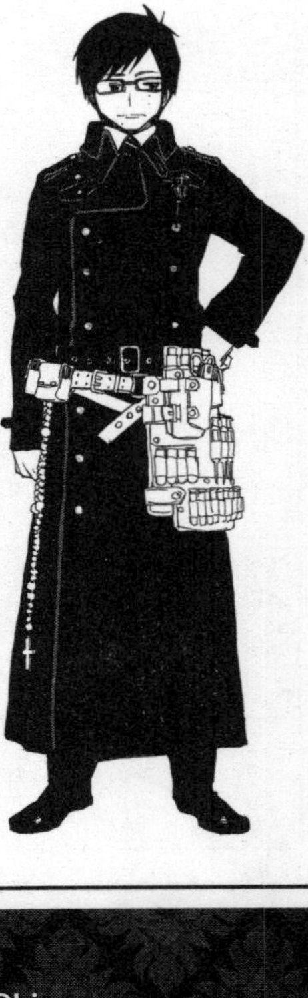

TRUE CROSS ACADEMY EXORCISM CRAM SCHOOL: EXORCISTS AND STUDENTS

True Cross Academy Exorcism Cram School: Exorcists and Students No. 0003

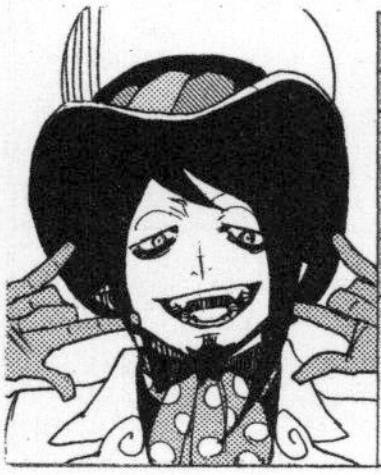

Name	Sex	Age
Mephisto Pheles	Male	(°ω°)

Status:

President, True Cross Academy
Head of Exorcism Cram School
Honorable Knight, Knights of the True Cross (Titles: ---)

Date of birth
(°ロ°) (◎益◎)
Blood type
(´–`)
Height
195 cm
Weight
74 kg
Pastimes and talents
Movies, manga, anime, video games, music, toys, subcultures
Average hours of sleep per night
1
Favorite food
Junk food
Favorite manga genres (Circle all that apply.)
Battle/action Gags Comedy Romance Horror Suspense/mystery Emotional drama Social drama Other (   )
Favorite type of girl:
Temptresses or elegant, beautiful girls

Details:

- Pretty good at party games, claw crane games and chess
- ↓These are his formal clothes.

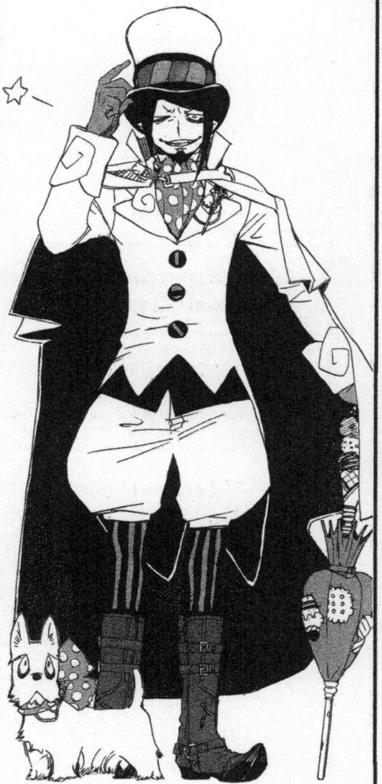

True Cross Academy Exorcism Cram School: Exorcists and Students No. 0004

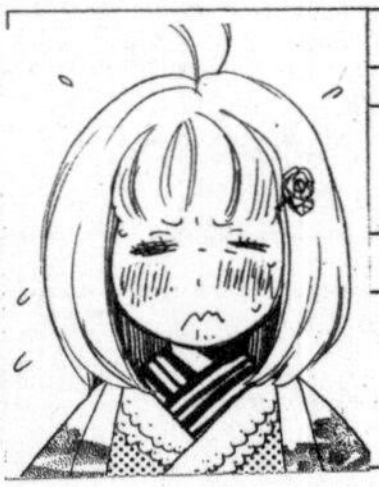

Name	Sex	Age
Shiemi Moriyama	Female	15

Status
Page, Exorcism Cram School

Date of birth:
March 6
Blood type
B
Height
165 cm
Weight
49 kg
Pastimes and talents
Gardening, making herbal teas, naming plants and flowers, baking cookies, lying in the sun
Average hours of sleep
8
Favorite food
Her grandmother's herb cookies
Favorite manga genres (Circle all that apply.)
Battle/action Gags Comedy Romance Horror Suspense/mystery Emotional drama Social drama Other (DOESN'T READ MANGA.)
Favorite type of boy
Nice guys

Details:
- Has only ever worn traditional Japanese-style clothing since she was born
- Blushes a lot
- Slightly allergic to pollen

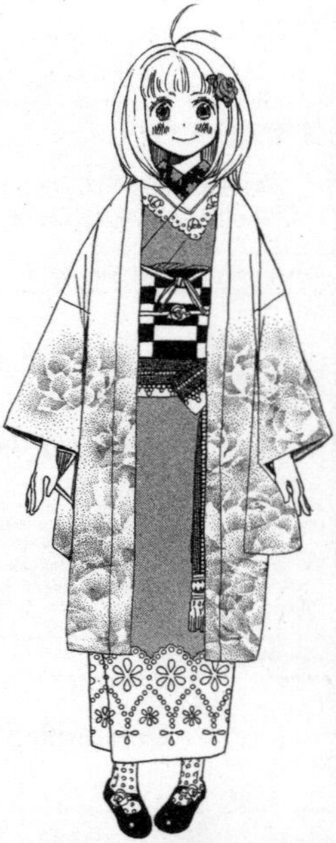

True Cross Academy Exorcism Cram School: Exorcists and Students No. 0005

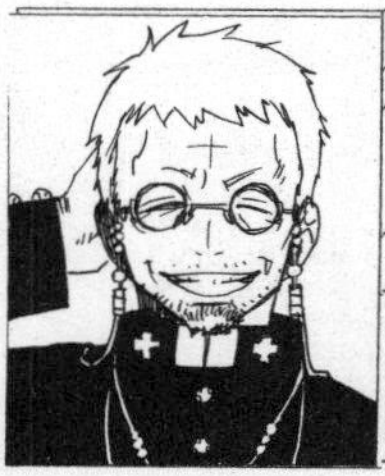

Name	Sex	Age
Shiro Fujimoto	Male	51

Status:

Exorcist, Knights of the True Cross (Titles: Paladin)
Priest, True Cross Church
Former first-year Demon Pharmaceuticals Instructor, Year One, Exorcism Cram School

Date of birth

May 10

Blood type

AB

Height

177 cm

Weight

62 kg

Pastimes and talents

Collecting dirty books, taking care of his glasses, falling asleep anywhere and anytime

Average hours of sleep per night

6

Favorite food

Oden (especially Japanese radish)

Favorite manga genres (Circle all that apply.)

Battle/action Gags Comedy Romance
Horror Suspense/mystery Emotional drama Social drama
Other ( )

Favorite type of girl:

Ones with big boobs

Details:

- Has known Mephisto for a long time
- Hasn't smoked for 15 years

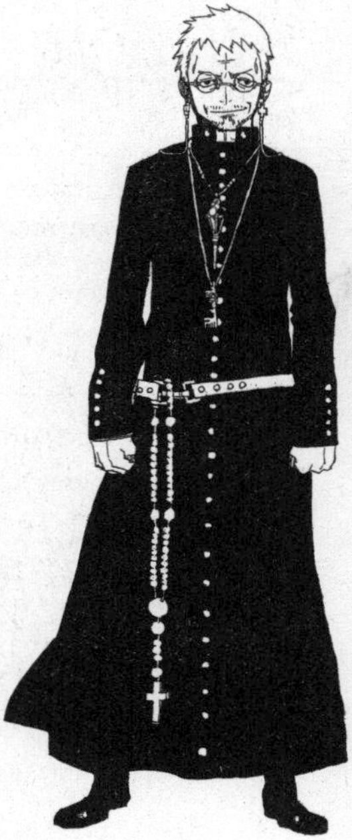

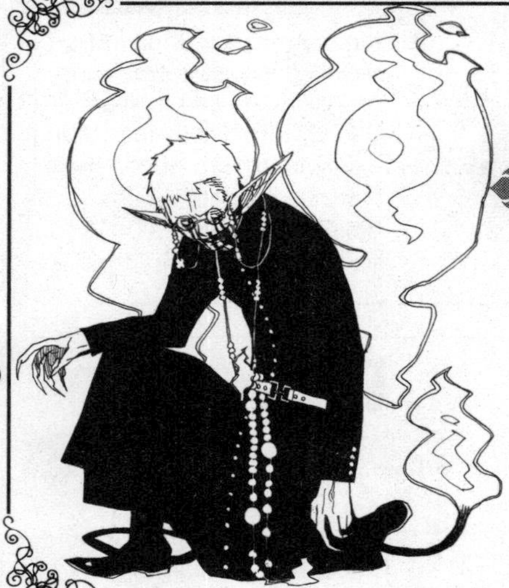

Satan

FILE 1

High level

Satan, God of Gehenna. Said to be the creator of all demons. Because of his great power, no material in Assiah can withstand possession by him. Even the strongest exorcist could not last more than ten minutes.

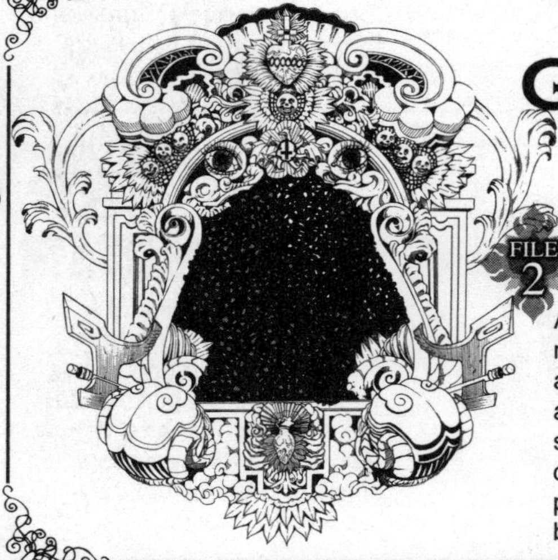

Gehenna Gate

FILE 2

Mid to High level

A demon that Satan can make while in Assiah. It allows travel between Assiah and Gehenna. The gate's size, appearance and abilities change depending on the properties and amount of blood used in making it.

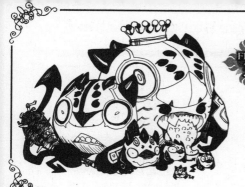

GOBLIN

FILE 3

LOW TO MID LEVEL

Kin of Amaimon, King of Earth. Mainly possesses small animals like rats and moles. Usually forms colonies around a king or queen. Hundreds of species may exist in any region. Hobgoblins are one particular type.

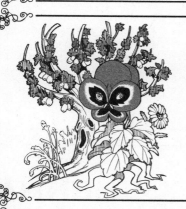

DEKALP

FILE 4

LOW LEVEL

Kin of Amaimon, King of Earth. Possesses plants and trees. Not usually very evil but enjoys conversation and playing tricks. Occasionally, one will deceive a human and grow violent.

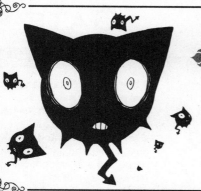

COAL TAR

FILE 5

LOW LEVEL

Kin of Astaroth, King of Rot. Possesses fungi. Gathers around dark, gloomy and unclean people, places and things. Coal Tars are the lowest level of demon that exists, but when a lot group up, they can be a real problem!

THE EARLIEST SKETCHES

An Initial Setting Image

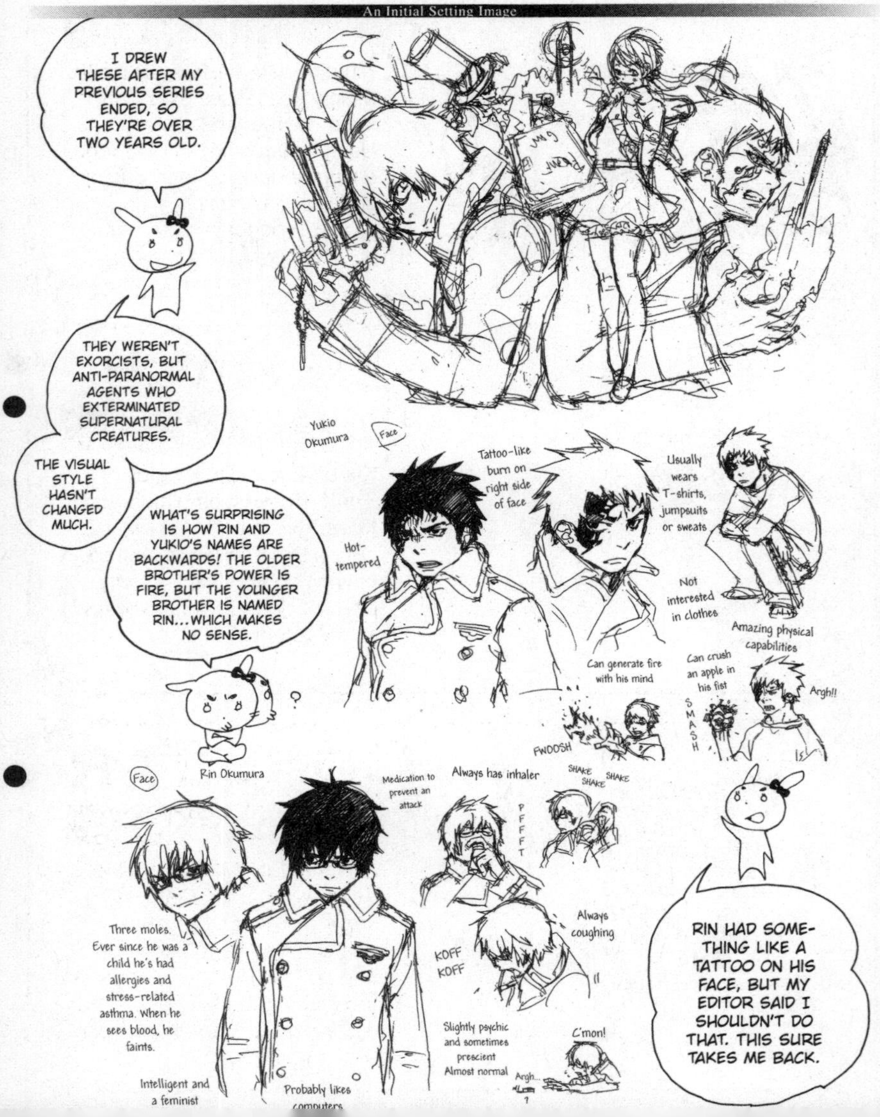

I DREW THESE AFTER MY PREVIOUS SERIES ENDED, SO THEY'RE OVER TWO YEARS OLD.
THEY WEREN'T EXORCISTS, BUT ANTI-PARANORMAL AGENTS WHO EXTERMINATED SUPERNATURAL CREATURES.
THE VISUAL STYLE HASN'T CHANGED MUCH.
WHAT'S SURPRISING IS HOW RIN AND YUKIO'S NAMES ARE BACKWARDS! THE OLDER BROTHER'S POWER IS FIRE, BUT THE YOUNGER BROTHER IS NAMED RIN...WHICH MAKES NO SENSE.
?
Yukio Okumura
Face
Hot-tempered
Tattoo-like burn on right side of face
Usually wears T-shirts, jumpsuits or sweats
Not interested in clothes
Amazing physical capabilities
Can generate fire with his mind
FWOOSH
Can crush an apple in his fist
SMASH
Argh!!
Rin Okumura
Face
Medication to prevent an attack
Always has inhaler
PFFFT
SHAKE SHAKE SHAKE
Three moles. Ever since he was a child he's had allergies and stress-related asthma. When he sees blood, he faints.
Always coughing
KOFF KOFF
Slightly psychic and sometimes prescient
Almost normal
C'mon!
Argh...
Intelligent and a feminist
Probably likes computers
RIN HAD SOMETHING LIKE A TATTOO ON HIS FACE, BUT MY EDITOR SAID I SHOULDN'T DO THAT. THIS SURE TAKES ME BACK.

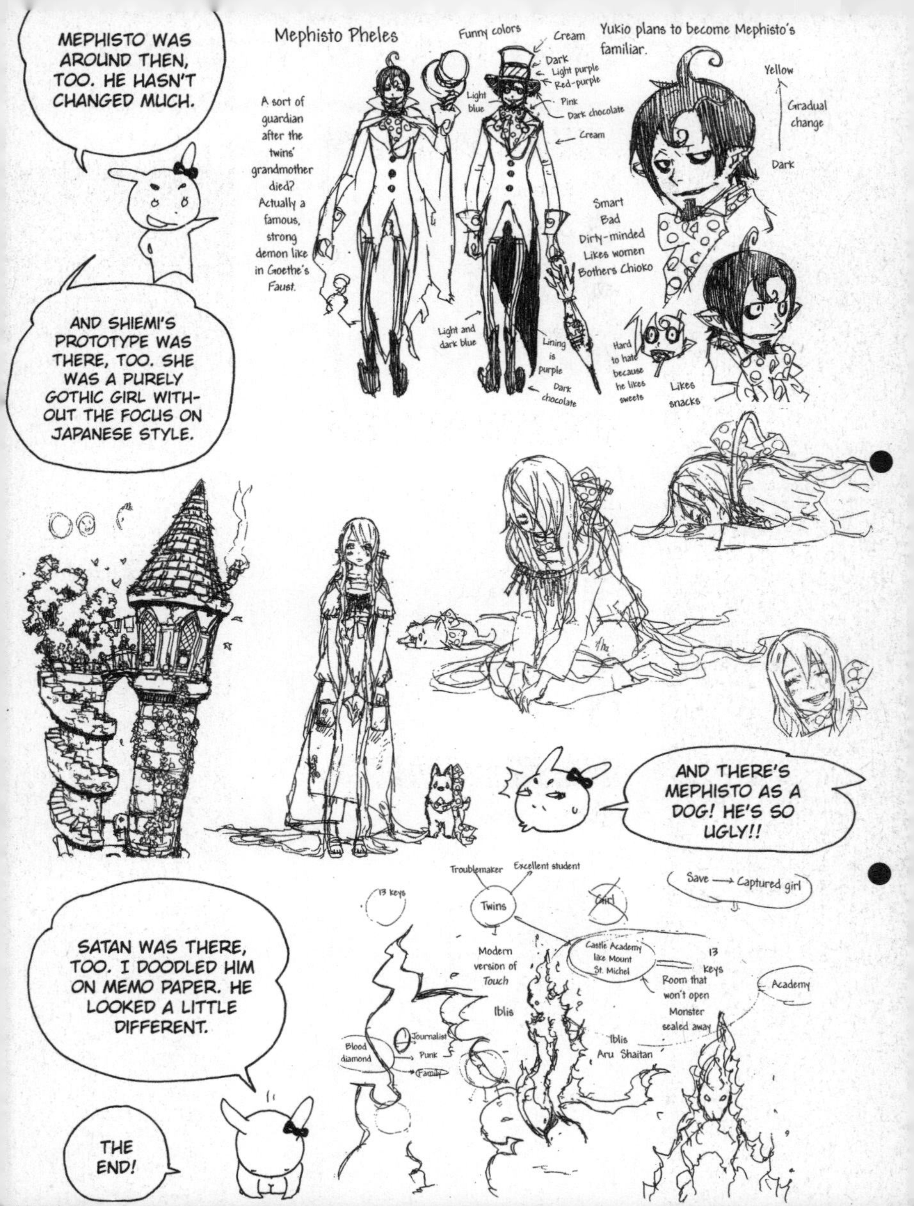

MEPHISTO WAS AROUND THEN, TOO. HE HASN'T CHANGED MUCH.
Mephisto Pheles
Funny colors
Cream
Dark
Light purple
Red-purple
Light blue
Pink
Dark chocolate
Cream
Yukio plans to become Mephisto's familiar.
Yellow
Gradual change
Dark
A sort of guardian after the twins' grandmother died? Actually a famous, strong demon like in Goethe's Faust.
Smart
Bad
Dirty-minded
Likes women
Bothers Chioko
Light and dark blue
Lining is purple
Dark chocolate
Hard to hate because he likes sweets
Likes snacks
AND SHIEMI'S PROTOTYPE WAS THERE, TOO. SHE WAS A PURELY GOTHIC GIRL WITHOUT THE FOCUS ON JAPANESE STYLE.
AND THERE'S MEPHISTO AS A DOG! HE'S SO UGLY!!
SATAN WAS THERE, TOO. I DOODLED HIM ON MEMO PAPER. HE LOOKED A LITTLE DIFFERENT.
Troublemaker
Excellent student
Twins
13 keys
Girl
Save → Captured girl
Castle Academy like Mount St. Michel
13 keys
Modern version of Touch
Room that won't open
Monster sealed away
Academy
Iblis
Blood diamond
Journalist
Punk
Family
Iblis
Aru Shaitan
THE END!

BLUE EXORCIST 1

Art Assistants

Shibutama
Uemura-san
Kamimura-san
Kimura-kun
Tae-chin
Hayashi-kun

Other Assistants

Sato-kun
Shimomura-san
Suzuki-taicho
Nakajima-san
Muto-san
Endo-san
Minoru

Editor

Lin Shihei

(in no particular order)

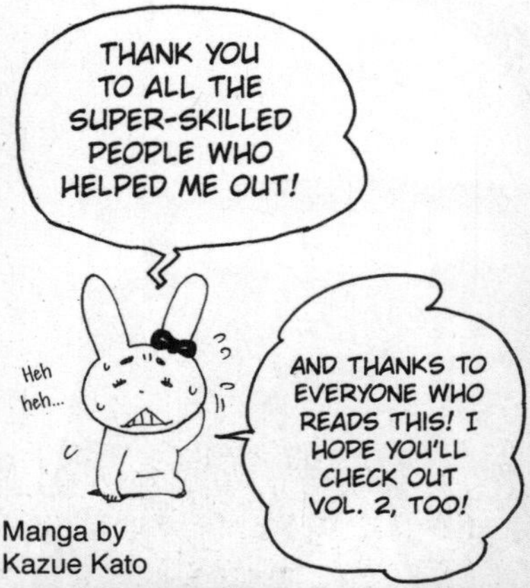
THANK YOU TO ALL THE SUPER-SKILLED PEOPLE WHO HELPED ME OUT!
Heh heh...
AND THANKS TO EVERYONE WHO READS THIS! I HOPE YOU'LL CHECK OUT VOL. 2, TOO!

Manga by
Kazue Kato

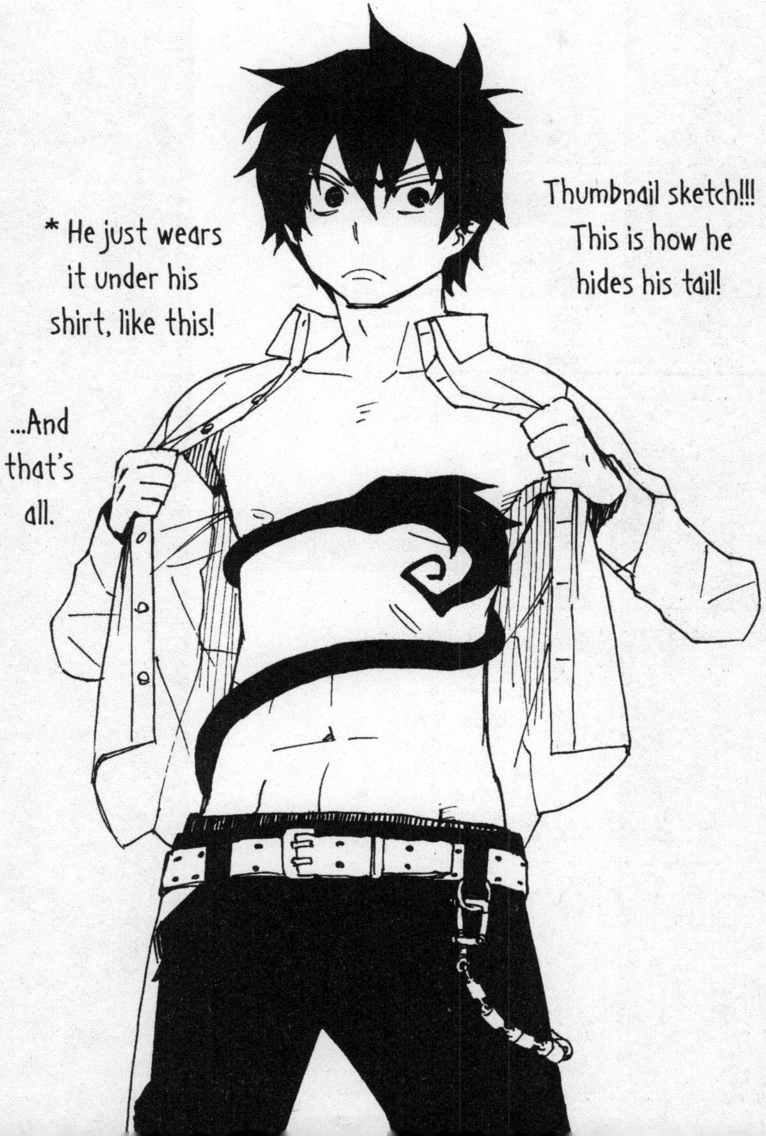
Thumbnail sketch!!! This is how he hides his tail!
* He just wears it under his shirt, like this!
...And that's all.

Playing with His Tail

...
Uh...
...ngh!
?!
Nngh! Guaah! Gyaaah!
flop flop
Eek! EEEE EEEK !!
thump thump
Riiin!!!
That joke's way too upsetting!!
WHAP

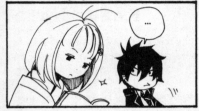

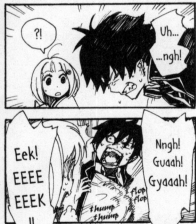

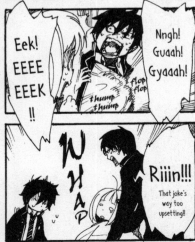

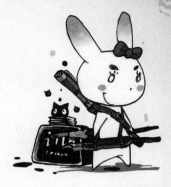

Kazue Kato

Hello and nice to meet you! This is my second series to appear in graphic novel format.

I'll be overjoyed if you have fun reading it!

BLUE EXORCIST

BLUE EXORCIST VOL. 1
SHONEN JUMP Manga Edition

STORY & ART BY KAZUE KATO

Translation & English Adaptation/John Werry
Touch-up Art & Lettering/John Hunt, Primary Graphix
Cover & Interior Design/Sam Elzway
Editor/Mike Montesa

Printed in Canada

Published by VIZ Media, LLC
P.O. Box 77010
San Francisco, CA 94107

15
First printing, April 2011
Fifteenth printing, April 2021

VIZ MEDIA
viz.com

SHONEN JUMP

ratings.viz.com
RATED T+ OLDER TEEN

PARENTAL ADVISORY
BLUE EXORCIST is rated T+ for Older Teen and is recommended for ages 16 and up. It contains violence, suggestive situations and some adult themes.

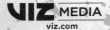

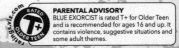

In the next volume...

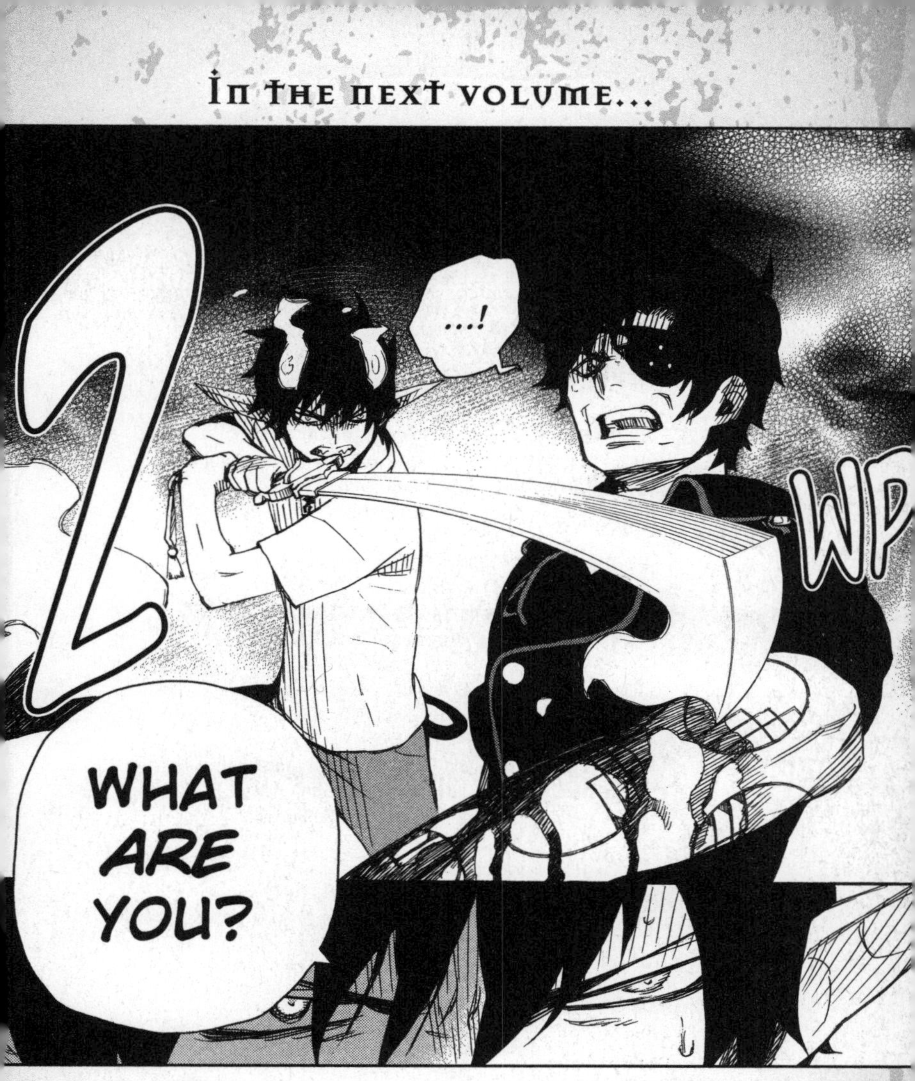
...!
2
WHAT ARE YOU?

Every great exorcist has to start somewhere, and for the students of the academy the first step is the Exwire examination. To prepare for the exam, the new pages in Yukio's class must undergo intensive training. Rin and his classmates have their hands full when a demon appears, but is this a test or something more sinister?

On sale now!

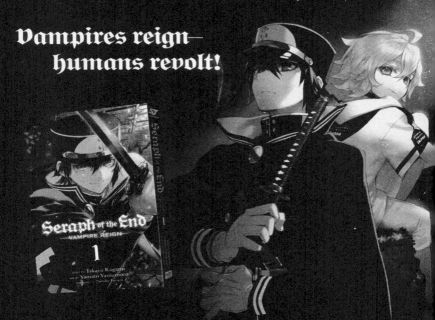

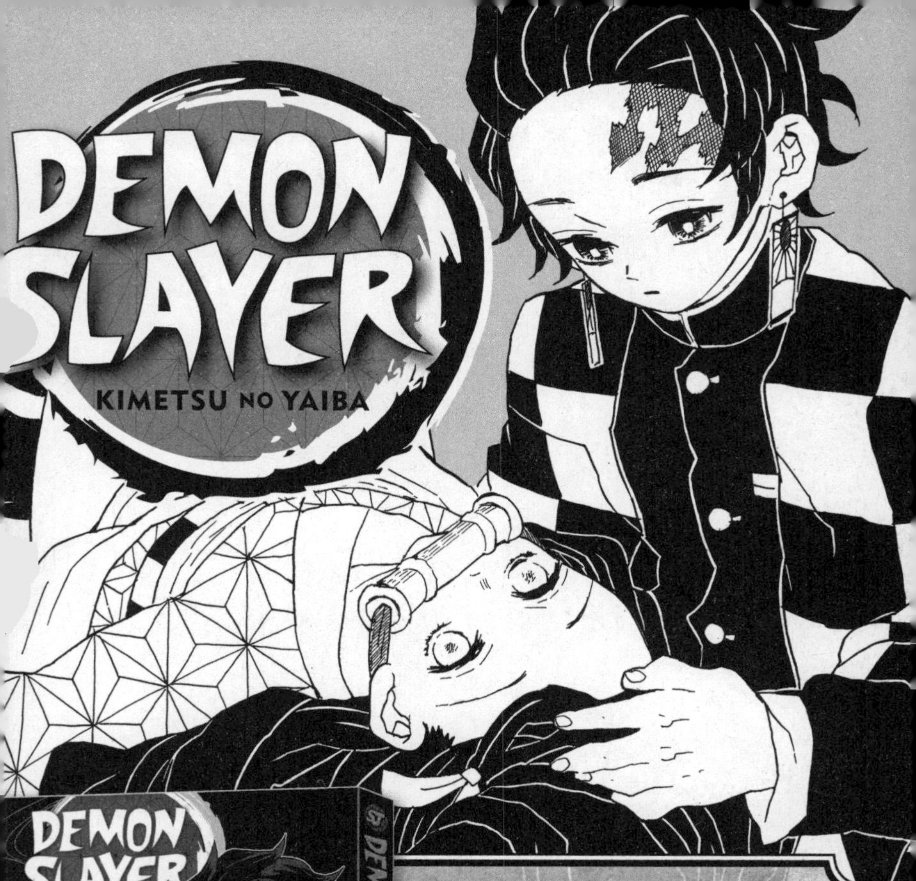

DEMON SLAYER
KIMETSU NO YAIBA

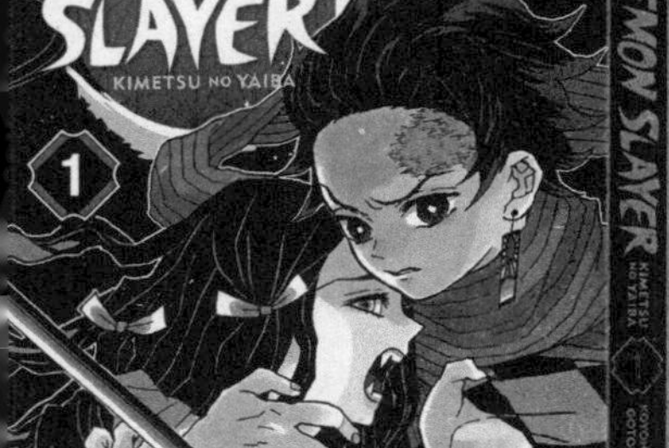

Story and Art by
KOYOHARU GOTOUGE

In Taisho-era Japan, kindhearted Tanjiro Kamado makes a living selling charcoal. But his peaceful life is shattered when a demon slaughters his entire family. His little sister Nezuko is the only survivor, but she has been transformed into a demon herself! Tanjiro sets out on a dangerous journey to find a way to return his sister to normal and destroy the demon who ruined his life.

RATED T TEEN

VIZ

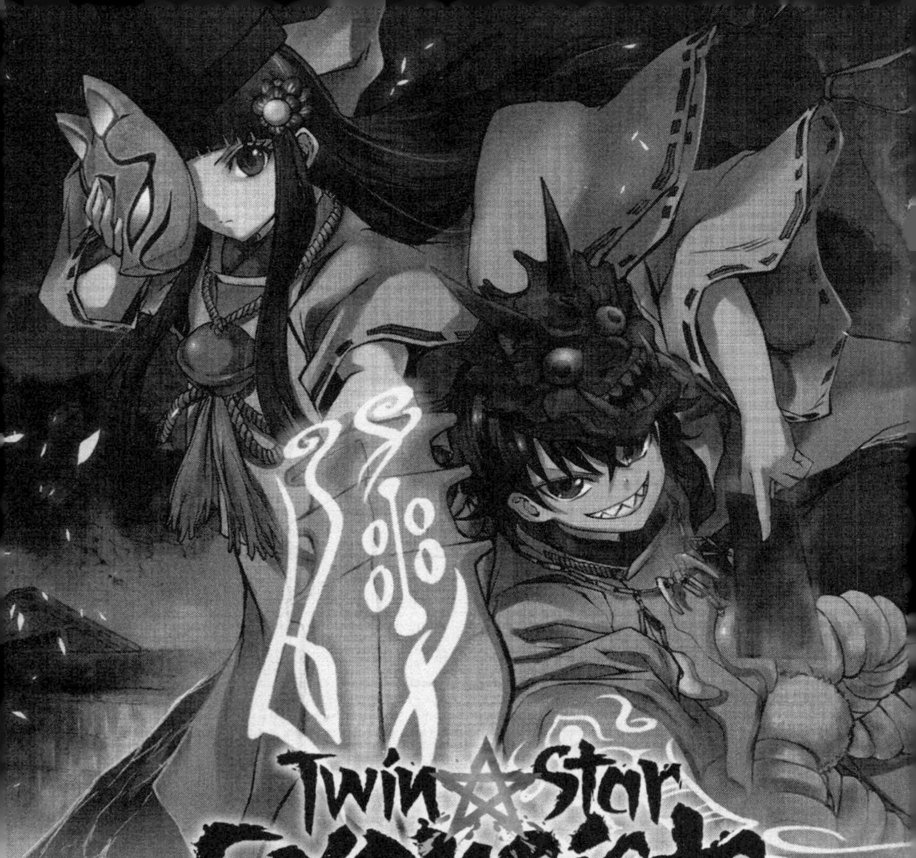
Twin Star Exorcists
ONMYOJI

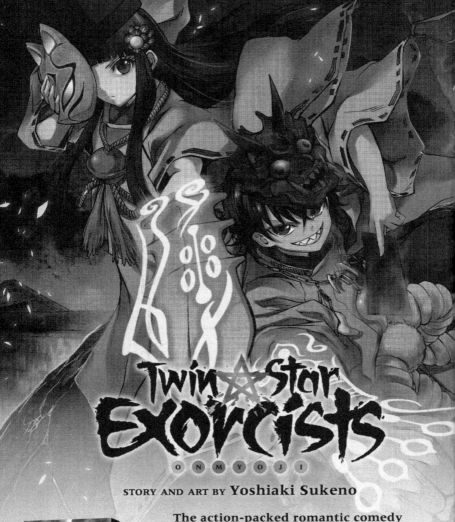

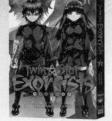

You're Reading in the Wrong Direction!!

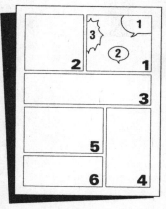

Whoops! Guess what? You're starting at the wrong end of the comic!

...It's true! In keeping with the original Japanese format, **Blue Exorcist** is meant to be read from right to left, starting in the upper-right corner.

Unlike English, which is read from left to right, Japanese is read from right to left, meaning that action, sound effects and word-balloon order are completely reversed... something which can make readers unfamiliar with Japanese feel pretty backwards themselves. For this reason, manga or Japanese comics published in the U.S. in English have sometimes been published "flopped"—that is, printed in exact reverse order, as though seen from the other side of a mirror.

By flopping pages, U.S. publishers can avoid confusing readers, but the compromise is not without its downside. For one thing, a character in a flopped manga series who once wore in the original Japanese version a T-shirt emblazoned with "M A Y" (as in "the merry month of") now wears one which reads "Y A M"! Additionally, many manga creators in Japan are themselves unhappy with the process, as some feel the mirror-imaging of their art skews their original intentions.

We are proud to bring you Kazue Kato's **Blue Exorcist** in the original unflopped format. For now, though, turn to the other side of the book and let the adventure begin...!

—Editor

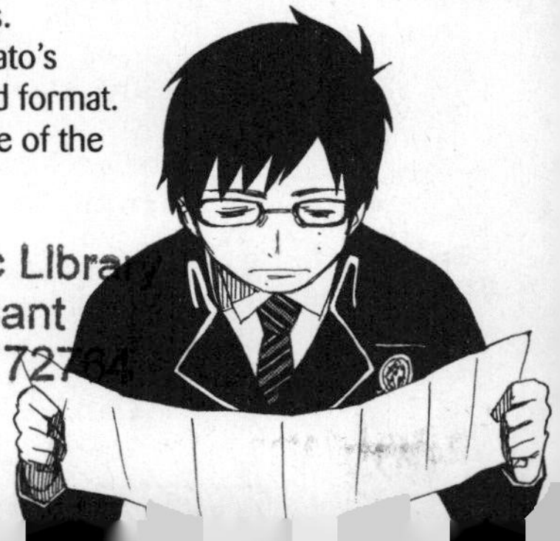